Reading
WOMEN
Writing

a series edited by
Shari Benstock and Celeste Schenck

Reading Women Writing is dedicated to furthering international feminist debate. The series publishes books on all aspects of feminist theory and textual practice. *Reading Women Writing* especially welcomes books that address cultures, histories, and experiences beyond first-world academic boundaries. A complete list of titles in the series appears at the end of this book.

GREATNESS ENGENDERED

George Eliot and Virginia Woolf

Alison Booth

Cornell University Press

ITHACA AND LONDON

To David, Emily, and Aaron

in the order in which we first met

Contents

Preface

Like all critical projects, this one has had a complex evolution curious to retrace, and one likely to yield surprising reflections on its author, as though it were an unwitting autobiography. I've often wondered why I should have become so attached to "Eliot-and-Woolf," and sometimes smiled as their initials vied with each other on the page like competing corporations, GE and VW. In the chapters that follow I acknowledge the ways my own role is situated within the horizons of this study (without pretending that it is possible to confess everything). I am aware that my historically and biographically grounded approach shares features of these authors' skeptical traditionalism. To continue to speak in terms intelligible to the arbiters of an English "great tradition" may appear to betray what Woolf calls "the difference of view," but for both Eliot and Woolf this strategy gained ground for subtle but radical dissent, while at the same time it won them their canonization. How the strategy worked lies at the core of my inquiry. In effect Eliot and Woolf are palace spies, consorting with patriarchal traditions to expose their flaws.

A few words about the terms of my discussion may be in order here. If I have, or would like to have, much in common with these two very different authors, I do not subscribe to their traditional feminism, with its longing for an essential, self-sacrificial womanhood (Eliot, and more often Woolf, can also see beyond essentialism to the historical construction of gender). In other words, I regard gender distinctions as treacherous conveniences for discussion rather than as reliable descriptions of different human beings. Thus I speak of the private sphere of domesticity, the focus of Eliot's and Woolf's historical narratives, as being associated with women (middle-class English women), and refer to the "feminine heroism" that is prescribed for women in English writings at this time, without assuming that Eliot, Woolf, or any other woman will cherish domestic privacy or self-sacrifice—or that men are incapable of espousing obscurity and selflessness. I focus on how Eliot, Woolf, and some of their contemporaries defined womanhood as a selfless mission, and how this definition is played out in the works that led readers to call Eliot and Woolf great. If, as I proceed, I appear to take canonical standards for granted, I invite the reader to put every use of the word "great" in quotation marks and to note that I read the crowning of "genius" as a process rather than as a miracle.

As I look back to the origins of this project—"the make-believe of a beginning," as Eliot puts it in *Daniel Deronda*—I recall that I started out convinced of Eliot's greatness and wisdom, and not so comfortable with Woolf. As I got to know Eliot, meaning that as I read biographies, her letters and essays, and feminist critiques of her views on womanhood and her treatment of heroines, I fell out of love with my vision of Marian Evans Lewes/"George Eliot." (Perhaps I have been unable to resist Woolf's disenchanting vision of a pompous, headachy woman of genius in a horrible cultural predicament.) Yet the textual George Eliot that I recreate as I read the writings published during her lifetime—a creature distinct from that rather depressing Victorian woman—still convinces me of greatness and wisdom, but not the naive concept of greatness I had once bought along with the "great tradition," and not primarily the wisdom that speaks in direct narrative commentary. I am still awed and moved by the paragraphs, the metaphors, the bitter and hopeful shapes the Eliot books find in the social embers. . . . But it is too Victorian to catalog what one loves in an author, and one no longer worships authors but instead the writing that forever beckons to be read. To paraphrase a mother who had employed Charlotte Brontë as governess, rebuking a too-affectionate child: "Love the *author*, my dear!?"

Almost the opposite change to that in my view of Eliot has occurred in my outlook on Woolf. I approached Woolf with a slight prejudice against modernism as I had been taught it. That is, I was aware of preferring Victorians because they were willing to tackle ideological conflicts right out there on the page, and I thought Woolf eschewed all that to tinker with the sentence (wonderfully, of course; there was a time when I practiced writing Woolfian sentences). Modernists were formalists and elitist experimenters, rejecting the story line and the arduous (GE keyword!) effort of belief, dazzled by fashionable uncertainties that I thought I had outgrown. It was the Woolf of *A Room of One's Own* that I was attracted to—and here you could say she is closest to the Victorian sage. I never loved Virginia Stephen Woolf as I once loved Marian Evans Lewes/"George Eliot." I was actually embarrassed by the biographical celebrity; I was not going to write a book on her lesbianism and suicide. What I have found in working on this project is a textual creature, Woolf, whom I would go to the ends of the earth for; she can write me any way she likes. And to my surprise, I have evinced a thoroughly common emotion for the biographical woman, the voice of the letters and diaries; I might be any old Woolf fan, though still desiring texts, not a real woman (the written woman of course fictionalizes the one who lived). Perhaps my sweetest revenge for the passion Woolf's writing inflicts on me is to redesign her as a new George Eliot.

It is not that I must transfer my loyalties or choose between these authors, but that much of the best in each of them (to me) is that which corresponds with the other, in every sense. Aligning two authors, with all their differences, and placing them in relation to a gender ideology and historical vision that evolves from the earlier writer's age may reveal my unregenerate desire to derive origins and to arrive at consensus. I recognize some such desire as a habit of my mind, one that must derive from my father's milk and my mother's word. I try to resist monolithic derivations or blinding agreement, making the best of this rewarding mental tropism (one shared by Eliot and Woolf) by watching it at work.

Of course I did not begin this project intending to be so personal, either toward myself or toward the authors considered. I first chose Eliot and Woolf because they were historians of a sort; I wanted eminent Victorian and modern novelists who also wrote essays, who were accepted as authorities on tradition and culture; they were great writers who happened to be female. My continuing encounter with feminist criticism and theory in these intervening years has dispelled such a dream of objective greatness and fostered a much more exciting project, in which the problem of "being personal" can be discussed (though I will focus on this problem for the women authors, not myself). I recall an inspiring course with Margaret Doody on the historical novel, which began the transformation, and dialogue with feminist theory groups and with students at Princeton and the University of Virginia, which urged me to go further. Sharon Davie and the Women's Studies community, and Kathleen M. Balutansky, Nancy Essig, and the editorial board of "Feminist Issues," a series at the

University Press of Virginia, have given me the pleasure of belonging to an active circle of feminist scholars and have fostered my development in ways I deeply appreciate. The University of Virginia itself has generously supported this project, with four Summer Research Grants and a Fourth-Year Associateship. The Department of English staff, above all Ida Garrison, have given countless hours to the many drafts of this book, and I thank each of them heartily.

Portions of my Introduction and of Chapter 2 appeared in modified form as "Biographical Criticism and the 'Great' Woman of Letters: The Example of George Eliot and Virginia Woolf," in *Contesting the Subject: Essays in the Postmodern Theory and Practice of Biography and Biographical Criticism*, ed. William H. Epstein (West Lafayette, Ind.: Purdue University Press, 1991). Excerpts from my interpretation of *Felix Holt* in Chapter 6 will appear in modified form as "Not All Men Are Selfish and Cruel: *Felix Holt* as a Feminist Novel," in *Gender and Discourse in Victorian Literature and Art*, ed. Antony H. Harrison and Beverly Taylor (DeKalb: Northern Illinois University Press, forthcoming). A portion of Chapter 7 appeared in a different version as "Incomplete Stories: Womanhood and Artistic Ambition in *Daniel Deronda* and *Between the Acts*," in *Writing the Woman Artist: Essays on Poetics, Politics, and Portraiture*, ed. Suzanne W. Jones (Philadelphia: University of Pennsylvania Press, 1991); this material is reprinted by permission of the editor and the publisher.

Like any authorship, mine is a kind of collaboration, and it might be best to thank these times of academic ferment and feminist inquiry. But it is more purposeful to thank my known collaborators. U. C. Knoepflmacher was muse, prophet, interpreter, editor; his fine red script flowered beside many a hedge of my scholarship, enriching the project immeasurably, while he himself inspired my respect and confidence. Maria DiBattista similarly helped me to gauge my distance from possible goals, offered judicious criticism, and lent me her courage and expertise as a feminist and mother. Karen Chase, Susan Fraiman, Deborah McDowell, Patricia Meyer Spacks, Herbert Tucker, and Anthony Winner have each contributed insightful and generous readings as the book evolved. Jerome McGann more than anyone helped that evolution leap over slow ages of development; our discussions repeatedly transformed my aims. My father's fine suggestions and example have generated much of the pleasure I have had in rewriting this work; he has been a demanding, dedicated, loving editor. Throughout, David Izakowitz has been my best and truest collaborator; though he has not been the wife who selflessly typed it all, we have managed both spheres, the home and careers, together, and to him and to our children I owe my happiness.

ALISON BOOTH

Charlottesville, Virginia

Acknowledgment of Copyright Material

I gratefully acknowledge The Estate of Virginia Woolf and the Hogarth Press for permission to reprint excerpts from *Women and Writing* by Virginia Woolf, ed. Michèle Barrett. Excerpts from *Virginia Woolf: A Biography* by Quentin Bell, copyright © 1972 by Quentin Bell, are reprinted by permission of Harcourt Brace Jovanovich, Inc. Excerpts from *Essays of George Eliot*, ed. Thomas Pinney, are reprinted by permission of Routledge.

Excerpts from the following works by Virginia Woolf are reprinted by permission of Harcourt Brace Jovanovich, Inc.: *Between the Acts*, copyright 1941 by Harcourt Brace Jovanovich, Inc., and renewed 1969 by Leonard Woolf; *Collected Essays*, vols. 1 and 2, copyright © 1966 by Leonard Woolf; *Collected Essays*, vols. 3 and 4, copyright © 1967 by Leonard Woolf; *Common Reader, First Series*, copyright 1925 by Harcourt Brace Jovanovich, Inc., and renewed 1953 by Leonard Woolf; *The Diary of Virginia Woolf*, ed. Anne Bell (vol. 1 copyright © 1977 by Quentin Bell and Angelica Garnett; vol. 2 copyright © 1978 by Quentin Bell and Angelica Garnett; vol. 3 copyright © 1980 by Quentin Bell and Angelica Garnett; vol. 4 copyright © 1982 by Quentin Bell and Angelica Garnett; vol. 5 copyright © 1984 by Quentin Bell and Angelica Garnett); *The Essays of Virginia Woolf*, copyright 1986 by Quentin Bell and Angelica Garnett; *Flush: A Biography*, copyright 1933 by Harcourt Brace Jovanovich, Inc., and renewed 1961 by Leonard Woolf; *A Haunted House and Other Short Stories*, copyright 1944 and renewed 1972 by Harcourt Brace Jovanovich, Inc.; *Jacob's Room*, copyright 1923 and renewed 1951 by Leonard Woolf; *The Letters of Virginia Woolf*, ed. Nigel Nicolson and J. Trautmann (vol. 2 copyright © 1976 by Quentin Bell and Angelica Garnett; vol. 3 copyright © 1977 by Quentin Bell and Angelica Garnett; vol. 4 copyright © 1978 by Quentin Bell and Angelica Garnett); *Moments of Being*, copyright 1976 by Quentin Bell and Angelica Garnett; *Mrs. Dalloway*, copyright 1925 by Harcourt Brace Jovanovich, Inc., and renewed 1953 by Leonard Woolf; *Night and Day*, copyright 1920 by George H. Doran Company and renewed 1948 by

Frequently Cited Works

Unless otherwise specified, George Eliot's essays are cited from Thomas Pinney's edition. Her letters are cited from Gordon Haight's edition, indicated by *"GE Letters"* with volume. The biography of George Eliot by Gordon Haight is cited throughout as "Haight." The following editions of the novels are referred to parenthetically with appropriate initials (e.g., M for *Middlemarch*).

Eliot, George. *Adam Bede*. New York: Rinehart, 1948.
——. *Daniel Deronda*. Harmondsworth, Eng.: Penguin, 1967.
——. *Essays of George Eliot*. Ed. Thomas Pinney. London: Routledge & Kegan Paul, 1963.
——. *Felix Holt*. Harmondsworth, Eng.: Penguin, 1972.
——. *The George Eliot Letters*. 9 vols. Ed. Gordon S. Haight. New Haven: Yale University Press, 1954–78.
——. *Impressions of Theophrastus Such*. Vol. 21. The Complete Works of George Eliot. New York: Harper, n.d. [1910].
——. *Middlemarch*. Boston: Houghton Mifflin, 1956.
——. *The Mill on the Floss*. Boston: Houghton Mifflin, 1961.
——. *Romola*. Harmondsworth, Eng.: Penguin, 1980.
——. *Scenes of Clerical Life*. Oxford: Clarendon, 1985.
——. *Silas Marner*. Harmondsworth, Eng.: Penguin, 1967.
Haight, Gordon S. *George Eliot: A Biography*. New York: Oxford University Press, 1968.

Woolf's essays appear in *Women and Writing*, edited by Michèle Barrett, unless otherwise specified. When her essays are cited from *Collected Essays*, they will be noted parenthetically thus: (CE 4: 230). Her letters are cited from the Nicolson and Trautmann edition, parenthetically identified by *"VW Letters"* with volume. Woolf's diary is similarly cited: *"VW Diary."*

The three pieces by Virginia Woolf exclusively on George Eliot are abbreviated as follows:

"GE" [1919]: "George Eliot." *Women and Writing*. Ed. Michèle Barrett. New York: Harcourt Brace Jovanovich, 1979. 150–60.
"GE" [1921]: "George Eliot 1819–1880." "Books of To-day and To-morrow." *London Daily Herald*. 9 March 1921. 7.
"GE" [1926]: "George Eliot" [Review of *The Letters of George Eliot*, Selected with an Introduction by R. Brimley Johnson, Bodley Head]. *The Nation & Athenaeum* 40 (30 October 1926). 149.

The following editions of Woolf's books are cited parenthetically with appropriate initials (e.g., *Night and Day:* ND; *A Room of One's Own:* RO; *Three Guineas:* TG). Quentin Bell's biography is referred to parenthetically throughout as "Bell."

Bell, Quentin. *Virginia Woolf: A Biography*. 2 vols. New York: Harcourt Brace Jovanovich, 1972.
Woolf, Virginia. *Between the Acts*. New York: Harcourt Brace Jovanovich, 1941.
——. *Collected Essays*. 4 vols. New York: Harcourt Brace Jovanovich, 1967.
——. *Common Reader, First Series*. New York: Harcourt Brace Jovanovich, 1953.
——. *The Diary of Virginia Woolf*. 5 vols. Ed. Anne Olivier Bell. New York: Harcourt Brace Jovanovich, 1977–84.
——. *Flush: A Biography*. New York: Harcourt Brace Jovanovich, 1961.
——. *Jacob's Room and The Waves*. New York: Harcourt, Brace & World, 1959.
——. *The Letters of Virginia Woolf*. 6 vols. Ed. Nigel Nicolson and Joanne Trautmann. New York: Harcourt Brace Jovanovich, 1975–80.
——. *Mrs. Dalloway*. New York: Harcourt, Brace & World, 1925.
——. *Night and Day*. New York: Harcourt Brace Jovanovich, 1948.
——. *Orlando*. New York: Harcourt Brace Jovanovich, 1956.
——. *The Pargiters*. Ed. Mitchell A. Leaska. New York: New York Public Library, 1977.
——. *A Room of One's Own*. New York: Harcourt Brace Jovanovich, 1957.
——. *Three Guineas*. New York: Harcourt, Brace & World, 1966.
——. *To the Lighthouse*. New York: Harcourt, Brace & World, 1927.
——. *The Voyage Out*. New York: Harcourt Brace Jovanovich, 1948.
——. *Women and Writing*. Ed. Michèle Barrett. New York: Harcourt Brace Jovanovich, 1979.
——. *The Years*. New York: Harcourt Brace, 1937.

Greatness Engendered

Introduction:
The Great Woman Writer, the
Canon, and Feminist Tradition

In a 1941 collaborative obituary of Virginia Woolf, the novelist Rose Macaulay, herself a descendant of literary Victorians, records Woolf's mimicry of a Victorian voice: " 'Is this a great age?' [Woolf would ask] or, 'can there be Grand Old Women of literature, or only Grand Old Men? I think I shall prepare to be the Grand Old Woman of English letters. Or would you like to be?' " (317). It is a brief moment in a short memoir, possibly invented as a novelist invents dialogue. But the gloss on Woolf's relation to literary tradition is telling: Woolf, with mock solemnity as well as genuine skepticism about the notion of unique literary greatness, seems to acknowledge her peculiar role as the leading *woman* writer of her age. She had succeeded to the title that only George Eliot had won before her, that of the Grand Old Woman of English Letters. The title, as Woolf's remark suggests, was deeply ironic, since the grandeur or greatness seemed calibrated with the writer's ability to suppress the disqualification of womanhood. The female laureate might as well have been male, she had become so representative of the age.[1] Yet Macaulay's memoir constructs the kind of female literary tradition that has become so dear to feminist

---

[1] Such is the logic implied in T. S. Eliot's contribution to the same tribute; Woolf appears to belong to the masculine category of "great writer." T. S. Eliot affirms that Woolf became "the centre . . . of the literary life of London," "the symbol" of the "Victorian upper middle-class" cultural tradition. T. S. Eliot dwells more on his own views than on Woolf herself (the memoir begins, "It has only been under peculiar conditions that I have ever been able to interest myself in criticizing . . . contemporary writers" [313]). Other contributors to this obituary include Vita Sackville-West, William Plomer, and Duncan Grant, in two issues of *Horizon: A Review of Literature and Art;* 3:17, 18 (1941): 313–27, 402–6. In 1928 Woolf suspected that she and Macaulay were jealous of each other's success (*VW Diary* 3: 185).

critics who follow Woolf; Macaulay's first sentences create a literary heroine: " 'She had animation; she had sensibility; she had elegance, beauty and wit.' Thus Jane Austen, doing her descriptive utmost, might have approved Virginia Woolf." Through a timeless Austen's approval of Woolf, Macaulay performs for Woolf the memorial service that the latter had performed for so many women of letters before her, but for no one more fully than for George Eliot.

Macaulay touches on some of the same elements that we find in Woolf's 1919 centenary essay on George Eliot. She focuses as Woolf does, for instance, on the predecessor's oracular presence in literary circles, but she notes that the twentieth-century sibyl is irreverent in a most un-Victorian manner. Woolf's admiring visitors encountered not an edifying discussion of culture but the sheer "entertainment" of "a flashing, many-faceted stream" of "conversation." The pilgrims to Eliot's house, the Priory, according to Woolf encountered the full force of Eliot's unplayful intelligence. Yet it is manifestly difficult to arrive at an accurate understanding of the famous woman writer of the past. Reassessing Eliot, Woolf marvels at "the credulity . . . with which, half consciously and partly maliciously, one had accepted the late Victorian version of a deluded woman who held phantom sway over subjects even more deluded than herself" ("GE" [1919] 150). Like Macaulay's obituary portrait of Woolf, the 1919 elegy, "George Eliot," strives to reconcile a peculiar disparity between the private woman and the public persona of the famous writer, as though both women of letters were reclusive outsiders yet full participants in the spirit of the age.[2] I seize on Macaulay's playful evocation of Woolf's speech as a guide to Woolf's understanding of her own vocation: she was to be—playfully—the grand old woman of English letters in her age, as she acknowledged Eliot had been in hers. To win the title would be to struggle with an idea of cultural history that excluded the personal qualification of womanhood from the realm of greatness.

This study of Eliot and Woolf addresses the problem of greatness

[2]Macaulay notes the great woman writer's ambiguous persona as both private and representatively public: "[Woolf] was sometimes pleased ironically to pose as the recluse who watched life from a quiet, drab corner." Yet "her going seems symbolic of the end of an age," Macaulay writes. Woolf consciously reenacted the ritual of visits to the great writer, as Daniel Mark Fogel recalls with regard to her response to Henry James. In 1907 she wrote to Violet Dickinson, "But when I am old and famous I shall discourse like Henry James" (VW Letters 1: 306). In one version of "A Sketch of the Past," she wrote, "I remember . . . the ceremony of our visits to great men. . . . Greatness still seems to me a positive possession; booming; eccentric; set apart; something to which I am led up dutifully by my parents. . . . But it never exists now" (Fogel 56–58). That the greats were men of the past did not prevent her reviving a female legacy of a different greatness.

for the woman writer, not only in biographical terms—how does she achieve "greatness"?—but in terms also of a feminist revision of history to admit the not-"great": the selfless, feminine, common, other. I hope to establish the extent to which Eliot and Woolf thought in common within a certain feminist tradition that affirms a supposed feminine selflessness as it rejects the masculine self-assertion that has conventionally fueled notions of greatness. While I wish to assess the implied debt that Woolf owed to Eliot (arguably her most substantial literary inheritance), this is not so much an "influence" study as it is a study of an ideal of feminine influence—as antidote to masculine egotism—that both authors incorporated in their texts with much equivocation. How did these authors, intent on their own success within a masculinist tradition, redefine heroism and greatness in feminist terms? Eliot's narrator sardonically observes Will Ladislaw's and Mr. Brooke's discomfort under a noble admonition from Dorothea: "A man is seldom ashamed of feeling that he cannot love a woman so well when he sees a certain greatness in her: nature having intended greatness for men" (M 285). Eliot, like Woolf after her, is quite skeptical about the "intention of nature" argument that separates male and female spheres according to gender stereotypes—man for greatness, woman for self-sacrifice. Yet in both Eliot's and Woolf's writings we can detect a fondness for feminine self-sacrifice, a nostalgia for separate spheres and for an essential, inborn gender.

Much of my argument in the following chapters turns around the vexed dualism and essentialism of such thinking, particularly the heavily gendered dichotomy between public and private spheres. First, the biographical question: How could the Grand Old Women of English Letters be both "women" and "great" in a tradition that defined greatness, like history itself, in terms of the masculine, public "sphere" of action? As Mary Poovey has shown, the Victorians found diverse uses for a cult of the impenetrably private sphere of woman, but in the process they subverted the binary opposition of spheres on which the cult rested (8–9, 21–22). Thus these women of letters can be seen traversing, in the design of their careers and authorial personas, the culturally defined spheres of womanhood and of masculine greatness. Second, their works can be read as historical narratives that promote commerce between the spheres—all private life has its history, all history is determined by the developments of private life—in specifically gendered terms.

These unusually privileged women writers give utterance to history's silencing of women (if not lending speech to women themselves). Woman, most simply, figures as the other in history—even as the "other half," the lower classes, are feminized. To speak from the point of view of this other, as these authors' works in part attempt to do, might be to challenge the hierarchy of the spheres, subverting the predominance of the masculine self, the public realm, and the ruling classes. Or it might remake woman in man's image, raise the common life to the condition of the middle class, reaffirm the masculine model of the ego and authority. According to the logic of this view of sexual destiny, in attaining authority within tradition women lose their privacy and they may lose the virtues of their difference, violating the sacrificial feminine ideal that I will call the ideology of influence. Eliot and Woolf appear to launch an attack on masculinist myth—particularly egotism—in the form of a celebration of the feminine selflessness and influence that have traditionally been considered the harmless underside of patriarchal myth. The harm that feminine influence might do to patriarchy had of course been underestimated, as we see in so many Victorian texts, but the harm this ideal might do to its own exemplars, the characters and women authors themselves, bears a careful reexamination.

The most fundamental challenges to the woman who wishes to become a "great writer" in a male-dominated literary tradition are, on the one hand, to suppress the modifier "woman"—though how this is done remains mysterious even in the instances of literary women's acknowledged "greatness"[3]—and on the other hand, to come to terms with the masculine norm inherent in the individualistic concept of greatness. No woman writer, of course, has ever successfully proved the complete irrelevance of her womanhood, but at the height of her reputation for greatness her sex must somehow seem either incidental, intriguing, or all the more cause for admiring her transcendence of ordinary life. Eliot and Woolf come to us almost uncontested as the greatest British Victorian and modern women novelists, and this chain of dubious modifiers helps us avoid deciding on "real" relative merit, forestalling any comparison, for example, to Dickens or Joyce. The literary lives and narrative strategies of Eliot and Woolf, however, shun the delimitation "woman."

Women writers face not only the obstacle of preconceived womanhood, but also the perhaps more daunting problem of the conception of greatness itself. To be great, in patriarchal culture, is to resemble the male hero, and certainly it is to have some standing in a public

---

[3]Ellen Moers illustrates this difficulty, faced even by the female feminist critic, when she begins her preface to *Literary Women: The Great Writers:* "The subject of this book is the major women writers, writers we read and shall always read whether interested or not in the fact that they happened to be women" (ix).

story; in modern, post-Romantic European culture, to be great is to embody an individualistic ideal. The great artist, at least in most popular accounts, is urged to forfeit all conscious "thinking in common"; *he* must be *original*. Woolf's vision of tradition as a "thinking back through" rejects the artist as self-made solitary, especially by urging women to think back through "our mothers," since mothers are notorious for threatening the dissolution of the ego, their own as well as others'. The institutionalized ambivalence toward the mother that Nancy Chodorow and Dorothy Dinnerstein have analyzed haunted the tradition that Eliot and Woolf worked within, and undoubtedly influenced their own childless careers and their own efforts at greatness. As though to become the grand and old mothers whom later generations would think back through, they threaten their characters with the dissolution of ego (they are especially severe on heroines), and they cultivate a selfless authorial persona, dedicating themselves to a collective cultural progress.

Eliot was accepted by her contemporaries as a sage who served the advancement of the common life. Her doctrine, if it had to be expressed in a sentence, teaches the sin of egotism and the virtue of self-denying fellow-feeling. Egotists like Rosamond Vincy and Gwendolen Harleth show that femininity and egotism readily coincide, but society lends women one advantage in their moral education by teaching them to yield to others in spite of their unruly desires. The narrator of *Middlemarch* observes: "We are all of us born in moral stupidity, taking the world as an udder to feed our supreme selves: Dorothea had early begun to emerge from that stupidity, but yet it had been easier to her to imagine how she would devote herself to Mr. Casaubon . . . than to conceive . . . that he had an equivalent centre of self, whence the lights and shadows must always fall with a certain difference" (156–57). Less overtly didactic, Woolf teaches much the same doctrine and makes the gender dynamics of egotism more explicit, repeatedly mocking the phallic "I, I, I" (RO 103–4; TL 160; Y 361). Her work increasingly enacts the breakdown of ego boundaries—as in the six equivalent centers of self in *The Waves*—to turn to the first-person pronoun "we." Although at times she concedes that women may share with men a desire for dominance, she finds hope in women's conditioning if not in their nature; as outsiders, they will emerge from moral stupidity.[4] Any woman might resist the loss of supreme self,

---

[4]Naomi Black notes Viscountess Rhondda's query about *Three Guineas:* "In my heart I find . . . all the pride, vanity and combativeness I ever see in men." Woolf replied, "[Such feelings] are in us of course; I feel them pricking every moment. But again they have so little encouragement in us. . . . If we emphasise our position as outsiders and

might wish to declare the centrality of her "I," but she cannot avoid
seeing with a certain difference, athwart the male point of view. Such
moral awareness cannot, however, earn her cultural eminence—or so
the myths of Dorothea, Mrs. Ramsay, and other women in the works
of Eliot and Woolf imply—unless true greatness can be redefined as
a participation in an historical common life, "our" life.

In my view, Eliot and Woolf succeed in redefining greatness in this
way; their greatness for me—their almost inexhaustible worthiness to
be read and reinterpreted—is due largely to the persuasiveness of the
myth they variously narrate, the myth of a shared, progressive life
beyond individuality. Yet in attributing the myth to them, I identify
their individuality. They appear as distinct cultural deities in a mythology of impersonality. Quite simply, the tension of this contradiction
propels this book.

My ironically charged worship of the great women of letters is
conditioned by changing histories of reception; in particular, this study
would have been impossible without the foundation of feminist criticism in the American academy. At the same time, this book inevitably
lives in the world of studies of canonical authors. We—a suspect
pronoun that I have decided to use, as much as possible in the diversi-
fied yet collective spirit in which Eliot and Woolf try to use it—we
cannot help mythologizing the writer whom large numbers of people
have agreed to read, and whom we in turn have agreed to talk and
write about. The literary name perpetuates the myth, so that every
time I write "Eliot" or "Woolf," or in the more specialized myth I am
constructing here, "Eliot and Woolf," an illusion of a unified author
or pair of authors rises to solicit our desire to keep reading and talking.
It appears impossible to look at authorship or discuss canonical authors without at moments believing that the texts we have read *are*
the woman or man who wrote them, a knowable, historically fixed
source. But I try to recall that the grand old women of letters are
for us textual constructs, even when considered as apparently real,
biographical beings. It is precisely to observe the workings of such
myths that I have chosen to study canonical women authors, trying
meanwhile to keep myself from falling into great-traditionism, cult-
of-genius-ism, Eurocentrism, and other acts of exclusion that I consciously deplore. In reconstructing the tradition of Eliot and Woolf,
then, I hope also to unsettle our reading of it, directing our practical
need for a female literary tradition into a more considered revision of

come to think it a natural distinction it should be easier for us than for those unfortunate
young men" (Black, "Woolf and Women's Movement," 192, citing *VW Letters* 6: 236–
37).

the terms on which we grant authorial greatness or "traditional" status. And let me say at the outset that "I" make no claim to unique originality; I am "thinking in common" in a tradition, one that most will agree in tracing back to that original, Woolf (with her debts to Coleridge, Arnold, and their debts . . . to Sappho, Felicia Hemans, or some hypothetical Mrs. Ayres?).

Victorian to Modern, Eliot to Woolf:
The Genealogical Record

As the obituary with which I began reveals, the literary executor is charged with the task of memorializing the past author in terms useful for unfolding literary history in the present. Thus Woolf's reading of Eliot, as we shall see, has a complex bearing on her self-construction as a woman of letters as well as on her sense of modernity, of living in a new age. For Woolf, the very definition of her "age" raised gender issues obscured by the standard tradition, so that she generally resorted to metaphors of the family romance rather than the vocabulary of science employed by T. S. Eliot, Pound, or the Futurists (Ian Bell 181, 191). The title as well as the substance of Woolf's modernist manifesto, "Mr. Bennett and Mrs. Brown," obliquely suggest that the famous change in human character is no gender-neutral aesthetic transition but a challenge to patriarchal dominance, as my later discussions of this essay will show. But Woolf is as capable as T. S. Eliot of erasing personality and gender in her depiction of cultural history.

Like other writers after the turn of the century, she covered the tracks that led her out of the Victorian age. In "How It Strikes a Contemporary," she claimed to have lived through a cataclysmic upheaval even as she invoked a favorite Victorian image of geological epochs:

We are sharply cut off from our predecessors. A shift in the scale—
the sudden slip of masses held in position for ages—has shaken the
fabric from top to bottom, alienated us from the past and made us
perhaps too vividly conscious of the present. Every day we find
ourselves doing, saying, or thinking things that would have been
impossible to our fathers. And we feel the differences which have
not been noted far more keenly than the resemblances which have
been very perfectly expressed.

Critics who are no longer direct successors of the Victorians now sense
that it is the resemblances between the moderns and the Victorians
that have been overlooked. Woolf contributed to a rhetoric of "novelty" that enabled the significant innovations of modernist writers
("How It Strikes a Contemporary," CE 2: 157–58; a title borrowed from
Browning), and she seems at times capable of using a phrase like "our
fathers" without wincing. But the paternal metaphor seems peculiarly
real in Woolf's case, as she held what T. S. Eliot calls "a kind of
hereditary position in English letters" (315); her understanding of the
generational *and* gender conflict in the family of letters was most
immediate.

   Woolf was herself reared among literary Victorians, as her portraits
of Mr. Ramsay (based on Leslie Stephen) and Mrs. Hilbery (modeled
on her aunt Anne Thackeray Ritchie) testify. Yet for the most part she
obscured the fact that her work had a corresponding upbringing in
Victorian literature. Indeed, she seemed to feel that the career of the
eminent writer "Virginia Woolf" would never have been born at all if
the figures of father and mother—her real parents and the literary
prohibitions they had come to represent—had not died. In "Professions for Women," she advises the young woman writer to slay "The
Angel in the House" (59), the Victorian ideal (invoked perhaps more
religiously in our feminist retrospectives than at the time) that haunted
Woolf in memories of her own mother, Julia Stephen (Rosenman,
Invisible Presence, 15, 70). Similarly, many critics have noted Woolf's
sense of release from Leslie Stephen's prohibitive influence: "Father's
birthday. He would have been 96, 96, yes, today; and could have been
96, like other people one has known: but mercifully was not. His life
would have entirely ended mine. What would have happened? No
writing, no books;—inconceivable" (*VW Diary* 3: 208). The absence of
both parents was as instrumental to her writing as the modernist sense
of having been "sharply cut off from our predecessors." Woolf's great
"elegy," *To the Lighthouse*, for example, would have been inconceivable
without the deaths of her parents, as Margaret Homans points out
(285).[5] As Woolf put it, "writing The Lighthouse laid them in my
mind" (*VW Diary* 3: 208).

   Works such as *To the Lighthouse* succeeded in laying to rest—and
simultaneously marking with indelible epitaphs—Woolf's literary as

---

[5]Homans effectively traces Woolf's ambivalence toward the representation of the
mother, who like Mrs. Ramsay has both access to the literal (pre-oedipal) language of
maternal presence and a well-trained subservience to the figurative discourse associated
with male mastery (279–81).

well as literal forebears. She betrays her sense that her "resemblances" to great predecessors would be "perfectly expressed." Woolf's impressive innovations in her 1927 novel may distract us from her equally impressive reworking of literary antecedents, in such details as the fact that Minta Doyle loses the final volume of *Middlemarch* on the train (Homans 277–78), and in larger patterns such as the madonnalike grandeur of Mrs. Ramsay, a modern Saint Theresa or Dorothea Brooke grown up (and married to a counterpart of Casaubon). Such reworkings are complexly ironic and at the same time surprisingly in harmony with the precedents offered by Eliot's works. Woolf laid George Eliot to rest, like another Mrs. Ramsay, in her centenary essay of 1919 (Jacobus, *Reading Woman*, 28–29), while perpetuating Eliot's literary spirit in her own writings.

Searching through English literary history like a genealogist, Woolf never fixed her own pedigree, male or female. Male writers "never helped a woman yet," Woolf asserts (RO 79), naming some (such as Thackeray and Dickens) who very much assisted her reading-apprenticeship in her father's library. In the facetious preface to *Orlando*, she obliquely honors her debt to a literary tradition almost exclusively male: "Defoe, Sir Thomas Browne, Sterne, Sir Walter Scott, Lord Macaulay, Emily Brontë, De Quincey, and Walter Pater" (vii). More than clownishly turning this tradition on its head, however, Woolf elsewhere parades before our eyes what appears to be a brand new tradition, the succession of her literary foremothers: "many famous women, and many more unknown and forgotten, have been before me, making the path smooth, and regulating my steps" ("Professions for Women" 57). Smooth and regulated may not be equally positive qualities for a writer trying to make her own way. But on the whole, Woolf's outlook on the female literary tradition is less adversarial than we have been led to expect, modeling our study of women writers on a separate-but-equal anxiety of influence.[6] In spite of Woolf's warning to slay the motherly Angel in the House, she seems eager to rescue rather than to slay precursors more overshadowed than overshadowing.

The individual author's claims to originality should be waived, ac-

---

[6]Sandra Gilbert and Susan Gubar draw on Woolf in their constructions of a female tradition of "anxiety of authorship," but Woolf's depiction of the literary landscape is far less bloody than *The Madwoman in the Attic* (187–88, 17). See Gilbert and Gubar's " 'Forward into the Past,' " *No Man's Land* 1: 192–93: "In the twentieth-century . . . Freud-derived Bloomian paradigms like . . . our own 'anxiety of authorship' must give way to a paradigm of ambivalent affiliation." See Showalter, *Sexual Anarchy*, 60, 77.

cording to Woolf, especially as women authors recognize the sufferings they have in common:[7] "For masterpieces . . . are the outcome of many years of thinking in common, . . . so that the experience of the mass is behind the single voice. Jane Austen should have laid a wreath upon the grave of Fanny Burney, and George Eliot done homage to the robust shade of Eliza Carter—the valiant old woman who tied a bell to her bedstead in order that she might wake early and learn Greek" (RO 68). Like Austen and Eliot, Woolf owed a tribute to her forerunner, but she paid it most in a few critical essays and in the kind of covert elegy I have briefly noted in *To the Lighthouse*. Woolf seems content that the public tributes seldom be paid, since the most characteristic yield of a woman's literary tradition is the masterpiece of submerged provenance: it is by "Anon." While Woolf more than anyone before labored to restore a female literary tradition, and explicitly honored a number of female predecessors, most notably the Brontës and Austen besides Eliot, she left us to detect in her far from anonymous masterpieces how much she owed to them. At the same time, she labored to be beautiful in a tradition that regarded itself as beyond gender or personality. The modern Grand Old Woman of English Letters, like the Victorian, paradoxically aspired to literary greatness, on the one hand by suppressing her identity as a woman and honoring the great tradition, and on the other hand by striving to dismantle the tradition of "our fathers."

This very problem, of how to be a "great" writer yet a woman, focuses the reasons for considering Eliot as the most important of Woolf's ancestors. As I shall argue, criticism of women writers almost invariably follows a biographical convention that divides artistic vocation from the normative plot of a woman's life, so that, for example, the wife and mother, if she writes, cannot be a *great* writer. Woolf at times seems to accept uncritically the dominant literary canon and standards of female greatness, as in her Mt. Rushmore of Jane Austen, Charlotte and Emily Brontë, and George Eliot, none of whom was conventionally married during her active writing career, and none of whom bore children.[8] Yet Eliot more than the others escaped womanly dependency on family: neither Austen nor the Brontës ever held a place in intellectual circles as Eliot and Woolf did; even Charlotte

[7]Janet Todd discusses Woolf's autobiographical portrayal of women writers as "female heroes or distressed ladies of sensibility," contrary aspects of her own self-portrait (107–9).

[8]See Showalter, *Literature*, 6–7. In her writings, Woolf helped rescue many lesser-known women writers and acknowledged some who integrated women's roles and professional writing. See M. Barrett, Introduction. Yet it seems that one of Woolf's criteria for greatness is the exemption from the usual womanly life.

Brontë was only a sojourner in literary London.[9] At the same time, Eliot must have seemed nearly part of Woolf's own family, having been friendly with Leslie Stephen and his sister-in-law, Anne Thackeray, both of whom somewhat skeptically joined in the author-worship on Sundays at the Leweses' Priory.[10] As important for Woolf as were many other figures, male and female, on the literary family tree, none but Eliot illustrated just how divorced the public persona of a great woman of letters might have to be from the traditional feminine role, defined by its privacy.

In her critical writings, Woolf might seem to disagree with my claim that Eliot is her most important female ancestor. Of the four "great" women writers of the English nineteenth century, Woolf often seems to give precedence to Austen rather than Eliot; Austen earns praise (as she did from George Henry Lewes and other Victorians) for her Shakespearean, "incandescent" unself-consciousness (RO 58, 71; "Phases of Fiction," CE 2:76; "Jane Austen" 109–20). Moreover, only Austen in this circle of great literary women was always the lady: in addition to her impeccable family credentials, she obeyed the commandment that women must "charm" rather than challenge (Todd 111–14). Paradoxically, in A Room of One's Own, Emily Brontë is linked with Austen for her single-minded disregard of the commandment to be ladylike. In effect, Woolf allows Emily and gentle Jane to drop one modifier, "woman," and add another, "great," because their artistic manners are self-effacing enough to remain feminine even in greatness. They have no biographies: readers know little about them, and their personal grievances never intrude upon the page. Charlotte Brontë and Eliot, on the other hand, are more easily criticized because they became notorious: their lives became matter for public debate.

The insistent personality of a writer like Charlotte Brontë offends a certain aesthetic code that dominated Woolf's day, and that had special implications for women writers. As Andreas Huyssen observes, the modernist dictum that art must be autonomous, non-referential, and detached from "everyday life" expresses in itself a strong bias against women and mass culture (53–54). Woolf curiously adapted this bias to her feminism by characterizing authoritative personality as masculine

[9]Elizabeth Barrett Browning and Elizabeth Gaskell, perhaps because of their well-known personas as wives and mothers, failed to engage Woolf's competitive interest in the same way, though she took pains to resurrect Barrett Browning in Flush and elsewhere.

[10]Stephen noted in his Mausoleum Book that "one had to be ready to discuss metaphysics . . . and offer an acceptable worship" at the Priory; Lady Ritchie wrote, "The shrine was so serene and kind that this authoress felt like a wretch for having refused to worship there before" (quoted in Showalter, "The Greening of Sister George," 293).

(Minow-Pinkney 15), so that writing beyond self-conscious personality might be considered writing "as a woman" or as an androgynous, Shakespearean mind (it is ironic that Shakespeare, the national hero, should be invoked as the impersonal ideal). Instead of achieving the universality of art, which Woolf concurrently figures as a feminine mode of egoless greatness, Charlotte Brontë declares herself to *be* a woman. One must write "as a woman who has forgotten that she is a woman," according to this aesthetic prescription, whereas Brontë allowed autobiographical protest about woman's lot to encroach on her novels (RO 96, 71–73).

Woolf certainly places Eliot higher in the pantheon than Brontë, in part because Eliot utters no personal outcry, though Woolf does detect awkward self-portraiture in Eliot's heroines.[11] It might almost seem that Eliot achieved the indifference to her womanly role that Woolf sought in the woman writer. Escaping the woman's sphere of the matchmaking novel of manners, Eliot according to Woolf was "one of the first English novelists to discover that men and women think as well as feel" ("GE" [1921]). Conversely, Eliot's command of the uncharming realm of thought seems to strike Woolf as a biographical monstrosity. Eliot moreover betrays the woman's "difference of view" ("GE" [1919] 160) with her masculine pseudonym and style (RO 80).

Eliot certainly breaks Woolf's rather unhelpful commandment to write as women write (and how is that?), though she does obey the concurrent commandment to write without (apparent) awareness of her own female personality. Perhaps Eliot makes her flight from female personality a little too obvious. For Woolf, the woman writer who writes like a man, instead of making a virtue of her limitations as Austen does, calls attention to those limitations (as Eliot was quick to point out in her own criticism of women writers). The fault of manliness, however, is at the same time for Woolf a major source of Eliot's importance, as it enabled Eliot to become the preeminent English woman of letters, largely escaping the usual patronizing criticism of female writers and extending the narrow sphere of the novel that Austen had so elegantly plotted out. Imagine a respectably genuine Mrs. Lewes being taken seriously by young Oxford men; imagine *The Wit and Wisdom of Mrs. John Cross.* Instead, the great literary figure overcame the identity of the fallen woman and eventually the male persona as well. As Gillian Beer puts it, Eliot transforms "the male

---

[11]When Woolf facetiously aimed to "sum up" her predecessor "once and for all" in the centenary essay, she noted the central problem of Eliot's heroines. Her reading notebook declares, "You may dislike her heroines but you don't get the full flavour unless you consider them" (Silver, *Notebooks,* 201–2).

persona . . . into her own image as a human scribe who is, historically, a woman" (*George Eliot* 16). Lauded as novelist and cultural critic, the colleague of leading intellectuals, George Eliot seemed to define the broadly "human" role Virginia Woolf adopted for herself.

Not long after Woolf's first article on Eliot appeared in 1919, she wrote in her diary a revealing response to the anxiety of publishing her own second novel:

> *Night and Day* flutters about me still, & causes great loss of time. George Eliot would never read reviews, since talk of her books hampered her writing. I begin to see what she meant. I don't take praise or blame excessively to heart, but they interrupt, cast one's eyes backwards. . . . I had rather write in my own way of "four Passionate Snails" than be, as K[atherine] M[ansfield] maintains, Jane Austen over again. (*VW Diary* 1: 316)

In another characteristic moment, when she writes in a letter to Margaret Llewelyn Davies of the task of reading all of Eliot for the 1919 article, she immediately moves from intimidating critical standards to the personality of the earlier author: "Its rather humiliating, reading other peoples novels. George Eliot fascinates me. Did your father know her? or was she too much under a cloud? Nobody called on her, so she says; and yet her virtue seems to me excessive—but there's no room left" (*VW Letters* 2: 385). It almost seems that Woolf would generate a whole novel (if there were room in the letter) about such a virtuous victim of scandal, such a learned and famous Maggie Tulliver, whom Woolf's father knew well.

When Woolf conjures up her most important predecessor she seems inevitably to follow the pattern of most readings of any woman novelist: she casts her as a literary *heroine*, creator of autobiographical heroines. It is one sad limitation of the colloquy I am initiating here that Woolf has all the last words, whereas Eliot must remain strangely silent on her successor. But if we were to borrow Rose Macaulay's license and allow the precursor to speak as the creator of the successor-heroine, Eliot may be imagined to say (as she wrote of her heroines Dorothea, Romola, Maggie, and Gwendolen): "Virginia Woolf 'had that kind of beauty which seems to be thrown into relief by poor dress. . . . She was open, ardent, and not in the least self-admiring; . . . her imagination adorned her sister with attractions altogether superior to her own.' She was reared in 'the world' of 'her father's books.' She wished to 'make [herself] a world outside [of love], as men do,' and there was 'an alarming amount of devil' in her; she was 'inwardly rebellious against the restraints of family conditions' but not one of the 'practically reforming women'; 'a soul burning with a sense of what the universe is not, and ready to take all existence as fuel, . . . nevertheless held captive by the ordinary wirework of social forms'; she was 'not going to do as other women did'; she was finally 'likely to seek martyrdom' " (M 5–7; R 104; MF 361, 328; DD 83, 168).

The portrait, of course, is more that of the composite Eliot heroine than of Woolf herself, but I submit that in general outline it would do not only for Eliot's supposed response to Woolf but for Eliot herself as well—not in either case the "real" woman, of course, but the "career author" recreated in a reading of her works (Booth 126–34). Woolf's portrayal of Eliot, as we shall see, corresponds with this model, as to some extent do all readings of these authors that grant their greatness. Woolf reconceived the Grand Old Woman of English Letters who preceded her: "The whole of the nineteenth century seems to be mirrored in the depths of that sensitive and profound mind which lies buried . . . under Mr. Cross's tomb" ("GE" [1926]). Aren't we tempted likewise to exhume Woolf as well as Eliot as a vessel of human history? How are we to reread Eliot and Woolf?

Not, it seems to me, by imposing a logical argument: my suggestions throughout this book for rereading Eliot and Woolf take the form of a series of colloquies or cross-breedings arranged in an associative narrative. First, in the rest of this introduction, I attempt to uncover the basis of the myths of Eliot and Woolf—the circumstances of their canonization, particularly in feminist discourse. It's lonely at the top: how many securely canonized women authors are there? How did they do it? Are we simply to admire the genius, like Shakespeare's, that from time to time lands in the wrong gender or class? Whatever the causes, the effects are manifest; the phenomena "George Eliot" and "Virginia Woolf" seem secure from literary oblivion—as far as we can see.

The question of how they have been *read* precedes, to my mind, the question of how *they* read the concepts of womanhood and tradition (taken up in Chapter 1), and subsequently, the question—addressed in the second chapter—of *how* they designed their works, personas, and careers to be read: what were the causes of their literary eminence? Chapters 3 and 4 focus on Eliot's and Woolf's revisions of history and of heroism, respectively—the two main axes of their feminist conception of greatness. The remaining chapters engage pairs of novels as parallel reinscriptions of the feminine in history. At successive stages in their careers (and here my narrative becomes chronological), Eliot and Woolf both speculated, first, on aristocratic heroines as stand-ins for the great women of letters, as leading ladies of historical romance (*Romola* and *Orlando*, Chapter 5). Then, chastening these individualistic fantasies, they wrote realistic histories of the common life with a conflicted feminist agenda, as private and public spheres, feminine and masculine, struggle for predominance (*Felix Holt* and *The Years*, Chapter 6). Finally, this struggle becomes impossible to ignore in the last novels, in which individual greatness and the feminine ideal, public history and the darker currents of private experience threaten to declare war, though the authors seek the arbitration of ancient myth (*Daniel Deronda* and *Between the Acts*, Chapter 7). With this trajectory in mind, I turn first to the biographical myth.

The Canon and the Canonized

I have been aware of a certain inevitability as well as improbability in this project: the inevitability of considering together the two most rounded and renowned English women of letters; and the improbability that a comparison will yield much more than certain striking similarities in literary biography. How unlikely it must seem that they have much in common: the female Victorian sage, with her intrusive philosophical narrator, and the "feminist-modernist" (Gubar, "Birth of the Artist," 39) with the disembodied voice, eddying rather than edifying. The contrast between these voices underscores the changing context of feminism and of literary modes over the years. A careful examination of these two profoundly related writers should help restrain a tendency to extrapolate from the circumstances of women novelists of the nineteenth century in England the supposedly universal circumstances of the woman writer. In many respects, the personas of Eliot and Woolf foil a desire to generalize about women writers.

The manly Victorian and the ladylike modern certainly went about their achievements in different spirits. Yet in their success they are not divided: they are among the few women writers ever to be welcomed into the canon without delay, though not without the usual fluctuations. As an outspoken feminist who eschewed the masculine narrative persona, Woolf not incidentally encountered resistance to her work as overrefined and elusive, as, in a word, ladylike. Eliot's literary persona can seem just the opposite, as Woolf remarked: "In fiction, where so much of personality is revealed, the absence of charm is a great lack [telling word!]; and her critics, who have been, of course, mostly of the opposite sex, have resented, half consciously perhaps, her deficiency in a quality which is held to be supremely desirable in

women" ("GE" [1919] 152). For some decades after her death, Eliot's
reputation sank under the ponderous image of the manly female sage.
Yet the canonized personas of Eliot and Woolf have much in common
besides the success that underlies these different styles.

Woolf was raised in Eliot's Victorian milieu,[12] but coming later could
more openly confront the obstacles in a woman's path toward literary
eminence, whereas Eliot had to play the role of the exceptional being
to whom the norms of her sex somehow never applied (Carroll, *Heritage*, 13–14; Beer, *George Eliot*, 26; D. Barrett 1–13). To be the sibyl, to
be the first woman of the age, may have been a handicap for Eliot, as
Woolf saw it, but she herself felt the strain of eminence, being "the
only woman in England free to write what I like," yet "being a figure
. . . being a martyr" to criticism (*VW Diary* 3: 43, 4: 251). Woolf's stance
as outsider in society and insider in moments of being replicates in
many ways Eliot's persona.

Readers of Eliot and Woolf have constructed many versions of these
personas, most of them images of greatness, but some of them high-
lighting the lack attributed to womanhood. Eliot could be appropriated
as a paragon of womanhood or a great man of letters; thus Mathilde
Blind in 1883 published the laudatory *George Eliot* in the "Famous
Women" series, but then in 1902 Leslie Stephen placed her among the
"Men of Letters," where her womanhood became a glaring fault.
Generations of biographies, guidebooks to Warwickshire artifacts, and
editions of the complete works certify the great author's canonicity.
Several editions of Eliot feature illustrations not of the author or of the
text itself but of the aura of greatness: photographs of her houses, or
of great men such as Goethe (the subject of a biography by George
Henry Lewes), whose statue and portrait endorse a 1910 edition of
Impressions of Theophrastus Such (Harper's *Complete Works*).

Woolf has yet to make it to gold-leaf "Complete Works," but biographies and guidebooks to Bloomsbury are hastening to outdo the
Eliot pattern, while the monumental volumes of diaries, letters, and
essays already exceed Eliot's remains, reminding us that the Victorians
customarily destroyed their most personal effects to protect the image
of greatness. Our tastes have changed; if we must love the great, we
must have some intimacy with private failings, and Woolf has amply

---

[12]Through her father, whom Eliot consulted on details of college life for *Daniel Deronda*
(Haight 476), Woolf knew many of her predecessor's eminent contemporaries. Henry
James, for instance, visited at the Priory in 1869 and at the Stephen home in the
1890s (Haight 416–17; Bell 1: 32). Woolf's great-aunt Julia Cameron brought a gift of
photographs to the Priory and wanted to photograph Eliot (Haight 450); Virginia Woolf
wrote an introduction to a volume of Cameron's work.

documented her privacy. Not everyone has loved Woolf, of course, any more than Eliot's immediate successors loved her. Some still doubt Woolf's significance. An eccentric but perhaps authoritative example is Hugh Kenner, who sets Woolf in a dead-end tradition as heir to Henry James, with "no descendants." The editions of letters and diaries are "a fine catafalque" that claims, as she would *not* have done, "that she was her time's regnant sensibility" (75, 165–66). Though Woolf was eager enough to crown herself as the spirit of the age (and to laugh at such monarchy), Kenner is right to view the scholarly memorialization with suspicion. As Thomas Caramagno charges, Woolf may have been turned into a "Lady of Shallot [sic] . . . more beautiful dead than alive" (10).

Much academic criticism prides itself on being less personal than the above biographical judgments, but the purest study of texts is governed by judgment of an author's worthiness on one scale or another. These days, no critic has to defend her choice to study Woolf, unless it be against charges of redundancy. Woolf is well entrenched in the academic battlefield: the *MLA Bibliography* for 1981 through March 1991 lists 732 items on her and 667 on George Eliot, who for decades was one of the three assuredly "major" English women writers (with Austen and Emily Brontë); each year the count of work on Woolf pulls farther ahead of the total for Eliot. Woolf has taken Eliot's place as a figure of intense biographical interest. The stir over Eliot's private life has subsided, while the political and formal aspects of her work seem to require the mediation of experts. In contrast, Woolf's revival has been sparked by the warm reception of her amply documented life and of her feminist politics, both of which have a wide if controversial appeal.[13] Eliot seems more firmly than ever grouped with the great sages, conversing over a rather thin gruel of Feuerbach and Comte, though studies such as those by Graver, Myers, and Welsh (in 1984 and 1985) have succeeded in reviving her as an independent and complex social critic, while works like Barbara Hardy's 1959 *The Novels of George Eliot: A Study in Form* have long established her astounding control of structure and imagery.

[13]Eric Warner notes that he was slow to assemble the only centenary conference on Woolf in England (at Fitzwilliam College, Cambridge, 20–22 September 1982), and that otherwise the British media were silent on Woolf's centenary (1–3). American enthusiasm for Woolf has been seen by Quentin Bell and others as a misguided belief in Woolf's feminist commitment and literary importance. See Jane Marcus, "Quentin's Bogey," and Bell, "Reply." Marcus notes a lingering "undecidability" in Woolf's reputation in spite of "canonization"; *The Waves* has been included in the Cambridge Landmarks of World Literature (1986), but there is continuing hostility, mostly among male British critics ("Lycanthropy" 109, 102–3).

Woolf has similarly required being rescued from exclusive masculine company, not that of the social philosophers but of the formalist innovators (Freedman 3–7). Recently, Jane Wheare has rightly challenged the formalist bias of earlier Woolf criticism: the neglect of Woolf's "dramatic" novels (e.g., *The Years*) by those who insist on Woolf as a modernist experimenter (Wheare 1–3; Black, "Life of Natural Happiness," 310). The dramatic novels reveal Woolf the realistic social commentator and feminist, as Wheare shows, but it is misleading to suggest that Woolf simply exploits realist conventions in these works. Woolf is as much a literary experimenter in a novel like *The Years* as she is a social commentator in a work like *Between the Acts;* the formal and the social innovator are one, much as "the personal *is* the political" (Cuddy-Keane, "Politics of Comic Modes," 273).

The same concert of political and formal elements appears in Eliot's work, as well as the same tendency of critics to lay claim to one or the other of these inseparable images of the great writer. Either she is aloft in the impersonal, apolitical ether of art, or she is muscling it out in the trenches of a Cause; in either case, certain aspects of the woman writer's persona become a liability. This is not the place to retrace the arguments in the tugs-of-war over these authors, but to point out that arbitrary divisions between formal, ideological, and biographical interests can be used to tear the writers apart.

Instead, many critics such as myself try to unite the different interests without arbitrarily reconciling them, implying that the contradictoriness itself is indicative of greatness—or of worthiness to be talked about. Ralph Freedman, taking stock of the battling versions of Virginia Woolf in 1980, wrote what could apply almost as well to Eliot as to Woolf: "She was both elitist and nonelitist, playful and earthbound, self-conscious about her art and socially conscious as well. If some critical opinion has become polarized to reflect her own dialectic, this is precisely the symptom of the condition that has returned her to the center of the literary stage" (8).[14] The composite character described here, a kind of stage heroine who encompasses a textual dialectic as well as a dialectic of public responses, seems to be the generic Grand Old Woman of Letters. Her greatness, our willingness to watch her at center stage, depends on her own difference from herself, her doubling of appearances to meet the contradictory demands of her audience. Such a burden of personality, which I discuss more fully in

[14]Marcus in 1989 discerned a similar variety of personas: "an anarchist Woolf next to a feminist, the class-bound Woolf next to the class-conscious. The daughter obsessed with the mother next to the modernist deconstructor" ("Lycanthropy" 110).

the second chapter, has subtly determined Eliot's and Woolf's changing roles in the canon.

Feminist criticism of Eliot and Woolf has further determined their
canonicity by stressing the womanhood that once had to be cordoned
off from their greatness. Of course, even before feminist criticism, few
critics ever forgot that Eliot *was a woman;* thus I somehow picked up
in college the insight that the harsh treatment of pretty Hetty Sorrel
or Rosamond Vincy must be the revenge of an ugly woman. Gilbert
and Gubar's Angel of Destruction, a vast improvement over Eliot as
jealous hag, remains for many the true George Eliot, in contrast with
a victimized Woolf who only harmed herself.[15] In the last fifteen years
or so, Woolf has far outstripped Eliot as an enabling foremother in the
"female literary tradition." While Woolf's literary eminence has been
perhaps as daunting to successors as Eliot's,[16] in general the response
of literary women to Woolf has been grateful rather than rebellious.
After all, Woolf has encouraging as well as restraining words for those
coming after: if she had set out to nourish her daughters in feminist
criticism, she could hardly have offered a richer source than *A Room
of One's Own* (Stimpson). Eliot has remained central; books of feminist
readings, whether neo-Marxist, neo-Lacanian, or variously poststructuralist (e.g., Newton, Homans, Langbauer), will predictably contain
a chapter on Eliot, but her presence is relatively passive: what can be
done to her to make her a feminist? The Grand Old Woman of Victorian
Letters counseled resignation, it seems: an ideal of selfless devotion
especially recommended for women who have little choice. Woolf, by
happy contrast, wrote two books avowedly addressing what in Eliot's
day would have been called the Woman Question, and she wrote
many articles on women writers; these writings provide volatile fuel
for our contemporary feminist controversy. I take it as significant that
Woolf, not Eliot, is invoked by feminists of every camp (e.g., Marshall;
Showalter, "Feminist Criticism"; Moi; M. Barrett, "Ideology," 77), in
spite of the fact that Woolf's feminism harks back to many of the tenets
of Eliot's and other Victorians' belief in womanhood.

Both Eliot and Woolf have disappointed many feminists in their

---

[15]Recent works by Uglow, Dorothea Barrett, Taylor, and Beer have complicated the
biographical image based on Cross's and Haight's defining works. Analogous revision
of Bell's Woolf has been instigated by Gordon, DeSalvo, Abel, and others.

[16]Elaine Showalter draws on Woolf's "Professions for Women": "A woman writer
must kill the Angel in the House. . . . For Charlotte Brontë and George Eliot, the angel
was Jane Austen. For the feminist novelists, it was George Eliot. For mid-twentieth-
century novelists, the Angel is Woolf herself" (*Literature* 265). See Marcus's corrective
of Moi's reading of Showalter on Woolf ("Lycanthropy" 103).

appeal to womanly influence, in their somewhat patronizing views of women writers, and in their implicit loyalties to tradition and explicit distrust of political action (Showalter, "Greening," *Sexual Anarchy*, 57–75, and *Literature*, 264–65, 280–282; Gilbert and Gubar, *Madwoman*, 466; Moers 194; Stimpson 135–38). If feminist critics concur in canonizing Eliot and Woolf as great *women* of letters, how do they account for these disappointing features in the authors' ideology?

Taking a cue from Woolf, feminist critics often reproach Eliot's works for their narrow conception of woman's sphere: her heroines tragically submerge themselves in familial duty (Z. Austen 549–51). Yet Woolf herself is open to the charge not only of privilege (easy for her to say, £500 a year and a room of one's own!) but also of resorting to the strategies of feminine influence. Rather than objecting to her portrayal of women (count her lesbians and spinsters!), some of Woolf's successors deplore the polite manner of her feminist writings. *A Room of One's Own* offends a certain feminist commitment by suppressing anger (Rich, "When We Dead Awaken," 37; M. Barrett, Introduction, 20), while *Three Guineas*, so openly angry as to seem "hysterical," appears to invite "educated men's daughters" to secede from the politics of their menfolk as though it were a matter of withdrawing from the port and cigars after dinner.[17]

Such distrust of Woolf's manifestos may derive from the lingering odor of Victorian feminine sanctity about them. Earnest feminists may feel they are being handed the kind of "woman's mission" sop that Eliot seems to dispense in the Finale of *Middlemarch*—though these feminists may themselves be heirs to the ideology of influence, arguing for example that we would all be better off for a return of matriarchy or a polity of mutuality rather than domination. Woolf's conception of the feminine does to an extent harmonize with Eliot's, as I will show, while her novels record much the same outlook as Eliot's on woman's narrow sphere. Feminists who believe in political activism and an eradication of difference are rightly suspicious of Woolf's traditional brand of feminism. And yet many of them rely on her as a predecessor, much as Woolf, critical of Eliot's masculine persona and refusal to create a heroine of Eliot's own stature, drew on the most lauded Victorian woman novelist as a guide to resist as well as follow.

The mixed terms in which Eliot and Woolf have been canonized,

---

[17]Showalter coincides with Q. D. Leavis ("Caterpillars of the Commonwealth Unite!") in charging that in *Three Guineas* Woolf is out of touch with ordinary women, though Showalter would ask for more propaganda rather than less. Both critics center on Woolf's personality: a heavily diagnosed invalid with a "deadly . . . disembodied" "vision of womanhood" (Showalter, *Literature*, 294–97). See Minow-Pinkney 187–88.

particularly in feminist criticism, call for a study such as this, which reconsiders not only the two authors in light of each other but also the critical and canonical standards. Thus the examination of Eliot's and Woolf's versions of feminism, while it throws new light on an important feminist tradition, also challenges the categories that have recently been imposed on feminist theory, inviting an eclectic method. From one point of view it appears that these writers could be differentiated according to the feminist theoretical treatment they invite: Eliot the Anglo-American empiricist mode with its preference for nineteenth-century realism, and Woolf the French psycholinguistic school with its privileging of modernist or postmodernist texts.[18] But just as many critics have challenged the geographical categorization of Anglo-American and French feminisms, I would question the utility of aligning Eliot with a naive empiricism and Woolf with an enlightened awareness of the contingencies of discourse. In spite of Woolf's skepticism about biographical truth and method, she like her "Anglo-American" heirs promotes the historical quest for maternal sources of meaning (however deferred); her reading of Eliot and of other women writers of the past anticipates the search for spiritual mothers by writers such as Alice Walker (who almost inevitably quotes *A Room of One's Own* at length; 235, 239–40).

At the same time, however, Woolf may be championed as a pioneer of *écriture feminine* (Marcus, *Languages*, 13, 170) or as an outsider strangely allied to whatever male modernists or postmodernists (Joyce or Proust, Derrida or Lacan) the cosmopolitan feminist theorists invoke.[19] Eliot in turn can be shown to have anticipated deconstruction in figuring language as a web of metaphor strung on illusory difference, "pinched into its pilulous smallness" by the touch of interpretation (M 16). Moreover, *Daniel Deronda*, for instance, figures women as "other," associated with the oppressed (colonies) and the repressed (the unconscious) (Hertz; C. Chase; Graver 224–43). Significant as distinctions among feminist schools may be for some purposes, in this book I make no attempt to segregate them, though clearly I read Eliot and Woolf for the most part through the lens of a feminist criticism they helped to form, often called "liberal" or "Anglo-American."

[18]Just as the origins of psychoanalysis may be linked to the probing of the unconscious in novels such as Eliot's, later psycholinguistic innovations on Freud could be seen as indebted to modernist experiments in the disintegration of discourse and consciousness. As if to confirm this, Cixous and Kristeva invoke modern writers such as Woolf and Joyce. See Minow-Pinkney on Cixous and Woolf (10, 15) and Kristeva and Woolf (23). See also Gilbert, "Introduction: A Tarantella of Theory," xv.

[19]Jacobus and Homans show how readily Eliot or Woolf can be adapted to psycholinguistic theory, turning the canon of Anglo-American feminism francophile.

My readings render Woolf more Victorian and Eliot more modern (and feminist) than many readers will comfortably allow. Although numerous readings of Woolf have highlighted her Victorian origins or qualities (e.g., Beer, *Past*, 117–82; Hill; Marcus, *Languages;* McLaurin, *Woolf;* Meisel; Paul; Rosenbaum), and some have noted her debt to Victorian conservative feminism, most have assumed Woolf's own stated view that her most valuable contribution is that of "novelty." Indeed, without the modernist credentials, she might have been viewed, at least temporarily, as another faded Rose Macaulay. I believe, however, that an alignment of Woolf with Eliot, and particularly with Victorian gender ideology, is not only one of the most instructive and most neglected ways to view Woolf now, but also a way to revive rather than eulogize her, freeing her from the exclusive company of Joyce, T. S. Eliot, and other modernist worthies as well as from the burden of being everybody's favorite feminist.[20]

There are of course pitfalls in placing eminent women writers in a new feminist canon. I am wary of the element of nostalgia in feminist studies of nineteenth-century women authors, as well as in the cult of Woolf, though I do not automatically repudiate nostalgia (or avoid it even when I try). The search for a mother-past, like Lily Briscoe's forsaken cry for Mrs. Ramsay ("to want and not to have" [TL 266]), can be a dubious quest, reinstating masculinist desire for Woman. But if Mrs. Ramsay, or the woman writer of the past we choose to search for, is understood as Eliot's and Woolf's writings encourage us to understand character, not as a fixed center of meaning but as a deferred process, the historical-biographical quest itself may be a process that will answer feminist purposes (Gilbert and Gubar, *No Man's Land* 1: xi–xii). If, moreover, we can laugh off our inclination to rescue work—that is, our desire to rescue women writers of the past for feminist respectability in the manner of genteel Victorians redeeming women of the streets—we may be able to reinterpret women's literary history and the history of feminist thought, reshaping it for purposes defined as "respectable" or worthwhile in our day.

Our rescue work in the female literary tradition often seems too eager to wash away the sins of history, that is, the particular historical conditions that render women different from each other in spite of their common sex and gender. Until recently, much feminist scholarship has been devoted to honoring female heroes, proving their great-

[20]Modernism ain't what it used to be: by now many eminent female modernists have escaped the shadows of T. S. Eliot and Ezra Pound to form their own marginal center. Works by Shari Benstock, Mary Lynn Broe and Angela Ingram, and Bonnie Kime Scott in particular have shifted the canon.

ness because they *too* speak for "us" all. By the 1990s, one really ought to be beyond that, ought to be rescuing more marginal voices. But there are still many silences in the few already dominant women's voices, and I listen for differences as well as concurrence within these. I have no stake in denying the significant changes in literary climate for these two authors, or in denying the exclusivity of that middle-class, English climate. Nor would I wish to ask readers to forget that Marian Evans Lewes Cross died in 1880, wholly innocent of the two World Wars and the myriad other factors that created a sense of the "modern," let alone unaware of the birth of Virginia Woolf in 1882. In the pages that follow, however, I am willing to let George Eliot and Virginia Woolf seem to speak to each other or even at times in unison, not as universal, ahistorical voices but in all their idiosyncracy and frequent dissonance. In this performance, I am drawn as so many feminist critics have been to the mode of Woolf's own biographical criticism. According to Barbara Currier Bell and Carol Ohmann, Woolf often "personifies the works of a writer: so she presents us not with a series of texts but with some*one*, a man or a woman" (their emphasis; 55). Bell and Ohmann make clear that for Woolf this personification is the essence of the biographical author contained in the texts, not a waxwork of the real personage who wrote them.

These authorial personas are usually read as offering contradictory responses to the Woman Question, Eliot conservative and Woolf radical. But feminist readers have often struggled with the hard fact of each author's skepticism about direct political action in spite of her close association with activists. This skepticism is in keeping with the feminist tradition in which I place both Eliot and Woolf. This tradition, upholding feminine influence in opposition to masculine authority, has generally confined its political action to the realm of rhetoric in the most honorable sense, that is, to teaching, art, and writing of all kinds, not (or not simply) from a ladylike reluctance to make a scene. Force is always wrong, we are shown in the satire of the rabble in *Felix Holt* and of Rose Pargiter's suffragette brick-throwing in *The Years*. The vote means little in the face of inequalities of education and opportunity—so the private and public writings of Eliot and Woolf maintain.

The ideology of influence as I characterize it is certainly more conservative than the agenda of most feminists in the United States in the 1990s (the pro-choice and pro-influence positions seem irreconcilable, for example), but the influence of that ideology itself has far from disappeared. Hence Eliot and Woolf are important to an understanding of feminist traditions. They articulate a skepticism about political reform based on a belief in the priority of private experience over public life that has remained with the movement. Many feminists now are persuaded that legislation will never shake the dominance of men in private relations; as Mary Evans puts it, "The universal subordination of women . . . is unlikely to be altered by changes in legal and administrative practices." Indeed, the slogan "the personal is political" should be seen as a late-twentieth-century equivalent of the demonstration in nineteenth-century novels that political reform is insufficient: the power plays of home life are the foundation of the state (Evans 15–17).[21]

One of the great benefits of feminist analysis has been to provoke readers to storm the mental barricades that separate history and the political world of men from everyday life and the domestic world of women, to challenge, as Eliot's and Woolf's writings do, the priority of public politics over private, or even to challenge the clear distinction between what is public and what is private. But there is always the risk of jumping over to the underprivileged side and adding sofa cushions and kitchen chairs to the barricades, thus reinforcing the dualism (and inevitable hierarchy) of public/private, male/female. The suspicion that demonstrations or legislative reforms may be simply new moves in a game always already fixed ought to warn us against assuming that those who abstain from playing necessarily approve things as they are.[22] Indeed, a certain radical glamor has been cast over the (inevitably political) move of abstention by French theorists who, like Eliot and Woolf, eschew the term "feminism" or hold aloof from the movements for parity for women with men in law or work. These French theorists compellingly charge that the desire for equality reinforces the phallocentric discourse of the "same"; liberation movements are bourgeois efforts to invert the dualist hierarchy of masculine/feminine without escaping hierarchical dualism (e.g., Irigaray, *This Sex*, 30–33). Yet this sophisticated argument is directed by women with Ph.D.s against women whose bedfellows are not Nietzsche, Heidegger, Derrida, or Lacan. Abstention, then, may often be the

---

[21]Claudia Johnson suggests that, in the aftermath of the French Revolution, simply to portray female independence was to express revolutionary sympathies (xxiii–xxv). In another regard, gender relations are more far-reaching than "politics"; Simone de Beauvoir belatedly realized sexism will not vanish after the ever-postponed revolution (Moi 91–92). See MacKinnon 234–35; Nicholson.

[22]An entire book could be written on the current phenomenon of critics rushing to make their ideological affiliations explicit and beating the bushes for political actions by writers of earlier times, while themselves busily writing, teaching, going to an occasional rally, or sending in their check to Amnesty International. Eliot and Woolf were after all rather busy writing, and agonizing over it to boot.

ironic privilege of women—such as Eliot and Woolf, not incidentally—
whose access to the patriarchal tradition or counter-tradition was undoubtedly hard-won and would not have been possible without earlier
reform movements. Nevertheless, the few women so privileged seem
determined to resist being lumped with ordinary women.

We can see a similar conflict in a bizarre minor tradition within
academic feminist criticism, a tradition of acknowledgments of the
"others," from Annette Kolodny's reference to "the millions of women
who labor in poverty" (163), to Moi's subsumption of black and lesbian
criticism in a text on feminist theory as a whole (86–87).[23] Often it
appears that feminist academics, like Eliot and Woolf, are finding
voice out of women's general silence: keep the few women in the
men's club by refusing admittance to the shrill petticoat (or radical
chic) rabble. We should be wary of this familiar move—and I perceive
it in my own discussion of two canonical writers—but it is not clear to
me that the politically laudable choice of scholarly subject or theoretical
vocabulary leads to more rapid defeat either of destructive ideology
or of the oppression intertwined with it. The written line may bear
some resemblance to a trench, but most of us know not to flatter
ourselves with the analogy. The written "front" is not imaginary, but
defers any victories to future consciousness; meanwhile the student
who has been raped by her roommate's boyfriend, the secretary who
can't collect child care payments from her ex-husband, the over-
crowded shelter for battered wives here in town are no better off if I
earn the order of merit on the page. Knowing that our gratifications
are perforce delayed may drive us in frustration to attack each other's
jargon or apparent lack thereof, but energies can be better directed. I
admire and engage with "theory" without wishing to *be* it, and in
many ways I infuse a poststructuralist critique of phallocentrism in
my study of Eliot's and Woolf's eccentric or *alter*-native evocations of
identity, history, and heroism or greatness. But my sympathies lie
more with the far-from-neutral tone and perspective of the far-from-
univocal liberal tradition that fostered Eliot and Woolf.

[23]Other instances of awkward bows to those outside the white, middle-class heterosexual enclave include Patricia Meyer Spacks's notorious disclaimer in *The Female Imagination* (see Smith 172; Gardiner et al. 639–40; and Carby 9–10) and the affirmative-action
table of contents of Showalter's *The New Feminist Criticism* (one article about lesbian
criticism, two about black and lesbian criticism). It is easier to attack the effects of
privilege than to avoid them, however. We should also grant that feminist critics have
been more responsive than some scholarly guilds to charges of exclusivity, as is indicated
by Showalter's inclusion of Smith's article in her own edition. Moreover, Spacks's was
one of the first admissions that "we" were not speaking from a universal platform; she
might have offended more if she had been more of an integrationist.

In resisting the compulsion to choose sides, I may not wholly please either. My point in what follows is to keep negotiations open; the conflicting loyalties and insights of Eliot and Woolf can never be reduced to complicity with patriarchal discourse and cultural privilege. Self-contradictory, they strove for the truth universally acknowledged at the same time that they demolished the One supposed to know such contested truth. And like most practicing academic feminists, they sought to transform the discourse in which human beings in all their variety apprehend women and men, while themselves purchasing a place as women of letters in a tradition blinded to difference.

1

Something to Do:
The Ideology of Influence and the
Context of Contemporary Feminism

Feminist critics have turned eagerly to both Eliot and Woolf as magnificent contradictions of all those prohibitions against women in the sanctum of art—"Women can't paint, women can't write," says Charles Tansley to Lily Briscoe (TL 75)—yet they are often disturbed to find in the novels an insistence on the suffering and silence of women. The authors appear to declare the rights of women to a place in history, yet also to depict that place as an obscure, retiring one. What presuppositions about the nature of womanhood and sexual difference governed their fiction as well as their writings on womanhood, on women's education and vocation, and what gender ideology guided their own rather reserved association with women reformers? The answers I offer to these questions suggest the need for a more fully elaborated ideological history of the women's movement. Instead, I can only trace here some especially intriguing intersections of Eliot's and Woolf's ideology of influence with that of some contemporaries.

Eliot and Woolf on the Nature of Womanhood

Like most nineteenth-century partisans of women's interests and like many feminist factions today, these English women of letters waffle in the debate about nature versus nurture. On the one hand, their narratives can be shown to undermine the illusion that historically conditioned differences in gender are natural and inevitable. On the other hand, they can be caught again and again conflating biological sex with cultural gender, smuggling into their texts a sentimental belief in the inherent and timeless (if not literally innate) femininity—

and superiority—of women. Why this fondness for what we would grandly call "difference" persists among some of those who have speculated most profoundly about sexual roles is an intriguing question, since a mystified "womanhood" has been the shibboleth of oppression. But it is certainly true that Eliot and Woolf both leaned toward this mystified difference.

Eliot and Woolf are in good company in their desire to preserve some aspect of the "nature" of womanhood from the effects of historical conditioning; the many feminists who have resisted seeing difference as an entirely historical construct have shared at least one compelling reason for doing so (besides the obvious—itself historically conditioned—basis of biological sex). If culture were entirely responsible for a perceived femininity, what would become of the virtue of *not* resembling the patriarch in the event that all oppressive conditions were rectified? If everyone were "like men," aggressive, calculating, power-hungry (and in many Victorians' view, uniquely sex-hungry), etc., etc., history would be a merciless chronicle. Hence the temptation to invoke what I call the ideology of influence: a belief that women have a direct line to the sources of human emotion, and that their self-sacrificing love (or in a current version, their interest in relationships rather than power or justice) "mitigates the harshness of all fatalities," in Eliot's words. This ideology of influence, which came into full flower after the 1830s as industrialization exaggerated the division between men in the workplace and women in the home (or in underpaid, segregated labor [Hartmann 207–13]), sought to redefine womanhood as a mission rather than a mere handicap. Thus, even if one protested the sacrifice of "many Dorotheas," one could without sense of treachery exalt the influence of the women sacrificed (M 612). The alternative might be no alternative, or alterity, at all. The norm of masculine egotism, of a struggle for domination in the political and economic realm, might govern all human existence. The logic of polarities thus generates a mystified historical other, even as those who invoke it try to reach beyond polarities: women's influence is toward reconciliation, what Eliot envisioned as a harmony of the sexes, and Woolf as an androgyny beyond sexual self-consciousness.

Eliot's writings exhibit all the ambivalence of her contemporaries when they criticize the historical position of women yet defend the special qualities of influence. Eliot's earlier writings, preceding the more widespread agitation for women's causes in the 1860s, show more inclination to hasten the progress toward equality of the sexes that she assumes is inexorably underway. At times claiming that women exert "a conservative influence" almost by nature ("The Natural History of German Life" 275), she nevertheless succinctly states the case for a cultural view of the "sex/gender system" (Rubin 168) when she acknowledges the radical innovations of such women as Margaret Fuller and Mary Wollstonecraft. An oppressive society has created feminine inferiority:

> On one side we hear that woman's position can never be improved until women themselves are better; and, on the other, that women can never become better until their position is improved. . . . But we constantly hear the same difficulty stated about the human race in general. There is a perpetual action and reaction between individuals and institutions; we must try and mend both by little and little. . . . Unfortunately, many overzealous champions of women assert their actual equality with men—nay, even their moral superiority to men. . . . But we want freedom and culture for woman, because subjection and ignorance have debased her, and with her, Man. ("Margaret Fuller and Mary Wollstonecraft" 205)

It may seem promising here that Eliot will not overzealously claim women's moral superiority, and that she calls for a wider field of endeavor for women because they have been defined by oppressive customs; whatever the nature, nurture has much to answer for (compare Lewes, "Lady Novelists," 7).

Eliot has little love for idolized women as they are. Thus she praises Wollstonecraft and Fuller but objects to that domestic monstrosity, the "doll-Madonna in her shrine"; warbling in her gilded cage like Rosamond Vincy, she is often a harpy who debases a "man of genius."[1] Indeed Eliot can be almost as hostile as Woolf toward the Victorian domestic idol, the Angel in the House, though Eliot follows tradition in commiserating with the Angel's husband rather than her daughters. Hints of direct conflict with the feminine ideal, however, make Eliot uneasy. She cannot kill the Angel in the House as Woolf advises the woman writer to do; she merely condemns her to a hell of falsity and selfishness.

It seems that Eliot cannot sustain her historical analysis of gender and the subjection of women. When women verge on Romantic egotism, she tends to revert to arguments of innate femininity. She praises

---

[1] "Margaret Fuller and Mary Wollstonecraft" 204. Without the added story of "Miss Brooke," *Middlemarch* might appear to retell the old misogynist story of genius destroyed by woman. But Dorothea in contrast to Rosamond could really have helped a man if he were indeed a genius. The artificial product of Mrs. Lemon's school and the bourgeois drawing room, not a concept of female nature, is being criticized.

the "brave" and "strong" Margaret Fuller and Mary Wollstonecraft because they are *not* the demon opposites of household angels: they still listen to "the beating of a loving woman's heart, which teaches them not to undervalue the smallest offices of domestic care or kindliness" (201; compare Woolf on Wollstonecraft, "Four Figures," CE 3: 193–99). Here we suspect a sentimental association of women's innate tendencies ("heart") with domestic self-sacrifice, only in a more active and unselfish mode than the doll-Madonna's. Eliot's ideal woman's role might be called the domestic public servant: a woman ministering to human need in the marginal realm of charity or social causes, whereby, for example, the hospital can be seen as the household sickroom "multiplied."[2] Her own role as novelist likewise bridges the private moment of the reader at home and the public domain of epochs in the national life, as well as the massive "public" or audience conjured up by her novels. (In N. N. Feltes's Althusserian interpretation, Eliot "interpellated a special audience," as she won her bid for "professional status," in part by "displaying publicly" her unwomanly individual rights [49].) Thus the apparent egotism of the public woman, from Wollstonecraft to herself, may be exonerated if the woman's "heart" still conceives its vocation in domestic terms (Homans 153).

An appeal to the womanly "heart" was almost universal in Victorian writings on the woman question, but it was sometimes accompanied by a less essentialist conception of women's role, especially among the women and men who like Eliot were familiar with the ideas of Spencer, Comte, John Stuart Mill, and others associated with the Social Science Congress (Myers, *Teaching of Eliot*, 5–9). Eliot's interest in developmental or evolutionary social science helped her to call attention to cultural variations, as when she notes the achievements

---

[2]Austen seems to recognize early on the parallel vocations of nurse and woman novelist when Mrs. Smith praises Nurse Rooke in *Persuasion:* "Hers is a line for seeing human nature. . . . Call it gossip if you will; but . . . nurse Rooke . . . is sure to have something to relate that is entertaining and profitable, something that makes one know one's species better." Anne Elliot and Mrs. Smith agree that "a sick chamber may often furnish the worth of volumes" (168; Spacks, *Gossip*, 57). Anna Jameson in 1855 and 1856 delivered lectures urging ladies to take up public charity "to perform socially the household-work"; "a woman begins by being the nurse, the teacher, the cherisher of her home, through her greater tenderness and purer moral sentiments; then she uses these qualities and sympathies on a larger scale, to cherish and purify society." Advancing civilization "multiplie[s] and diffuse[s]" the complementary domestic relations of man and woman (*Sisters of Charity* 5–6; Bauer and Ritt 81–82). Though Eliot could not have attended Jameson's lectures (she was not in England in February 1855, when the first was delivered, and she was not welcome in polite female circles), she would probably have read the published versions, in which her acquaintance expresses views quite similar to her own on women's potential influence.

of cultivated French women during the Enlightenment ("Woman in France: Madame de Sablé" 54, 58). Yet this same empiricist bias betrays her when she too readily attributes biological origins to perceived characteristics. Eliot would undoubtedly have concurred with John Stuart Mill when he noted in *The Subjection of Women* that "unnatural generally means only uncustomary" with regard to sexual roles; yet we see in her works an unacknowledged clinging to what Mill calls the "moralities . . . and . . . sentimentalities" that tell women "it is their [duty and] nature, to live for others" (22, 27).

For Eliot, the idea of a biological burden is readily transposed into a moral mission. As she wrote to John Morley in 1867 apropos of the debate over Mill's amendment for the franchise for women,

> I would certainly not oppose any plan . . . to establish as far as possible an equivalence of advantages for the two sexes, as to education and the possibilities of free development. . . . I never meant to urge the 'intention of Nature' argument, which is to me a pitiable fallacy. I mean that as a fact of mere zoological evolution, woman seems to me to have the worse share in existence. But for that very reason . . . in the moral evolution we have "an art which does mend nature"—an art which "itself is nature." It is the function of love in the largest sense, to mitigate the harshness of all fatalities.

The "zoological" difference between men and women is a boon in that it teaches humanity to recognize its own progress toward "a more clearly discerned distinctness of function (allowing always for exceptional cases [such as herself?]. . .)," while the inequalities of this difference are "a basis for a sublimer resignation in woman and a more regenerating tenderness in man."[3] Nature, or the womanly art of love which *is* nature, seems to be the only certainty in a tenuous struggle toward "equivalence of good for woman and for man."[4] Thus the "pitiable fallacy" of biological destiny creeps back in in spite, or *because,*

---

[3] The belief in progress as an increasing organic differentiation was a favorite with such writers as Spencer (see "Progress: Its Law and Cause" [1857], 13: 14–17); Eliot here calls it "the one conviction on the matter [of sexual roles] which I hold with some tenacity." See Levine, "Eliot's Hypothesis," 8. I quote the letter to John Morley from Haight, *Selections from George Eliot's Letters*, 331–32, because the complete edition omits the phrase "—an art which 'itself is nature,' " and because it has: "I meant to urge the 'intention of Nature' argument" (*GE Letters* 4: 364–65).

[4] Eliot, borrowing the Bard's authority, contributes to the tradition of horticultural imagery that I later discuss, when she alludes to Polixenes' debate with Perdita over the propriety of hybrids (*The Winter's Tale* IV.iv.78–135). By affirming that cultivation also *is* nature, Polixenes alerts us to the inverse idea that no nature is not also culture.

of an attempt to represent women as active partners in human progress. Without innate difference, and hence without the need for "resignation," Eliot implies, there would be no regeneration for men, nothing but harsh fatality.

Eliot wrote similarly equivocal pronouncements to her friend Emily
Davies, the pioneer of women's higher education, during the height
of the struggle to found Girton, the first women's college affiliated
with "Oxbridge." The letter begins with a self-censorship that is also
weighty advice to the woman who will be addressing the public:

> Pray consider the pen drawn through all the words and only retain
> certain points . . . as a background to all you may . . . say to your
> special public.
>   1. The physical and physiological differences between women and
> men. . . . These may be said to lie on the surface. . . . But . . . the
> differences are deep roots of psychological development. . . .
>   2. The spiritual wealth acquired for mankind by the difference of
> function founded on the other, primary difference; and the prepara-
> tion that lies in woman's peculiar constitution for a special moral
> influence. In the face of all wrongs, mistakes, and failures, history
> has demonstrated that gain. And there lies just that kernel of truth
> in the vulgar alarm of men lest women should be 'unsexed' [by
> education]. We can no more afford to part with that exquisite type of
> gentleness, tenderness, possible maternity suffusing a woman's be-
> ing with affectionateness, . . . than we can afford to part with the
> human love, the mutual subjection of soul between a man and a
> woman—which is also a growth and revelation beginning before all
> history.
>   . . . Complete union and sympathy can only come by women
> having . . . the same store of acquired truth or beliefs as men have,
> so that their grounds of judgment may be as far as possible the same.
> (GE Letters 4: 467–68)

Here Eliot envisions historical change—increasing education for
women—as a means of *restoring* a kind of Platonic, pre- or ahistorical
union between man and woman. At the same time she cannot resist
the vulgar anxiety to preserve a feminine ideal that depends on separate "grounds of judgment." Like Mary Wollstonecraft, in other
words, Eliot would have males and females educated together in order
to promote mutual understanding, but unlike Wollstonecraft (86, 107–
9) she distrusts a monolithic, masculine norm for all human beings.
What would we do without difference? Like the Victorian opponents

of equal education whom Ray Strachey describes, Eliot wishes to preserve "that special and peculiar bloom which they regarded as woman's greatest charm, . . . that valuable, intangible 'superiority' of women" (Strachey 143). Eliot's sibilant words, "gentleness, tenderness, possible maternity suffusing . . . with affectionateness," seem nervous approximations of an ideal very much like Ruskin's in "Of Queen's Gardens."

But Eliot is not quite the advocate of arrested female development that this likeness to Ruskin and the guardians of bloom suggests. It is less the intention of nature that concerns Eliot than the intention of women: they must retain their selflessness to mend the "hard nonmoral outward conditions" that men more directly contend with (*GE Letters* 4: 365). In *The Mill on the Floss*, at least in the early books, Eliot treats the notion of womanly "bloom" with bitter sarcasm, disparaging the system that prevents Maggie from learning Latin. But the novel implies that if a masculine education cultivates the sword-swinging and cruel "justice" of her brother Tom, Maggie is better off learning through her suffering.[5] Most readers undoubtedly side with Maggie, though we may resist the novel's pressure to concur in her sacrifice.

This sympathy for Maggie is not only a rhetorical effect, I believe, but also an effect of prejudice in favor of the feminine: many of us still feel the attraction of the myth of the "intangible 'superiority' of women." Less dubiously, I think we need not be ashamed of wishing to see "gentleness, tenderness, . . . affectionateness" incarnated in powerful forms, preferably female and male, without the prescription that those born female must be more selfless than those born male. Bloom and influence are deeply sinister ideals as the strategies of the marginalized, but it would be misguided therefore to value only self-interested plain-dealing on the masculine model. If most feminists now abhor the silent, disembodied lady of the Victorian imagination, they do not therefore repudiate all things "feminine" as though women must advance by becoming "manlike." Eliot's and Woolf's defense of feminine or selfless heroism seems an attempt to escape the dichotomy between the man's ability to exploit and the woman's ability to remain chaste. If Maggie's sacrifice to the flood and family history seems more disturbing than Miss La Trobe's immolation, at the end of *Between the Acts*, in a flood of words for the sake of a new

[5]Tom has a promising moment early in his education—a process of plowing and harrowing—when he takes the feminine point of view of the field being "plowed and harrowed." "Tom became more like a girl than he had ever been in his life," and he even resembles the benighted " 'masses' " (MF 124–25; Jacobus, *Reading Woman*, 69–74).

history of the human family, both can be seen as offering an escape from self that might also be an end to essentialized gender.

Woolf persists in the Victorian hopes for women's education and the alteration of the nurture that has suppressed women, but she also shares the Victorians' nostalgia for natural difference. In *A Room of One's Own* she eulogizes "that extremely complex force of femininity" that has infused the rooms of civilization for ages, and she suggests that it be preserved (though she also speculates that womanhood itself may become obsolete): "For if two sexes are quite inadequate, considering the vastness and variety of the world, how should we manage with one only? Ought not education to bring out and fortify the differences rather than the similarities?" (RO 91). Such differences might even be biologically based: "The nerves that feed the brain would seem to differ in men and women" (81). In tracing a history of women's cultural advancement, however, she seems to reject the oppressive virtues of woman's mission: "Do not dream of influencing other people," she advises her audience of university women (115). In *Three Guineas*, she nevertheless revives the Ruskinian belief in a separate sphere or mission: she urges educated men's daughters to shun the avenues to power newly opening to women and instead to consolidate their outsiders' influence. Yet in recommending the virtues of "poverty, chastity, derision, and freedom from unreal loyalties" to old institutions (TG 79), she is partly reinstating the conditions that have subordinated women in history. In her vision of the harsh fatalities of patriarchy, of fascism, war, and all systems of oppression, a new assertion of feminine otherness appears to be the only mitigation: not a practical measure, not indeed the quickest route to the success (in society's current terms) of the greatest number of women, but a subversion of the whole existing order. Like Eliot, Woolf charged that a peculiar feminine potential till now had been stunted, but no good would come of promoting it in the image of masculine power.

In the spirit of many Victorian reformers, then, Eliot and Woolf retain an ideal of feminine "suffering and sensibility" as a moral advantage ("GE" [1919] 159), in the name not of a clearer separation of the spheres but of a nearer approach to sexual harmony. If femininity is an art which paradoxically *is* nature, it artfully *mends* nature by asserting women's influence on culture. Through education, Eliot and Woolf hope, women may fully develop beyond the past when they were seen as outside and opposed to culture. Yet Eliot's and Woolf's visions of sexual harmony echo the Platonic myth of the sexual spheres, a myth underwriting the patriarchal tradition. Eliot proposed (anticipating Woolf's metaphor for personality, the rainbow): "Let the whole field of reality be laid open to woman as well as to man, and then

. . . we shall have that marriage of minds which alone can blend all the hues of thought and feeling in one lovely rainbow of promise for the harvest of happiness" ("Woman in France " 81). In *A Room of One's Own*, Woolf imagines a similar "marriage of minds": "When I saw the couple get into the taxi-cab the mind felt as if, after being divided, it had come together again in a natural fusion. . . . One has a profound, if irrational, instinct in favour of the theory that the union of man and woman makes for the greatest satisfaction, the most complete happiness" (RO 101–2). The dream of gender without oppression still attracts these women of letters as they try to awaken from the nightmare of historical subjection.

Woolf's desire to preserve feminine bloom is more conscious of its own perversity, its conflict with her open desire to promote women's free development. Her confession of an instinctive heterosexism is explained, tellingly, by her having witnessed a tryst between "people in the street" whom she looks "down on," as though the common life around her were another state of nature. In the same passage she describes the alienation when, instead of thinking "back through [her] fathers" she "thinks back through her mothers": when, "in walking down Whitehall, . . . from being the natural inheritor of that civilisation, she becomes . . . outside of it" (101). The position of outsider is, she acknowledges, uncomfortable and difficult to sustain. Hence the relapse into a "state of mind . . . without effort," in which one can believe in the reconcilability of sexual difference in its customary costumery: "a girl in patent leather boots, and . . . a young man in a maroon overcoat" (100–101).

Such a vision suggests that Woolf's most effortless outlook on sexuality was the essentialist one she first learned in a Victorian milieu (Gordon 5). Yet Woolf unlike Eliot cannot feel at home in Whitehall for long; she finds no comfort in affirming women's "worse share," except to justify her preference for them. "I like their unconventionality. I like their subtlety. I like their anonymity" (RO 115). The terms in which she expresses this preference suggest that she still clings to the nineteenth-century ideology of "woman's sphere" while proclaiming women's moral superiority even more explicitly than Eliot would do.

The Context of Social Movements: Ladies and Heroines as Reformers

We are now in a position to take a closer look at these authors' complex affiliations with contemporary women's causes. I have already touched on two reasons for the authors' distrust of conventional politics. The first is the ideology of influence, which exalts qualities that have been shaped by oppression and perhaps depend on it for their existence. The second reason is closely related to the first: a profound distrust of public forms of power, both that of male leaders and that of the common people. Legislated reform cannot respond with novelistic subtlety to the feminine "art" of "nature," or to the complexities of emotions and consciousness. Ordinary people, similarly, tend not only to be poor readers but also to threaten the sensibility (and at times the security) of ladies, no matter how readily ladies acknowledge common cause with them. The refined private insight of cultivated women, strangely enough, is the force with which Eliot and Woolf propose to combat the evils of things as they are: the oppression of common people as well as of all women. At the same time, as women these authors could expect their critics to associate them with the threatening masses and with low art, no matter how ladylike, rarefied, or impersonal their manners. Neither Eliot nor Woolf could be said to have languished amid the mass readership; indeed, they have been reproached for their supposedly unquestioning identification with elitist values, whether those of the liberal intellectual or the upper-class "social parasite" (Cottom 3–31; Leavis 386). Yet both were persistently seized with anxiety about their right to speak, and retained a sense of themselves as outsiders, albeit cultural aristocrats (Hertz 79-80; *VW Diary* 2: 168, 321).

Defining themselves as outsiders within an elite, as ungendered beings speaking for a feminine common life, Eliot and Woolf necessarily betray inconsistent political affiliations. Indeed, their known relations to contemporary political movements reflect the politics of their own vocations as women of letters. They each lent assent to their associates' efforts to win for women unrestricted education, more just marriage practices, and equitable opportunities to earn a livelihood and control property—all matters that had direct bearing on the career of a woman writer (David 204–6). The sibylline woman writer, like the early women's movements as a whole, must stand aloof from the usual politics of men and the subjection of ordinary women and common people. In so doing, the woman of letters gathered influence to promote sexual and social harmony—or she justified the selfishness of aspiring to greatness as writer or reformer. A closer look at the interconnection of these women of letters and contemporary reform movements should help define both factors: what was the role of the great woman as writer or reformer, and how did contemporaries formulate the "woman question"?

It seems likely that Eliot's cautious approach to the women's movement was conditioned by her own position. She did sign Barbara Leigh Smith's petition for the Married Women's Property Bill in 1856 (Herstein 84), but having "eloped" with Lewes in 1854 she would of course have been excluded from the benefits of that reform. She must have felt all the more reluctance, because of her anomalous status, to take part in the political action on women's behalf that increased over the following decade. There was already a precedent for discrediting feminism by citing the extramarital liaisons of Mary Wollstonecraft. It seems likely that Eliot might have associated more with the "ladies of Langham Place," or contributed to *The English Woman's Journal*, founded by Barbara Leigh Smith and Bessie Parkes in 1857, if her social position had not been so equivocal, and if indeed she had not been preoccupied with gaining the authority of a male novelist.[6] Her apolitical, "objective" stance is not a coincidence of temperament, but rather the position that enabled her to aspire to "greatness."

Eliot consistently writes as the "natural historian" of culture rather than the reformer of particular laws. She expressed uncertainty about the value of the vote for women (Zimmerman, *"Felix Holt,"* 432–37); in *Felix Holt, the Radical* and "Address to Working Men, by Felix Holt," for example, she diverts the issues of the recent Reform Bill of 1867, with the concurrent debate about women's rights, to the context of the first Reform Bill in 1832, arguing that working men (and presumably women even more so) are unfit for the franchise in their current state of ignorance. That Eliot did not confine politics to such party matters is demonstrated in her portraits of Harold Transome and Mr. Brooke, gentlemen "radicals" (and misogynists) for differently muddied "personal" reasons, and in her implication of Mrs. Transome and Esther, Dorothea and Rosamond, in public political events. But the great writer strives to appear unimplicated; her art must not serve politics, though she elaborates a definition of politics in her art that evidently implicates everyone.

Woolf was similarly restrained in her contribution to "the cause," fearing the censure of her own work as polemical. Whereas Eliot had cautioned against abruptly legislating change, Woolf asserted that new legal rights had not altered the "cause"—shared by women and men—against "tyranny," "the same fight that our mothers and grand-

[6]Helsinger, Sheets, and Veeder 2: 147; Feltes 45. Eliot termed "second-rate" the literature in Parkes's *Waverley Journal* (predecessor to *The English Woman's*) (Haight 243; *GE Letters* 2: 379–80; Lacey 218). Eliot wrote to Barbara Leigh Smith (later Bodichon) that essays revealing hardships of poor women "will make the Journal a true organ, with a *function*"; but she deplored the bad reviewer: "I wish Bessie felt more keenly about the immorality of such slack writing" (*GE Letters* 3: 153, 225–26). See Uglow's lucid account, "George Eliot and the Woman Question in the 1850s," 65–81.

mothers fought" (TG 102), a matriarchal lineage that included Emily
Davies and Barbara Leigh Smith Bodichon, as well as another associate
of Eliot's, the physician Elizabeth Garrett Anderson (TG 183n.38,
186n.44). Woolf's "cause," then, is given genealogical respectability,
bound closely to the maternal past, though it might seem eager in
other ways to break with it.[7] "Revisionist rather than revolutionary"
(Rosenman, *Invisible Presence*, 46), she declares, in E. M. Forster's
words, that "women must not condone this tragic male-made mess."
Her feminism is indeed "old-fashioned" as Forster says, not as he
claims because it is obsolete suffragism but because it takes the revenge
of opting out, at least as old as *Lysistrata* (Forster 33; TG 147n.10). In
comparison, Eliot shows less solidarity with the history of women's
resistance to oppression and more respect for the public channels of
reform: there is no real opting out in Eliot's deterministic world,
neither for men who wish to put women and domestic life behind
them nor for women ignorant of the "great" movements of politics
and culture.

Like Eliot's, Woolf's public position on the women's movement of
her day was equivocal, though more active. She took part in some of
the suffrage work that Mary Datchet undertakes in *Night and Day*.
From January 1910 she addressed envelopes for the Adult Suffrage
movement, at the suggestion of Margaret Llewelyn Davies (Bell 1:
161), who was the original of Mary Datchet and of Eleanor Pargiter in
The Years (Marcus, *Languages*, 26–27), as well as being the niece of
Eliot's friend Emily Davies. Woolf worked closely with the younger
Davies, and in June 1913 she attended a meeting of the Women's
Cooperative Guild (an outgrowth of the nineteenth-century socialist,
trade-unionist, and women's-rights movements), yet in her introduction to Davies's collection of the testimony from this meeting, *Life as We
Have Known It*, she expressed her sense of remoteness from working
women's experience ("Introductory Letter" xix; "Memories of a Working Women's Guild," CE 4: 134–48).

In Woolf's day it was far less possible than in Eliot's to restrict the
women's movement to middle- and upper middle-class reform, and
the newly democratic perspective made Woolf uneasy. She herself,
like Eliot, would have had no desire to join riots and hunger strikes
to gain the vote, thereby forfeiting educated women's difference both
from men and from the working classes who likewise fought for the
franchise. Safe as a small-scale heiress, Woolf's narrator in *A Room of*

[7]Woolf's mother signed Mrs. Humphry Ward's anti-feminist petition of 1889. Woolf,
"The Compromise," 171; Marcus, Introduction, xix; Bauer and Ritt 260–62.

One's Own can afford to view financial independence as a greater benefit for women than the vote (37); basic economic needs press on women of all classes, but only an educated elite can regard the preconditions of writing as the most elemental rights. Specialized as her concern for the evolution of educated women at times appears, Woolf had broader motives as well for emphasizing intellectual freedom over electoral power. She believed that all women were qualified to join in a collective resistance to forces that oppress all human beings. She withheld her endorsement from the term "feminism," calling it "corrupt" and obsolete (TG 101), largely because it seemed to clamor for equality at the cost of women's "difference," while obscuring the more fundamental cause against "the tyranny of the patriarchal state" (TG 101–3). The vote, if it wedded women to war and all the injustices of patriarchal power, would be an instrument of such harmful indifference.[8]

The women's movement with which Eliot and Woolf were allied derived primarily from liberal individualism, though it also advocated an impersonal altruism. Thus the early "cause" could be read as a heroic narrative of a few ladies who broke out of passive anonymity into the activity of history. In this light, historical women and heroines in novels by Eliot and Woolf may appear to strive for human progress on the same plane, though the purely fictional figures accomplish less (in practical terms) than their counterparts in life. The kinship between some actual lady reformers and these authors' female characters suggests that there were ideological advantages to conceiving women's social action as tending to quixotic idealism (though women's practicality was prized in the home). Generous failure on pure-minded principles somehow earns greatness for reformers and heroines alike.

According to Lytton Strachey's sister-in-law, Ray Strachey (and Woolf adopts this view in *Three Guineas*), the first movements toward feminism in Britain grew out of the philanthropies organized by ladies whose activity outside the home had traditionally been limited to charity among the poor of their parish; as Strachey puts it, "The feminist movement began through the awakening of individual women to their own uselessness" (13, 44; Bauer and Ritt 80–81). This derivation is true enough for the activists whom Eliot and Woolf

---

[8]Woolf notes that women won the vote because they helped fight the Great War (TG 148n.12), and it was members of the Women's Social and Political Union who handed out white feathers to goad men to enlist (TG 182n.35; Rowbotham 116). Rhetorically, *Three Guineas* tries to elide difference because fascism is dividing "sexes" and "races": "The daughters and sons of educated men are fighting side by side" (TG 102–3).

personally knew, but it ignores the widespread organization of working-class socialist women's groups alongside the Owenites and Chartists (Strachey does briefly mention these groups: 30–32; Killham; Rowbotham 42; MacKinnon 230–31). Eliot's works epitomize the complex loyalties of the early lady reformers, women who retained their upper-class superiority to the objects of their charity, the poor and the sick, and seldom questioned their allegiance to educated men.

One of Eliot's friends, Bessie Rayner Parkes, advocated the ladylike vocation of systematic charity in terms that read like a rough draft of the Prelude and Finale of *Middlemarch:*

> Among the comparitively [sic] affluent ranks women lament a monotony of existence resulting from the narrow sphere of action assigned them. This becomes the source of an indescribable *ennui* by which they reproach society, and almost Providence. . . . It is the prerogative only of a few rare natures to find sufficient incitement to exertion. . . . Numberless temptations beset this life-torpor. . . . [I]t is to the finest capacities that inactivity proves most detrimental. In such cases there is a consciousness of aspiration for which no available medium of realisation appears. . . .
>
> It is in the power of women to become invincible agents in the work of charity. The very attributes of feminine nature are of essential value in such a cause. Funds, programmes, and committees . . . can only partially effect the good which results from . . . charity. Kindly and sympathetic contact, the expression of benevolence ardent and sincere, is needful and irresistible. . . . ([1859]; quoted in Bauer and Ritt 83)

Here, the ardor of a lady like Dorothea, her capacity to feel for others, is offered as both her greatest danger (the temptation of discontent) and her saving grace.

The institutionalization of charity coincided with the rise of movements for women's emancipation, as though the deflection of altruism into public channels, answering the personal question "What can I do?," rendered that question at once more pertinent to the nation as a whole. Rosamond Vincy's passive-aggressive "What can *I* do?" is not, it turns out, antithetical to Dorothea's and the lady reformers' desire to do whatever needs to be done (Lydgate himself compares the two ladies' responses to hardship, recalling Dorothea's unselfish appeal to him on behalf of her husband, "think what I can do" [432–34]). In a later context, both the idle and the helpless appeals turn into a healthier demand: let me do whatever I am best at—for the betterment of all—and change the laws that prevent me. To the reader in 1871–72, after successive attempts to change the divorce, property, and suffrage laws as well as educational practices, Dorothea must have seemed decidedly a throwback to the first, more hampered lady reformers, as Eliot well knew (this is an aspect of her historical reading of the 1830s).[9]

That Woolf too should have lingered over madonna-like figures of influence such as Mrs. Ramsay suggests their lasting appeal, not simply as historical curiosities extinct like the "Dodo" (Celia's nickname for Dorothea). Mrs. Ramsay, having found what she can do, has an instinct to visit

> this widow, or that struggling wife in person with a bag on her arm, and a note-book and pencil with which she wrote down in columns . . . wages and spendings, employment and unemployment, in the hope that thus she would cease to be a private woman whose charity was half a sop to her own indignation, half a relief to her own curiosity, and become . . . an investigator, elucidating the social problem. (TL 17–18)

In this way, ladies of "the finest capacities" were encouraged to find an activity that would not openly compete with men's administration or violate class structures but that would assume responsibility for "the social problem." Dorothea and Mrs. Ramsay conceive the problem economically, and never lose sight of their difference from the poor and uneducated whom they care for. But their authors clearly include gender with economics and class as a factor in "the gentlewoman's oppressive liberty" (M 202). As a lady, Dorothea can only solve social problems that directly pertain to men in her own circle: the housing on Sir James's estate, Lydgate's and Farebrother's moral and economic standings. Similarly, Mrs. Ramsay busies herself unobtrusively with poor widows and wives, matchmaking, and the well-being of her

[9]Dorothea Beale was a well-known ladylike reformer who educated girls "so that they may best perform [their] subordinate part" (R. Strachey 135), as she assured the Social Science Congress in 1865. Nina Auerbach notes the popular fear of even such conservative reformers, reflected in the ditty "How different from us,/ Miss Beale and Miss Buss!" (*Woman*, 119). Beale (1831–1906) directed Cheltenham Ladies' College and founded St. Hilda's College, Oxford, for rescue work: the reform of prostitutes. She appears in Leslie Stephen's *Dictionary of National Biography*. Frances Mary Buss (1827–1894) founded the North London Collegiate School for girls. Both favored women's suffrage, but Beale was most concerned with "duties rather than rights" (Banks). Dorothea Beale suggests to me one prototype for Eliot's Dorothea Brooke, but the real woman was foundress of something.

household, never venturing to attack the order that subordinates women and the poor while separating women of different classes. Both Dorothea and Mrs. Ramsay remain private women though others around them testify to their widespread influence.

The Victorian hope that more enlightened, organized charity would reconcile both women and the poor to their lots by moderately improving them is dramatically represented in the portrayal of Romola, the Eliot heroine who most distinctly represents the political role of Victorian ladies. Romola has at least two originals, distinguished Victorian women who happened to be cousins, Barbara Bodichon and Florence Nightingale, both of whom came of English "intellectual aristocracy" as the Stephens did (Annan 1–7). Barbara Bodichon became perhaps Eliot's closest friend; among other causes, she founded an innovative school for the poor and organized committees for the Married Women's Property Bill in 1855 and for women's suffrage in 1866, as well as promoting women's higher education. Romola also figures as Eliot's "Lady with the Lamp"; she learns to minister to the ailing masses like Bodichon and like the more famous Florence Nightingale. The latter eminent Victorian had "the highest lot ever fulfilled by woman, except women Sovereigns," according to Harriet Martineau; she achieved "an opening for her sex into the region of serious business" (196; Jameson, *Sisters*, 112–14).

Far from a feminist, Nightingale nevertheless epitomized the Victorian Public Lady. "She was no declaimer, but a housewifely woman" and thoroughly "lady-like," Martineau assures us (202)—herself severe on unladylike feminists such as Wollstonecraft (81). Nightingale's one loud protest against the idleness of ladies, *Cassandra,* now well-known, remained unpublished at the time. To judge by Eliot's novels, she would have advised against publication; her own heroines emulate the quiet good deeds of Nightingale nurses without assuming the public recognition and power of the prototype. Ministers of state consulted Nightingale, whereas Romola cannot prevent her uncle's politically engineered execution. Dorothea dreams of founding a cooperative agricultural community, but she ends by helping Ladislaw behind the political scenes. Fittingly, Nightingale objected to Eliot's portrait of Dorothea as a poor substitute for the successful housing reformer Octavia Hill.[10] Eliot, it seems, was rather more discouraging than some of her contemporaries as to the range of achievement for women (or at least heroines) who bore their charitable vocation outside

[10]Showalter, "Greening," 305–6. Woolf discusses Hill in *Three Guineas* (165n.35). Eliot donated £200 to a fund supporting Hill's projects (*GE Letters* 6: 31). Hill was a kind of daughter-in-law to Eliot, as sister-in-law to Lewes's son Charles.

the home. Yet her most honored heroines, Romola and Dorothea, are close cousins of the early lady reformers.

Woolf, in contrast, was more likely to exalt than to disparage these ladies' achievements. She loyally calls for the preservation of the charm of the nineteenth-century lady reformers, the "unpaid-for education" that made them "civilized human beings" eschewing "egotism" and love of "fame." She cites Florence Nightingale, Anne Clough, Mary Kingsley (TG 76–79, 82), Josephine Butler, Sophia Jex-Blake, and Barbara Bodichon as well as Elizabeth Barrett, Charlotte Brontë, and Mrs. Gaskell (TG 130–37)—all contemporaries, acquaintances, or close associates of Eliot—and she elaborates on the obstacles to women's achievement that these reformers courageously overcame. Woolf nevertheless seems to savor their role as rebellious daughters, as new Antigones, which would be lost if they had not in some sense failed like the literary heroines (TG 81, 169n.39). Like Eliot exalting an obscure Romola or Dorothea, Woolf honors the civilized selflessness of Victorian ladies as the pearl of patriarchal oppression (TG 78–79).[11] Women's influence was offered as a compensation for their ostensible powerlessness; influence could, to a degree, tangibly improve conditions for the less fortunate. Like Mrs. Ramsay as well as Julia Stephen, Eleanor Pargiter in *The Years* visits the poor and even helps construct more and better housing for them, as though fulfilling the promise of Dorothea as well as of Octavia Hill.

The model for both the public reformers and the fictional heroines derives from an ideology of influence that itself was influenced by a shift in the perspective of social thought. For middle-class women at mid-century, the most immediate crisis was the lack of education and employment for "redundant," that is unmarried, middle-class women (Poovey 1–15). The discovery of this redundancy through the 1851 census was itself symptomatic of a new tendency to regard society as a subject of study like any aspect of natural science. Just as Eliot herself worked closely with Herbert Spencer and her "husband," a self-trained scientist, many women reformers were allied with the rising social sciences, which, while promising to demystify the bases of the social order, could also serve to justify individual suffering as part of a progressive plan. At the same time, the methods of social science helped organize charity on a scale to influence lawmakers, by docu-

---

[11] I discuss the use of the Antigone prototype in Chapter 4, but here I note that Woolf speaks for Eliot as well when she claims that "ridicule, obscurity and censure are preferable, for psychological reasons, to fame and praise," and that women especially must avoid prostituting themselves; art must be pursued "for the sake of the art" (TG 80).

menting the abuse of women and children in factory labor, for instance. The National Association for the Promotion of Social Science, founded in 1857, was one of the first learned societies to admit women and to allow them to read papers at meetings (Bauer and Ritt 80). The new social science offered women "something to do" as investigators of the social problem from the vantage of educated circles. Many readers of Eliot have supposed that she defined her vocation in terms of a sociological "something to do," but few have traced the particular utility of Comtean positivism, a source of the new sociology, for her vocation as a lady reformer (Vogeler 407). Indeed, scholars have focused on Comte's positivism to the neglect of his adaptation of current ideas of woman's "Mission," obscuring the gender politics that supported sociology, like other empiricist science, from the beginning (Harding 85–92). Envisioning "woman as the moral providence of our species," Comte promotes a new "Positive Religion" in which women are the saints, duty-bound to remain chaste, abstain from politics or work outside the home, and espouse motherhood or perpetual widowhood as their highest goal.[12]

Both Eliot and Woolf could interpret the destructive inconsistencies of such an ideal, yet they remained attracted to it. In spite of her skepticism about Comte's philosophy, Eliot tended to exalt as he did women's superior capacity for submission to a communal good (Newton 135–37), and her heroines often stand in for saints. For Woolf, chastity and behind-the-scenes influence on social cohesion remain ideals. Like Sarah Lewis in *Woman's Mission*, the author of *Mrs. Dalloway* might have argued that influence is more effective than power as it commands "unconscious acquiescence" (Lewis 13); Clarissa, who sleeps alone in her narrow bed, serves goddess-like to unite the many souls at her party. The "intellectual chastity" Woolf espouses for educated men's daughters in *Three Guineas* might be a polemical caption

[12]Comte aims "to direct the *thoughts* of women and working men to the *question* of a thorough renovation of the social order" (emphasis added; *The Catechism of Positive Religion*, 14, 20–38). This work was published in English by Eliot's former intimate, John Chapman, early in her career as a novelist (1858). Earlier, Harriet Martineau had translated and condensed Comte's *Positive Philosophy* (*Comte and Positivism* 69–306). The Positivist Calendar assigns a great name to every month and day of the year, and among the great men includes "Heloise," "Joan of Arc," and "St. Theresa," as well as "Sappho," "Mme. de Staël," and "Miss Edgeworth," among twenty or so other women. An "Additional Day in Leap Years" would be honored as the "Festival of HOLY WOMEN" (*Comte and Positivism* 472–73). Martha Vogeler points out how *Middlemarch* violated Comtean doctrine: the wife of a man of science destroys him rather than "inspiring him by superior moral virtue," while the widow of a scholar remarries (417). Comte himself defies the establishment of "pure science" in which woman figures as the passive *body* of Nature penetrated by man (Harding 118; Showalter, *Sexual Anarchy*, 128–33).

for the Comtean tableau that Romola, perpetual widow, arranges at the end of Eliot's novel (Myers, *Teaching*, 96–97; Levine, "Hypothesis," 3; Marcus, *Languages*, 117).

Education, Class, and Hothouse Cultivation

Most of the Victorian reformers sought to establish a less treacherous basis than Comte's for the ideology of influence, while they disparaged the association of all women with working-class outsiders (except through sympathy). Rather, they endeavored to gain for women of the middle and upper classes the same access to cultural privilege as their brothers enjoyed. As a reform movement, the cause of higher education for women was relatively unthreatening, since there was little danger at first of including untold masses in the scheme (Altick 143; Brantlinger 238–39, 246–47). Eliot endorsed women's educational reform, including the efforts of her friends Barbara Bodichon and Emily Davies to raise support for Girton College; she contributed £50 "from the author of *Romola*"—in itself a statement (given Romola's broken ambitions) that the vocation of charity, not learning, was most fitting for women (Redinger 453). Ironically, under the ladylike auspices of Girton, Eliot was not welcome (as a Victorian Romola would have been) to visit the college openly, and had to enter by the back drive (Bradbrook 14–15). As Ray Strachey observes, her support of the college was "of no use in reassuring the public about [its] absolute respectability" (147). Such was Eliot's authority, however, that she was later consulted as to the propriety of the women's acting in college theatricals in men's costumes; in spite of her own use of a male pseudonym, Eliot concurred with other authorities that "Hamlet must be played in a skirt" (Woolf, "Two Women," CE 4: 64; compare Lucy Snowe's compromise as the male lead in a girls' school theatrical in *Villette*). Such also was the lasting importance of Eliot as a leading example of female achievement that Margaret Llewelyn Davies donated a sketch of George Eliot to Girton College in 1923 (Haight 339).

Like Eliot and her associates, Woolf focused her feminism on education. Sandra M. Gilbert offers a persuasive reading of *A Room of One's Own* and *Orlando* as manifestos for a liberal education on women's terms ("The Battle of the Books"); in *Three Guineas*, moreover, Woolf invents her own women's college (Marcus, *Languages*, 116). *A Room of One's Own*, originally delivered as lectures at Newnham and Girton, pictures a visit to "Fernham," much as though Woolf herself were calling on her cousin Katherine Stephen, principal of Newnham (Marcus, *Languages*, 82). Woolf is, of course, welcome to enter by the front door. In Woolf's day, lady reformers appear to have been less anxious to preserve the propriety of gender than the propriety of class, as the latter hierarchy no longer could be invoked as natural. Educational reform had taken a much more democratic cast, and the spectacle of the suffragette movement had dramatized the distinct differences between the interests of all women and those of all men, regardless of shared interests between sexes within each class. Thus Woolf has her own version of the bloom that must be preserved, not of chastity but of cultivated privilege and impractical beauty.

In "Two Women," a review of Lady Stephen's book, *Emily Davies and Girton College*, Woolf obliquely addresses the interrelated issues of women's education and of class. In Woolf's view, Davies and other exceptional women such as Barbara Bodichon overcame the middle-class woman's "negative education" in how to be useless. Woolf contrasts their ambitious achievements with the sequestered, placid life of Lady Augusta Stanley. The conclusion is uncertain: "There is something in Lady Augusta's power to magnify the common and illumine the dull which seems to imply a very arduous education behind it. Nevertheless, . . . one cannot doubt that Miss Davies got more interest, more pleasure, and more use out of one month of her life than Lady Augusta out of a whole year of hers" (CE 4: 66). The lady herself " 'wished to be a fellow of a college,' " and did in fact join Davies's cause to create a women's college. Woolf imagines that this cause brought about a "union of the middle-class woman and the court lady"—like her own wishful union with an Orlando/Sackville-West—bearing "some astonishing phoenix of the future who shall combine the new efficiency with the old amenity, the courage . . . [and the] charm" (CE 4: 66). Woolf would perhaps conceive herself as that future being, combining all Eliot's learned yet charmless force with an aristocratic "power to magnify the common."

Like Martineau assuring us that Nightingale was "lady-like," Woolf prefers her female predecessors to be civilized ladies; it is even preferable that they should have been defeated in their goals than that they should stridently have demanded too much. In her 1919 essay on Eliot, Woolf seems to betray her own resentment that Eliot was not really a lady, raising the class issue that dominates the question of women's access to privileged culture. "We know . . . that the culture, the philosophy, the fame, and the influence were all built upon a very humble foundation—she was the grand-daughter of a carpenter" ("GE" [1919] 152; see also the opening sentence of "GE" [1921]). For Woolf, the great-granddaughter of a Master in Chancery, the privilege of class meant certain literary privileges, the power to charm critics of that class; Eliot, supposedly, was "out of her element" "in middle-class drawingrooms" ("GE" [1919] 158).[13] But Eliot had done everything she could to extricate herself from the provincial society of Dodsons and Tullivers that so strictly limits women's education and development. The novels from *Romola* on might seem repeated demonstrations that the author was perfectly at home in middle-class drawing rooms, and that her advocacy of women had no tinge of vulgar demands for personal rights.

Along with concerns about class and ladylike respectability, the question of the education and cultural achievement of women seems by a kind of reflex to raise images of the garden or conservatory. If women have the art which does mend nature, which *is* nature, *are* women in themselves a cultivated form of nature? Rather than resorting to the ancient analogy between women and animals, those who wished to maintain the innate lack of passion and appetite in women readily imagined them as flowers or fruits. Curiously, advocates of the liberation of the sex often called up the age-old imagery of the enclosed garden in answer to those who would plant women there.

In one of the most eloquent arguments against the "intention of nature" fallacy (and one of many disturbing liberal analogies between slavery and womanhood), John Stuart Mill claims that slaves have at least been allowed some "liberty of development" as to their character,

> but in the case of women, a hot-house and stove cultivation has always been carried on of some of the capabilities of their nature. . . . Certain products of the general vital force sprout luxuriantly . . . in this heated atmosphere and under this active nurture . . . , while other shoots . . . left outside in the wintry air . . . have a stunted growth, and some are burnt off with fire . . . Men . . . indolently believe that the tree grows of itself in the way they have made it grow, and that it would die if one half of it were not kept in a vapour bath and the other half in the snow. (*Subjection* 39)

Mill is not deliberately longing for a natural, organic womanhood, since his entire treatise insists that development be understood as the result of environmental influence, but he can't help arousing our sentiment for the vulnerable tree and how it might have grown with-

[13]The relation between Woolf and Eliot might be compared to the first confrontation between Katharine Hilbery and Ralph Denham, two representatives of the middle class, one who must "live up to . . . ancestors" and the other who must live down his "dull," bill-paying family (ND 17–18).

out man's interference. The desire to protect womanhood from the distortions of civilization can be seen in writings on both sides of the question of women's education and rights.

Both Eliot and Woolf, like their contemporaries, seem drawn to what for convenience I will call horticultural imagery. We might consider these images as a literalization of the metaphor of culture (Jacobus, *Reading Woman*, 72–73). In the conservatory, how can one tell the intention of nature from the nurture that has artfully mended it? Eliot, picking up on the current aspersions on the cultivation of girls, plays out these images in the portrait of Gwendolen Harleth, herself serpentine and meaning to lead. Gwendolen scoffs at "reforming women," yet is "inwardly rebellious against the restraints of family conditions" (DD 83); she tells Grandcourt that feminine bloom, confined to the domestic hothouse, often grows "poisonous" from boredom (171). Eliot attributes the serpentine corruption of young women like Rosamond or Gwendolen to a cultural law of supply and demand: "Men's taste is woman's test" (DD 132). Girls are artificially cultivated to be sold in the market for idle ladies, and the taste might well prove poisonous. In the eyes of many, however, girls like Gwendolen had been spoiled by promiscuous exposure to a man's world; too much rather than too little education was to blame. As Meredith's Egoist, Sir Willoughby Patterne, exclaims to himself, "Without their purity what are [women]!—what are fruiterer's plums?—unsaleable. O for the bloom on them!" (114). Even some educators like Anne Jemima Clough were anxious to segregate female education to preserve the bloom.[14]

As a connoisseur of bloom, Ruskin could insist that woman is not to be the "shadow" or "slave" of man but that she should enjoy chivalrous influence over him as "Queen" of her "Garden"; like Mill, he objects to the artificial cultivation of girls.

> You may chisel a boy into shape. . . . But you cannot hammer a girl into anything. She grows as a flower does,—she will wither without sun; she will decay in her sheath, as the narcissus does, if you do not give her air enough; she may fall, and defile her head in dust, if you leave her without help . . . ; but . . . she must take her own fair form and way. . . . Let her loose in the library, I say, as you do a fawn in

[14]B. A. Clough, *Memoir of Anne Jemima Clough* (1897), 195, in Hollis 6; R. Strachey 143. Martineau asserted that girls could learn everything their brothers did with greater facility, freeing a third of their day for studying the household arts (118, 120). Woolf notes that Charlotte Yonge blamed women for their own "inferiority": "She reminded her sex of a painful incident with a snake in a garden" ("Two Women," CE 4: 62).

a field. It knows the bad weeds twenty times better than you; and the good ones too. (50, 66–67)

This apparent permissiveness, it becomes clear, is only due to Ruskin's assumed confidence that a woman will grow into a willing tender of other flowers, and that she will acquiesce in her domesticity ("home is always around her . . . home is yet wherever she is" [60]). The emphasis is still on nurture, on the civilized containment in dwelling or garden of what might otherwise simply *be* nature.

Most partisans of women's genuinely unlimited development were not so confident that the garden analogy was benign. Mary Wollstone-craft, back in 1792, blamed "a false system of education" for women's "barren blooming," "like the flowers which are planted in too rich a soil" (85). In the 1850s and later, some feminist reformers suspected educational hothouses might only be a new cover for patriarchal venom. Emily Davies called the offer of separate examinations for women a "serpent" (Strachey 143), suggesting the negative side of the garden imagery, with its inevitable Miltonic and biblical associations. Feminists could exonerate Eve in attacking the serpent, perhaps, but they might also deplore the feminine weakness of some of the latter-day products of the garden, as Wollstonecraft does. Josephine Butler described women trained for the profession of marriage as "Brazilian creepers . . . which sprawl out their limp tendrils . . . to find some-thing to hang upon" (Introduction, *Woman's Work and Woman's Culture* [1869], in Hollis 10); the conservatory is a deadly place, apparently, and robust women must grow elsewhere.

Woolf, like her Victorian predecessors in the women's movement, resorts to imagery of exotic, domesticated nature when considering women's education, but she was as likely to defend the protected, "natural," Ruskinian education of the girl at home (indeed, this was the mode of her own education) as she was to criticize the artificiality of such cultivation. In spite of her admiration for Lady Augusta's protected charm, she deplored an excess of femininity: "The power of sympathy, when so highly developed . . . tends to produce a hothouse atmosphere in which domestic details assume prodigious proportions and the mind feeds upon every detail of death and disease with a gluttonous relish. [The volume of Lady Augusta's letters] is all per-sonal, emotional, and detailed as one of the novels which were written so inevitably by women" ("Two Women," CE 4: 65). The poisonous intimacy of the hothouse does not, however, drive Woolf into the "masculine" open air; unlike Emily Davies, she would not have in-sisted that women's education must be in all things equal to men's.

In a commentary on *Euphrosyne* written in 1906, Woolf defends "that respectable custom which allows the daughter to educate herself at home. . . . which preserves her from the omniscience, the early satiety, the melancholy self-satisfaction" of her university-educated brothers (Bell, appendix C, 1: 205). The criticism of masculine smugness is telling, as though the brothers are the ones who grow poisonous on too rich a soil.

Woolf herself contributed to the education of working women by teaching history and composition at Morley College from 1905 to 1907, and we see her depicting her pupils as inarticulate nature, though without the delicate bloom of flowers—perhaps because they are not ladies. Impressed with working women's uncultivated intelligence, she takes the place of the "masculine" cultivator: "It would not be hard to educate them sufficiently to give them a new interest in life; They have tentacles languidly stretching forth from their minds, feeling vaguely for substance, & easily applied by a guiding hand to something that [they] could really grasp" (Bell, appendix B, 1: 203). In the portrait of Rachel Vinrace, in *The Voyage Out*, Woolf's imagery is less monstrous, as befits a lady. Rachel's education is Ruskinian, typical of "the majority of well-to-do girls in the last part of the nineteenth century"; she has only a smattering of confused information gleaned from private tutors, but she has been allowed to indulge her talent for music, and she has "abundant time for thinking." Her sense of captivity in an artificial social system is concentrated on the memory of the "sickly horrible" scent of "the little hall at Richmond laden with flowers on the day of her mother's funeral" (VO 33–36), and her doom is met in the jungle.[15]

The association of women with nature, usually the liminal nature of domesticated exotics, is directly bound to images of death and loss, as *The Voyage Out* suggests. Education indeed threatened the bloom; it would figuratively open the hothouse and let women breathe as human beings, at peril to their existence as ladies. The serpent of man's supremacy or desire to possess the woman already lurks in this already-fallen garden; the plants themselves are raised to be poisonous, tempting others and dying prematurely, as Wollstonecraft says: "The flaunting leaves, after having pleased a fastidious eye, fade, disregarded on the stalk" (85). Even the most enlightened attempts to

---

[15]Clarissa Dalloway recalls Sally Seton "like some bird or air ball that has flown in, attached itself for a moment to a bramble." Walking together on the terrace, "passing a stone urn with flowers in it[,] Sally stopped; picked a flower; kissed her on the lips" (MD 51–52). Isa Oliver is clearly associated with the greenhouse in *Between the Acts*, while Mrs. Ramsay is preoccupied with repairing the greenhouse roof.

protect women from the early doom of sexuality by cultivating their intellects and their independence seem haunted by danger. That a women's college could itself become a kind of conservatory is suggested by the anecdote about Eliot's covert visit to Girton, as though the strong-minded woman were a more dangerous serpent even than men; the pioneering project had to be especially vigilant against the blight of scandal.

In Woolf's view, Eliot must have been better off exploring the territories of learning on her own than attending a college modeled on men's institutions ("Two Women," CE 4: 66). Conceiving the predicament of cultivated Victorian women in the conventional horticultural terms, Woolf explicitly figures Eliot as a greenhouse captive much like Gwendolen or the other heroines. Reviewing *The Letters of George Eliot*, edited by R. Brimley Johnson, Woolf wrote of Eliot: "Fate had planted her in such surroundings that it was only by breaking the pot itself that she could escape. . . . To dream of seeing 'the bread fruit tree, the fan-palm, and the papyrus,' and at last actually to see them at Alton Garden were scarcely enough to fill a life" ("GE" [1926]). Earlier, in the centenary essay, Woolf had pictured Eliot both as one who escapes the confines of her upbringing and as an interloper in the garden: "She must reach beyond the sanctuary [of womanhood] and pluck for herself the strange bright fruits of art and knowledge" ("GE" [1919] 160).

Eliot and Woolf were closely associated with the feminist efforts of educated men's daughters in their day, as we have seen, but they found that the Grand Old Woman of English Letters must ambivalently subscribe to the ideology of influence, because a publicly politicized stance on women's issues would preclude the cultural privilege they struggled to gain. In this light we may be less surprised by their loyalty to prescribed differences between the sexes; it is as though they believe that the garden or conservatory must remain inviolate even when the "natural" products of such nurture have grown poisonous with resentment and frustration. They were urgently writing like women who had forgotten they were women—obliterating whatever might distinguish them from any "human" writer—while what they wrote posed over and over the vexed question of womanhood, the dangers and appeals of the ideology of influence. Questioning the constitution of the human, and demonstrating in their works the interpenetration of public and private spheres, they still retained the ideal of feminine selflessness as though it were the quality of mercy to soften the "justice" or injustice of a deterministic, masculinist world.

2

The Burden of Personality:
Biographical Criticism and
Narrative Strategy

If Eliot and Woolf share in an ideology that prizes women's sacrifice to a common good, how can their own eminence be accommodated to this ideology? To unmask the productive contradiction between their visions of selflessness and their own cultivated distinction, I need to address the vexed issues of authorial identity and biographical criticism, which not incidentally relate to the ambiguities I have been unearthing in Victorian ladylike reform. When we personify canonical authors, whether women or men, how can we not reinforce an exclusive metaphysics of origins? How do Eliot and Woolf design themselves as authors, earning greatness in spite of womanhood, while at the same time appealing to an alternative to masculine identity and authority?

That postmodern proclamations of the death of the author should coincide with the "second wave" of feminism and a burgeoning interest in female authorship is perhaps no accident. Feminism itself owes much to humanism and the long historical movement toward an elaborated concept of the individual, but it quickly emerges as a challenge to notions of autonomy and authority underwritten by patriarchy. Instead of equality for the unified *female* subject, many feminists turn to an ideal of feminine selflessness or deconstruction of the subject; instead of inserting more women's biographies in a single cultural history, they attack the specious unity implied in the concepts of a "life" and a "universal" history. Yet as the word itself indicates, selflessness might range from a subversive *jouissance* to a coerced submission; the Angel in the House, after all, is conceived as essentially selfless. Moreover, many theorists' insistence on the breakdown of all grounds for authority may reveal an unconscious resistance to sharing cultural privilege with the marginalized groups who are beginning to grasp at it (Morgan 6; Jardine 45–46). In any case, much as feminist thought has been enhanced by a distrust of models of identity and authority, feminist literary criticism (like feminist scholarship generally) could hardly have launched itself without regard for the existence of certain individual, historical women, such as those in the supposedly dead role of "author."

The limitations of biographical criticism are obvious, but the tendency to conflate author and work in such criticism reveals some subtle aspects that should not be dismissed. First, there is the fact that criticism of women authors has seldom escaped being biographical. Many feminist critics have traced the historical effects of an enforced intimacy between women and their writing. Writer and text are liable to be mistaken for each other, and to be read aesthetically as trivial and morally as loose (Ellmann 29). Access to the privacy of the author seems more intensely desired when the author is a woman, given the charged cultural value of a woman's privacy. It would seem, then, to be a sign of progress that women writers be accorded the ability to distance themselves from their work as men are allowed to do. Second, however, such distancing has its drawbacks for women: to place the author at an aesthetic remove—indifferent, paring *his* fingernails— may not be for a woman quite what it is for a man. Obscurity and self-effacement for her may be qualities that preclude authorship rather than help her assume godlike authority. It has been the task of many literary women to invent ways to display exceptional powers that seem to transcend ordinary identity (mere womanhood) yet never to claim the self-determined authority of masculine hero or author (Waugh 8–10).

Humility is conventionally demanded of women and their works. In 1847 George Gilfillan praised Felicia Hemans as a great woman poet precisely because she would not compete for greatness in masculine terms: "Sympathy, not fame, was the desire of her being"; instead of being a "*maker*" herself, "her life is a poem" (Helsinger, Sheets, and Veeder 3: 28 29). Greatness, for Eliot and Woolf if not for Hemans, entailed fame as well as sympathy: the brazen authority as well as the careful distinction between self and work, along with the affirmation of "others." Their heroines may be honored for an unambitious servitude, like that of Mrs. Hemans, to art and sympathy; Dorothea Brooke is told she *is* a poem (M 166). But to be indistinguishable from the art which does mend nature is to risk oblivion; no "poem" was ever immortalized as an *author*.

The successful writer, male or female, must carefully tend the fiction of authorial personality as the ground on which the work stands, but for women writers this has been a particularly unsteady fiction to sustain. In this chapter I examine how Eliot and Woolf sustain this fiction. I offer a reading of their lives in terms of Woolf's feminist biographical criticism, consider briefly some of the preconceptions of women's unfitness for authorship against which they contended, and finally, analyze the apparently distinct strategies of the masculine and androgynous narrators as two versions of an aesthetics of *im*personality.

Virginia Woolf on George Eliot

Although I have already presented some details of Woolf's reading of Eliot's authorial personality, the full story of the Victorian Grand Old Woman of Letters must be told as Woolf reconstructed it for her own use. Here as in all her biographical criticism of women writers, Woolf contends with the model that generally shapes the lives of heroines in biography as well as fiction, a model divided between irreconcilable erotic and ambitious plots (to adapt Nancy Miller's use of Freud's terms in "Emphasis Added" [346]; D. Barrett 17–19). To some extent, Woolf inherited her reading of Eliot, especially from Leslie Stephen's biography;[1] this inherited reading stresses the erotic plot, or the suffering-woman-behind-the-book. She reiterates her father's criticism of the novelist's *womanly* faults; in *George Eliot*, Stephen attributes Eliot's limitations to a natural feminine diffidence and desire for respectability. Woolf, more generous, assumes that those limitations were culturally imposed: Eliot's narrow range (as compared to Tolstoy's, for example) is due to the enforced "suburban seclusion" of a woman living with a married man. Yet at the same time, Woolf seems to hold Eliot's struggles with her reputation against her, as a kind of self-imposed handicap "which, inevitably, had the worst possible effects upon her work" ("Women and Fiction" 47; RO 73–74).

Eliot is difficult to pity as feminine victim, though Woolf eventually

[1]Woolf retains the Victorian reading of Eliot more than Showalter allows. Woolf does not share in the "malice, rivalry, and cant" of women novelists who were Eliot's contemporaries, but not because she "had never sat down to the task of being George Eliot" ("Greening," 292–97). Perhaps under the influence of more recent Woolf scholarship, Showalter implies a closer relation between Woolf and Eliot in her very different version of this essay in *Sexual Anarchy* (69). Besides her father and Edmund Gosse, Woolf's 1919 essay relies on Lady Ritchie for a portrait of Eliot as "not exactly a personal friend, but a good and benevolent impulse" (152). J. Russell Perkin briefly retraces Woolf's reception of Eliot (105–8).

devises a way to do so. The greatest obstacles for the biographical critic of Eliot, Woolf finds, are the masculine narrative persona and the ambition and charmlessness of the historical woman. The textual George Eliot is obviously too manly; she "committed atrocities with" the "man's sentence" (RO 79–80). The imposing stature granted to her by the Victorians as an exception among women—Herbert Spencer admitted her novels, "as if they were not novels," to the London Library ("GE" [1919] 150–51)—frustrates an impulse to love and pity the woman, but it helps that she is dead and has come to be laughed at. More useful still is the indescribable ugliness (physical appearance usually rears *its* ugly head in criticism of a woman's work):

> Her big nose, her little eyes, her heavy, horsey head loom from behind the printed page and make a critic of the other sex uneasy. Praise he must, but love he cannot; and however absolute and austere his devotion to the principle that art has no truck with personality it is not George Eliot he would like to pour out tea. On the other hand, . . . Jane Austen pours, and as she pours, smiles, charms. ("Indiscretions" 72–73)

A critic of the same sex, Woolf is uneasy until she can treat Eliot as "an Aunt": "So treated she drops the apparatus of masculinity which Herbert Spencer necessitated; indulges herself in memory; and pours forth . . . the genial stores of her youth, the greatness and profundity of her soul" (75). Although Woolf sets Eliot in a catalogue that includes the "maternal" Gaskell and culminates in a Diana-like Austen, whom "we needs must adore," it is the "inimitable" Aunt who inspires Woolf's most passionate literary "indiscretion" ("Indiscretions" 75–76; compare "Phases of Fiction," CE 2: 78–80). Woolf here treats Eliot as neither the inhibiting mother-saint nor the equine sibyl, but an aunt-novelist (like Anne Thackeray Ritchie) to put writers of the same sex at ease.[2]

Woolf needs to discover a precursor at once truly great, by masculine standards she is unwilling to abandon, and truly feminine. Thus she claims that the mind that created was one and the same as the woman

[2]Thackeray's daughter, Anne, the sister of Leslie Stephen's first wife, was the only contemporary novelist besides Trollope that Eliot admitted to reading toward the end of her career (*GE Letters* 6: 123, 418), and her marriage to a younger man, Richmond Ritchie, provided Eliot with reassuring precedent for her own marriage to John Cross (*GE Letters* 6. 398; Haight 536). In 1879, Edith Simcox recorded Eliot's remark that she had visited her friends "Mrs. Ritchie . . . and Leslie Stephen" (*GE Letters* 9: 267), and Lewes's son Charles visited Mrs. Ritchie on 23 May 1880 to explain Eliot's marriage (Haight 542).

who suffered; a false patriarchal convention divided the personality that the female successor can reunite. "I can see already that no one else has ever known her as I know her. . . . I think she is a highly feminine and attractive character—most impulsive and ill-balanced . . . and I only wish she had lived nowadays, and so been saved all that nonsense. . . . It was an unfortunate thing to be the first woman of the age" (*VW Letters* 2: 321–22).[3] Perhaps "nowadays" an ambitious woman might avoid monstrous disguises.

In keeping with her need to confirm the woman's feminine personality, Woolf recreated a Victorian image of the works as chronicles of rural life. She shared many early readers' preference for the works that drew on "the genial stores" of Eliot's upbringing in Warwickshire, *Scenes of Clerical Life, Adam Bede, The Mill on the Floss,* and *Silas Marner* (Carroll, *Critical Heritage,* 2, 16–20). The author of robust country scenes might be viewed as more masculine than feminine, and it was only in the early works that "George Eliot" was accepted as the genuine name of a man. Yet the details of "the homespun of ordinary joys and sorrows" in a lost past inevitably carry feminine associations ("GE" [1919] 154). As I consider in the next chapter, Eliot's emulation of Dutch realism could gratify nostalgia for the maternal and for a lost sense of community (Graver 250–55) while defying the classical artistic order and gender hierarchy that trivialize domestic detail (Carroll, *Heritage,* 17; Schor).

The nostalgic reading of Eliot was not enough for Woolf, however; she refused to "confine her to village life and lament the book-learned period which produced *Middlemarch* and *Romola.*" In other words, Woolf rescues the woman writer from the feminine sphere of letters. In Eliot's hands, the novel, no longer "solely a love story, an autobiography, or a story of adventure" ("GE" [1921]), becomes the narrative of a collective history particularly associated with women. Woolf insists that the later novels forfeit the early charm for the sake not of bluestocking pedantry but of "wider scope" ("GE" [1921]). The loss of the charm associated with home and the past is thus no repudiation of the authority of feminine experience but a means of expanding its influence.

For Woolf as for Eliot the challenge is to command "wider scope" without assimilating the masculine norm of human experience; indeed

---

[3]In quoting this passage I have omitted a piece of the sort of gossip Woolf treasured for casting predecessors as suffering heroines (the editors swiftly put down the charge as "quite unfounded"): "(Mrs. Prothero once told me that she—George Eliot that is—had a child by a Professor in Edinburgh . . . the child is a well known Professor somewhere else—)." Was the great writer but a woman after all?

in their writings the feminine itself seems to approximate an ideal universality. It is for awakening a dormant, feminine common life that Woolf values Eliot most of all: for having expressed not only everyman's "ordinary joys and sorrows" but also the sufferings of women who never escape "the common sitting-room" (RO 69, 118; "Women and Fiction" 46). "The romance of the past" fades from the novels after *The Mill on the Floss* ("GE" [1919] 156), but they gain power to express "the ancient consciousness of woman, charged with suffering and sensibility, and for so many ages dumb." Eliot's heroines come to represent the yearning of all women torn between romantic confinement and an unfulfilled desire for some less personal object; this yearning "brimmed and overflowed and uttered a demand for something . . . that is perhaps incompatible with the facts of human existence. George Eliot had far too strong an intelligence to tamper with those facts. . . . Save for the supreme courage of their endeavour, the struggle ends, for her heroines, in tragedy, or in a compromise that is even more melancholy" ("GE" [1919] 159–60). The heroines' story of feminine self-sacrifice "is the incomplete version of the story of George Eliot herself." Eliot, unlike her heroines, found fulfillment in "learning" and "in the wider service of [her] kind," "confronting her feminine aspirations with the real world of men." In short, she transcended her fated personality as a woman, though "the body . . . sank worn out" (159–60). While Woolf certainly wished to attain Eliot's wide range of cultural achievement through other means than Eliot's, she honors the "triumphant" great writer and loves the woman who sank under the burden of personality, decking her *visited* tomb with "laurel and rose" (160). She portrays the Victorian author as the incomplete version of the story of Virginia Woolf herself.

Woolf's heroines are also incomplete versions of their author's own story, though she does grant artistic fulfillment to the unmarried, childless Lily Briscoe and Miss La Trobe, as well as improbable fame and family fulfillment to her magical, aristocratic poet, Orlando. Both authors' heroines must to a large extent typify feminine "suffering and sensibility"; they must preserve a degree of womanly silence even in triumph (or erupt in destructive, disfiguring rage, like Mrs. Transome or Rose Pargiter) so that Eliot and Woolf may articulate the untold story of "universal" feminine experience. The story is generated in the gap between the female characters' potential and their achievement, in their struggle with the burden of personality. As feminist biographical critics, we repeat this move; our subjects, the women writers, might be heroines in a plot of women's education and ambition that necessitates suffering because of the "facts" of oppression—setting aside the circumstances of women outside the modern English middle class. *We* presumably never end in Woolf's tragedy or Eliot's melancholy compromise.

The Biographical Common Ground

If Eliot and Woolf, then, complete the heroine's story by fulfilling the ambition of a woman of letters, it is not without strain on the more private plot of womanhood. The biographies of these two women writers suggest similar ingredients in their erotic and ambitious plots: similar pressures, strategies, and achievements.[4] At the same time they suggest some of the reasons why an understanding of the author's life adds a crucial dimension to our reading of a text, preventing the illusion of a universal context. Many feminist theorists have joined in the assault on biographical criticism, yet all feminist criticism, however chastely textual, ultimately refers to the specificity of female experience; the "feminine" is never simply a writing-effect, but also registers the living effects of female human beings.

Anglo-American feminist criticism, in its so-called second stage, the study of the female literary tradition (Showalter, "Feminist Criticism," 248), has been most openly biographical in its approach to works by women. At times this approach does draw too direct a correspondence between a woman's sexual identity and her authorship; it is a deterministic prejudice as old as men's criticism of women's writing. I hear the echo of Leslie Stephen's reading of Eliot: "In spite of her learning and her philosophy, George Eliot is always pre-eminently feminine" (*George Eliot* 74). To restore value to the writing of women does not necessarily challenge the mode of thought that defined the feminine other in the first place. Thus Peggy Kamuf charges feminist critics who are preoccupied with "women's language, literature, style or experience" with reinstating humanistic epistemology, "with its faith in the universal truth of man" (44). Toril Moi admonishes readers of American biographical feminist criticism: "For the patriarchal critic,

---

[4]I wish to avoid any deterministic reading of these careers: the varied styles of literary life devised by women in their day suggest that there is no prescribed female writer's strategy. Consider Eliza Lynn Linton, who, according to Haight, at the outset provided Marian Evans with the example of a woman making a living by writing (81), who later married and became an outspoken antagonist of women who spoke out, and who resented Eliot's unconventional success as woman and novelist (Anderson 288, 297). Or take Rose Macaulay, who became a kind of Anglo-Catholic lay-sister while sustaining a prolonged affair with a married man and wrote novels like witty retorts to Mrs. Humphry Ward.

the author is the source, origin and meaning of the text. If we are to undo this patriarchal practice of *authority*, we must take one further step and proclaim, with Roland Barthes, the death of the author" (62–63). Similarly, Mary Jacobus scorns the American feminist "flight toward empiricism" as part of the obsession with origins and authority that constitutes Western metaphysics. Yet Jacobus concedes, "The category of 'women's writing' remains as strategically and politically important in classroom, curriculum, or interpretative community as the specificity of women's oppression is to the women's movement" ("Woman in This Text?" 138).

We won't go far, I think, with a premature Foucauldian dismissal of the category "woman" along with the category "man," because in practice that is to deny the "specificity of women's oppression," including the distinctive burden of personality that arises when we modify "author" with "woman." From this more pragmatic angle, Nancy Miller counters Peggy Kamuf's anti-authorial stance: "To fore-close . . . discussions of the author as sexually gendered subject in a socially gendered exchange" may be to deny the material context of our theoretical discourse. Text-centered approaches, whether New Critical or Poststructuralist, have been used to evade the political context of the choice of text, which always entails the privileging of one kind of authorship (or particular author[s]) over another. Feminist critics may retain a concern with the signature or sexual identity of the author, Miller hopes, without naive empiricism or a demand for positive role models: "The author can now be rethought *beyond* traditional notions of biography" ("Text's Heroine" 50).[5] This is my hope, as well; as women authors or critics we risk appearing simple-mindedly *personal* unless we show ourselves capable of mastering theory (or any dominant cultural discourse), but we should not forfeit the ironic insights of the outsider's "difference of view" ("GE" [1919] 160; Jacobus, *Reading Woman*, 27–28; Christian 69). Like the women novelists, we may be damned if we do invoke biography or the personal, but we will be damned if we don't: the personal is always attributed to texts written by women whether or not the authors strove to write in an impersonal mode. With Cheryl Walker, I would advocate the inclusion of the author's biography and of historical context(s) as contributing, unfolding *texts* in an alert intertextuality (560).

Woolf herself laid a foundation for feminist biographical criticism, with her emphasis on the material and ideological conditions that

[5]Miller has continued to pursue a political yet deconstructed idea of writing and the author. "So why remember Barthes"? she asks, recalling his 1968 "The Death of the Author" ("Changing the Subject" 104–5). See *Subject to Change* 16; *Getting Personal* 1–30.

have constrained women's writing. In one sense, this tendency was true to her heritage; the biographical mode dominated nineteenth-century criticism, including Eliot's essays. As we would expect, Woolf's biographical criticism probes further than Eliot's would have done into private details and physical circumstances, while taking a more phenomenological approach to identity ("The New Biography," CE 4: 229–35). Yet both authors preferred reticence about the writer's intentions, doubting the relevance of biography to criticism of the novel.

Disapproving of gossip as Woolf does not, Eliot repudiates curiosity about authors in severe moral terms:

> I am thoroughly opposed in principle (quite apart from any personal reference to myself) to the system of *contemporary* biography. . . . The mass of the public will read any quantity of trivial details about a writer. . . . Even posthumous biography is, I think, increasingly perverted into [a time-wasting] indulgence. . . . It seems to me that just my works and the order in which they appeared is what the part of the public which cares about me may most usefully know. (*GE Letters* 6: 67–68)

Woolf characteristically granted that details may not be trivial (and Eliot's narrators often insist on their importance). Woolf condones a reader's interest in the "truth" behind the fiction ("nothing is more fascinating"), and she would indulge popular appetites. But she clearly dissociates the novel from the author, who can tell us about *himself* but who is probably unable to "say anything about his own work" (Introduction v–vi). The author is one thing, a very interesting thing, and the canon of "his" works is another.

Though Eliot and Woolf both engaged in biographical criticism themselves, it would not have been news to them that the living being who becomes an author has little final say as to what the book becomes in the hands of readers, and that he or she is profoundly unknowable, like Lydgate "a cluster of signs for his neighbours' false suppositions" (M 105).[6] Yet both authors share a biographical model of character as development largely determined by milieu and hence to a degree intelligible; Woolf's three pieces on Eliot confidently enlist the circumstances of Eliot's life as determinants of the works. Curiously, she passes harshest judgment where personalities and circumstances are

---

[6]We should bear in mind Eliot's early grounding in the Higher Criticism with its decentering of biblical authorship.

especially public; she is most lenient with the most obscure writers or with the great whose "lives" are lost. "The people whom we admire most as writers, then, have something . . . impersonal about them." We know too much about the Victorians, she claims: it is impossible to imagine "George Eliot gathering her skirts about her and leaping from a cliff" as Sappho did ("Personalities," CE 2: 275, 274). Though we know almost too much about Woolf's most private life, we still can romanticize her as having taken an abstract, sapphic plunge—perhaps because narrative conventions are stronger than unglamorous details.

In my Introduction I traced the canonization of these great women of letters. Here I am concerned with the intense fascination with the personalities of these authors, as though to read their works, not unusually autobiographical, were to read a woman. Both idolatry—of Eliot in her own day and Woolf in ours—and repudiation have fixated in either case on the author's appearance. Woolf's mournfully serene face has been reproduced so often in the photographs, and Bloomsbury has been so thoroughly palpated, that we confront a popular legend when we approach her work (Rose, *Woman of Letters*, 249–51). The few portraits of Eliot reveal, in spite of the disproportion of nose and chin, a face as evocative as Woolf's: the serenely mournful expression, the head elegantly tilted, the hair plainly drawn back (compare the illustrations in Bell and in Haight); Ina Taylor has located additional photographs of Eliot (though Eliot claimed never to have sat for any) that give images of the woman as various as her shifting names (xiv). Indeterminate as it was, Eliot's notorious ugliness seems to have haunted Woolf; it was not a trait ingratiating to the heir of great beauty on the mother's side. Woolf wrote in 1919, "The long, heavy face with its . . . almost equine power has stamped itself depressingly upon the minds of people who remember George Eliot" ("GE" [1919] 151). Woolf neglects to mention that those "who remember George Eliot" often perceived the great sage as highly feminine in person (Carroll, "Sibyl," 13–14). Instead she dwells on the public persona as an obstruction to the secret femininity that she privately discovered in Eliot's works.

Most interpreters of both writers, however, seem unable to distinguish the embodied woman from her narrative style, perceived as too masculine or too feminine. Defenders must compensate by uncovering a feminine Marian Evans Lewes and a masculine Virginia Woolf; one variation of the latter is the robust, political Woolf exhumed by feminists. Ugly and instructively wise, Eliot must be certified to be gentle (Haight entitles a chapter of his biography " 'Someone to Lean Upon' "). Beautiful, cultivated, and charming, Woolf must overcome the role of Invalid Lady of Bloomsbury (Bell 2: 146, 210; Plomer 324; Caramagno); her voice, we learn, was deep and strong (as was Eliot's [Marcus, *Languages*, 139; Bell 2: 200; Haight 11]), and her wit was as lively as any Cambridge Apostle's (Sackville-West, "Woolf III," 318, 320).

In *Seduction and Betrayal*, Elizabeth Hardwick provides an instructive variation on these schematic biographical readings of the women writers. Attacking American feminist critics for recuperating Woolf's "androgynous vision," Hardwick praises Eliot in contrast: "The 'masculine' knowledge a writer like George Eliot acquired from her youth in Warwickshire is way beyond anything Virginia Woolf could have imagined. . . . The aestheticism of Bloomsbury, the 'androgyny' if you will, lies at the root of Virginia Woolf's narrowness. It imprisons her in femininity" (139). This may be a unique instance of attributing Eliot's masculinity to her rural origins rather than her excessive learning, but it is a typical association of femininity with smothering narrowness— an association that itself motivated Eliot's masculine persona and Woolf's impersonal aesthetics.[7]

Hardwick's animosity to Woolf may of course also be fueled by the resentment many women feel toward ladies of unassailable refinement. Like the commandment to be charming, the commandment to be a lady has been enforced with great zeal, as though women more than men, even today as they enter the "LADIES" room, must emulate their betters in the class scale. Eliot's initial class standing was more likely to be pitied than resented, but each of her heroines beginning with Maggie Tulliver either is born a lady or becomes one. The pattern of marrying or blossoming "up," while it answers to the tradition of fairy tales and novels of manners, also follows Eliot's ascent, though hers was through cultural achievement rather than love or feminine "nature." For Esther, Rosamond, and Gwendolen the social ladder proves to be a trap, but for their author it proved enabling: she "rose" to the ranks of educated gentlemen.

Different as their origins certainly were, Eliot and Woolf can be read as heroines struggling against much the same odds with much the same success. Both women overcame the pieties of their upbringing, whether Evangelical or humanist (and Leslie Stephen's humanism owes much to Eliot), to consort with the freethinkers of their day; both

---

[7]Curiously enough, Hardwick chimes in with Woolf's argument in *A Room of One's Own* when she maintains that only artists who unite "masculine and feminine into a whole" can create universal art (139). If Hardwick felt that Carolyn Heilbrun's ideal of androgyny (*Toward a Recognition*) was somehow effeminate, many feminists since have attacked androgyny as a masculinist ideal.

triumphed over their educational disadvantages as girls to master classical and contemporary learning and literature. Both dutiful daughters understood that nursing the sick and pouring the tea must always supersede the translation project or the literary reviewing— until they escaped to homes of their own. Both lost their somewhat remote mothers while they were in their teens. They were both strongly attached to their fathers who, though they encouraged their clever daughters, expected them to lend domestic service. Each woman viewed her father as an inhibiting power. Mary Ann, before Evans's death, wrote: "What shall I be without my Father? It will seem as if a part of my moral nature were gone. I had a horrid vision of myself last night becoming earthly sensual and devilish for want of that purifying restraining influence" (GE Letters 1: 284). As a measure of the distance Woolf has traveled from Eliot's (and her own) early filial piety, her comment in 1928 on her father's death expresses no horror at her own propensities, but only a sense of release: his "life would have entirely ended mine. . . . No writing, no books" (VW Diary 3: 208).[8] After their fathers' deaths (and supported by small inheritances), they were able to begin careers in earnest, publishing translations or reviews and essays before building up confidence to write and publish eight or nine novels as well as biographies, poetry, or stories, while they kept up their correspondence and amassed notebooks and journals.

This might be the model narrative of success, but it would be dull without a hint of the great woman's suffering, and certainly we must not omit the love interest. Eminence took its toll: Eliot was often ill and despondent as she wrote her novels; Woolf went into severe depressions after every novel appeared. The suffering was mitigated for each woman by a fortunate union with a loving man of letters capable of tending her career, supplying confidence when she despaired. Lewes assisted at the labor of Eliot's novels much as she helped him with such works as Physiology of Common Life (1859). As their library testifies, they were true Victorians in their curiosity and erudition on countless subjects. The Woolfs were a similarly productive and versatile couple; the Hogarth Press was their version of the Victorian cottage industry of letters.

I would not want to exaggerate the woman writer's dependence on the tolerance of the men around her, but it seems certain that without

---

[8]In Three Guineas Woolf writes of the "infantile fixation" of fathers who claim complete possession of their daughters. Nevertheless, "it was the woman, the human being whose sex made it her sacred duty to sacrifice herself to the father, whom Charlotte Brontë and Elizabeth Barrett had to kill"—not the father himself (134–35).

some release from the conventional roles of daughter, wife, and mother neither Eliot nor Woolf would have excelled as they did. In spite of their famous departures from convention (Eliot's alliance with Lewes, Woolf's briefer one with Vita Sackville-West), both led quiet domestic lives, forfeiting with regret the right to have children (Haight 205, 413; Showalter, *Literature*, 272–73). The ban on childbearing suggests a similarity between the status of the mistress and the madwoman. An unmarried woman and a woman liable to suicidal bouts with insanity were equally denied the full status of motherhood, although Eliot welcomed the role of "Madonna" and "Mutter" to Lewes's sons and others (Beer, *Eliot*, 27, 109–12; Homans 22), while Woolf, though vicariously engaged in her sister Vanessa's mothering, tended to designate other women to mother her (Marcus, *Languages*, 96–114). Woolf herself points out that "the four great women novelists" (Austen, the Brontës, and Eliot) bore no children ("Women and Fiction" 45); although literary creation and childbirth were welcome analogies, they seemed to be antinomies in most women's lives.

Perhaps because of their unusual domestic circumstances, Eliot and Woolf were able to combine a reclusive private life with public prominence and wide access to culture. Woolf noted that Eliot played the retiring sibyl, and Rose Macaulay observed the same of Woolf, in spite of the fact that both hobnobbed with the cultivated and famous. Nor was Eliot the pitiable recluse Woolf imagines; she traveled frequently and extensively and associated with such prominent figures as Liszt, Martineau, Spencer, and Tennyson, not to mention the "mothers and grandmothers" of Woolf's feminism (TG 102). Bloomsbury was a province of its own and did not inevitably foster Woolf's cosmopolitan historical insight, as Clive Bell's jingoistic *Civilization* suggests. Both women of letters did strive to capitalize on the enforced privatization of a woman's life; Woolf urged the woman writer to find a room of her own (Showalter, *Literature*, 285, 297; RO 24), whereas Eliot expressed gratitude for her involuntary isolation from polite society, which afforded her a kind of room of her own. Whatever the cost, a certain retreat from the world seems to have been necessary for both Eliot and Woolf, perhaps because the personality of a famous woman seems especially assailable.

Woolf's insight into this vulnerability sometimes renders her blind to her predecessors' ambition and love of homage. Thus the great women become victims of convention and self-doubt. "It was the relic of the sense of chastity. . . . Currer Bell, George Eliot, George Sand, all the victims of inner strife as their writings prove, sought ineffectively to veil themselves by using the name of a man. Thus they did homage to the convention . . . that publicity in women is detestable" (RO 52). This picture of women writers as veiled inmates in a "harem" ("Indiscretions" 75) cannot explain the triumphant strategy of a writer such as Eliot. Woolf's belief in self-sacrificing femininity leads her to deny that Eliot is driven by "that romantic intensity . . . a sense of one's own individuality, unsated and unsubdued," that is usually associated with heroism and fame ("GE" [1919] 154–55). Yet few writers have been more intensely (and ambivalently) ambitious than Eliot.

It is true that like other women writers she found it difficult to assume the single-minded individualism expected of the great Romantic artist. The very definition of "greatness," according to George Henry Lewes, entails a self-determination culturally proscribed for women:

> The greatness of an author consists in having a mind extremely irritable, and at the same time steadfastly imperial:—irritable that no stimulus may be inoperative . . . ; imperial, that no solicitation may divert him. . . . A magisterial subjection of all dispersive influences, a concentration . . . these are the rare qualities which mark out the man of genius. In men of lesser calibre the mind is more constantly open to determination from extrinsic influences. (*Principles of Success* 33)

The gendered opposition here between terms of political power and "influences" is ominous: socialized as women, Eliot and Woolf could be easily marked out as less than men of genius because they remained open to "dispersive . . . extrinsic influences," the validated demands of others. In compensation, they devised magisterial, impersonal narrative personas that make a virtue out of susceptibility to others, to the extrinsic and distracting. *"Dispersed are we,"* intones the musical commentary in *Between the Acts* (95–98). The historian of Middlemarch, claiming to be dwarfed by the "great" predecessor Fielding, struggles like Lewes's lesser man against distraction: "All the light I can command must be concentrated on this particular web, and not dispersed over that tempting range of relevancies called the universe" (105). But like Miss La Trobe the playwright's self-effacement, this is no genuine expression of modesty, but a claim to greatness through selflessness, beyond gender, beyond the cult of personality and genius.

Judgments on Womanhood and Women Writers

In spite of their best efforts, both Eliot and Woolf faced the gendered biographical criticism of their day, which defined greatness according to the model of the imperial masculine self. Perhaps surprisingly, they turned around and applied the same tools in their criticism of other writers; in their cultural judgments they often sound like the voice of tradition. Women writers who seemed untrue to their innate "vocation" as well as those who appeared too womanly met alike with their disapproval: the unwomanly and the womanly were incompatible with greatness.

Though Eliot and Woolf defy gender stereotypes, they have often been characterized as representing (and preferring) opposite genders. Woolf appears to show a strong bias toward the feminine, whereas Eliot has usually been read as having pitched her tent in the masculine camp. In Ruby Redinger's terms, Eliot was a woman of "masculine identification" as opposed to Woolf, who celebrated androgyny (59). These characterizations correspond with the authors' different readings of other women writers to a large extent: Eliot seems severe, Woolf sympathetic. But Woolf too could be competitive and destructive.

The mocking denigration of minor women writers in Eliot's essay "Silly Novels by Lady Novelists" and the indulgent admiration for lesser women writers in many of Woolf's critical essays may seem representative. After all, Eliot never claimed to prefer women as Woolf did. In her essay on Fuller and Wollstonecraft, Eliot asserts that it would be "overzealous" to claim women's "actual equality with men," just as she disputes the authenticity of Dickens's saintly poor people and Stowe's virtuous slaves: "If the negroes are really so very good, slavery has answered as moral discipline" ("Three Novels" 327).

To me this skepticism remains a challenge to such champions of the oppressed as Woolf, who risk glorifying the effects of oppression. Woolf, however, is no simple sentimentalist of femininity, and she has foreseen a problem that Eliot largely missed, the problem of the masculine norm. In early, positivistic essays at least, Eliot upheld a standard of human development as though it were not fundamentally alien to those who have had no opportunity to measure up to it. Later, and in fiction, she questions the standard itself; she mocks those who prematurely answer the woman question: "If there were one level of feminine incompetence as strict as the ability to count three and no more, the social lot of women might be treated with scientific certitude" (Prelude, M 4; Blake 306). Woolf too denies the validity of standards belittling women: "There is no mark on the wall to measure the precise height of women. There are no yard measures"; the "universities" and "professions" have "hardly tested" the new element in their midst (RO 89). Both women authors might be restating Anne Elliot's charge in *Persuasion:* "Men have had every advantage of us in telling their own story. Education has been theirs in so much higher a degree; the pen has been in their hands" (237). Such remarks seem richly ironic, traceable as they are to the pens of women who had broken all standards for female achievement.

Eliot retained, however, a sense that men had not only the advantage over women but also inherently superior qualities that she preferred, in spite of her sympathy and admiration for womanhood. Like Woolf, she had throughout her life numerous intimate friendships with women, some of whom were drawn to her with romantic love, however unreciprocated. She admonished Edith Simcox, a journalist and women's labor organizer, "that the love of men and women for each other must always be more and better than any other." Eliot went on to say, according to Simcox, that "she had never all her life cared very much for women . . . that she cared for the womanly ideal, sympathised with women and liked for them to come to her in their troubles, but . . . the friendship and intimacy of men was more to her" (Haight 535). The womanly ideal was one thing, and a proposed lesbian bond quite another.[9]

Woolf's bonds with women reveal the opposite structure of power. In *A Room of One's Own* and *Orlando*, written during her affair with Vita Sackville-West, Woolf affirms a preference for womanly qualities. "Better is it," thinks Orlando, "to be clothed in poverty and ignorance, which are the dark garments of the female sex; . . . better to be quit of martial ambition, the love of power, and all the other manly desires" and to enjoy, instead, "contemplation, solitude, love" (O 160). In her later romantic attachment to the composer Ethel Smyth, Woolf said, "Women alone stir my imagination" (Cook 728; Abel 12, 37; DeSalvo 119, 303–4; Marcus, *Languages*, 80). Yet her advocacy of androgyny and her love of women never entirely erased her belief in a heterosexual norm of gender difference, while her fascination with spinsters can be traced to a lurking aspect of Victorian sexual ideology (N. Auerbach, *Demon*, 109–49; Oldfield).

---

[9]Dorothea Barrett draws a contrast between Marian Evans Lewes's expressed preference for men and the "bias towards her own sex" in George Eliot's fiction; "George Eliot is a feminist," but Marian Lewes was not (23, 175). I agree that the novels make a stronger feminist argument than can be constructed from the life, but I would not attempt such a clear demarcation; some statements in the letters and elsewhere are as feminist as anything in the fiction.

In spite of their different orientations toward women, Eliot and Woolf applied remarkably similar standards of judgment to women writers. They both assumed that a woman's disadvantage—which must become her strength—lay in her confinement to domestic life; her expertise must be in the detail of domestic experience, from counterpanes to courtship. This material was infinitely rich, as novels by men as well as women had shown since the beginning. But the woman writer, like a number of Eliot's and Woolf's heroines, continued to grow restless indoors and to violate her threshold by stepping out. Strangely, Eliot and Woolf can be seen standing outside the door telling her how much more seemly she appears within her familiar environs. It is fatal to the woman writer to write like a man; it only adds fuel to the male critics' inevitable ridicule if she pretends to learning or theology; and if she overindulges her imagination or raises a protest she positively fails in her duty. In short, if she is in every way as much like Jane Austen as she can be, she may do fine things as a novelist; otherwise, she is a woman thrown entirely on her own resources, like Jane Eyre in the wild.

This rendition of Eliot's and Woolf's counsel to women writers might also paraphrase the critical doctrine of George Henry Lewes and Leslie Stephen; it is not, however, a complete account of what Eliot and Woolf had to say about women writers. Eliot, for example, greatly admired Harriet Beecher Stowe and Charlotte Brontë, both of whom diverge markedly from Austen in their use of melodrama and social protest. Woolf similarly swerves from the Austen model by encouraging the Mary Carmichaels, the twentieth-century women novelists who write of women's relations to each other and to their work outside the home, as well as those writers of the future who will disregard altogether the injunction that women should write novels if they must write (RO 95, 80–81).

It is helpful to consider the preconceptions about women's literary style and vocation that Eliot and Woolf would have encountered, as Lewes and Stephen expressed them, if we are to understand their responses to other contenders for the role of grand old woman of letters. In "The Lady Novelists," Lewes claims: "To write as men write is the aim and besetting sin of women; to write as women is the real office they have to perform." Women are "better in *finesse* of detail, in pathos and sentiment" than men; their expertise on "domestic experiences" fits them to be novelists. (As though to contradict the notion of gender-specific style—or perhaps to affirm that Eliot's impersonation of the masculine essay style was opaque—this essay was misidentified as the work of George Eliot [Herrick 11–12]). Given his taste for domestic realism in women's fiction, Lewes not surprisingly considered Austen "the greatest artist that has ever written" in terms of economy of "means" to "end,"[10] and took it upon himself to counsel the young author of *Jane Eyre* to study Jane Austen. Charlotte Brontë repudiated Austen's genteel propriety as Jane Eyre spurns Rochester's offer of gilded captivity: "I should hardly like to live with her ladies and gentlemen, in their elegant but confined houses" (Gaskell 337). Brontë was not to be domesticated; she wrote Lewes, "I cannot, when I write, think always of myself and of what is elegant and charming in femininity" (386)—an interesting challenge to Woolf's claim in *A Room of One's Own* that Brontë's work was inhibited by her self-consciousness as a woman. Lewes's review of *Shirley* enraged Brontë: "After I had said earnestly that I wished critics would judge me as an *author*, not as a woman, you so roughly—I even thought so cruelly—handled the question of sex" (398).

It is impossible to judge whether Lewes had learned to set aside the question of sex when he came to nurture his "wife" as a novelist less than a decade later, but he certainly had not abandoned his predilection for Austen and domestic realism. Marian Evans, after she eloped with Lewes to "Labassecour" (as she put it, referring to Brontë's name for Belgium in *Villette* [Haight 147]), began to write fiction under Lewes's urging and guidance. Unlike Brontë, she accepted Lewes's commendation of Austen (Marian and George read Austen's novels aloud together in 1857 [Haight 225]). For her the model of Austen seems to have been instructive, opening rather than closing possibilities.[11] The novice George Eliot already possessed the powers of realistic description and sober judgment that Lewes urged Brontë to learn from Austen; what George Eliot needed, according to Lewes, was "dramatic power" ("How I Came to Write Fiction," *GE Letters* 2: 406–10). Austen, then, offered Eliot not a fenced-in garden but a liberation from dutiful translation or the first person plural of the *Westminster Review*. The Austen model would not, however, have deflected the cruel "question of sex" without the added authority of masculinity. Eliot's domestic critic seems to have been willing to treat "George Eliot" man-to-man.

Leslie Stephen, like George Henry Lewes, respected women novelists, and he certainly encouraged his daughter to write, though he

[10]Herrick 14. Like Woolf, Lewes compares Austen to Shakespeare and criticizes Austen in terms that would favor George Eliot: in Austen "there are neither epigrams nor aphorisms, neither subtle analyses nor eloquent descriptions" ("The Novels of Jane Austen," *Blackwood's* 86 [1859]. 101–9, in Kaminsky, *Literary Criticism*, 92–93).

[11]See Moers (48–52) on *Adam Bede* as an inversion of *Emma*, focusing on the agricultural fringe of Austen's world. I would add that Esther Lyon is another Emma, this time taught to choose the Robert Martin figure, Felix Holt.

imagined making an historian out of her (Hill 351–53; Rosenbaum 33; DeSalvo 219). His account of Eliot's late beginnings as a novelist seems prescriptive of his daughter's own: "Women who have the gift have been often kept back by the feminine virtue of diffidence" (*George Eliot* 52). Even more than Lewes, Stephen subordinates a supposed women's sphere of experience and hence literary achievement. In noting that the character of Adam Bede was largely a portrait of the author's father, Stephen revealingly remarks:

> Men drawn by women . . . are never quite of the masculine gender. . . . Adam Bede is a most admirable portrait; but we can, I think, see clearly enough that he always corresponds to the view which an intelligent daughter takes of a respected father. That is, perhaps, the way in which one would like to have one's portrait taken; but one is sensible that the likeness though correct is not quite exhaustive. (*George Eliot* 74–75)

Granting that a male author's heroine may be equally incomplete, Stephen persists in distinguishing George Eliot's outlook from that which "one," as a man of letters, shares with men of genius; it is assumed that a woman is limited to describing what she has experienced or reiterating what she has learned. The diary of Eliot's tour of Italy, for example, seems an unoriginal record, whereas the resulting novel, *Romola*, is " 'academic,' " mainly due to the "defect" of the author's womanhood, which Stephen almost claims to have discovered. "George Eliot, I have suggested, was a woman; a woman, too, of rather delicate health, exhausted by hard work; and, moreover, a woman who, in spite of her philosophy, was eminently respectable," and hence out of her depth in the male realm of history, among "the ruffian geniuses of the Renaissance" (120–21, 135–36).

Woolf may have sought to circumvent her father's prescriptive view of women's writing in her own ideal of androgyny: "The fully developed mind . . . does not think specially or separately of sex" (RO 103). But as we have seen, she too needed to insist that George Eliot "was a woman." In a 1918 review, she conditionally endorses R. Brimley Johnson's version of Stephen's judgment: "A woman's writing is always feminine. . . . For all her learning, 'George Eliot's outlook remains thoroughly emotional and feminine.' " She adds in her own assent to Stephen, "The absurdity of a woman's hero or of a man's heroine is universally recognized" ("Women Novelists" 70–71). She attempted to convert the old principle that women will write as women into an open opportunity to invent new forms of literature quite unlike the writings of men. Like Lewes's promotion of the Austen school, then, Stephen's patronage of George Eliot may have helped the beginning writer resist the foreclosure of her potential by identifying a female literary tradition. Ostensibly, Eliot and Woolf agreed with their domestic critics that this tradition centered on novels of domestic realism, but their own work was not about to stay at home.

Eliot and Woolf had reason to fear that the constriction on their experience as women would brand them as inferior "lady" novelists. Thus, Eliot needed to clear the ground for her own far-reaching development as a novelist when she wrote "Silly Novels by Lady Novelists" (1856) in the anonymous, gentlemanly voice she adopted for the *Westminster Review*. The essay is an intriguing attempt to anticipate the criticism she herself might attract as a novelist; she satirizes women's abuse of certain conventions she would endeavor to exploit to greater effect.[12] As though she has completely seen through the cult of woman's mission with its exaltation of minutiae ("trifles make the sum of human things," as Sarah Ellis says [1]), she heaps scorn on *"mind-and-millinery"* novels, with their combination of exquisite accessories and ignorant philosophies (compare the disjunction between Hetty Sorrel's beautiful "eyelashes" and weak "morals" [AB 155]). In these works, ill-educated heroines offer their influence as "a sort of dial by which men have only to set their clocks and watches, and all will go well" ("Silly Novels" 301–2), very much as Dorothea Brooke would more compellingly do. *Middlemarch,* not incidentally, proves the fateful importance of Lydgate's taste in trifles; his costly furniture and wife force him to set his watch to the common time.

In this review Eliot goes on to deplore the "mental mediocrity" of historical fiction by women. This exacting genre requires genius, wide learning, and "sympathetic divination, [to] restore the missing notes in the 'music of humanity' " (320–21)—faculties she would later exercise in her own historically inspired fictions. Though she pities impoverished ladies driven to ply their pen as they would the needle, she suspects that most women writers are motivated by vanity and a restless fantasy life; this unworthy majority, her competition, should cede the field to professionals who understand the responsibilities of art, and who will raise the reputation of the lady novelist. That this reputation remained low, or that Eliot at least wished not to belong to this class of writers even in her eminent success, is suggested by a satire on authoresses in her last published work, *Theophrastus Such.*

---

[12]For instance, the sinister baronet becomes Sir James Chettam; the dying first husband who blesses the match of the heroine and her lover becomes Casaubon forbidding Dorothea's union with Ladislaw.

Vorticella is a provincial hostess and the author of "The Channel Islands," a much-trumpeted, bad book. "What one would have wished . . . was that she had refrained from producing even that single volume, and thus from giving her self-importance a troublesome kind of double incorporation"; the plump lady and plump book should both have effaced themselves ("Diseases of Small Authorship," TS 155).

Woolf, neither so patronizing nor so rivalrous when she surveyed the possibilities for women's achievement in literature, tended to blame women's failures on societal pressures rather than on undisciplined silliness. "Outwardly, what obstacles are there for a woman rather than for a man?" she wrote. "Inwardly, I think, the case is very different; she has still many ghosts to fight, many prejudices to overcome." Yet the true novelist seeks "to be as unconscious as possible. He has to induce in himself a state of perpetual lethargy" ("Professions for Women" 61–62). If in conceiving this passive (and feminine?) state Woolf unthinkingly obeys the convention of the masculine pronoun, we must grant that the internal obstacles are very great indeed. The woman novelist can point to no external obstacles, and only has her own struggling self-consciousness to blame.

In *A Room of One's Own*, Woolf offers women a kind of catch-22, like Bardo's simultaneous praise of Romola for being unlike a woman and reproach for being nothing more.[13] Women must write as women write, yet they must not be mere women writers. Male pseudonyms may be ineffective veils, as she charges (RO 52), but they helped gain Eliot and the Brontës both "impartial criticism" and freedom "from the tyranny of what was expected from their sex" ("Women Novelists" 70). That tyranny extended over generic expectations: though Woolf's great women writers wrote novels, women should not be merely novelists ("Women and Fiction" 46): "The overflow of George Eliot's capacious mind should have spread itself when the creative impulse was spent upon history or biography" (RO 70). Eliot wrote poetry as well as historical and biographical essays, of course, and Woolf overflowed into history and biography. Indeed, Woolf gives voice to the restlessness both authors must have felt in the sphere of domestic fiction; their careers reveal their effort to command the impersonal realm of historical discourse, epic poetry, or drama. In spite of Woolf's rejection of women's meager generic portion, she rather tyrannically imposes a code of feminine decorum: "It is fatal for a woman to lay

---

[13]Dr. Malone, in *The Years*, emulates Bardo's criticism of his daughter's assistance with his scholarship: "Nature did not intend you to be a scholar, my dear" (81).

the least stress on any grievance . . .; in any way to speak consciously as a woman" (RO 108). In effect (whether describing or enforcing this code), she undermines the possibility of the specifically womanly writing she calls for.

Eliot's and Woolf's patronizing assessments of the handicaps on women writers at times seem to imply that they alone of all women shared the perch with men of letters. Like most contemporary critics they held the personality of the woman as well as the quality of the work up to scrutiny, demanding selfless devotion in both plots, the woman's life and the career. Eliot and Woolf did find some contemporaries and predecessors to admire according to these exacting criteria. They were not unwilling to grant the excellence of literary women such as Elizabeth Barrett Browning and Mary Wollstonecraft, either because these authors *were* able to reconcile artistic calling and womanhood or because they *refused* to reach a compromise.

Elizabeth Barrett Browning impressed both Eliot and Woolf as a distinctly feminine writer who seized a masculine artistic freedom. In her 1857 review of *Aurora Leigh*, Eliot calls Browning "all the greater poet because she is intensely a poetess," one who exhibits "all the peculiar powers without the negations of her sex." As Gillian Beer explains in citing this review, however, Eliot believes the feminine writer must, like Barrett Browning, incorporate masculinity along with femininity in order to achieve "liberty *from* sexual type: 'there is simply a full mind pouring itself out in song as its natural and easiest medium' " (16). Woolf's similar reading of *Aurora Leigh* expresses stronger misgivings about the feminine personality displayed in the work. "Elizabeth Barrett was inspired by a flash of true genius," Woolf allows, "when she rushed into the drawing-room and said that here, where we live and work, is the true place for the poet." Barrett Browning herself, according to Woolf, "was one of those rare writers who risk themselves . . . in an imaginative life which . . . demands to be considered apart from personalities." Yet the *poem* is too personal: "The connexion between a woman's art and a woman's life was unnaturally close." In *Aurora Leigh*, the feminine "genius," then, remains "in some pre-natal stage waiting the final stroke of creative power," because the woman poet cannot escape her personality after all ("Aurora Leigh" 137–44). Both great women of letters find in Barrett Browning, lauded as the greatest English woman poet in her day, the incomplete version of their own stories: a somewhat too easy, personal, feminine artist, though a great venturer in the poetic territory of the drawing room that Eliot and Woolf were to mine so profitably.

Like Woolf, Eliot viewed other women writers through the lens of personality, at times empathizing with suffering and admiring fidelity to womanly duty while praising the escape from the "negations" of personality. Eliot compared her own career with those of Harriet Beecher Stowe and Margaret Fuller, both noted partisans of the oppressed, and though Eliot might not entirely concur with their reforming zeal, she admired the combination of public mission and ladylike private life. Eliot sustained a long friendship in letters with Stowe, acknowledging her as one who properly fulfilled a dual vocation of womanhood and art (outdoing Eliot in the former at least): "Dear friend and fellow-labourer—for you have had longer experience than I as a writer, and fuller experience as a woman, since you have borne children and known the mother's history from the beginning" (*GE Letters* 5: 31). She praised Stowe's "rare genius": " 'Uncle Tom' and 'Dred' will assure her a place in that highest rank of novelists who can give us a national life in all its phases" ("[Three Novels]," 326).

The example of Fuller seems to have illustrated a conflict between vocations—as explicator of the national life and as woman—that was closer to Eliot's experience, as Thomas Pinney points out: "It is a help to read such a life as Margaret Fuller's," Eliot wrote in 1852 (before her union with Lewes); "I am thankful, as if for myself, that [the life] was sweet at last" (*GE Letters* 2: 15; *Essays* 199). Eliot perceived that the postponed romance plot in Wollstonecraft's and Fuller's ambitious lives was similar to her own; the late loving marriage after literary endeavor comes to Barrett Browning and Aurora Leigh as well. Eliot particularly admired Fuller's "calm plea for the removal of unjust laws and artificial restrictions, so that the possibilities of [woman's] nature may have room for full development." Fuller could be seen as a heroine of the ilk of Romola or Dorothea, a crusader who does no harm to Tennysonian "distinctive womanhood" ("Fuller and Wollstonecraft" 200). Indeed, Fuller's brother, in the edition of *Woman in the Nineteenth Century* that Eliot reviewed, reassures us (as Gaskell did in her biography of Brontë) that "literary women" and female reformers do not necessarily "neglect the domestic concerns of life." Rather, Fuller is remembered "as the angel of the sick-chamber," whose "gentleness was united to a heroism . . . truly womanly" (Preface, Ossoli iv–v). Her belated marriage and sudden death soon after make her a heroine like Gaskell's Brontë, while her drowning has a fortuitous literary respectability; Eliot recalls Wollstonecraft's earlier attempt to drown herself (*GE Letters* 5: 160–61) and rewrites aspects of these exemplary lives in Maggie Tulliver's drowning and Mirah Lapidoth's attempted suicide. It is difficult not to believe that Woolf was trying to write the closure of her own life into such a tradition.

Woolf as much as Eliot tries to read her literary women as heroines, linking text and personality, and she too discovers womanly greatness in Mary Wollstonecraft. But although both Eliot and Woolf rediscover the "loving woman's heart" in the legendary hyena in petticoats ("Fuller and Wollstonecraft" 201), Woolf is not certain that the feminine susceptibility is to the credit of the great reforming author. She admiringly paraphrases Wollstonecraft's doctrine: "Independence was the first necessity for a woman; not grace or charm." The reformer "won fame and independence and the right to live her own life," but according to Woolf she was always brought up short by her desire for domestic love. The woman herself embodies conflict: "These contradictions show[ ] . . . in her face, at once so resolute and so dreamy, so sensual and so intelligent, and beautiful into the bargain." Ultimately, like Dorothea, "she has her revenge" when woman and text form an immortal unity: "We hear her voice and trace her influence even now among the living" ("Wollstonecraft" 97–99, 103).

In other portraits of female predecessors Woolf is less tolerant of the conflict between womanhood and ambition, though it is clear that to compromise in favor of womanhood is to forfeit all claim to greatness. Mrs. Humphry Ward, whose books "we never wish to open" again, chose the route of "compromise" (the melancholy alternative to tragedy for Eliot's heroines, according to Woolf). Her fulfillment as a lady of letters, "beloved, famous, and prosperous," entailed no disinterested devotion to art, though she was active in public causes, including the ignoble anti-suffrage campaign. The worst is that "her imagination always . . . agrees to perch"; she has become mere historical personality ("The Compromise" 171–72). In contrast, Olive Schreiner seems to have some of Wollstonecraft's vision, and to share the honor of tragedy (in ultimate obscurity and isolation) rather than compromise, but her egotism prevents her from measuring up to Woolf's standard for greatness. Schreiner's "famous book," *The Story of an African Farm*, "has the limitations of" the Brontës' "egotistical masterpieces without a full measure of their strength. The writer's interests are local, her passions personal." Nevertheless, like a reverse of Mrs. Humphry Ward, Schreiner earns "pity and respect" as one of "those martyrs" to "the cause . . . [of] the emancipation of women." If she is "one half of a great writer" ("Olive Schreiner" 180–83), the other half is marred by egotism and politics (even if, unlike Ward's politics, Schreiner's are correct).

Apparently, Eliot's and Woolf's ideal of greatness for the woman writer would be almost impossible to fulfill, if one must be both genius and angel, must live *down* and live *by* one's personality as a woman.

These great women of letters deplored writers who sought a way out of this bind through a manly style, as much as they censured women (writers or heroines) who attempted to live egotistically for themselves as men appeared able to do. These prescriptions often concern the question of style. On the one hand, Eliot lauded the forgotten women of the French Enlightenment who created "a new standard of taste" combining exalted sentiment with simple language ("Woman in France" 54, 58), much as Woolf praised Austen's "perfectly natural, shapely sentence proper for her own use" (RO 80). On the other hand, no literary persona could be more transparent than a woman's "exaggeration of the masculine style, like the swaggering gait of a bad actress in male attire," in Eliot's words ("Woman in France" 53). Yet Woolf, like Eliot, would label self-consciously feminine writing "silly": "The women who wished to be taken for men in what they wrote were certainly common enough; and if they have given place to the women who wish to be taken for women the change is hardly for the better" ("Women Novelists" 70). But how were women authors to choose between dressing in ludicrous frills or in men's oversize suits? Their only hope, perhaps, was to suppress the cruel "question of sex" altogether by offering up work so authoritative as to constitute a kind of reinvention of the personality of the author.

Eliot's and Woolf's Strategies of Impersonality

Eliot and Woolf sidestepped their own intermittently held ideal of woman's anonymous mission and their own criticism of the disabilities of women writers to pursue careers as women of letters. They did not write as, according to their different lights, women were supposed to write. In their own narrative strategies and styles, Eliot and Woolf display their ambivalence toward women's role as outsiders in an androcentric tradition. The marginal vantage seemed an opportunity, yet at the same time a constraint they would not themselves accept. How *not* to think of themselves as women writers was the first difficulty. As Woolf, in spite of her introspective diaries, might have said of her own personality as well as of Eliot's, "For long she preferred not to think of herself at all" ("GE" [1919] 157). The great women of letters became powerful personalities that covered their works, yet the success of their narrative strategies depended upon a transmutation of personality as well as a difficult relation to an audience often seen as embodying patriarchal judgment.

Eliot had had painful experience, not only of the costs of sickroom heroism (in tending her father) but also of the consequences of over-stepping the bounds of woman's sphere. She would be genius *and* angel in spite of her notoriety as freethinking journalist and "wife" of a married man (Carlyle wrote her off as a "Strong minded Woman" [Haight 160–61]). First she acted the clerical gentleman, as though she intended to be a supremely convincing actress in male attire. Later she affirmed her "heart" as a sibyl selflessly devoted to art and human progress. Though as Gillian Beer puts it, " 'George Eliot' was name without person" initially, the author soon fled the clerical pose; the style outlasted the disguise, in the novels after *Adam Bede* (Beer, *George Eliot*, 22–24, 55, 17). Eliot went on to develop the freest possible approximation of "egolessness," which undoubtedly required that the author herself appear to retire from the public eye and that she present, in the novels, the evils of egotism and the virtues of self-sacrifice. The narrators of Eliot's later works seem to speak from the reservoirs of a mind that has survived the burden of a personal life: she, for one, is free to have a "human" voice. The narrative strategy, then, would seem to give the lie to Woolf's detection of an autobiographical femininity in Eliot's work, yet Woolf is also right. The very evasion of personality is an indication of the burden to be sloughed off.

Woolf's own narrative strategy is more difficult to identify, as to some extent it succeeds in avoiding the question of sex through a disembodied, interpersonal voice that freely penetrates all the characters. Virginia Blain describes Woolf's "life-or-death combat" in the early novels with "the masculine voice of the omniscient narrator"; her later impersonal narrators (like Eliot's "human" narrators) reveal "the gender consciousness that betrays a female perspective" (119, 133). Except for the parodically male biographer in *Orlando*, Woolf in general does not personify her narrators or allow them first-person commentary. Is this an attempt at the androgynous unself-consciousness she has shown is next to impossible for women, or is this a feminine narrative stance? I would argue that in other contexts Woolf would have defined such interpersonal indeterminacy as in itself feminine, but that she needed to perceive her own strategy as beyond gender.

Woolf's curious insistence on an identifiable gender of style was somehow not meant to apply to her own work. Yet as she defines women's writing, it resembles not only *écriture feminine* in Hélène Cixous's vision, but also her own egoless style. The theorists of *écriture feminine*, of course, insist on divorcing the actual sex of the author from the gender of style, much as Woolf seems momentarily to do in her definition of androgyny in *A Room of One's Own*.[14] But Woolf also reverts to a more essentialist view ("The book has somehow to be adapted to the body" [RO 81]), much as Cixous echoes old stereotypes of women's inherent qualities. Cixous defines feminine style as one of "flourishes . . . near and distant byways," "sweeping away syntax." Woman is likewise perceived: "Secretly, silently . . . she grows and multiplies . . . adventuring, without the masculine temerity, into anonymity . . . because she's a giver" (287, 290, 292). Eliot as well as Woolf would recognize such a style and being, the cousin of "Anon" and of the incalculably diffusive Saint Theresas. The persona-without-boundaries that Woolf devised for her narrators thus may have seemed to be a new way to be freely "human" in a hitherto suppressed feminine mode, but it sustains the ideology of influence.

Woolf's narrative ideal of androgynous unself-consciousness, like Eliot's narrative ideal of selfless objectivity, serves as a screen for female personality. In practice, the two writers' styles and narrative personas were of course various, and a close examination of each could engage a long study in itself. I reserve extended discussion of the novels for later chapters (particularly Chapters 5–7) and instead focus briefly here on the strategies Woolf and Eliot employ for constructing an audience, especially in their essays, in which both authors generally adopt a masculine, self-effacing persona. These guises were designed in response to an audience personified in terms of the gendered spheres: the authoritative audience of the essay was male, while the casual novel reader was female.

In "The Influence of Rationalism," Eliot satirizes the public she has won as a novelist: "The general reader of the present day does not exactly know what distance he goes; he only knows that he does not go 'too far.' . . . He likes an undefined . . . amelioration of all things: . . . something between the excesses of the past and the excesses of the present" (398). This opinionated gentlemanly reader has an earlier counterpart among the ladies: "Mrs. Farthingale, for example, who prefers the ideal in fiction" ("Amos Barton," SCL 41). Neither the liberal nor the sentimental reader is, of course, Eliot's ideal reader (Prince 9). Mrs. Farthingale, like the "world's wife" (MF 428), will be

---

[14]Woolf's famous comment on Dorothy Richardson's style tries to identify a nonessential gender: "She has invented . . . a sentence which we might call the psychological sentence of the feminine gender. It is of a more elastic fibre than the old. . . . Other writers of the opposite sex have used sentences of this description." But Richardson's sentence "is used to describe a woman's mind by a writer who is neither proud nor afraid of anything that she may discover in the psychology of her sex" ("Dorothy Richardson" 191).

even less lenient than the vaguely liberal gentleman in judging women like Maggie Tulliver and Marian Evans who go "too far." If the author had allowed herself to be vulnerable to such criticism of her work, she might have met the fate of the scholar Merman: "The gall of his adversaries' ink had been sucked into his system" ("How We Encourage Research," TS 49). Instead, she constructed a sympathetic coterie, the "we" or "you and me" of the meditative passages in *Middlemarch*, for example. The narrator him/herself cannot be charged with being either too detached, like the male reader, or too involved, like the female, since he/she, and the nonadversarial coterie, partake of both.

Woolf apparently shares Eliot's desire for a non-gendered collective of readers upon a common ground. Like Eliot, she invites "us" to join a club, but the modern club is, at least in theory, open to all. Her "common reader" has no professional key to culture, but "has, as Dr. Johnson maintained, some say in the final distribution of poetical honours." Yet Woolf instinctively invokes "the great man's approval" as though the honors will be distributed much as in the past ("The Common Reader" 1–2). Further, Woolf inadvertently signals the exclusion of women from the club of active truth-lovers: "For the true reader is essentially young. He is a man of intense curiosity; of ideas; open-minded and communicative, to whom reading is more of the nature of brisk exercise in the open air than of sheltered study" ("Hours in a Library," CE 2: 34). Like "George Eliot" personifying his associates as gentlemen, Woolf here conceives the ideal audience of literature as male; this essay, significantly, borrows its title from one of her father's books (and recreates the young mountain-climbing Stephen: the true reader "climbs higher and higher" ["Hours," CE 2: 34]). Woolf, too, hides on occasion behind the equivalent of a male pseudonym (notably in early essays such as this one written for *The Times Literary Supplement* in 1916). Yet in marked contrast to Eliot, she did broadcast a female voice in some feminist essays, books, and on radio (*VW Diary* 5: 83). At the same time she anticipates male adversarial response, humorously represented by a counterpart to Mrs. Farthingale, "Sir Chartres Biron" spying on her lectures to the women's college: "We are all women, you assure me?" (RO 85); Biron, fictional as he sounds, actually was the magistrate in the Radclyffe Hall obscenity trial, as Marcus reminds us (*Languages* 166). This personified censor helps consolidate a *female* subset of the consensual "we." For the most part, however, Woolf seems to rely on a trouble-free audience for her fiction, one that is never personified, gendered, or addressed (*Jacob's Room* and *Orlando* are examples of exceptions).

While both women of letters advised women to write in a style of their own, and while both tended to personify the critical audience as male, they devised such different styles that we must abandon any lingering desire to generalize about women's style. Yet there is a consistency in their need to write beyond gender and self. In nonfiction they come closest to speaking *in propria persona*—Miss Evans, anonymous editor of *The Westminster Review*, was known at least in London intellectual circles, while Mrs. Woolf was widely known to readers of *The Times Literary Supplement*. The risk of being read as an unmediated personality, however, is one that Woolf and Eliot especially guard against in the essays. Here they significantly assert a more masculine authority than seems necessary in their more mediated fiction.

Their different versions of the comradely essayist reflect in part the fashions of their times. To paraphrase Woolf regarding Mr. Birrell on Carlyle: there is a great gulf between Virginia Woolf on George Eliot and the essay which one may suppose that George Eliot would have written upon Virginia Woolf ("The Modern Essay," CE 2: 45). Woolf's essays range through cultural history and bring together unexpected relevancies as Eliot's do, but a piece by the modern writer will be a quick and elusive flight compared to the Victorian's essay, an expedition in search of conviction. It is safe to say that Eliot devotes two sentences to any point that Woolf, with twentieth-century efficiency, would express in one. Reading an essay of either writer, one attends to a voice of great mastery, well-read yet persistently curious, often satirical—a voice, especially in Woolf's case, distinct from that of her fictional narrators. Whereas Woolf poses more as her audience's companion than as an authority, Eliot impresses us as the collective voice of Victorian reason; yet both follow the "convention of the *male* reviewer" (Stange, "Voices," 317; Showalter, *Literature*, 290–93; Daiches 130–41).

In certain essays, Eliot and Woolf confidently survey the industry and profession of literature, satirizing the hackwork that makes life unpleasant for cultivated readers and writers like themselves. In two similar pieces, they turn from a good-humored survey to an attack, whether on the dilettante or the reviewer. Eliot's "Lord Brougham's Literature" begins: "It is matter of very common observation that members of the 'privileged classes,' who . . . find their time hang rather heavily on their hands, try to get rid of it by employments which, if not self-imposed, they would think rather pitiable." This caricature of aristocrats who dabble in superfluous crafts is intended as an emblem for Lord Brougham's *Lives of Men of Letters*, a collection of "third-rate biographies in the style of a literary hack!" Claiming no personal animosity toward Lord Brougham, and no resentment of any "hard-run literary man" really forced into mediocrity, this reviewer expresses boiling "indignation" against genteel self-indulgence, parasitical on the great originals: "If he has no jewels to offer us, at least polish his pebbles" (138–39). (This 1855 essay suggests that Eliot did not believe literary silliness to be a monopoly of lady novelists.)

Woolf's "Reviewing" similarly begins with an arresting image of amusing labor. "In London there are certain shop windows that always attract a crowd. The attraction is not in the finished article but in the worn-out garments that are having patches inserted in them." Like Eliot's aristocratic poker-makers, Woolf's "women at work . . . putting invisible stitches into moth-eaten trousers" reflect on the confusion between writing as a trade and as a vocation, but in Woolf's emblem, craft sides with literature rather than opposing it: the stitching women are "poets, playwrights, and novelists," the most impertinent passersby are reviewers. Like Eliot's essay, Woolf's sides with the misrepresented men (or persons) of letters, expressing boiling indignation against a different kind of hack: "The reviewer was a louse; his bite was contemptible; yet . . . in the nineteenth century . . . he had considerable power" (CE 2: 204–6). Since both Eliot and Woolf in such essays are writing with the reviewer's power, it is interesting to see their hostility toward minor men of letters who might be said to share their company; Eliot expresses "noble rage" against the fulsome and ignorant biographical critic (142), Woolf a sense of "public duty to abolish" the reviewer who cannot judge by "the eternal standards of literature" (208). It seems that such essays helped the women authors to carve out a place among men of letters who *did* consider those supposedly immutable standards of greatness.

If as essayists both Eliot and Woolf strive for authority high above the hacks, the same must be said of their strategies as novelists.[15] Yet we have seen that in novels as well as essays these authors exhibit differing strategies of impersonality, scarcely predictable from the fact of their being women; only Woolf's manners in fiction resemble the conventionally "feminine." Perhaps they have attained "liberty from sexual type," "apart from personalities," as they said Barrett Browning had done. Fair enough, let us not pester them to *be* women writers

---

[15]In a fascinating and slightly embarrassing letter never sent to *The New Statesman*, Woolf defines the ranks of culture and declares herself "proud to be called highbrow." The highbrow tradition (from Shakespeare through Henry James, with Austen, Brontë, but not Eliot thrown in) pursues art itself, and loves lowbrow "life itself," but scorns middlebrows obsessed with "money, fame, power, or prestige" ("Middlebrow," CE 2: 196, 199).

according to the tyranny of what is expected. But why then do they so persistently attempt to define what is expected of their sex, and why do we in turn question the narrative personas and styles of their writings as responses to certain historical patterns of gender expectation? Why, particularly, is Woolf offended by Eliot's air of authority, preferring Austen's "woman's sentence"? Perhaps because these women authors and feminist readers generally are in search of an engendered greatness that would not silence the experience of female personality.

In "Phases of Fiction" Woolf draws a comparison of Eliot and Austen that qualifies Woolf's apparent preference for ladylike charm, and that reveals her own negotiation of the problems of greatness and womanhood, authority and style. Austen, self-effacing, "went in and out of her people's minds like the blood in their veins," whereas "Eliot has kept the engine of her clumsy yet powerful mind at her own disposal" to analyze a hidden "state of mind which often runs counter to the action and the speech." This description of Eliot's method suggests a subversive ability to capture the elusive Mrs. Brown as Austen could not have done. The intrusive narrative persona troubles Woolf, however. Unlike Austen, Eliot "at once reveals herself as 'I.' . . . 'I' will do my best to illumine these particular examples of men and women with all the knowledge, all the reflections that 'I' can offer you" (CE 2: 78–80). Woolf identifies her predecessor's narrative persona (if not her actual style). Eliot's narrator repeats the claims of authoritative address—though not the phallic pronoun itself; this narrator is at the same time intimately feminine ("melancholy, tolerant, and perhaps resigned"). Yet Woolf's Eliot has not accepted Austen's womanly sphere of personal relations (she writes of relations "with God or nature" as well).[16]

Perhaps we see here a design for Woolf's own narrative persona. Eliot's crime is not self-assertion but an overexposure of her *personal* claim to knowledge and authority (the "grave mind" that "darkens and thickens the atmosphere" [CE 2: 79]). Woolf would claim every bit of Eliot's authority to show human relations with history, nature, or spirituality, though in a modern frame of mind. And she would

---

[16]CE 2: 78–79. When Eliot's narrator does use the first person singular, it serves personal memory and fellow-feeling, not hard self-assertion: "I remember those large dipping willows. I remember the stone bridge," intones the female Wordsworth at the opening of *The Mill on the Floss* (7). "Phases of Fiction" appeared in 1929, the same year as *A Room of One's Own*, suggesting that Woolf would have been attributing masculine ego to Eliot in using the repeating "I, I, I" (RO 103–4). The repetitions of the pronoun are also displacements, and can affirm *"connection* to others" in Woolf's usage, as Patricia Waugh notes (11).

retain Austen's feminine suppression of the "I," becoming the blood in her people's veins. Thus, finally, her incrimination of Eliot's manliness seems mainly a dread of the evidence that to succeed on men's terms a woman author must unsex or efface herself—must become an overbearing ego, just like a man, or a charming chameleon, like a lady. In the twentieth century, she hoped, that sacrifice would no longer be called for, though she still warns that manifest womanhood can be "fatal" to the writer and her text.

Woolf's debt to "the first woman" of her father's age was undoubtedly difficult to honor. But she wished to emerge from her heritage as a new voice; she cultivated a style, especially after *Night and Day*, like the flashing of fireflies compared to the steady desk lamp of Eliot's prose. If the style is the man, these different styles are precisely *not* the woman writer. In all their complexity, the rich utterances of Eliot's and Woolf's narrators must be seen as tacit bids for the textual immortality of the great writer. This greatness would be granted, in current terms, almost exclusively to texts that silenced the woman, erased the female origin. Readers of their novels knew full well (at least after *Adam Bede*) that a woman had written them, but they encountered implied authors who, unlike the more strictly gendered characters within the text, enjoyed the freedom of both spheres. If these narrators were female, they were also impersonal, able to speak in the collective first person: "we" transcend the individual, "we" commune with human greatness, "we," though especially intimate with a feminine common life, partake of an omniscience usually considered a masculine privilege. Ultimately, "we" are immortal, because these women authors and their "human" narrators are not dead; such is the liberal myth of culture that the grand old women of letters collaborate in writing. This myth of a collective history, a common life, which I turn to next, is both source and confirmation of their recognition as great women writers.

3

Eliot and Woolf
as Historians of
the Common Life

The traditional image of the historian is of a man calmly recounting past events from the heights of retrospect, authorized by his very disengagement to delineate general patterns in the dust of past particulars. Of course, this image remains unchallenged only in the realm of the ideal; in practice, historians and their audience always engage with history from a "proper" point of view. Yet objectivity, like godliness, remains an attractive aspiration whether or not one still believes in such things (it is certainly the most tempting convention for the critic). Thus Eliot and Woolf at times adopted the impersonal role of historian as though the ideal were intact; it was a means of escaping the boundaries of self while synthesizing the details of the past. At the same time their works shatter the illusion of objective order and challenge the possibility of manly indifference in historical interpretation. Their feminist perspectives on history force a revaluation of the class system of data—the privileging of certain public facts over the mass of private detail—while inviting us to examine the personal motives of a Casaubon or a Professor von X.

To what extent are the narrators in Eliot's and Woolf's novels implicated in the myths of objectivity and the conventions of realism? Do they simply embellish the big picture with authentic details of private, feminine, or common life, or can the altered emphasis change the entire aesthetic, epistemological, and even ethical frame? Such questions have continued to disturb feminist critics, particularly those who acknowledge their debt to a liberal, empiricist tradition shared (and challenged) by Eliot and Woolf.

Feminists of many varieties have been happy to attack objectivity as a masculinist myth; as Annette Kolodny puts it, "If feminist criticism calls anything into question, it must be that dog-eared myth of intellectual neutrality" (163). But as Kolodny herself would no doubt concede, it is difficult to combat bias, for example the bias of traditional history against the detail of women's lives, except on the grounds of a nearer approach to objective truth. *Our* ideological bent is less distorted than theirs; feminist history includes *more*—such at least is the unspoken motive for most feminist scholarship. Yet to claim the superiority of a feminist history is to posit an ahistorical standard, and we instead prefer to smash such figureheads and declare our bias at the outset. Even those in my feminist "we" who more rigorously eschew claims to truth-value than I do cannot avoid this dilemma if they grant that feminism at the very least presumes a standard that patriarchal culture and discourse have failed so far to meet.

One feature of this dilemma has been a predilection in feminist discourse toward positivist history and realistic fiction (Moi 47–49), both of which have helped to gather the neglected "data" of women's experience. It is surely no accident that women's growing awareness of themselves as an oppressed group coincided with the development of the first literary genre largely invented, sustained, and read by women (Spender 4–6; Armstrong 104–8). It is no more true, however, that all women's novels are realistic than that the novel form itself is essentially feminist—indeed it seems that novelistic convention is generally antipathetic to women's "cause." Faithful data-gathering, like patriotism, is not enough (to paraphrase Nurse Cavell in *The Years*); realistic copies of things as they are may rouse protest, but must themselves be subject to critique for failing to challenge the presuppositions of patriarchal discourse.

Eliot's and Woolf's fundamentally realistic mode of historical writing and their corresponding personas as historians must to some degree raise such a challenge for feminist readers. To focus for the moment only on the writer's role: Why should the woman writer who has her own way to make in the world wish to burden herself with history in the footsteps of Dryasdust? Would not the egotistical sublime of the Romantic artist open more inviting vistas? Certainly the Victorian sibyl and the modernist visionary owed something to the Romantic cult of genius, and never wholly effaced themselves as servants of little-known but illuminating facts. Yet they were suspicious of the conventional egotism of the Romantic artist. Like Mary Shelley, Eliot and Woolf must have sensed that this imperious image of the creator could be a potentially monstrous denial of femininity—of the material, contingent, or domestic (Homans 100–111; Schor 16–17, 35–38). The historian's role, if still conventionally masculine, at least entailed nearly anonymous service of a sort that Eliot and Woolf would have associated with the feminine. Moreover, the inspired historian might, like the poets, instill meaning in the mundane particular without egotistically presuming to create it as well.

If Eliot more than Woolf emulated the artistry of the historian, it was due perhaps to the greater optimism in the earlier age that an accurate history of ordinary experience might be written. Yet Eliot never practiced the kind of naive empiricism that Woolf parodies in *Orlando* ("to plod . . . in the indelible footprints of truth" [65]). Eliot's declared duty, "the faithful representing of commonplace things" (AB 182), did not, as Woolf claimed, subdue the Victorian author's "romantic intensity" or overweening individuality. The authoritative narrators of the novels frequently confess to their necessary bias, alerting us to the pains they take in selecting and interpreting the "data," and then tripping us up when our theories outrun the evidence presented.[1] Eliot's texts call attention to their own mimetic medium without pretending to transparency: the narrator of *Adam Bede*, for example, proposes to emulate the "Egyptian sorcerer" in recreating "visions of the past" with "a single drop of ink for a mirror" (1). Conversely, Woolf in her work tethered the Romantic "rainbow" of personality and vision to the "granite" of the commonplace. She hoped to capture the "state of mind" "wedged among solid objects" as faithfully as Eliot did. Such fidelity could become plodding duty, the historian's role suppressing the woman writer's vision (witness the torments of writing *Romola* or *Roger Fry*). But as Eliot and Woolf strained for a place in the center of tradition, they necessarily pledged the faith of contemporary historiography to some extent. As I try to assess just how far they held to this faith, I will also be exposing their heresy. Their historiographical realism always betrays a feminist bias toward the underprivileged detail, as well as a resistance to hierarchies of class and gender inscribed in mimetic narratives.

Historiography, the Idea of Progress, and the Common

Eliot's and Woolf's works display remarkably similar visions of history. Woolf, as we have seen, was fond of modernist declarations of independence. Her description of the outlook of the new age,

---

[1]"For there is nothing more widely misleading than sagacity if it happens to get on a wrong scent," we are reminded in *The Mill on the Floss*; Mr. Riley recommends Mr. Stelling as teacher for Tom Tulliver without ulterior motive. Ordinary life does not proceed by grand plot, in other words, but by small deeds, "hand to mouth" for "immediate desires" (MF 23).

however, would have been readily intelligible to Eliot. Alter only the impulsive style and the time scale (admittedly significant in themselves), and Woolf could be writing from a Victorian perspective:

> The mind is full of monstrous, hybrid, unmanageable emotions. That the age of the earth is 3,000,000,000 years; that human life lasts but a second; that the capacity of the human mind is nevertheless boundless; that life is infinitely beautiful yet repulsive; that one's fellow creatures are adorable but disgusting; that science and religion have between them destroyed belief; that all bonds of union seem broken, yet some control must exist—it is in this atmosphere of doubt and conflict that writers have now to create. ("The Narrow Bridge of Art," CE 2: 219)[2]

Set this side by side with the following passage from Eliot on the decline of superstition. Witch trials have given way to the latest spiritualism:

> At least we are safely rid of certain horrors; but if the multitude . . . do not roll back even to a superstition that carries cruelty in its train, it is not because they possess a cultivated Reason, but because they are pressed upon and held up by what we may call an external Reason—the sum of conditions resulting from the laws of material growth, from changes produced by great historical collisions shattering the structures of ages and making new highways for events and ideas, and from the activities of higher minds . . . with which the . . . multitude are inextricably interwoven. ("The Influence of Rationalism" 402)

Certainly Woolf's "mind" is more Paterian than Eliot's "higher minds": Woolf's spirit of the age is a kind of aggregate of idiosyncratic impressions. Eliot's processional prose is less steeped in aesthetics than in the new "sciences" of development, with their reassuring (if in our view ultimately dangerous) "laws" that subsume the individual in the mass. Nevertheless, these passages illustrate certain shared presuppositions: that "great historical collisions shatter[ ] the structures of ages" and that "events and ideas" contribute to changes in the "atmosphere," or the collective experience of the age; that the "multitude"

---

[2]Woolf here, in 1927, is writing of the inadequacy to modern experience of lyric poetry, which is "so intense, so personal, so limited" by belated Romantic egotism. An unflinching omniscient realism seems called for.

is "adorable but disgusting," submitting only to an unknown "control" or "external Reason"; that old forms of faith have broken down, and that some pressure must unite the alarming diversity of human beings to ensure continuing progress.

We would expect a Victorian writer to express a belief in progress or social evolution. Eliot, drawing a familiar analogy between natural and social law, declares that the "law of consequences . . . lights up what once seemed the dreariest regions of history with new interest; every past phase of human development is part of that education of the race in which we are sharing. . . . A correct generalization gives significance to the smallest detail" ("The Progress of the Intellect" 31). Yet even in her early positivist confidence, there is no assurance that "human development" will be individually experienced, by small details like ourselves, as benign or orderly. In later writings, though she retains much of her faith in the correspondence between the minutiae of common life and a collective, impersonal history, the "bright beam of promise on the future career of our race" ("Intellect" 31) has considerably dimmed. "Practically, we must be content to aim at something short of perfection. . . . While on some points of social duty public opinion has reached a tolerably high standard, on others a public opinion is not yet born" ("Authorship," in "Leaves from a Note-Book," 438). The grand design begrudges us our concluding moral and our prophecy; it is careless of the individual and careless of the type.

For Eliot there was comfort in conceiving human history as a vast organism evolving toward more unified complexity.[3] The latest development is by definition the most advanced because the most articulated ("Intellect" 29). Yet Eliot seems to have become increasingly alarmed by articulate diversity, by the masses awakened by social change beyond rational control. Moreover, her own progressive model of history alerted her to the historian's changing standpoint, undermining the hope of objective measures of progress; the historian becomes frightened by her own insight into the contingency of all points of view (cf. Hirsch 39–41). Eliot could accept the decentralization of truth more readily than the disintegration of social hierarchy. She scarcely disguised her fear of the breakdown of old cultural barri-

---

[3]Herbert Spencer attributed progress to "general natural causes" rather than such mysterious forces as " 'the hero as king' " or " 'collective wisdom,' " forces Eliot still favors as novelist (Spencer, "The Social Organism" [1860], *Essays* 1: 266). In "Progress, Its Law and Cause" (1857), Spencer cautions, as Eliot would do, against equating progress with teleology; increasing differentiation arrives at impersonal, perhaps undesired ends (*Essays* 1: 8–9, 35–38, 59–62).

ers: in notes first published in 1884, she deplored "that troublesome disposition to authorship arising from the spread of what is called Education." Yet she adhered to an ethical principle of progress: the self-sacrificing individual may add an increment to the sum of the common good, propagating in others a responsive altruism and faith in progress. Those who show "an alarming equality in their power of writing 'like a scholar and a gentleman' . . . can only be cured by . . . higher ideals in social duty" to aid the progress of "general culture" ("Authorship" 441–42). Her own alarming equality was always purified by its service to cultural progress as defined by European traditions.

More surprisingly, Woolf too conceived of a collective progress generated by sacrificial "unhistoric acts." Stimulated by her encounter with the "eager, egotistical" young women of Girton, she wrote, "I fancy sometimes the world changes. I think I see reason spreading" (*VW Diary* 3: 200–201). Here is no confident assertion of cultural evolution, however; as Gillian Beer argues, determinism and the Darwinian model were associated for Woolf with the patriarchal outlook of her father's generation (*Arguing with the Past* 118–21; *Darwin's Plots* 3–5). Though she accepts the cultural and individual decentering derived from anthropology and psychoanalysis, she resists the totalizing tendencies of such sciences, their subjection of all particulars to the general pattern. She insists on the power of "others," women and servants especially, to disrupt historically sanctioned hierarchies. Yet at the same time, Woolf like Eliot tries to purify such feminine excess or variability of what Eliot calls the "vanity and ambition" of cultural outsiders ("Authorship" 441); the cook breezing "in and out of the drawing-room" ("Bennett and Brown," CE 1: 320) should join the humble generations, "the common life" preparing for the female literary messiah in A Room of One's Own (117). A correct generalization— the honored tradition—gives significance to the smallest insubordinate detail.

For the most part, Woolf observes the spectacle of history as a literary critic rather than a sociologist; tradition is her organic medium of progress. "Books descend from books," she maintains, "as families descend from families" ("The Leaning Tower," CE 2: 163). Tempering her ancestor worship, she notes that the Renaissance man John Evelyn joined the popular pastime of watching a man being tortured, and hesitantly suggests that if all of our "humane instincts" were better developed than the Elizabethans', "we could say that the world improves, and we with it" ("Rambling Round Evelyn," CE 3: 47). Reservations aside, Woolf habitually reads history as Western cultural progress, especially the history of women: "The seventeenth century produced more remarkable women that [sic] the sixteenth, the eighteenth than the seventeenth, and the nineteenth than all three put together" ("The Intellectual Status of Women" 55). Yet at the same time, she entertains notions of cultural decline, of lost vitality. John Evelyn's imaginative faith is "now only to be matched by listening to the talk of old women round the village pump" (or to the babble of Florentines or Londoners in *Romola* or *Mrs. Dalloway*). The educated classes have lost a precious inventiveness; even in her own father's day, gentlemen could still "venture on private discoveries" as Evelyn did (45). Woolf frequently expresses a kind of pitying envy of the Victorians: novelists back then enjoyed "the vigour and splendour of youth" without "the more deliberate virtues" of a culture grown to manhood ("On Re-Reading Novels," CE 2: 128).[4] As though uncomfortable with history as a male bildungsroman, however, Woolf complicates the plot: the ages of literature are as likely to reveal "a circular tendency" as "an improvement" or a decline ("Modern Fiction," CE 2: 103).

Both Eliot and Woolf enter the lists in the tournament of Moderns vs. Ancients with some humor. Eliot in *Middlemarch* ironically honors Fielding as "a great historian . . . who had the happiness to be dead a hundred and twenty years ago, and so to take his place among the colossi whose huge legs our living pettiness is observed to walk under" (104–5). Yet she observes that back then "the days were longer," and Fieldingesque "chat" in a modern context "would be thin and eager, as if delivered from a camp-stool in a parrot-house" (M 105). Woolf similarly qualifies her admiration for the Olympians: "Fielding did well and Jane Austen even better," but they worked with "simple tools and primitive materials." Now, "in the crowd, half blind with dust, we look back with envy to those happier warriors, whose battle is won . . . we can scarcely refrain from whispering that the fight was not so fierce for them as for us" ("Modern Fiction," CE 2: 103). Both women writers figure tradition as a masculine conflict for precedence and intelligibility, but take pride in their belated battle with meaninglessness and disorder, their cognizance of "that tempting range of relevancies called the universe" (M 105). While Eliot appears more confident that her humanist outlook serves the advance of reason and

---

[4]This review of Percy Lubbock's *The Craft of Fiction* and of editions of Austen, the Brontës, and Meredith denigrates the Victorians (in the Lubbock spirit) as feminized men: "To build a castle, . . . reform a workhouse, or pull down a prison were occupations more congenial to the writers, or more befitting their manhood, than to sit chained at a desk scribbling novels for a simple-minded public" (CE 2: 129). Leave writing to the women?

fellow-feeling, and Woolf expresses more genuine doubts about the privilege and influence of a European intelligentsia ("in the crowd, half blind with dust"), the modern writer still situates liberal high culture in the vanguard of "universal" human progress. Woolf's famous assertion that "in or about December, 1910, human character changed," proclaiming a decentering rupture (with some facetiousness about the need to pick a date), nonetheless retains a monolithic idea of a spirit of the age or of "human character" traceable to events in the London art world ("Mr. Bennett and Mrs. Brown," CE 1: 320).

The presupposition of a collective spirit of an age, or of a progressive "common life," widespread in an age when historicist paradigms were reshaping every field of inquiry (Toulmin and Goodfield, chaps. 9–11; Buckley; Kern), could exonerate the ambitious outsider who defined her vocation as social service. The collective good would be embodied in anonymous masses, but it would be marked by great names authorizing great ideas. In 1855, Eliot affirmed "those impulses that tend to give humanity a common life in which the good of one is the good of all" ("Evangelical Teaching: Dr. Cumming" 188). In an essay of 1868, her spokesman Felix Holt reiterates this religion of humanity. Workers must earn a share in "the common estate of society: . . . that treasure of knowledge, science, poetry, refinement of thought, feeling, and manners, great memories and the interpretation of great records, which is carried on from the minds of one generation to the minds of another" ("Address to Working Men, by Felix Holt" 425).[5] Eliot elsewhere defines morality in terms of rational obedience to an indomitable tradition; her ethical heroes "have their impulses guided . . . by the intellect of human beings who have gone before them, and created traditions and associations which have taken the rank of laws" ("Evangelical Teaching" 166). The Napoleonic overreacher like Tito Melema in Romola is no hero in Eliot's account of history; the multitude of martyrs are more truly heroic. Yet if "the growing good of the world" (M 613) depends on countless sacrifices to the coming generations,[6] it

---

[5]According to Eliot's Feuerbachian faith in humanity, fellow-feeling dissipates the "common mist" of prejudice and superstition ("Birth of Tolerance," in "Leaves from a Note-Book," 449; "Evangelical Teaching" 187). Although Eliot, like Woolf, is almost exclusively concerned with Western cultures, her humanitarian views embrace within those cultures the "Negro" ("[Three Novels]," 325–28) and the Jew ("The Modern Hep! Hep! Hep!" [TS 191] and Daniel Deronda). See Myers on Eliot's assumption of the objectivity that Marx criticizes in Feuerbach (Teaching 103–5).

[6]Edward Hallett Carr argues the necessity of some concept of progress, or of duty to "generations yet unborn. To justify these sacrifices in the name of a better world in the future is the secular counterpart of justifying them in the name of some divine purpose" (158). Eliot offers the secular justification because of the ethical consequences: "Things are not so ill with you and me as they might have been" (M 613).

remains difficult to account for progressive *change* rather than repetition; change is usually credited to disruptive individuals with the prestige to guide that disruption toward good ends.

Woolf too takes the sacrificial view of history, though she advises women rather than working men to distrust rather than to obey their allegiance to a paternalistic tradition. Again, the many are to place their hope in a collective enterprise: after the visit to Girton in 1928, her diary notes, "How little anyone counts; . . . & how all these thousands are swimming for dear life" (*VW Diary* 3: 201). The famous conclusion to *A Room of One's Own* echoes with great fidelity Eliot's narrative of a common life struggling to produce the rare redeeming individual, like a modern, literary Saint Theresa:

> For my belief is that if we live another century or so—I am talking of the common life which is the real life and not of the little separate lives which we live as individuals . . . if we escape a little from the common sitting-room and see human beings not always in their relation to each other but in relation to reality . . . then the opportunity will come and the dead poet who was Shakespeare's sister will put on the body which she has so often laid down. Drawing her life from the lives of the unknown who were her forerunners, as her brother did before her, she will be born. . . . I maintain that she would come if we worked for her, and that so to work, even in poverty and obscurity, is worth while. (RO 117–18)

Here, as in Eliot's usage, "common" serves a double function: it suggests the universality of an age-old organism of humanity as well as the commonplace particularity of our "little separate lives" in the "common sitting-room"—the realm, Woolf has already made clear, of women (RO 91).

Eliot's notion of "higher minds . . . with which the . . . multitude are inextricably interwoven" might be a drier precursor of Woolf's tale of Shakespeare's sister: an anonymous progress of the intellect in which unknowns may proudly share. The great woman poet's future success will be the justification for our unacknowledged sacrifice, much as the relative well-being of "you and me" is the justification of Dorothea's sacrifice. Though Woolf allows for the triumph of one great woman, her peroration seems to join Eliot in endorsing the slow progress of an intact hierarchy, with only a trace of the irony at play throughout *A Room of One's Own*. No Napoleonic heroine, Shakespeare's sister will succeed by her very dependence on "traditions and associations" created by "human beings who have gone before," as

Eliot puts it. Here and elsewhere, Woolf counsels women to labor on their education and give little thought to the costly fight for public power (TG 14), in a manner reminiscent of Felix Holt's admonition to the working men: the oppressed must not selfishly seize their share too soon. Nevertheless, Woolf takes more of the position of an outsider than Eliot; in *Three Guineas* she seems to ask, Who would want a share of that patriarchal pie anyway?

The idea of a history of the common life can serve, then, both to subordinate the individual (how little anyone matters) and to exalt any individual as contributor to grand historical developments, which in turn must be seen as the cumulative effects of multitudes of common lives. History, as George Henry Lewes put it, "is not the chronicle of events . . . —it is the *Life of Humanity as evolved by human beings.*"[7] This typical Victorian reappropriation of history for the individual is paradoxically a universalizing move, as that individual, the humanist subject, is presumed to be the representative white, European, middle-class male.

Eliot and Woolf, while they intermittently displaced that egocentric individual's horizons by taking a more pan-cultural perspective (for example in their attacks on anti-Semitism or fascism), most consistently challenged the norm of masculinity. A history redefined as the aggregate of obscure lives was, their works imply, a history of the feminine, that is, of what had been silenced in patriarchal discourse. On the more literal level, it was a history that comprehended the subordinated individuals—workers, the poor, and women generally—as the hidden prime movers of developing humanity. Further, such a history could justify the hubris of the historian who claims to serve the more comprehensive truth.

This shift of focus was not, of course, unique to Eliot and Woolf, though they give it what to me are its finest expressions. The developing novel form itself marked a turn from battlefields to drawing rooms, from high circles to the middle class, and from the world of men to the world of women (Doody 277, 289). Viewing history and fiction as allied forms of interpretive narrative,[8] Eliot and Woolf addressed more explicitly than most contemporaries the specific issues

[7]Lewes's italics; "History by Modern Frenchmen," *British Quarterly Review* 14 (1851): 405–6, in Graver 41.
[8]Eliot and Woolf would have subscribed to Collingwood's principles: "All knowledge of mind is historical," and "the body of human thought . . . is a corporate possession" (219, 226). See White, *Metahistory,* 30–31, on the historian's "poetic" prefiguration of the field of study; Mink, "History and Fiction," 541–45. The kinship of history and fiction, while anciently acknowledged, became increasingly problematic after the eighteenth century; see Carr 20–35; Davis.

of gender and historical interpretation that they believed had come to a crisis in their day. While questioning the conventions that made gender roles appear natural, they nevertheless claim an inevitable association between the silenced "other" and womanhood, between domestic life and the experience of women. Woolf's historical project remains consonant with Eliot's: to probe "the lives of the obscure—in those almost unlit corridors of history where the figures of generations of women are so dimly, so fitfully perceived." We need "a faithful picture of the daily life of the ordinary women" to "turn history wrong side out" ("Women and Fiction" 44). Yet as Bradford K. Mudge has shown, Woolf left the traditional standards of cultural achievement almost as she found them (202). Turning history wrong side out serves to "account for the success or failure of the extraordinary woman as a writer," Woolf writes, signaling a history on which to found her own greatness ("Women and Fiction" 44).

In their focus on the "wrong side" of history, both authors wavered in their allegiance to the truly ordinary and hitherto unhistoric, insisting on the one hand that it is arbitrary to single out a heroine among the "many Dorotheas," and on the other hand that we rightly worship certain rare spirits who influence those around them for the better—hence the madonna-like stature of Dorothea or Shakespeare's sister. Eliot and Woolf evoked the rare "types" of female self-sacrifice whom they considered at the same time "common" or representative; their fictional histories mitigate the harsh fate of those sacrificed by showing the resulting incremental progress. The authors took the tragic rather than the sociological view of "woman as the moral providence of our species," but on the collective scale the genre is more comic than tragic. The narrator of *Middlemarch* remarks, "That element of tragedy which lies in the very fact of frequency, has not yet wrought itself into the coarse emotion of mankind." Properly understood, such acts as Dorothea's marriages present to us an intelligible pattern of errors to be left behind as we recognize our "imperfect social state" and as we work, in "nameless, unremembered" ways, to change it. We must take pleasure in that "keen vision and feeling of all ordinary life" (M 144, 612) as a new form of historical art. The challenge in Woolf's day was still as Eliot had presented it, though the modern consciousness may seem to have become obsessed with the tragedy of frequency. "The flight of time . . . hurries us so tragically along," writes the narrator of *Jacob's Room;* "merely to see the flash and thrust of limbs engaged in the conduct of daily life is better than the old pageant of armies" (153, 163). Attention must be paid to the very commonness that generates the data to which we ascribe historical meaning (Faris 81–83).

Such an ambivalence toward the common has a marked effect on Eliot's and Woolf's treatment of heroism, but it also governs their expressions of sympathy for the unheroic multitude. It was easy to attribute a (perhaps involuntary) selflessness—as well as a kind of femininity—to the masses who seldom stood out as individuals, and who like women might be perceived as closer to nature and the past. Conversely, history's pawns might become monsters of vengeful passion when unleashed. Less ambivalently, one might seek to discover unsung glory in the obscure but less wild middle classes. Those incapable of fellow-feeling, who cannot empathize with the mediocre Casaubon or Mrs. Brown, are condemned to a silence less sociable even than hell, an egotism that will dry up or wall in human discourse.

In keeping with this doctrine of fellow-feeling, Theophrastus Such rebukes the man of letters (perhaps a figure for Eliot's dread of the critics) who in the name of Truth destroys the reputation of rivals; his "arrogant egoism, set on fire," evaporates "the dews of fellowship and pity" as he carves an opponent's face or pours salt in his wounds ("The Watch-Dog of Knowledge," TS 108–9). The failure of fellowship and pity threatens an author with nothing less than the death of the text, it seems. Woolf in a less paranoid phase similarly attributes selfishness to her literary rivals as she celebrates her own invention of a form to "enclose the human heart . . . everything as bright as fire in the mist. . . . I suppose the danger is the damned egotistical self; which ruins Joyce & [Dorothy] Richardson to my mind" (*VW Diary* 2: 13–14). As such passages suggest, Eliot and Woolf approached the field of letters in an adversarial spirit to match the hostility they expected, yet they hoped to perfect a more generous, secure position in their writing, that of an author beyond egotism who freely empathizes with the common experience. The danger lay not only in egotism but also in that vulnerable virtue, selflessness. Hence the rich complexity of their evocation of the common life as the feminine undercurrent of history (indeed, as the medium of progress), and the corresponding ambiguity of their role as self-effacing historical authorities.

Histories by Eliot, Woolf, and Their Contemporaries

It is important to recognize the extent to which both Eliot and Woolf centered their oeuvres on what might be called "the history question"—so intimately linked for them to "the woman question." Though both authors have been canonized according to predominantly formalist standards, Eliot owes much of her acclaim to her *Wit and Wisdom* (the title of a collection based on Alexander Main's Eliot scrapbook, *Wise, Witty, and Tender Sayings in Prose and Verse* [1871]), whereas Woolf has generally been viewed as ill-suited to the role of historical thinker (Rosenbaum 35; Zwerdling 9–15). Yet both writers aspired to historical authority within the very tradition that had consistently obscured "Anon"—the wives, mothers, sisters, daughters of the acknowledged agents of history (David viii–x, 175). Contributing their own revisionary historical writings to a literature predominantly by men, they made every effort not to remain anonymous themselves while giving voice to those whose unclaimed expressions often ironically bear the label "traditional."

They reveal an abiding preoccupation with history throughout their careers. The works mount up: Mary Ann Evans's Chart of Ecclesiastical History (planned in 1839, then abandoned [Haight 24]); George Eliot's thoroughly researched reconstructions of past periods, especially *Romola, Felix Holt, Middlemarch,* and *Daniel Deronda,* her historical poem *The Spanish Gypsy,* as well as her essays on historical writers and translations of Strauss and Feuerbach; Virginia Stephen's "A History of Women" (a lost manuscript [Bell 1: 51]); Virginia Woolf's frequent essays on the everyday life of past ages (e.g., "The Pastons and Chaucer," CE 3: 1–17), her fictional histories such as "The Journal of Mistress Joan Martyn," *Orlando, The Years, Between the Acts,* and her late plans for "a Common History book" on English literature (Squier and De-Salvo 237–39; Silver, " 'Anon' and 'The Reader,' " 356–68). In such works, these women authors defined themselves both within and against the great outpouring of English historical writing in the eighteenth and nineteenth centuries as well as our own.

Eliot and Woolf shared in the impulse to tell of ordinary people in a form that would certainly appeal more to these people themselves as readers. "Real solemn history" excludes and hence repels common readers such as Catherine Morland: "the men all so good for nothing, and hardly any women at all" (*Northanger Abbey* 84). Historical novels at their best, in the works of Sir Walter Scott for instance, might amplify history with an entertaining perspective on the common life. Scott and his imitators, taking the cue from accounts of that history-making crowd scene, the French Revolution, fleshed out the history of kings and battles with the experiences of private Waverleys—and a few women who are something besides stock heroines. History was dramatized in such novels as the living past, even as historiography itself became more novelistic.[9]

[9]Fleishman, *English Historical Novel,* 16–23; Lukacs 23–51. Well after history began to be an academic discipline in England (in the 1850s), Scott's style of anachronistic historical romance continued to be replicated (Simmons 27–55).

The fascination with history in Eliot's and Woolf's writings is symptomatic of their schooling in writers widely admired by the Victorians. Two such figures, Walter Scott and Thomas Carlyle, serve to illustrate how these women writers could shade tribute to a literary master into criticism of his self-promotion and his neglect of the feminine in historical life. Scott dominated Mary Ann Evans's and Virginia Stephen's childhood love of novels (Haight 7, 15, 39, 66; DeSalvo 219–27), and he remained an influential literary model for them, referred to explicitly in their most autobiographical novels, *The Mill on the Floss* and *To the Lighthouse*, and elsewhere. Both later novelists seemed to value Scott especially for having integrated common people into the drama of history. In "The Natural History of German Life," Eliot cites Scott, along with Wordsworth and others who had portrayed common life, as having done more "towards linking the higher classes with the lower . . . than by hundreds of sermons." For Eliot, historical fiction, by extending social sympathies, became itself an historical agent "levelling" classes, nations, and ages, as well as counteracting egotism and "the vulgarity of exclusiveness" (270). Scott, however, lapsed from his social duty and became a kind of tradesman pandering to popular demand ("Authorship" 440–41). Himself failing to be truly heroic, Scott furthermore failed to serve feminine sufferers; his gendered roles are oppressively conventional. Maggie Tulliver calls for a story "where the dark woman triumphs . . . to avenge Rebecca and Flora MacIvor and Minna."[10]

Woolf too appreciated Scott's promotion of an historical perspective on social class, though she saw his influence on readers as divisive rather than unifying. She suspects him of trying to "show[ ] up the langour of the fine gentlemen who bored him by the immense vivacity of the common people whom he loved" ("Sir Walter Scott," CE 1: 141). She shared her Victorian father's devotion to Scott,[11] but she debunks the cult of manly heroism in the Waverley novels through the Scott-chanting figure of Mr. Ramsay in *To the Lighthouse*. The great man is a commercial showman, earning love for his failings but not gratitude for his conventional treatment of gender.

Another example of an influential reformer of Victorian historical

[10]MF 291. *The Heart of Mid-Lothian*, along with *The Scarlet Letter*, may have been less objectionable in this regard: both provided a foundation for *Adam Bede*. See the epigraph to chap. 57, *Middlemarch*; Haight 268, 235; Eliot's "[Westward Ho! and Constance Herbert]" 128, and "[Three Novels]" 326–27. See Baker, *Libraries*, 104–6.

[11]See Stephen, "Sir Walter Scott," 1: 186–229. Woolf disparages Scott's narrative style and claims "he no longer influences anyone" (Silver, *Notebooks*, 160, 143); yet she calls him "a great writer" whom any woman must be "head over ears in love with" ("Indiscretions" 76).

writing, Carlyle, reveals a similar pattern in Eliot's and Woolf's response: admiration for his extension of social sympathies, critique of the great man, and rejection of the biased assignment of gender roles. Carlyle's most influential insight, I would argue, is not the famous assertion that history consists of the biographies of great men, but rather the earlier recognition that ordinary lives form the substance of history. Like a Wordsworthian poet, a Carlylean historian finds "glory" in the commonplace: "We do nothing but enact History," which "is the essence of innumerable Biographies" ("On History" 84, 86; *On Heroes* 245; B. Rosenberg 2). Besides stressing the significance of the quotidian, Carlyle himself became the heroic proponent of a widespread outlook that can be traced in Eliot's and Woolf's own historical writings: that is, skepticism about actual large-scale historical tendencies coupled with cautious meliorism regarding individuals. In "Signs of the Times," Carlyle declares: "To reform a world, to reform a nation, no wise man will undertake; and all but foolish men know, that the only solid, though a far slower reformation, is what each begins and perfects on *himself*" (82; cf. Eliot, "Shadows of the Coming Race," TS 225–32).

Eliot and Woolf seem to share Carlyle's curious blend of determinism and faith in self-reformation. In the private sphere, through "unhistoric acts" and "little daily miracles" some progress will be made (M 613; TL 240). In effect, these authors' virtues as novelists, their grasp of individual, experiential detail, made them appear somewhat in sympathy with Carlylean conservatism: the slow reform of the relations of men and women would more radically change the world than conventional political action. Their political heroes, then, were those writers who altered perspectives on experience. Accordingly, they valued Carlyle's own biographical example more than his public precepts with which they could not concur. Though spurning Carlyle's projection of a "theocracy with the 'greatest man', as a Joshua who is to smite the wicked (and the stupid)," Eliot praised his own "great and beautiful human nature," "influential on the formation of character" ("Thomas Carlyle" 214; "[The Life of Sterling]" 49; see Haight 36, 430). Woolf still admired Carlyle's writings but doubted the beauty of his nature and his continuing influence (Bell 1: 50–51; DeSalvo 220). The hero who wrote of heroes had become less palatable for the modern colleague of debunkers like Lytton Strachey, though Woolf held Strachey up to the standard of Carlyle (*VW Diary* 2: 110; "Mr. Bennett and Mrs. Brown," CE 1: 335).

Traces of Carlyle appear in Eliot's and Woolf's novels, especially the earlier ones, reflecting his emphasis on the telling detail of everyday life but reversing his bias toward great men. The narrator of *Adam Bede* conjures up Carlyle (and Pickwick):

> Leisure is gone. . . . Ingenious philosophers tell you, perhaps, that the great work of the steam-engine is to create leisure for mankind. Do not believe them: it only creates a vacuum for eager thought to rush in. Even idleness is eager now. . . . Old Leisure was . . . a contemplative, rather stout gentleman. . . . Life was not a task to him, but a sinecure: he fingered the guineas in his pocket, and ate his dinners, and slept the sleep of the irresponsible. . . .
>   Do not be severe upon him, and judge him by our modern standard: he never . . . read *Tracts for the Times* or *Sartor Resartus*.

The Carlylean historical comparisons that are respectfully parodied here are undermined by "Old Leisure's" lack of "lofty aspirations": the patriarchs did nothing to advance human progress. Eliot also challenges Carlyle in the perspective on the "great man" offered elsewhere. The narrator points out, for instance, the "superfluous existences" of the Rev. Irwine's spinster sisters. The Rector's sacrifice on their behalf is a form of heroism that outweighs his "generic classification" as a worldly clergyman. The narrator invites us to inspect the household humanitarian behind the self-serving public man, at the same time reminding us, in an un-Carlylean gesture, that a public humanitarian may be cruel to the dependent women in his home (AB 525, 65–69). In other words, we must redefine our heroes in terms of their domestic relations; our historical categories have been cast in public terms, terms that exclude powerless women.

Woolf's variations on the bildungsroman and on biography, *Jacob's Room* and *Orlando*, also parodically adapt Carlyle's idea of historical heroes while they rework his insight into the epochal import of material life. In Jacob's college room we see an essay entitled "Does History consist of the Biographies of Great Men?," a "prize" volume of Carlyle, and a trace of the great woman, "Jane Austen . . . in deference, perhaps, to someone else's standard" (JR 39).[12] Carlyle can be wielded against false pieties and the marginalization of the commonplace; thus *Sartor Resartus* and the clothes philosophy pervade *Orlando* (e.g., 78). Nevertheless, the undervalued female influence, the Austen smuggled into a man's world, reminds us of what has been missing from Carlylean history. In the manuscript version of *Orlando*, the heroine

---

[12]See Schlack, *Continuing Presences*, 41–43; Schlack suggests a connection between Woolf's brother Jacob and Eliot's (35).

pays a call in Chelsea, only to be turned away by the sage's protective wife (Moore 337–38). Like Eliot bringing spinster sisters into the foreground, Woolf looked past the great man to inquire after his wife: was not her suffering the living price of his achievement? Her own family offered an example like that of the Carlyles (*Moments of Being* 41), and she insisted that the days of such blind exploitation were over: "Read the *Agamemnon*, and see whether, in process of time, your sympathies are not almost entirely with Clytemnestra. Or consider the married life of the Carlyles and bewail . . . the horrible domestic tradition which made it seemly for a woman of genius to spend her time chasing beetles, scouring saucepans, instead of writing books" ("Bennett and Brown," CE 1: 320–21).[13]

Though championing the neglected history of women less explicitly than Woolf was to do, Eliot too called for a shift in genre and in the outlook of readers that in effect challenged gender prescriptions. In defining her task as an historian, Eliot struck a medium between "real, solemn history" as Catherine Morland sees it and the fantastical fictions that lighthearted readers like Catherine are conditioned to prefer ("Historic Imagination," in "Leaves from a Note-Book," 446–47). As I have suggested, Eliot's emphasis on "individual lots" in the mode of realistic fiction was characteristic of her times, though she carried it further than most contemporary historians. Thomas Babington Macaulay's popular *History of England*, for example, purportedly borrowed the novel's resources for capturing "revolutions . . . in dress, furniture, repasts," to give "the English of the nineteenth century a true picture of their ancestors" (3).[14] Yet in practice Macaulay and others still produced a public history, writing of Prime Ministers' cabinets, not what their daughters were wearing to dinner. As Woolf later observed, the history of "Wars and Ministries" written by "gentlemen in tall hats in the Forties who wished to dignify mankind" (i.e., Macaulay) ignored "modes and manners—how we feel and dress" ("Modes and Manners of the Nineteenth Century," *Essays* 1: 331). Woolf disparages the guise of objectivity as well: the "sweeping asser-

[13]See "Geraldine and Jane," CE 4: 27–39. Woolf read Carlyle's *History of Friedrich II of Prussia* while studying the monarch's sister, Wilhelmina (Silver, *Notebooks*, 175).

[14]Lewes and Eliot read Macaulay aloud together in 1854 and 1861 (Haight 174, 342). See Baker, *Libraries*, 89–90. Woolf read Macaulay's *History of England* in 1897 (Bell 1: 50) and in 1936 (Silver, *Notebooks*, 57–58). For a wonderful contest of greatness between Woolf and Strachey, with Macaulay as standard, see *VW Diary* 2: 114–15. Macaulay published antiquarian ballads in the manner of Scott, underlining the literary art of history, in 1842 (Preface, *Macaulay's Lays of Ancient Rome*, 27), reissued in 1928 with an introduction by his great-nephew, Trevelyan (vi). In "Clio, a Muse" (1913), Trevelyan stresses that history is an "art of narrative" that modern historians have mistaken for a " 'science,' " in reaction to Carlyle, Macaulay, and others (14).

tions and undeniable convictions" in Macaulay's essays seem dissociated from "anything so minute as a human being" ("Addison," CE 1: 85). Minutiae are implicitly, subversively feminine, like women's concerns with emotions and fashion.

In *A Room of One's Own*, Woolf reminds us that women are "all but absent from history"; she notes that G. M. Trevelyan's popular *History of England* (1926) refers only in passing to women's marital slavery. Trevelyan, as his great-uncle Macaulay had done, divided history into chapters with such titles as "The Hundred Years' War" and persisted in ignoring the evidence of the common life of women in "parish registers and account books" (RO 44–47). Yet in Woolf's own terms, Trevelyan's frankly interpretive history must have marked an improvement from the historiography of Eliot's day, as we see from a passage in his *History of England* that she quoted in her late unfinished essay, "Anon," and in *Between the Acts*. Significantly, she was drawn to Trevelyan's depiction of prehistory, which had come to be included in the popular narrative of human evolution. In the "untamed forest," Trevelyan's "story of the Mingling of the Races" tells us, the forest "floor was hidden from heaven's eye" by "woven . . . tree-tops" resounding with the "wild music of millions upon millions of wakening birds": "A troop of skin-clad hunters, stone-axe in hand, moved furtively . . . , ignorant that they lived upon an island, not dreaming that there could be other parts of the world besides this damp green woodland with its meres and marshes, wherein they hunted, a terror to its four-footed inhabitants and themselves afraid" (2–3; Silver, *Notebooks*, 187; Silver, " 'Anon,' " 357, 382).

This tableau depicting hunters, presumably men, may have appealed to Woolf as a kind of parodic dramatization of the origins of the sexual division of labor, but it may also have seemed like a refreshing counter-image to the "common sitting room" that she urges women to escape in *A Room of One's Own*, as well as to the mode of objective "political" history.[15] In civilized drawing rooms, the primitive past may well up: in *The Years*, the Pargiter women wonder if they in turn will be looked back on as primitive cave-dwellers, while in *Between the Acts*, the Olivers themselves revert to life among the rocks. The scope of history, like the concept of geological time, had greatly expanded

[15]Trevelyan also seems useful to Woolf for his fanfare of the imperialist, patriarchal sentiments that she would align with fascism in *Three Guineas*. For example: "The universality of the Englishman's experience and outlook . . . is due to his command of the ocean . . . as explorer, trader, and colonist. . . . Thus, in early times, the relation of Britain to the sea was passive and receptive; in modern times, active and acquisitive" (xix–xx). This imperial ontogeny, so to speak, offers the disturbing pretext for *Between the Acts*.

since Eliot's day, undermining further the confident centrisms of present civilization. Departing from conventional historiography to challenge the clear demarcation of historical progress, and of dichotomies such as civilized/primitive, public/private, and masculine/feminine, Eliot and Woolf created their own innovative histories of the common life.

History as the Biographies of the Common Life

In the spirit either of Victorian fellow-feeling or modern aestheticism, both Eliot and Woolf invite a more or less privileged audience to see beyond the privileged terms of conventional history to the common elements in private experience. On closer examination, we realize that Eliot's humanitarianism is also an aesthetic program, just as Woolf's aesthetics are, if not precisely humanitarian, then ethical. They each arouse our faculty of comparison as well as our discrimination of detail in portraits of everyday domestic life—long considered the province of women writers—even as they force us to recognize that province as an almost limitless domain with a world-shaping history. Eliot holds that "every judgment exhibits itself as a comparison, or perception of likeness in the midst of difference," in which the two terms alter each other ("The Future of German Philosophy" 151–52). The privileged term, be it public history, the masculine, or the heroic, will be compromised by the comparison to private life, the feminine, or the common. How did Eliot and Woolf adapt their literary inheritance, the woman's sphere of the novel, to meet the demand for historical narratives of the common life, narratives to alert us to the sameness-in-difference in multitudes of neglected others? Did their sympathetic comparisons truly dethrone traditionally privileged terms?

Eliot, in essays and narrative commentary, explicitly calls for the imaginative recognition of what we have in common: "Art is . . . a mode of amplifying experience and extending our contact with our fellow-men beyond the bounds of our personal lot" ("German Life" 271). The implication is that art, like empirical science, guides the observer toward an objective basis for comparative judgment; art should expand the horizons of the ego to intersect with others' horizons. The most ample experience may approximate objectivity, but it also casts suspicion on the presumption of a monopoly on knowledge or truth. Neither the personal standard of pleasure or good nor the "universal" judgments of common sense can be implicitly trusted; one ego or an entire province can be sorely mistaken. There must be a persistent questioning of one's vocation, that it may truly serve the greatest good and not, like Bulstrode's hypocritical philanthropy, merely serve one's personal providential myth. Thus, when Eliot assumes the duties of the Arnoldian "higher mind" steering the multitude, she is not posing as a self-guided devotee of art for art's sake but as the chosen voice of a people; her most exemplary hero, Daniel Deronda, like a steadier Will Ladislaw, leaves behind aestheticism for the life of a public reformer.

Yet the taint of egoism touches all mortals, perhaps the more so as they aspire to immortality. Hence the streak of satire in Eliot's work that surfaces completely in *Theophrastus Such*. Woolf claims that Eliot imbues her work with a "spirit of sympathy. She is no satirist" ("GE" [1919] 155). Yet the sympathy and the satire should be seen on a continuum of painful insight into competing centers of self and the distortions of point of view, an insight particularly sharp when it pertains to those who mean to lead. She is more likely, then, to anatomize the wounded vanity of the ambitious Bardo, Savonarola, or Casaubon than to celebrate, with Woolf, an hospitable, collaborative tradition to which each aspiring author contributes before passing on.

The Victorian need for biographical history of great cultural prophets may have guided Eliot's sympathetic satire of those who aspire to eminence. Certainly this need is recalled in Woolf's portrait of a more lovable and venturesome Casaubon, Mr. Ramsay, who wishes always to be reassured, "Oh, but your work will last" (TL 161). Such egotistical closure of horizons or monopolization of sympathy appears obsolete in a modern vision of a tradition built not by higher minds but by the common life. For Woolf, culture may be "some vast building, which being built by common effort, the separate workmen may well remain anonymous" ("How It Strikes a Contemporary," CE 2: 161). With E. M. Forster, Woolf imagines "the English novelists" " 'seated together in a . . . sort of British Museum reading-room—all writing their novels simultaneously.' . . . Richardson insists that he is contemporary with Henry James. Wells will write a passage which might be written by Dickens" ("The Art of Fiction," CE 2: 51; cf. "How Should One Read a Book?" CE 2: 8–10). As in Eliot's idea of a moral tradition, the individual submits to a larger plan; accordingly, Woolf and Eliot would be contemporaries, simultaneously writing their parts in a vast collaborative work. Thus, like Eliot, Woolf views art as a means of dissolving identity and extending our contact, in her case with divergent writers or works as much as with "fellow-men." Rather than being called on to master an objective historical order of the best that has been known and thought, the reader is invited to indulge in a collective reverie on sameness-in-difference, the selfless influence of writer on writer. The frequent tragedy of what might have been, of the almost-great, becomes, in the long run, "part of the human gain" (TL 74).

Eliot and Woolf not only conceive of a tradition that, cruelly or benignly, subsumes individual claims of authorship, they also conceive of history, literary or otherwise, as the cumulative biographies of all who have contributed to it. As I have already noted, biographical criticism dominated the literary field in Woolf's day as well as Eliot's. Though a relatively young genre, biography might be said to have had the omnivorous capacity that Bakhtin (and Woolf) attributed to the novel, since it shaped not only criticism but also poetry, fiction, and history; the genre of women's biography, younger still, might be said to have grown out of the novel. The fascination with biography generally hinges on the wish to amplify the public portrait with private background, as well as to account for cultural and historical change in familiar terms, confirming the inherent importance of whatever resembles ourselves. As a narrative model, biography may serve thus to extend our sense of what we have in common while endorsing the belief in the unique importance of each individual.

Biography, like history, had tended to place undue value on great men, as though they had sprung into being above and beyond ordinary experience. Instead, Eliot and Woolf maintained, writers must fill in the picture with details of the multitude of lives. Characteristically, Woolf explicitly theorized about the practice of collective biographical history, as she participated in the modern revolution in biographical writing, whereas we find Eliot formulating her biographical practice primarily in fiction. Yet Woolf's claims apply almost equally to her predecessor's program. "Until we have more facts, more biographies, more autobiographies," Woolf wrote, "we cannot know much about ordinary people, let alone about extraordinary people" ("The Leaning Tower," CE 2: 162). (Compare the refrain in The Years: "We do not know ourselves, ordinary people" [281].) Overcoming the traditional isolation of great writers from the common life, both writers and readers are learning to plunge into ordinary memoirs ("Hours in a Library," CE 2: 37–40). "The unknown . . . instead of keeping their identity separate, as remarkable people do, . . . seem to merge into one another, their very boards and . . . innumerable pages melting into . . . the fine mist-like substance of countless lives . . . from century to century" ("The Lives of the Obscure," CE 4: 122). Woolf's vision, like Eliot's, still requires the granite-like biography of the great individual, the focus on Dorothea or Daniel, to anchor the rainbow of common life.

Much as we might characterize Woolf as a poet of the incommunicable, the tendency to rhapsodize about boundless *communion* is more marked in Woolf than in Eliot, largely because the modern writer believes more in the magic of art than in stern necessities of social evolution. The stern evolutionist Theophrastus Such assumes that, instead of blending together, people are solid entities connected only by great intellectual effort. He extends his "keen interest in the natural history of my inward self" to the study of different fellow beings, as though comparing the similar "natural history . . . of continents widely apart" ("How We Come to Give Ourselves False Testimonials, and Believe in Them," TS 132–33). Yet in "A Political Molecule," Theophrastus affirms that even the selfish common man serves "larger ends": "Society is happily not dependent for the growth of fellowship on the small minority already endowed with comprehensive sympathy. Any molecule of the body politic . . . gets his understanding more or less penetrated with the fact that his interest is included in that of a large number" (TS 79). This is not simply the atomism of the utilitarians but an approach to the modern desire for a collective natural history or biography of the mind. On the scale of molecules rather than continents, individuals may become mist-like. The myth of the difference between remarkable individuals and the mass dissolves in a "universal" history of private experience such as psychoanalysis.

Eliot frequently appears to be adding to the sympathetic minority by supplying the privileged information of a character's biography and encouraging our faculties of comparison with other common stories. She narrates such biographies not as their inventor but as a natural historian of human data, dwelling on the tension between the individual's notability and his or her commonness. The narrator of *Middlemarch*, for example, supplies a biography "to make the new settler Lydgate better known to any one interested in him than he could possibly be even to those who had seen the most of him." The narrator hints that Lydgate's story will become that of "the multitude of middle-aged men": "The story of their coming to be shapen after the average . . . is hardly ever told even in their consciousness." But for now the young surgeon aims high, and Eliot's readers should compare him to any "great man" starting out:

Most of us, indeed, know little of the great originators until they have been lifted up among the constellations and already rule our fates.

. . . Each of those Shining Ones had to walk on the earth among neighbours who perhaps thought much more of his gait and his garments than of anything which was to give him a title to everlasting fame: each of them had his little local personal history. (M 105–9)

Though Eliot seems to retain the ideal of the "great originator" (invariably male), the very capitalization of "Shining Ones" suggests the ironic treatment this ideal will receive in a work in which the "little local personal history" triumphs. To extend fellow-feeling by revealing the "spots of commonness" in great men or men who might have been great may paradoxically flatter us into doubting the difference between the "great" and you and me. The "average" is shown to share in the same human stuff of which greatness is made, while greatness and the myth of the objective man of science are demystified.

The story of how a *woman* escaped the mold of the average to become a great originator could not be told without straining the genre of realistic biographical history, a mode that insists, as Elizabeth Ermarth points out, on the potential interchangeability of individuals. The specificity of womanhood seemed to resist a realistic drive toward the "average," or "collective . . . consciousness" and "consensus," to borrow Ermarth's terms. To achieve such consensus was a prime motive for Eliot's invention of a narrator without a particular biography (66–67). Yet in spite of the clear distance between Eliot's own biography and her narrative role as "Destiny" or historian, her works illustrate the dangers of licensing such a dissociation between life and work—in part because not everyone can exercise such license alike. For one thing, plausibility dictates that female greatness be of a circumscribed sort, always tied to "life." Few women have been Shining Ones of great "works," few have enjoyed the possibility of a duplicitous biography: the domestic or private story *is* their only story. Oddly enough, to affirm that women may be shapen after the collective average may be one way to prepare for female Shining Ones such as Shakespeare's sister; hence Eliot's grand female "failures."

Her men who would have shone, like Casaubon or Tito, fail because they cannot measure up on both public and private scales, cannot reconcile their emotions and ambitions. Theophrastus Such insists "that the relation of the sexes and the primary ties of kinship are the deepest roots of human well-being," though he refuses to call an "unscrupulous" man "moral" simply because he "comes home to dine with his wife and children" ("Moral Swindlers," TS 168). Respectable lawyer Jermyn, at home with his wife and daughters, remains the villain of his own double biography. The women who remain at home may not know the whole, double truth of the men's biographies, but they have the fullest knowledge of the private life and rarely can be accused of not having one. Eliot's attacks on men's hypocrisy seem to have a special motive in her experience of the punishment meted out for her own public admission of an irregular private life. The "village gossips" merely dictate that the forms be observed, so that a "treacherous" king is esteemed because he was "not lewd nor debauched" (TS 167); a woman is esteemed *only* if she is chaste, and seldom has the opportunity for political treachery.

Woolf is even more critical of hagiographies of "Shining Ones," even more suspicious of facile summaries of public character. She acknowledges her debt to those male originators, Chaucer, Montaigne, Boswell, or Sir Thomas Browne, who called attention to "the curious shades of our private life" ("Montaigne," CE 3: 18; "The Elizabethan Lumber Room," CE 1: 51), though she also countenances the rediscovery of unknown women who led the way (Stanton 6; "The Pastons and Chaucer," CE 3: 8–15). We have already glanced at some of her biographical criticism of women writers, with its stress on personal details. The mundane particular, a perhaps feminizing impertinence in the biography of a great man, becomes the key to a revised standard of greatness. In this spirit, the first work Woolf ever had accepted for publication—"Haworth, November 1904," on the Brontës—attempts to excuse biographical interest in women writers (Gilbert and Gubar, *No Man's Land* 1: 200). Though "pilgrimages to the shrines of famous men" may well be "sentimental journeys" ("It is better to read Carlyle in your own study chair than to visit the sound-proof room"), the peculiar circumstances of the Brontë sisters are a necessary context for their works. Rewriting Gaskell's description at the opening of *The Life of Charlotte Brontë*, the young Virginia Stephen notes the "commonplace" village, and especially "the little personal relics, the dresses and shoes of the dead woman." Surprisingly, such "trifling and transient" details bring Brontë "to life, and one forgets the chiefly memorable fact that she was a great writer" ("Haworth, November 1904" 121–23). The Brontës are true shining ones who transform the common by their very loyalty to it; Charlotte's shoes become sacred relics or Cinderella's slippers. On the other hand, Carlyle, that proponent of the biographies of great men, has a personal story too notorious to bear repeating, at least for the young woman beginning her writing career.

Woolf participated in a modern revision of biography, altering the public, adulatory emphasis of Victorian three-volume "lives."[16] The revolution would bring greater respect for the ambiguity of inner life, it would slough off the public persona, and it would recognize the neglected "common" experience. The revolution, promoted by Strachey and others as well as Woolf, curiously enough was an outgrowth of such subversive "biographies" of public men as Eliot's portrait of Bulstrode or Dickens's of Gradgrind or Merdle. The subject, mysterious and split, would like Lydgate be an intermixture of commonness and greatness, and like Orlando, would become representatively female (cf. Armstrong 8). Biographical histories of the common life would span sympathy and satire, the recognition of the imperious desires of the ego and the insistence on the greater truth and good of a "selfless" perspective. Out of tolerance for sameness-in-difference, out of a dream of cultural progress guided by exemplary minds, Eliot and Woolf strove for the effect of consensus in writings distinguished or rendered extraordinary by fidelity to the ordinary.

Discrimination and the Realism of Feminine Detail

Eliot's and Woolf's biographical history, then, appeals to our capacity for recognizing interdependence and the permeability of the ever-changing self, at least potentially without limit. Ideally, the common detail of life could be fully sensed, like the roar on the other side of silence. Woolf hoped, in the new form she felt she had discovered in 1920, to "enclose everything" without "scaffolding," illuminating "the heart, the passion, humour" but escaping "the damned egotistical self" (*VW Diary* 2: 13–14). All-inclusiveness is only an ideal, however. More poignantly, these authors also make us aware of the necessary deafness, the need to discriminate. In social practice, the limits are very marked; one may single out representatives of the lower classes, but it is more difficult, and perhaps aimless, to direct sympathy toward an indiscriminate mass. At the same time, for all one's humanitarian aesthetics or aestheticist humanitarianism, the commonplace must often be pitilessly censured as the vulgar. Artistic greatness, at least, seems antithetical to the run-of-the-mill, much as heroism would seem by definition out-of-the-ordinary. Such ambivalence toward the com-

[16]The narrator of *Orlando* claims that every detail of a writer's spirit and experience is writ large in his works, thus rendering biographical criticism superfluous (209). Yet this claim is made by a persona of the author of *Roger Fry, Orlando,* and *Flush,* all biographies of writers or cultural figures. See "The New Biography," CE 4: 229.

mon informs these writers' attitudes toward detail itself: a trifle may be invested with value as the representative trace of human agency, like the artifact that tells of an entire civilization; it may also be rejected as the sign of indiscriminate taste.

As Naomi Schor has made clear, detail has conventionally played a feminine role in aesthetics, while the concern for realistic portrayal of domestic matters was historically associated not only with the rise of subordinate classes but with the emergence of women's writing. In neoclassical aesthetics, a prejudice against detail and the feminine combined in the denigration, noted by Svetlana Alpers, of the Dutch school as appealing mainly to women's taste for "a flood of observed, unmediated details drawn from nature" ("Art History and Its Exclusions," quoted in Schor 20). As Schor goes on to observe, the novel itself could be charged with pandering to such a taste, as a genre written largely by and for women. Aesthetically, detail is "threatening" because of "its tendency to subvert an internal hierarchic ordering of the work of art which clearly subordinates the periphery to the center, the accessory to the principal, the foreground to the background." Politically, the insubordination of the detail (associated with realism) figures as the "revolutionary mob. . . . The crowd and the female are on the same continuum in the nineteenth-century male imaginary" (Schor 20–21).

I would argue that Eliot's espousal of Dutch realism was not only an acceptance of what Lewes and others had set aside as woman's sphere in art (women excel in domestic detail), but also a challenge to the history (and art history) that had devalued commonplace detail, the feminine, and Dutch realism together. Instead, as a broadly "human," ungendered narrator, she could render the "feminine" universal and control the mass of detail by a kind of "external Reason."[17] This endeavor to universalize private particulars is no more inevitably feminist than populist; we have seen that Sarah Ellis quotes the platitude "Trifles make the sum of human things" to reinforce the middle-class woman's domestic prison. But even in Ellis's hierarchical tableau of the home, feminine detail threatens insubordination, *becoming* the big picture.

In their close-ups of the tragedy and comedy of everyday life or of little daily miracles, Eliot and Woolf exalt the lowly detail. In doing so, they remain to a certain extent within the tradition of Ruskinian aesthetics and of Victorian analogical thinking generally, which sees

---

[17]Laurie Langbauer offers a rich interpretation, in light of Schor's argument, of realism and the specular treatment of feminine detail in Eliot's fiction (188–232).

the world in a grain of sand, or the spirit of the age in its material surroundings. Eliot and Woolf approach the ethics of aesthetics as severe critics both of those who cannot perceive the subtle significance of the ordinary, and of those who sentimentalize the vulgar. To dignify the commonplace inevitably raises questions of class and taste. It is no use reading nobility into the petty folk, nor beauty into crude imitations of beauty.

Both authors flee popular taste as a sign that trifles have no hope of adding up to the sum of human things. Bad taste generates bad opinions, Eliot warns us: "The ugliness of our streets . . . the vulgarity of our upholstery" are symptoms of a moral disease. Eliot associates emotion, sensation, daily context with the feminine, and attributes to it an historical import overlooked by the masculine, though "men" may be the agents to reform the historical outlook: those "men who are trying to banish ugliness . . . are modifying men's moods and habits, which are the mothers of opinions," as determining "as the responsible father, Reason" ("The Grammar of Ornament," Herrick 189–90).[18] While Woolf also assumes a connection between the feminine sphere of feelings and taste and the wide world of ethos or opinions, the relation is mysterious; "modes and manners" have magical power over the body—as when women, "instead of swimming" in the crinoline, "mince about the streets" in tight skirts—but such effects (as *Orlando* repeatedly shows) can be absurdly irrelevant to the individual spirit within ("Modes and Manners of the Nineteenth Century," *Essays* 1: 333–34). When it comes to high art, Woolf is less of a modern relativist, however. As Eliot presumes that a "savage" is improved by his response to "a grand church organ" ("Ornament" 190), so Woolf trusts that a common reader benefits from an acquaintance with Arnoldian touchstones. The highly select consensus of tradition may be modified, it may begin to crumble as in "The Leaning Tower" (1940), but Woolf cannot abandon "inherited" concepts of "genius" and "taste" (Mudge 215). Woolf particularly enjoyed mocking Victorian middlebrow taste; she concurs with Eliot's (and Ruskin's) judgment that a proliferation of hideous things characterized that age.

Sharing in the kind of reaction to the blight of urbanization and mass production that led to the crafts of Morris & Co. or the Omega Workshop, Eliot and Woolf reject popular taste, yet insist that we pay attention to its manifestations in the lives around us ("Leaves from a Note-Book" 448; "Phases of Fiction," CE 2: 101; "The Modern Essay,"

---

[18]Eliot's essay, a venture in semiotics, quotes Carlyle's Teufelsdröckh, who credits the advent of printing with "creating a whole new democratic world" (189).

CE 2: 48). What both authors call for is writing that somehow captures a (past) glory while not belying material existence. Hence Woolf's famous critique of the materialists revises but does not abandon the realist project. "Life is not a series of gig lamps symmetrically arranged; life is a luminous halo, a semi-transparent envelope surrounding us from the beginning of consciousness to the end" ("Modern Fiction," CE 2: 106). It may seem that Eliot's concern with upholstery is incompatible with Woolf's aim at intimations of immortality; at least, in this image of "life," which is art's *matter*, there is little hint of material detail (though there is a swerve from the linearity associated with the masculine). In both writers, however, matter and spirit interfuse, with particular emphasis on women's cultural assignment, that of tending to trifling matters while remaining pure in spirit.

For women especially, it seems, practical conditions betoken moral state. Women are bound to domestic trifles, like Esther Lyon fussing about tallow candles, or Milly Pargiter fraying the wick under the kettle to make it boil. But Esther's fastidious taste in her homely surroundings hints that she was born for a wider life, while the Pargiters' restless drawing-room rites bespeak their Victorian servitude. The authors deplore the claustrophobic concerns of these young women, but they never dismiss them as immaterial.

Themselves far from captives of the drawing room or kitchen, and certainly not subject to vulgar affectations of taste born of limited perspective—after all, they stand on the heights with the historians—Eliot and Woolf nevertheless challenge our ability to extend our sympathies to those who must magnify the importance of trifles. They thereby also expose the narrowness of our own supposedly wider perspective. Even as they uphold putatively universal aesthetic standards, they shift authority to the "mothers of opinion."

In critical tradition, Eliot and Woolf have come to represent the opposing modes of traditional realism and modernist stream of consciousness, based on their official statements of purpose and on texts read in an ungendered light. Their aims, however, nearly harmonize beneath the strains of changing contemporary modes. Eliot, in advocating realism, must clear away the idealizing conventions of romantic fiction (with the dubious determinism of the marriage plot), whereas Woolf must oppose the overly literal realism or materialism of her day, which in general had only objectified woman further. Eliot herself never practiced such photographic representationalism. For all his adornment of Dorothea as muse, Ladislaw appears to speak for Eliot's conscience when he protests, "The true seeing is within; . . . I feel that especially about representations of women. As if a woman were

a mere coloured superficies!" (M 142). Eliot had begun in the Wordsworthian mode of pursuit of the middling truth: to strive to see "by
the 'light of common day,' without the lamp of faith" ("Introduction
to Genesis" 257). Her model would be the "Dutch paintings": "I find
a source of delicious sympathy in these faithful pictures of a monoto-
nous homely existence" (AB 180); instead of nude goddess or madonna, the ordinary woman at her chores might become the center of
interest. In the course of her career, however, Eliot evolved her own
form of philosophical and idealized realism (Knoepflmacher, *Early
Novels*, 34–35; Levine, "Hypothesis," 3; McGowan 173–74) as though
to escape both the designation of woman as aesthetic object and the
relegation of women's lives to the realm of the commonplace. On an
aesthetic and ethical scale, Maggie Tulliver must appear closer to Our
Lady of St. Ogg's than to a "friendly bar-maid," but we must also
believe that her part in the "sordid life" "on the banks of the Floss"
contributes to an "historical advance of mankind" (MF 431, 238–39).

Setting aside—according to custom—the question of the representation of women, Lewes and Eliot as well as Woolf considered mere
detail to be vulgar materialism. Lewes claimed that "realism" had
become a fad for "unessential details," "coats and waistcoats," and
bourgeois manners, "delight[ing] the tailor-mind" (*Principles of Success*
84), much as Woolf was later to censure the writers who outfitted life
like "Bond Street tailors" ("Modern Fiction," CE 2: 106). Not that Woolf
despised factual detail in fiction (Paul 35). She admired "truth-tellers"
like Defoe, with their version of Dutch realism, and savored the precise
delineation of "personal relations" in Jane Austen, but she regarded
such realisms as too transparent. Instead, George Eliot according to
Woolf developed the intrusive omniscient narrator who alerts the
reader that "the end of life is not to meet, to part, to love, to laugh,"
revealing instead a hidden consciousness that "runs counter" to the
surface ("Phases of Fiction," CE 2: 78–80). Instead of a colored superficies, we have subversive psychological depths and an ambition to
encompass all of "life"; Woolf's own fiction would represent those
overpowering forces, not just marriage and manners.

The nineteenth-century novelists might be seen as having made the
first assaults on the mystery of the "ordinary mind on an ordinary day"
("Modern Fiction," CE 2: 106) without having made full allowance
for the "astonishing disorder" of the inner life as Woolf and other
"Georgians" sought to do ("Bennett and Brown," CE 1: 333, 336).
Though Eliot can be seen as a pioneer of psychoanalysis, she exhibits
a Victorian reticence, out of "piety" and "fellow feeling" for "our
common nature," as Theophrastus Such puts it ("Looking Inward,"

TS 4). Such tact can be a handicap; Woolf herself felt the restraints of Victorian decorum, if not about unseemly private thoughts then about female desire and the body. Was a retreat from external realism one way to avoid writing a body no longer circumscribed by Victorian reticences? In any case, Woolf's trifles of everyday thought retain a sense of decorum while attempting to overcome the propriety of gender and identity.

Woolf remained in the tradition of Eliot's representational fidelity and continued to figure the object of art as feminine (to "describe beautifully if possible, truthfully at any rate, our Mrs. Brown" [CE 1: 336]); she turned from the colored superficies to the internal registers of experience while seeking "some more impersonal relationship" ("The Narrow Bridge of Art," CE 2: 225). The realism of a Dutch painter and that of an impressionist thus differ somewhat (Albright 96–97; Praz 383). If Eliot admits that her "mirror is doubtless defective" (AB 178), she nonetheless offers a framed representation. For Woolf, however, the Romantic faith in correspondences, "how beauty outside mirrored beauty within," has been irreparably shattered (TL 201–2). She anatomizes phallocentric discourse in a harsher light than Eliot, and she seems more doubtful than Eliot of the adequacy of her artistic medium. Yet even from the beginning, Eliot's "faithful account of men and things as they have mirrored themselves in my mind" allows for the contingencies of perspective and of language that make the latter-day artist so anxious: "dreading nothing, indeed, but falsity, which, in spite of one's best efforts, there is reason to dread" (AB 178, 180; Hillis Miller, *Ethics*, 61–63, 71). Woolf had merely taken the next logical step in questioning mimetic art, without abandoning the aim of representing reality as she knew it in order to rouse readers' sympathetic awareness of common experience.

For both authors, moreover, the speculation on mimetic art entails a critique of (and some participation in) the relegation of woman to represented object. The mimetic order has always privileged reality over appearance, and figured woman as reflected image or blemished incarnation, a falling away from inward truth. Eliot's defense of Dutch realism explicitly sides with the feminine and common: "Do not impose on us any aesthetic rules which shall banish from the region of Art those old women scraping carrots with their work-worn hands, those heavy clowns taking holiday in a dingy pot-house" (AB 181). A passage in *To the Lighthouse* similarly objects to aesthetic rules that subordinate feminine detail (Mario Praz traces the "everyday lyricism" of Woolf and other modern writers back to the aesthetics of Dutch genre painting [25]). Those who seek the meaning of "sea and sky"

encounter some feminine details "out of harmony": "an ashen-coloured ship . . . a purplish stain upon . . . the sea as if something
had boiled and bled, invisibly, beneath." Both the vessel and the
bloodstain (suggestive of Mrs. Ramsay or of Mr. Carmichael's desired
youth, Andrew) disrupt "the most sublime reflections," interrogating
all gender dichotomies modeled on Man vs. Nature.

> Did Nature supplement what man advanced? Did she complete what
> he began? With equal complacence she saw his misery, his meanness,
> and his torture. That dream, of sharing, completing . . . was then
> but a reflection in a mirror, and the mirror itself was but the surface
> glassiness which forms in quiescence when the nobler powers sleep
> beneath? (TL 201–2)

The passage ends with the bracketed information that Mr. Carmichael
published a book of poems, a kind of elegy for Andrew and the
youth destroyed in the war, suggesting that those who pace the beach
dreaming of complementarity are still male Romantics. She, woman,
relegated to nature and silence, takes her revenge in indifference,
among the "nobler powers" that may return from the repressed but
that do not answer. These things are a parable, as Eliot might say, for
the resurgent power of feminine detail in Eliot's and Woolf's writings.

These Things Are a Parable: Feminine Trifles
Make the Sum of Common Life

In centering on "trivial" detail, Eliot and Woolf adopt the realism
and apparent objectivity of historians yet at the same time gain the
intimacy of vulgar gossips, frequently dignifying the kind of feminine
detail only novelists, not historians, would admit onto the page. Objects, such as Charlotte Brontë's (or Jacob's) shoes, take on a life of
their own, chastening our sense of all-importance. Eliot and Woolf
furnish instructive parables that nod both to the selfless perspective
gained by philosophy (a vocation for men) and to the particular,
contingent view of women (in their household occupations).

Chapter 27 of *Middlemarch* introduces an episode in the egotistical
flirtation of Rosamond with Lydgate by way of a parable:

> An eminent philosopher among my friends, who can dignify even
> your ugly furniture by lifting it into the serene light of science, has
> shown me this pregnant little fact. Your pier-glass . . . made to

be rubbed by a housemaid, will be minutely and multitudinously scratched in all directions; but place now against it a lighted candle as a centre of illumination, and lo! the scratches will seem to arrange themselves in a fine series of concentric circles round that little sun. (194–95)

The "serene light of science" suggests a phallocentric sun, beyond the questioning of a housemaid, but it is she, if anyone, who knows that pier-glass. The "pregnant" little facts suggest that philosophy must acknowledge its relation to female materiality, as Lydgate must concede that Rosamond is her own "little sun" rather than his moon. The eminent philosopher and the housemaid, a nobody, might each be able to tell you "that the scratches are going everywhere impartially," yet both observers share the human tendency to believe in "the flattering illusion of a concentric arrangement." Nothing in the passage suggests either that understanding (or education) will exempt one from egotism, or that the furniture and housemaid are not indeed a bit commonplace though they must be attended to. Notably, the narrator numbers philosophers among her friends, and addresses those who own the furniture, while satirizing the interlocutors' agreement that "any person now absent" is egotistical (195).

In *To the Lighthouse*, Lily Briscoe ponders the dependence of the eminent philosopher Mr. Ramsay on "people's praise" but attempts to excuse the vanity of a great thinker:

Whenever she "thought of his work" she always saw clearly before her a large kitchen table. It was Andrew's doing. She asked him what his father's books were about. "Subject and object and the nature of reality," Andrew had said. And when she said Heavens, she had no notion what that meant. "Think of a kitchen table then," he told her, "when you're not there."

So now she always saw, when she thought of Mr. Ramsay's work, a scrubbed kitchen table. It lodged now in the fork of a pear tree. . . . And with a painful effort of concentration, she focused her mind, not upon the silver-bossed bark of the tree . . ., but upon a phantom kitchen table, one of those scrubbed board tables, grained and knotted, whose virtue seems to have been laid bare by years of muscular integrity, which stuck there, its four legs in air. Naturally, if one's days were passed in . . . this reducing of lovely evenings . . . to a white deal four-legged table (and it was the mark of the finest minds so to do), naturally one could not be judged like an ordinary person. (TL 38)

Here a dignified piece of furniture is rendered comic by a woman, in this case an artist not unlike the know-nothing housemaid ("Heavens, she had no notion"), who is trying to understand the egotistical blindness of a man gifted to see with the serene light of science. Terms like "virtue" and "muscular integrity" suggest that the table has been scrubbed by Mr. Ramsay's manly efforts to come to terms with things in themselves, in the phallocentric Western tradition. But any Woolfian kitchen table must have been laid bare by the labor of (female) servants when neither Lily nor Mr. Ramsay was there. Mr. Ramsay seems more capable of a kind of objectivity than Lily (or than women, Woolf implies), but less capable of conceiving a world in which he is not there.[19] Further, in her selfless vision Lily shows her superior gift to adorn "angular essences" with imaginative details (she notes "fish-shaped leaves," "flamingo clouds" [38]).

Such resonant object-lessons suggest that Eliot and Woolf will insist on the significance of commonplace details even as they urge a non-egocentric perspective; at the same time they will stand with "us" and the philosophers or artists judging the limitations of "any person now absent." Thus there is some condescension as well as tribute in their impressions of commonplace women.

In *The Mill on the Floss*, for instance, the Dodson sisters' absurd provincial fashions bespeak their outlook, station, and mood, a semiotic system begging to be read. Mrs. Glegg selects from among her "curled fronts" of hair according to the occasion, wearing her most "fuzzy and lax" front when visiting Mrs. Tulliver, to criticize that woman for wearing her own blond curls. Mrs. Glegg's clothes are similarly expressive: they announce her principle never "to wear her new things out before her old ones." "One would need to be learned in the fashions of those times to know how far in the rear of them Mrs Glegg's slate-coloured silk-gown must have been; but from certain constellations of small yellow spots upon it . . . it was probable that it belonged to a stratum of garments just old enough to have come recently into wear" (MF 48–49). The details of personal effects themselves become historical facts, implying a host of associations from the past. A new science must be called up to interpret such details, and no one should assume fashion is trivial because women are concerned with it (compare RO 77).

---

[19]Lily can accept the idea that her painting will be rolled up in an attic, but Mr. Ramsay is tormented by the idea that his little light will be extinguished in cultural history. Lily silently praises Mr. Bankes: "You are entirely impersonal; . . . finer than Mr. Ramsay; . . . generous . . . heroic" (39). Mrs. Ramsay meditates that her husband, like "all the great men," was "blind, deaf, and dumb, to the ordinary things" (107–8).

Woolf examines her own human documents from obscure, old-fashioned sectors of society. Take for instance Mrs. Brown, "one of those clean, threadbare old ladies whose extreme tidiness . . . suggests more extreme poverty than rags and dirt." From observable details, Woolf extrapolates a personal history that in turn takes the form of material details expressive of a certain social milieu and code of honor: "I thought of her in a seaside house, among queer ornaments: sea-urchins, models of ships in glass cases. Her husband's medals were on the mantelpiece" ("Bennett and Brown," CE 1: 322, 324). The method Woolf felt she had discovered on her own in 1920 and sketched out in "An Unwritten Novel" was certainly freer than Eliot's style, with dashing use of the present tense, apposition, and ellipsis, yet it emulates the realists' use of historically located detail to flesh out a character (Bell 2: 42).

As in "Mr. Bennett and Mrs. Brown," in "An Unwritten Novel" an elderly woman in a railway carriage comes to life for the observer, who tentatively invents her context and past.[20] "Minnie Marsh" dwells between spirit and matter:

It's the spirit wailing its destiny, the spirit driven hither, thither, lodging on the diminishing carpets—meagre footholds. . . .

But then—the muffins, the bald elderly dog? Bead mats I should fancy and the consolation of underlinen. . . . After all, the tea is rich, the muffin hot. . . . (19; my ellipses)

In Woolf's writings, quotidian detail is less charged with intentionality or empirical accuracy than it is in Eliot's; the underlinen and threadbare gloves of Minnie Marsh are frank speculations on the part of the interpreter. In a more modern temper, Woolf allowed things their obdurate materiality and allowed the observer great license; she resisted, for example, the symbolism of jewels and artworks that Eliot devised in such novels as *Romola* and *Middlemarch*, or she ironically adapted such symbolism, as in *Orlando* or *Between the Acts*.

The affinity between these authors' modes of substantiating a common character in representative detail is nowhere better displayed than in the famous manifesto for modern fiction, "Mr. Bennett and Mrs. Brown," a paper Woolf read to the Heretics at Cambridge on May 18, 1924, and in the passage most often cited as the constitution of Eliot's state in the world of fiction, the beginning of chapter 5 of

[20]Rachel Bowlby astutely retraces the railway journey with its passing glimpse of woman in Woolf's writings.

"The Sad Fortunes of the Rev. Amos Barton" (1857), the first fiction Eliot published (reissued as the first part of *Scenes of Clerical Life* in 1858). Neither declaration of artistic intent prepares us for the kind of fiction Woolf or Eliot later wrote, but in both pieces the authors dissociate themselves from a kind of contemporary fiction and espouse a realistic depiction of character and milieu in all its commonplace detail, exhorting their readers to lend aesthetic sympathy to the "others" in history. Both authors claim as the material of their fiction the unheroic life of the particularized Everyman or Woman. Eliot's Mr. Barton is Woolf's Mrs. Brown. Eliot, with ironic modesty, cajoles:

> Perhaps I am doing a bold thing to bespeak your sympathy on behalf of a man who . . . was palpably and unmistakably commonplace. . . . But, my dear madam, it is so very large a majority of your fellow-countrymen that are of this insignificant stamp. . . . Yet these commonplace people . . . have their unspoken sorrows, and their sacred joys. . . . Nay, is there not a pathos in their very insignificance,—in our comparison of their dim and narrow existence with the glorious possibilities of that human nature which they share?
> . . .As it is, you can, if you please, decline to pursue my story farther; and you will easily find reading more to your taste, since I learn from the newspapers that many remarkable novels, full of striking situations, thrilling incidents, and eloquent writing, have appeared only within the last season. ("Amos Barton," SCL 41–42)

Woolf addresses her audience less disingenuously but in a similar strain, likewise championing an undistinguished individual (one of many reproduced by the same "stamp") against a horde of flashy publications:

> In the course of your daily life this past week . . . you have overheard scraps of talk that filled you with amazement. . . . In one day thousands . . . of emotions have met, collided, and disappeared in astonishing disorder. Nevertheless, you allow the writers to palm off upon you a version of all this, an image of Mrs. Brown, which has no likeness to that surprising apparition whatsoever. . . . Hence spring those sleek, smooth novels, those portentous and ridiculous biographies . . . which pass so plausibly for literature at the present time. (CE 1: 336)[21]

[21]Woolf appears to define a virile modernism: readers' undue respect for writers seems to "emasculate" literature and leads to a "milk and watery criticism" (CE 1: 336). But she also debunks the cult of the individual genius and the male norm of experience.

Notably, there has been some change in gender roles between "Amos Barton" and "Mr. Bennett and Mrs. Brown." Pseudonymous "George Eliot," in his debut, entertains gentlemen with the follies of silly lady readers who are blind to the pathos of an ordinary clergyman's life, while the story as a whole centers on the women unmentioned in the title, Mrs. Barton and the spectacular Countess Czerlaski. Virginia Woolf, well-known literary lady, alerts college men that life itself is in actuality an unknown old woman, counterbalancing in her title the famous man and the truly great fictional spirit. Yet the fundamental appeal is much the same: we, educated "men," must recognize lives of the obscure, the biographies of those who are precisely *not* great men.

Both passages alert us to an unwelcome truth: that people we shun or overlook in fact typify common humanity; our uniqueness is really one detail in a vast picture without clear focus or boundary. The rhetorical strategy has shifted, of course: the noble "unspoken sorrows" and "sacred joys" become "thousands of emotions . . . in astonishing disorder." Eliot's writing is actually more rooted in the commonplace than Woolf's, however. Elsewhere, Eliot disparages "that deficient human sympathy, that impiety towards the present and the visible, which flies . . . to the remote, the vague, and the unknown" ("Worldliness and Otherworldliness" 385). Conversely, Woolf quarrels with "Mr. Wells, Mr. Bennett, and Mr. Galsworthy" as "materialists . . . concerned not with the spirit but with the body. . . . The sooner English fiction turns its back upon them . . . and marches, if only into the desert, the better for its soul" ("Modern Fiction," CE 2: 104). The betterment of the soul may require a deliberate flight to the remote and unknown, but Woolf is only fleeing "the body" as literally conveyed by male Edwardians, not failing in Eliot's call for sympathy with the experiential present. Mrs. Brown is corporeal enough, but eludes her unsympathetic male observers. Realism, though for Eliot it was a means of honoring the sacred, feminine, common life, could become yet another masculine version of history, a secular catalog of ordinary goods. Yet as I have noted, Woolf retains a realist's fidelity to common experiential detail, however impressionistic the medium of representation. If Woolf's otherworldly artists become saints in the desert, their vocation like Eliot's still recalls traditional pieties. At the same time, Woolf's stress on spirituality, like her stress on impersonality, seems aligned with a masculine modernism in conflict with her desire for the concrete personality of Mrs. Brown.

Mr. Barton and Mrs. Brown impress their stories upon us, much as Eliot, a "woman of flesh and blood," emerges in Woolf's account from behind "the solemn pedant of legend" ("GE" [1926]), or as Woolf comes alive in the diaries and letters, the elusive feminine spirit suppressed by literary history. Like Eliot's heroines in Woolf's view, Barton and Brown are the incomplete stories of the historian-narrators who observe them. Common "others," they vanish without grasping a large share of greatness. Look closely at the human beings next to you, Eliot and Woolf seem to say, and imagine what stories their lives make for them. Dreary as these stories generally are, there will be moments in which the common life appears to be an exalted progress; let these great authors illuminate the glorious possibilities of narrow existences.

Class and the Single Writer: How to Read the Common Life

Mr. Barton and Mrs. Brown are emblematic of a vast collection of biographical histories in the works of the great women of letters. These works reflect ambivalent loyalties to the dominant tradition and to those whom it excluded or oppressed, calling divided attention to the big picture and to the obscure detail that adds to the mass. Aesthetic questions of selection and emphasis implicate questions of class and gender, while authors find themselves implicated as social teachers no matter what their dreams of the detachment of high art. As I have suggested, the trespasses of outsiders like Eliot and Woolf could be forgiven if they construed their vocation as service to the common life. Yet the great author must take care that her teaching not resound as explicit propaganda for the oppressed, or lose her favor with the "coterie." Eliot and Woolf reflect on the precarious role of author in a world of social change.

Eliot equates the role of writer, male or female, with "the office of teacher or influencer of the public mind" ("Leaves from a Note-book" 440). Yet a baldly didactic novel would fail as art, she warned herself while writing *Romola* and *Felix Holt*, both works in part designed to temper the rebellious spirit. Though she was far from approving the status quo, her writings everywhere betray a wariness of change. We ought to be pleased by "all guarantees of human advancement," Eliot's narrator admits. Nevertheless, we do have "moments" when "imagination does a little Toryism on the sly, revelling in regret" ("Amos Barton," SCL 7). For the writer starting out, the loss of privilege can be an opportunity: "It is no longer the coterie which acts on literature, but literature which acts on the coterie; the . . . *public*, is ever widening" ("Woman in France"

60). That wider public had welcomed a great woman novelist, but to the last, Theophrastus Such cannot decide between sly Toryism and progressivism: "Many ancient beautiful things are lost, many ugly modern things have arisen; but invert the proposition and it is equally true" ("Looking Backwards," TS 21). The role of great sage did not increase Eliot's enthusiasm for an indiscriminate public, nor did it shake her nostalgia for art as a sphere of privilege.

Woolf shares Eliot's ambivalence toward trends of democratization; the modern writer confesses her confused allegiances, and even celebrates her elitism: "I want . . . old coronets . . . that carry land with them and country houses; coronets that breed simplicity, eccentricity, ease" ("Am I a Snob?" *Moments of Being*, 186). She has qualms about such Toryism when it comes to literary progress, however; she recalls a "republic of readers" ("How It Strikes a Contemporary," CE 2: 154), but traces "a change . . . from a small audience of cultivated people to a larger audience of people who were not quite so cultivated," a "change . . . not altogether for the worse" ("The Modern Essay," CE 2: 45). She liked to imagine the privileged reader in the library of a country house, one of the "little fortresses of civilization" ("Reading," CE 2: 16); but she also needed to rely on a regenerative image of the common reader in the public library. Her own role as great novelist still carries with it some of the burdens Eliot bore as sage, to try to sway that common reader toward sympathy for the common life (we must "know ourselves," *The Years* insists). Thus she frequently steered her "fiction . . . dangerously near propaganda" (*VW Diary* 4: 300), especially as, in the crisis of world war, she felt the imminent death of a culture of the coterie. "Literature . . . is common ground . . . English literature will survive this war" only in the hands of "commoners and outsiders like ourselves." The gesture of solidarity between the cultivated woman and her audience (she was speaking to the Workers' Educational Association in 1940) would have been inconceivable to Eliot, yet Eliot and Woolf held similar positions as "outsiders" who had broken the monopoly of "a small class of well-to-do young men" ("The Leaning Tower," CE 2: 181).

There are limits, of course, to these authors' allegiance to commoners and outsiders. The uneducated and working classes occupy a central place in Eliot's novels, yet the early editions of her novels, like most Victorian fiction, were priced beyond the reach of many in the literate minority, except through the lending libraries (Feltes 21–27; Sutherland 37–40, 188–205); moreover, she appealed, in the designedly unpopular *Romola* and other later works, to a certain intelligentsia within her "public," without whose approval her portraits of common life could not have been deemed great. Woolf wrote in what she considered more democratic times but in an atmosphere of increasingly rarefied artistic experimentation. The three-volume novel and the lending library were fossils, and literature could be a cheap commodity; but still the great woman writer had to hold herself aloof from the people, as though hand-crafting books to be read by E. M. Forster in order to preserve her freedom from the popular market.

Making a kind of privacy out of their public, both Eliot and Woolf nevertheless strained against the literary class system. Woolf seems to have been more troubled by exclusive conventions; she claimed that the great change in human character, "that shift in the whole pyramidal accumulation" (MD 246), meant a greater intimacy between all orders and an insubordination of the female: the cook has risen from "the lower depths" ("Bennett and Brown," CE 1: 320). Yet that cook plays quite a marginal role in Woolf's novels; Alex Zwerdling notes in Woolf's fiction "a refusal or inability to describe anyone below the rank of the middle class in persuasive detail" (96). Eliot, though she described servants in persuasive detail at times, could also enjoy the idea of an insubordinate cook without abandoning the social hierarchy. In "Servants' Logic" she satirizes a cook's resistance to orders from her superiors. An enlightened gentleman's belief in human progress is sorely tried by representatives of humanity in his household: "We may look to the next century for the triumph of our ideas, but it is impossible to look there for our dinners" (392). This essay, for the *Pall Mall Gazette* in 1864, still seems to converse with a coterie of gentlemen, though it points out that trifles governed by women have a way of deflating men's grand theories about progress.

The undeniable "dignity" and "beauty" of upper-class life are the age-old perquisites of literature, Woolf claims ("Reading," CE 2: 16). That the novel should have forfeited this privilege is a source of amusement to the narrator of *Middlemarch:* "Whatever has been or is to be narrated by me about low people, may be ennobled by being considered a parable. . . . Thus while I tell the truth about loobies, my reader's imagination need not be entirely excluded from an occupation with lords" (M 249–50). Clearly a conventional preference for high life is not being condoned here, but neither is Eliot confining us to the hovels of loobies. As in the parable of the pier-glass, the "low" detail is elevated to the perspective of the educated classes. This middle-class perspective seems far more shifting and defensive in Eliot than in Woolf, as Eliot's noble artisans often stand for lords, born gentlemen with mechanical skills. Social mobility (such as Robert Evans and his daughter possessed) rather illustrates than resolves the class contradictions in Eliot's idea of the common life. Woolf, perhaps because she had little to gain from climbing the class scale, rarely depicts such a climb in her fiction, though she frequently touches the nerve of class differences; she often appears to construct an upper middle-class enclave almost impervious to change. Only in *To the Lighthouse*, *The Years*, and *Between the Acts* do any sustained passages from a servant's point of view appear, and these works are typical in centering on a cultivated family circle, a metonym for humanity rather than a Victorian microcosm of a specific social organism.

Centering in different ways on the middle class, Eliot's and Woolf's novels reflect not only the authors' positions but also generic convention and the demands of realism; characters in novels are typically and most convincingly middling. They wrote most about what they knew, and except in the historical excursions *Romola* and *Orlando*, largely avoided the aristocracy as much as the lower classes. They seemed to believe that the danger lay in generalizations that reduced people to statistics or types, or that exalted the unworthy. Still, we find them conceiving of the "masses" collectively in both idealizing and denigrating terms. Many of the same qualities attributed to women in the ideology of influence accrue to the common people: anonymity, historical obscurity, more immediate access to the past, to nature, and to human emotions, and above all a tendency to be *many* rather than *one*. Nevertheless, Eliot and Woolf resist sentimental clichés about the folk much as they resist the doll-madonna.

In Eliot's and Woolf's novels, a generalized crowd of the emerging classes frequently functions as chorus, like the brutish miners in *Felix Holt* or the street criers in *The Years*, but sometimes the crowd takes on a life of its own, as in *Romola* or *Mrs. Dalloway*. Uncultivated people are readily romanticized as vestiges of more primitive phases of culture. Woolf notes this especially in Eliot's early works, in which "the whole fabric of ancient rural England is revived" as though by "a natural process" ("GE" [1919] 155; cf. "GE" [1921]). The simple folk, romantically distanced from bourgeois reading rooms, seem to speak of a happier past and a more integrated humanity.

Woolf herself shares in a certain post-Romantic exaltation of a common ancestry among rural people; she praises their "humour which has been . . . finding expression over their beer since the pilgrims tramped the Pilgrim's Way; which Shakespeare and Scott and George Eliot all loved to overhear." Peasants do not "stand out as individuals"; as Eliot claimed, "The cultured man acts more as an individual; the peasant, more as one of a group" ("German Life" 274). "They compose a pool of common wisdom," Woolf continues, "a fund of perpetual life." While heroes and heroines come and go, the folk "remain" as the "hope for the race" ("The Novels of Thomas Hardy," CE 1: 259–60). Woolf may seem far removed from Eliot's or Hardy's aim to preserve dialect and folkways, yet she still believed, as they did, that the anonymous classes are guardians of the common past.

According to such a vision, the common life forms a kind of archaeological text interpolating fragments of the past in up-to-date histories. Like many of their contemporaries, Eliot and Woolf seek out the origins of present civilization among social groups that have eluded scrutiny and hence erasure. The rural weavers in a village like Raveloe, "on the outskirts of civilization," represent "remnants of a disinherited race." Traces of earlier belief survive: "Echoes of the old demon-worship might perhaps even now be caught by the diligent listener among the grey-haired peasantry" (SM 51–53) (compare Woolf's "women round the village pump" ["Evelyn," CE 3: 45] and the peasant "ancestry" in *Romola* [193]). This appeal to common people as blurred incarnations of history appears not to threaten the historical observer's own civilized individuality. Eliot remarks that contemporary German farmers resemble English farmers of fifty years ago ("German Life" 274), whereas Woolf asserts that the typical remote English village preserves the "perfect existence" of an ancient Greek community ("On Not Knowing Greek," CE 1: 1–2). During the pageant at Pointz Hall, the villagers whose names are in the Domesday Book wear a path in the grass as venerable as the Pilgrim's Way. The common life can pronounce forgotten languages and beliefs, perhaps as alternatives to patriarchal, European, Christian culture.

Woolf indulges more than Eliot in nostalgia for a natural common life, though not without irony. Her ambivalence toward common women is powerfully displayed in "Memories of a Working Women's Guild": "What images and saws and proverbial sayings must still be current with them . . . and very likely they still keep the power which we have lost of making new ones." "We" have fallen from nature into self-consciousness, but perhaps we gain imagination by this fall. Working women "were indigenous and rooted to one spot. Their very names were like the stones of the fields, common, grey, obscure, docked of all the splendours of association and romance" (CE 4: 141, 138). Woolf here seems to be revising Wordsworth as well as recalling Arnold's dismay over "Wragg is in custody," with the mixture of pity, attraction, and revulsion for the poor.[22] Both Eliot and Woolf find

[22]Leslie Stephen shares the Arnoldian snobbish cultural history: "The process [of change] proceeds at varying rates in different social strata. The vulgar are still plunged in gross superstition, from which the educated have definitively emerged" (*History of English Thought* 7). See Arnold, "The Function of Criticism at the Present Time."

limits to their affection for common people when the masses rise up as unruly agents. Thus the lust of the crowd for Tito's or Savonarola's blood, the assault on the ladies of Treby Manor barely averted by Felix Holt, and the riots of the Turkish rebellion in *Orlando* suggest the more threatening side of the crowd. Similarly, the heroine's fantasy that she may rule among the gypsies is met in *The Mill on the Floss* and *Orlando* by the fact that the gypsies are hostile both to women and to the life of the mind.

Eliot was particularly anxious to dispel sentimental myths about the rural poor. An honest observer sees "the slow gaze . . . the slow utterance, and the heavy slouching walk, remind[ing] one rather of that melancholy animal the camel." Such blunt description is paradoxically kinder than the literary (or demagogic) lie, such as Dickens's portrayal of the "preternaturally virtuous poor," that glosses over social ills ("German Life" 269, 272). Of course, Eliot portrays her own style of noble common people, but she sets plausible limits to their exemption from general conditions. Woolf jars readers with the hideous violet-seller in *The Years* or the prehistoric woman singing beside the tube station in *Mrs. Dalloway*. The greater intimacy with so-called undistinguished people in Eliot's works no doubt has some basis in the fact that Eliot had grown up among them; Woolf regrets that for her, the class "barrier is impassable" ("Women's Guild" 141). Each in her way struggling to read resistant texts with sympathy, to acknowledge the otherness of irreducible details, Eliot and Woolf nevertheless resort to a romanticized common life as a source of both historical continuity and mutual understanding. The spectacle of the unknown classes threatens the distinguished woman writer, yet it furnishes some of her most enabling material.

In "Woman in France: Madame de Sablé," Eliot recalls the forgotten women of the influential French salons. She recognizes that Madame de Sablé's name lies below "the surface of literature and history": "She was only one amongst a crowd—one in a firmament of feminine stars which, when once the biographical telescope is turned upon them, appear scarcely less remarkable and interesting" (80). This is the very telescope Woolf is still wielding in the next century. As Woolf puts it, "A hundred years ago it was simple enough; [women] were stars who shone only in male sunshine," but now we must consider the "ordinary woman" on whom the "extraordinary woman depends"— the stars in a newly discovered firmament ("Indiscretions" 75; "Women and Fiction" 44). For both authors, the relation between the great woman and the sacrificial common life is what must be interrogated. Woolf consulted the biographies of famous women, "Florence Nightingale, Anne Clough, Emily Brontë," and others, as though to approach obscure lives: "It is much to be regretted that no lives of maids . . . are to be found in the *Dictionary of National Biography*" (TG 79, 166; cf. O 305–6). Though Woolf's own work, as an alternative to the DNB, includes few "lives of maids," she is as eager to ally herself with an inarticulate tradition as to affirm her ties to great female predecessors. Her own *greatness* might be defined by her narration of a collective biographical history. Eliot and Woolf invert their daring bids for eminence in their loving attentions to women who never had a chance.

Little Old Ladies Make the Sum of Human Things

What could be more distinctly the opposite of greatness than the ordinary little old lady? Here, in what seems an obscure feature of their works, Eliot and Woolf locate a source of women's power to influence the course of history, or to shift the terms of the discourse altogether. Deprived of the temporary power of youth and beauty, the elderly woman (often a widow) is by definition a dependent; the fortunate few who still have authority and property seem all the more aware of their handicap as women. A number of prominent female characters in these authors' works have reached the age of outward powerlessness, including Mrs. Transome, the Alcharisi, Eleanor Pargiter, and Mrs. Swithin, but each retains the privileges of her class while accruing some of the powers of the sorceress or sibyl; only in Woolf's vision are these powers playful rather than bitter (Oldfield). Just as often the old or solitary woman is a minor character indeed, without even the notoriety of a witch. Framed for a moment like Mrs. Brown in a railway compartment between stations, these women appear as a reminder of common life, a kind of answer to the conventional privileges of narrative history: "but why always Dorothea?" indeed (M 205).

In Eliot's espousal of the "vulgar details" of "Dutch paintings," the old woman is the most prominent emblem. "I turn, without shrinking, from . . . sibyls, and heroic warriors, to an old woman bending over her flower-pot, or eating her solitary dinner, while the noonday light . . . falls on her mob-cap, and . . . her spinning-wheel, and . . . all those cheap common things which are the precious necessaries of life to her" (AB 180–81). She is almost motionless among the reified conditions of her life, like Silas Marner a vestige of the past. Like Mrs. Brown, she is recognizable as a picturesque motif in art who demands greater attention.

Eliot repeatedly introduces dependent spinsters as nodes of sympathy and measures of the public man's ethical stature. As I have noted, the Rev. Irwine in *Adam Bede* is best known by the details of his consideration for his spinster sisters and widowed mother. From the point of view of "any person of family within ten miles," "it was quite a pity handsome, clever Mrs Irwine should have had such commonplace daughters." The local poor people, instead of seeing the daughters as "inartistic figures crowding the canvass of life," worship them as sources of true charity. The narrator, too, can share in the popular reverence for these "prosaic" women, challenging the aesthetic and socioeconomic rankings: "The existence of insignificant people has very important consequences in the world. It can be shown to affect the price of bread and the rate of wages, to call forth many evil tempers from the selfish, and many heroisms from the sympathetic, and, in other ways, to play no small part in the tragedy of life" (65–66). If heroism and the price of bread are indisputably historical factors, so are "old women and clowns" (AB 181).

A similar family scenario is more deftly and humorously displayed in *Middlemarch*, to the same purpose of distinguishing the sympathetic from the selfish and of linking great and small. The Rev. Camden Farebrother's devotion to his mother, spinster aunt, and sister shows him in "rather a changed aspect" to Lydgate. Though Farebrother's "womankind" regard him "as the king of men and preachers," they treat him as "in much need of their direction. Lydgate, with the usual shallowness of a young bachelor, wondered that Mr Farebrother had not taught them better." Miss Winifred Farebrother appears "nipped and subdued as single women are apt to be," while Miss Noble steals treats from the tea-table for poor children,

> reverting to her tea-cup with a small innocent noise as of a tiny timid quadruped. Pray think no ill of Miss Noble . . . fostering and petting all needy creatures being so spontaneous a delight to her, that she regarded it much as if it had been a pleasant vice. . . . Perhaps she was conscious of being tempted to steal from those who had much that she might give to those who had nothing, and carried in her conscience the guilt of that repressed desire. (125–27)

Lydgate ignores this mousy Robin Hood, whereas Ladislaw, a more altruistic bachelor (with future aims of redistributing social goods), befriends her. Again, the insignificant spinster, like a version of Miss Bates in *Emma*, serves as an index to justice and fellow-feeling. Only once does Eliot portray "a thriving and independent 'old maid,' "

Gillian Beer observes (*Eliot* 112–13); Priscilla Lammeter, in *Silas Marner*, need not regret the single state because like Emma she has enough money to lend her significance. *Impoverished* old maids may, as Emma quips, be "the proper sport of boys and girls" (*Emma* 77), or even of female authors, as when Eliot's narrator mocks "Rumour" as "a very old maid, who puckers her silly face by the fireside" (FH 191).

Poor spinsters are by definition marginal, their very meaning lying in the neglect they endure. In Eliot we see them subjected to powerful mothers, substitute patriarchs who take a speaking role in the action. These maternal figures too can suffer neglect, however, like Mrs. Transome in "helpless bondage" to her son and her ex-lover. She seems forced to pose for "a charming picture of English domestic life. . . . But the artist would have felt it requisite to turn her face towards her husband and little grandson, and to have given her an elderly amiability of expression" (FH 198–99). The framed and falsified image seems to hold women captive, whether they are powerless or ostensibly powerful.

Woolf creates similar emblems of women, frequently posing the little old lady in the railway carriage, as we have seen, but presenting other framed images as well. As in *Adam Bede* or *Middlemarch*, the obscure female figure may seem superfluous or inartistic (though presented to our aesthetically self-conscious gaze), but she points up the gender conflicts between public and private spheres, and seems to argue for the idea of a collective life in "the world as a whole." In *The Voyage Out*, for example, Rachel Vinrace posits the existence of "an old widow in her room, somewhere . . . in the surburbs of Leeds," hoarding "tea, a few lumps of sugar" according to the economics determined by politicians such as Richard Dalloway. "Still," she tells him, "there's the mind of the widow—the affections; those you leave untouched." Richard, as "citizen of the Empire," counters with his own emblem: "the state as a complicated machine," dependent on "the meanest screw." The narrator, speaking for Rachel, says, "It was impossible to combine the image of a lean black widow, gazing out of her window . . . with the image of a vast machine." Yet Rachel soon intuits what will be the insight of that spritely widow, Mrs. Swithin, that all such incongruities indeed combine as all ages are overlaid: "If one went back far enough . . . everything was in common; for the mammoths who pastured in the fields of Richmond High Street had turned into paving stones and boxes full of ribbon, and her aunts" (VO 66–67).

The widow and the machine evolved out of the mammoths, and remain interdependent with them. A similar syncretic point of view is reached by Clarissa Dalloway when, in the midst of her party, she goes alone to the window to face her distorted mirror image: an old lady "going to bed, in the room opposite." Clarissa unites in a triadic, dissonant chord the solitary old woman, the society hostess, and the defiant suicide, Septimus: "The young man had killed himself; . . . with the clock striking the hour, one, two, three, she did not pity him. . . . There! the old lady had put out her light!" (MD 283).

In "Time Passes," grotesque Mrs. McNab struggles to preserve the Ramsays' house and past, the legacy of one woman, Mrs. Ramsay, from "the fertility, the insensibility of nature. . . . It was beyond the strength of one woman, she said" (TL 207). Decay threatens to overrun the place like the resurgence of mammoths in the high street, but united, women combat irreversible time and disintegration: Mrs. McNab, Mrs. Bast (her name perhaps borrowed from Forster's common man, Leonard Bast in *Howards End*), and Lily Briscoe (two widows, perhaps, and a spinster) revive the house. Though this interlude genders an indifferent, destructive nature as feminine, it appears that if not for the sacrificial labors of forgotten women the whole edifice of civilization, the property of men haunted by maternal idols, would crumble into oblivion. Inarticulate Mrs. McNab through her housekeeping—her scrubbing of that kitchen table, perhaps—reconstitutes the very possibility of narrative.

In these instances we glimpse what Eliot and Woolf conceived as the role of ordinary women in history, as figures of silent endurance, vessels of unifying emotion, and powers to resist oblivion. Alongside the grand figures of the heroines, these fleeting reminders of the unremembered represent the complex interdependencies of history. Like insubordinate details challenging the aesthetic hierarchy, like embodied testimony against the fallacy of objectivity and a history of the biographies of great men, the little old women are monitory figures. There but for certain graces of artistic achievement go the grand old women of letters. Feminine examples of the common life are honored, but never overcome their subordination. Indeed, they are seldom mentioned in discussions of the great works by Eliot and Woolf. Like Austen's Emma claiming to wish to remain unmarried, the narrators may endorse a Ladislaw or Knightley who champions a Miss Noble or Miss Bates, but the authors never honestly wish to be reduced to uttering Miss Noble's inarticulate sounds or Miss Bates's inconsequential babble. Instead, the narrators are learned, artful, great; they are arbiters of history, showing how the insignificant masses sacrifice themselves to the progress of the common life.

4

Miracles in Fetters:
Heroism and the Selfless Ideal

Few novelists, even in twentieth-century avant-garde movements, have had the fortitude to dwell for long among the insignificant masses. It proves irresistible to adorn the homely with significance, to spice up that little old lady's dinner, or even to turn away from her to grander personages less likely to bore us. Readers consider it their privilege to *identify*, if not in the usual sense of identifying with a character, then in the sense of being able to distinguish remarkable characters or knots of meaning in the common wood. As I turn now to the heroines (without intending any slight to the heroes),[1] I follow perhaps the most common route in the interpretation of novels, next to consideration of plot. Reading the "characters," especially the heroic "shining ones," we may flatter our sense of selfhood. The grand old women of letters, while dissenting from the cult of individualism, single out certain characters for godlike eminence much like their own. Yet as I hope to show in this chapter, they adapt the conventions of heroic character to accord with a feminine ideal of selflessness.

Readings of any novel by a woman often seize on female characters as keys both to the author's experience and to her views on womanhood. Eliot's and Woolf's heroines, however, are instructive in part because they *cannot* be reduced to author surrogates.[2] As Eliot and Woolf define femininity, and hence feminine heroism, their own story

[1]Woolf's handling of characterization and plot may seem so radically different from Eliot's that it is difficult even to speak of her heroines or heroes. I use the terms loosely for female and male protagonists but recognize that these functions are often dispersed, in Eliot to a lesser extent than in Woolf. What is Rhoda in *The Waves?* what is Septimus Smith in *Mrs. Dalloway?* Extremes of the advocated selflessness, in suicide they extend the more dominant hero or heroine, Bernard or Clarissa.

[2]It may be that Eliot's and Woolf's place in the canon required their suppression of autobiography to some extent; their heroines are less easily mistaken for autobiographi-

is so unfeminine as not to be repeated in respectable fiction. A character who would strive toward published greatness as the authors did
would violate the virtue of the unpublicized common life (ambitious
characters, male as well as female, are generally condemned to obscurity or death in these novels). Conversely, those who abandon the
narrow designs of the self must fail to distinguish themselves, and
thus may seem to fall short of heroism and greatness—unless, of
course, the masculine norm of heroism might be discarded in favor of
a more collective mode.

Eliot and Woolf, like many contemporary writers, conceive a form
of heroism in keeping with an ideal of feminine selflessness—and
with realistic depiction of circumstances that actually limited women's
achievements (Martin 22). This conception of a feminine heroism reflects the development of a newly engendered, literate middle class,
a development often narrated in literary history. Terry Eagleton draws
on Jean H. Hagstrum's argument in *Sex and Sensibility* (24–49) that the
"feminization" of bourgeois culture associated with the rise of the
novel in the eighteenth century entailed a "domestication of heroism"
(Eagleton 14); according to Eagleton, this domestication marked a shift
from the belligerent ethos of a masculine aristocracy to a fashion for
the "sensibility, civility, and *tendresse*" associated with women. At the
same time, there was a new emphasis on "possessive individualism"
and a stiffening of the hierarchy of the patriarchal family, so that
women's confinement to domesticity and their indoctrination in
selflessness were further assured. As Eagleton puts it, "The 'exaltation' of women . . . also serves to shore up the very system which
oppresses them" (14–15). The contradictions of this oppressive exaltation were not lost on some of those who experienced it. Ann Richelieu
Lamb protested in 1844, "Woman, chained and fettered, is yet expected to work miracles" (*Can Woman Regenerate Society?* in Murray
31). Like many nineteenth-century novels, Eliot's and Woolf's fictional
experiments with heroism seem less disposed to protest the chains and
fetters than to acclaim the miracles performed by women in spite—or
because—of them. The very fettered privateness of women is seen as
a source of widespread influence and possible greatness. At the same
time, such novels help cast doubt on the assumption that those
"shapen after the average" are male, and that the female sphere is a
lesser, deformed part of the whole, "Man."

What could be the benefits of supposing that privacy *and* social

---

cal stand-ins than, say, Dorothy Richardson's Miriam Henderson. Though I may frequently suggest a correlation between these authors' treatment of heroines and their
views on women's actual roles in history, it is as important to distinguish the fictions
from the practical positions as it is to distinguish characters from authors.

conscience are somehow feminine virtues? It seems dangerous to maintain, as some feminists still do, that even in a possible nonsexist world women would excel in collaboration rather than in Herculean exploits. But it may be useful to suppose that because patriarchal culture denies women and other marginal groups the illusion of independent identity, they are conditioned to know that the subject is decentered. The norm for the autobiographical self, for instance, has been European, implicitly *male*, and "individualistic"; thus Georges Gusdorf claims that the author of autobiography must "feel himself to exist outside of others" as members of some cultures are not able to do ("Conditions and Limits of Autobiography" 29–30, in Friedman 35). Susan Stanford Friedman tries to convert such a disability of the marginal into a strength: women's autobiography is generated by the very conditions that in Gusdorf's view *prevent* autobiography. "Autobiography is possible," Friedman writes, altering Gusdorf, "when 'the individual does not feel *herself* to exist outside of others, and still less against others, but very much *with* others in an interdependent existence' " (her emphasis). Friedman, following Sheila Rowbotham and Nancy Chodorow, affirms women's capacity for a collective identification as "potentially transformative" of the human community (Friedman 35–42). Such endorsements of a decentered feminine subject retain the spirit of the nineteenth-century ideology of influence, though no latter-day feminist intends to mystify women's "fetters" in the old-fashioned way. Friedman's hope of basing another kind of self-inscription in women's culturally conditioned "interdependent existence" seems to me to continue the kind of endeavor to reconceive a feminine heroism that I trace in Eliot's and Woolf's works. Those bound to live in others might gain an insight that transforms the chains and fetters into the preconditions of a more authentic and pervasive heroism.[3]

Eliot's and Woolf's most honored characters, female or male, emulate an ideal of self-sacrificing, altruistic, or—taking the essentializing risk that these authors take—feminine heroism, either as anonymous vessels of the common life or as near-legendary shining ones. These characters' spectacular vanishing acts succeed in commanding our reverence—Eliot's and Woolf's novels are read seriously—but if we for a moment imagine the authors as impresarios on stage touting silence and suffering and incurable stage fright, we can see the incongruity of the performance. Of course, the great women of letters never

---

[3]Too often, the benefits of alternative concepts of the self and of heroism have misled reformers. No one should postpone any effort to remove material and practical chains because of the conditioned strengths of the chained.

have recourse to the bullhorn; their narrators like their heroines appear self-effacing, though Eliot's narrators are willing enough to speak for us all. But the gap between the understood authorial origin—the famous woman—and the textual doctrine of selflessness is most instructive.

A nineteenth-century model of feminine heroism, based on the ambiguity of the term "selflessness," shapes the characterization in Woolf's as well as Eliot's novels, I would argue, though many would prefer to emphasize in these works the heroism of anger and resistance. As evidence *against* my claim that the heroic is diverted to selfless ends in these novels, one might highlight the demonic rage and desire in Maggie, Mrs. Transome, Gwendolen, or the Alcharisi, and the sinister egotism in Hetty or Rosamond. Or add to the account of feminist resistance the facts that Rachel, Katharine, Mrs. Dalloway, Mrs. Ramsay, Sara Pargiter, and Isa all preserve a fierce chastity of inner life, and Lily, Orlando, and Miss La Trobe refuse to trade in sympathy. Yet interdependent existence is ultimately affirmed for each of these characters; if anything, it is more enforced in Woolf's fiction, as her permeable characters have only moments rather than chapters to reign as the queen in exile.

Although Woolf attempts to slay the Angel in the House, she turns around and hooks up life-support systems to keep that Angel alive for the sake of counter-individualist and historically evocative fiction. "Feminine" heroism, the standard for both male and female characters in Eliot's and Woolf's works, emphasizes interrelation, living for others as the notorious Angel does, forfeiting the spectacle, the credit, the excitement. Feminine heroism arises when an exceptional individual paradoxically, perhaps even boringly, becomes most representative of a social group: the heroine or hero earns quiet honor by subsuming her or his self in the common life.

Obviously, the idea of heroism raises recalcitrant gender questions. Both male and female characters are being held to a selfless, feminine ideal (McKee 25–26), yet their deeds can only be deemed heroic if they affect the public sphere in some way. Lee R. Edwards, in order to make way for the "female hero," redefines heroism as any action, by women or men, that strives toward an impersonal end in some form of knowledge or love, an end that "brings about a change from an old idea of community to a new ideal" (Edwards 11–13; compare Pearson and Pope 13). Although this definition has the advantage of opening careers to female talent, it alerts us to the difficulty for women to meet this criterion, if they are conventionally defined as incapable of striving for impersonal, grand, or public goals (Holtby 52–53). Indeed, Edwards arbitrarily designates as a mere "heroine" any female protagonist who lapses into the private, non-militant life (Edwards 16, 95).[4] The idea of community and public influence does seem inseparable from the idea of feminine heroism, at the risk of forfeiting femininity. If a female character abandoned the private sphere to engage herself not to one man but to society and public welfare, the disruptive potential would be great indeed. Such is the potential that Eliot tentatively explores in *The Spanish Gypsy* and *Romola*, significantly choosing remote historical settings and at the same time stressing the heroines' voluntary loyalty to patriarchal tradition. In sacrifice to a collective identity, Eliot's and Woolf's heroines may expand the merely local and domestic contours of their lives and find some form of public influence not incompatible with the prescribed privacy and anonymity of women.

After briefly considering some of the ways canonical nineteenth-century novels conceive of a heroic selflessness applicable not only to female characters, I focus in this chapter on the emblematic contrasts between sisters and brothers in *The Mill on the Floss* and *Between the Acts*, the resurgence of Antigone as heroic prototype in several texts, the transformation of living women artists into fictional heroines (like the portraits of lady reformers), and finally the pressure on individual characters to fuse with the "many" in *Middlemarch*, *Jacob's Room*, *Mrs. Dalloway*, and *To the Lighthouse*. Each of these instances reveals various means of working miracles in fetters: infiltrating the public sphere with feminine influence, achieving celebrated selflessness, or obscuring oneself in the common life for the growing good of the world.

Feminine Heroism: Some Definitions

When Eliot and Woolf, like many Victorian and later novelists, single out a female character for a privileged role, they generally obey the provisos of the realist tradition: (1) that she be self-effacing; (2) that her ambitions fail, apart from succeeding in marriage and influence; (3) that she be poor, homely, plainly dressed, an orphan, or humbled in

---

[4]The advantages of a gender-neutral term "hero" seem outweighed by the disadvantages of isolating female characters who do not behave with proper self-determination as "heroines," a kind of lesser, third sex. I prefer to imagine a rejuvenated term, "heroine," freed of its diminutive connotations yet affirming difference. My intention is not to erase the history of salutary attempts to deny difference in *moral* responsibility; Wollstonecraft and others needed to shatter a double standard by which a heroine's virtue might consist simply in her chastity (Kirkham 19).

some other way; (4) that she be intelligent, sensitive, and talented, but a thorough amateur (or else that she fail as in [2]); and (5) that she be representative of many, of a collective experience, while remaining in private life.[5] One kind of heroine, a favorite in romance and popular fiction, has every advantage; she may be a beacon illuminating a text— "handsome, clever, and rich" like Austen's Emma—but she should also learn humility, so that she does not outshine those who suffer more under the common burden of womanhood. Austen provides another model for the heroine, at the opposite extreme from that of Emma: that of Fanny Price, without commanding charms but with the self-sacrificial "heroism of principle" (*Mansfield Park* 265, in Butler 247; compare Little Dorrit).

Charlotte Brontë undoubtedly made the most of this second type, letting us see the superwoman lurking in the mild-mannered nobody. The extreme privacy of such heroines seems not to have satisfied other novelists, who repeatedly sought to carve out a sphere of action in which ordinary women—albeit almost exclusively ladies of some leisure and education—might figure as more than mere pawns of history. In this third, more middling type of heroine, we see a woman of somewhat uncommon endowments stepping into that semi-public arena, the represented world of the novel, with its select social and domestic scope and its implied general public (primarily subscribers to the lending libraries) who nevertheless read in the privacy of home. As amateur prototypes of the social worker, such heroines could challenge men's predominance in history and culture. Gaskell's Margaret Hale, Dickens's Esther Summerson, not to mention Romola, Dorothea Brooke, Mary Datchet, or Eleanor Pargiter, offer instances of the limited but deeply benevolent effect hoped for from such ladies. But at what might seem their most heroic strain, when they display power rather than insinuate influence, heroines violate the code that has determined the feminine heroic ideal. How heroines (or women writers) may overreach their sphere yet do "homage to the convention" of feminine "anonymity" is then the challenge, as Woolf indicates in *A Room of One's Own*.

It could be argued that "publicity" has been "detestable" (RO 52) in male *or* female characters in realistic fiction: that the humbleness of common life is especially favored regardless of any gender ideology. Yet any reader can perceive that something more is expected of female

[5]Terry Eagleton notes the double bind of realist fiction (which parallels the double role of these representative individuals): "caught . . . between its local persuasiveness and generalizing force," such fiction-that-might-be-history must provide plausible details that do not deny its exemplary status (19).See McKee 3–50.

representatives of the common life: a specially enforced privacy and yet a specially interdependent social duty. Male characters in the novel tradition have frequently offered humble instances of heroism (e.g., the Vicar of Wakefield, Waverley). But there have been many grander heroes who distinguish themselves on the public stage of history. The model of the Carlylean Great Man, unlike the feminine model I am examining, cannot be adapted to either sex without severe alterations (N. Auerbach, *Woman and Demon*, 4; Edwards 14, 20). The plausible heroine must compromise with the demands of domestic life; if like Mrs. Jellyby she too zealously takes up the cause of Borrioboola-Gha, she becomes a slattern who neglects her home and family.

The typical nineteenth-century heroine faces a strange form of private life in which her selfhood or individuality is publicly suspect: she must learn to suffer in secret, while at the same time she must appease an intense communal interest in defining her, usually as a term of exchange in marriage or gossip (Homans 251–76). Molly Gibson, in Gaskell's *Wives and Daughters*, discovers that to move freely about town even on a mission to rescue her friend is to forfeit her reputation; she is finally most heroic when serving unobtrusively in the sickroom. For heroines more than for heroes, self-determination becomes associated with sexual transgression—female chastity is still the underlying concern in the nineteenth- as in the eighteenth-century novel—but romantic error may be forgivable if suitably converted to altruism. A figure like Dickens's Lady Dedlock, hiding her past love even as the newspapers inspect her smallest movements, offers a sinister exemplum at another extreme from Molly Gibson; her ill-gained eminence as well as her outlived passion are punishable by death. But when we are privy to her motherly self-sacrifice, her scarcely retraceable wanderings, we forgive her.[6]

In keeping with what we might call the commandments of anonymity and collectivity, Eliot devises an all-purpose excuse for her aspiring heroines: their representative or "common" failure. Nowhere is this strategy more brilliantly displayed than in *Middlemarch*. Here the narrator informs us that heroic women must fall "unwept into oblivion" (though the novelist teaches us to weep). The community asserts its right to interpret the secret motives of any woman who in the least sets herself apart from her kind: the "many Theresas . . . alternated between a vague ideal and the common yearning of womanhood; so that the one was disapproved as extravagance, and the other con-

[6]Lady Dedlock is not so much the heroine of *Bleak House* as Esther is, of course, but since mother and daughter are frequently mistaken for each other, they seem avatars of the same feminine principle.

demned as a lapse." So defined, female heroism becomes extremely difficult to detect, since to "common eyes" a woman who attracts notice has probably lost either common sense or her sense of propriety. Yet privileged readers, recognizing "spiritual grandeur," will not mistake the distinction of a heroine like Dorothea Brooke for self-aggrandizement (M 3). We smile at the slight vanity and inconsistency of Dorothea's self-denial in the scene of sharing out their mother's jewels with her sister, but we later see that her hobby of giving up has become an arduous vocation. There is nothing arbitrary in the author's decision to have Dorothea give up in the end; it is a necessity of the convention of feminine heroism that she be "absorbed into the life of another," as the crowning glory of her selfless dedication to the common life (M 611).

We should ask why the agony rather than the exploit becomes the favored mode of female heroism, and why so much is expected of heroines *because* of their lack of independent selfhood.[7] How active or how effective is the ideal, heroic woman to be? Any appearance of conscious motive—let alone the daring often expected of a hero—endangers a heroine's reputation, yet mere decorous idleness in the safe zone is decidedly unheroic and usually reserved for a heroine's foils. (Compare Jane Eyre and Dorothea Brooke to their respective Rosamonds.) Instead of narrow domesticity, Eliot would most admire the dedication of a new Saint Theresa, a heroine who fulfills a public mission rather like that of the grand old woman of letters, provided she—unlike Daniel Deronda's mother but like Romola—forgo self and honor household and cultural gods. Woolf famously repudiated the feminine heroine, but she seems to have been exceptionally intimate with her, as I have noted. The Angel in the House as Woolf describes her is precisely the Victorian heroine, but in her wifely and motherly phase, after the end of most novels:

> She was intensely sympathetic. She was immensely charming. She was utterly unselfish. She excelled in the difficult arts of family life. She sacrificed herself daily. If there was chicken, she took the leg; if there was a draught, she sat in it—in short she was so constituted that she never had a mind or a wish of her own. . . . Above all . . . she was pure. ("Professions for Women" 59)

Woolf hints that this creature of fiction has been impossible to kill: "It is far harder to kill a phantom than a reality. She was always creeping

[7]Pearson and Pope anachronistically claim that "the female hero does not martyr herself for others," while they note the actual selfishness of the traditional "helpmate." "Undertaking a heroic quest to discover the true self" is paradoxically less selfish (14).

back when I thought I had despatched her" (60). Specifically, she must slay her in order to gain her own independence as a writer, but in other respects she wishes to revive Angels of the past who transposed the selfless virtues *out* of the house.

We have seen that Eliot and Woolf share with many Victorians an expectation that moral guidance will emanate from womanhood, a hampered but vital source.[8] Women's forced specialization in domesticity was transformed into a socially redeeming vocation by writers as diverse as Harriet Martineau and Sarah Ellis. Martineau, calling for genuine female learning, also urged the lesson of humility: "Let [woman] be taught that she is to be a rational companion to . . . the other sex . . . that her proper sphere is *home*." Having mastered the domestic arts, some exceptional women may, without agitating "the cause of Woman," join the ranks of public servants and great thinkers (91–93, 82–83). Ellis maintained that humble benevolence rather than knowledge was the aim of the cultivation of women: "The most servile drudgery may be ennobled by the self-sacrifice, the patience, the cheerful submission to duty, with which it is performed"; through unobtrusive example, women thus may raise "the *moral* character of the nation" (her emphasis; 38–42).[9]

Edward Bulwer-Lytton adapts Ellis's woman's-mission line to the realm of literary culture; women "are the great dictating portion of the reading world," and must use their "influence" "nobly" rather than debasing art and the artist to the level of drawing-room entertainment.

> With women, whose organization renders them so susceptible to new impressions—who are ever prone, when their emotions are deeply roused, to forego and forget self—who, in all great revolutions of mind . . . are the earliest to catch the inspiration and lead on opinion—with women it will always rest to expedite and advance

[8]Victorian writers on the woman question define an ideal that was still resonating for Woolf in the 1920s and 1930s, much as she tried to silence it. In the controversy over the "New Woman" in the 1890s (Jordan 19–20) and the furor over the suffrage movement from the 1890s till the Great War, the tone of the debate changes, as a new kind of female heroism, forthright and aggressive, comes before the public.

[9]Martineau, though anxious to suppress women's "self-exaltation," rejects the Ellis doctrine of noble drudgery: "If 'great thoughts constitute great minds,' what can be expected from a woman whose whole intellect is employed on the trifling cares . . . to which the advocates for female ignorance would condemn her?" (91–93). Ellis explicitly narrows the sphere of feminine greatness: "A high-minded and intellectual woman is never more truly great than when . . . performing kind offices for the sick; and much as may be said . . . in praise of the public virtues of women, . . . a response would be heard throughout the world, in favour of woman in her private and domestic character" (42).

the career of Social Reform. (quoted in Helsinger, Sheets, and Veeder 3: 8)

Susceptible, prone, impressionable, emotional, women may yet form the vanguard of history according to this view, but only as a mass, not as self-defining individuals—as readers and hostesses, not as authors. The individualism of Martineau's program for women's progress—go out and show what you can do on your own—certainly seems to have been the exception among the Victorians, though common enough among successful women then and now. Generally, women are portrayed as an anonymous, collective influence on history, embodying rather than directing change—if they are not figured as a conservative mass to resist change of any sort.

But what is heroism if not an active differentiation from the common mass? Eliot and Woolf seem attuned to a potential ambiguity in any form of the heroic: a conflict between desired recognition—without which it is no heroism in effect—and the dangers of egotism or of the refusal to share recognition with fellow beings. *Utterly* unsung heroism is a contradiction in terms, just as greatness must be named in at least *one* narrative to be known as such. The favored compromise in realistic fiction is that the protagonist's public fortunes not be great, and that the recognition come from readers more than from the community within the narrative. Thus Eliot articulates a well-established tradition when she insists on the literary eligibility of the Rev. Amos Barton, though she deliberately carries it further than most in choosing a middle-aged, married, clerical gentleman. "Depend upon it, you would gain unspeakably if you would learn with me to see some of the poetry and the pathos, the tragedy and the comedy, lying in the experience of a human soul that looks out through dull grey eyes, and that speaks in a voice of quite ordinary tones" (SCL 42).

The point of demonstrating Barton's significance is that he is *common*, one of many. Doing without the opium of Romantic egotism, according to Eliot, will earn us the more widespread infusion of the heroic in the everyday. Woolf's vision of the "semi-transparent envelope" of vital experience may be less flattering to any one center of self, but the Romantic gleam still shines upon the commonplace, perhaps all the stronger for being impersonal. According to Woolf's theory at least, consciousness is no respecter of persons. It is not the novelist's task to evoke sympathy for dull grey eyes, but to dignify the slightest impressions concentered on any ordinary being like Mrs. Dalloway. In practice, however, Mrs. Dalloway displays heroic gifts of sympathy; her ordinary day is full of poetry and pathos, tragedy and comedy.

The opium of personal glory proves to be a literary addiction more or less irresistible. Adam Bede, not Amos Barton, sets the pattern that Maggie, Romola, Felix, Dorothea, and Daniel follow (Silas is the only protagonist in the novels who conforms to the wholly unobtrusive Barton model). These are heroic creatures of extraordinary eyes and voices, clearly differentiated from the common mass. Like Adam they make the stranger and reader "turn[ ] round to have another long look," but they remain for the most part "unconscious of the admiration" they win without trying. Adam is both Saxon and Celt, the true British ideal of the common man, though "uncommon clever" and "an uncommon favourite wi' the gentry"; he is the type to save his country: "We want such fellows as he to lick the French" (9, 13). Here we are asked to admire greatness in common form, to anticipate the historic service to be rendered by the representative commoner (one of many "such fellows as he"), and finally, to like rather than envy or resent the unpretending one who is singled out for centrality in the text.

Woolf too preserves heroism from the triumph of the commonplace, singling out rarities. Yet she presents the one-among-many with less fanfare than Eliot does, indeed with considerable irony toward greatness, and she allows a heroine to assert her self as equivalent to a man's. In *Mrs. Dalloway*, the famous motorcar in Picadilly seems an empty vehicle that the worshipful crowd fills with tenor or meaning. "But there could be no doubt that greatness was seated within; greatness was passing, hidden, down Bond Street, removed only by a hand's-breadth from ordinary people"; it must be the immortal "majesty of England." Mrs. Dalloway, an ordinary mortal, decides that it is the Queen inside (23), yet she herself seems to embody the greatness that people vainly try to locate in the motorcar. She is a heroine to her maid, who takes Mrs. Dalloway's "parasol . . . like a sacred weapon which a Goddess, having acquitted herself honourably in the field of battle, sheds" (43–44). Such epic similes recur throughout, affirming through comic overstatement the truth-to-life of a narrative *not* about deities and monarchs, and at the same time revitalizing the possibility that greatness passes by us, hidden, all the time.[10]

Clarissa, with a gifted susceptibility to others yet an "indomitable egotism" scarcely admitted among Victorian heroines, has a queen's

---

[10]Many have noted the affinity of Woolf's mock-epic with *Ulysses*. See DiBattista, "Joyce, Woolf, and the Modern Mind"; Richter.

dignity though her private life is exposed to our scrutiny. She silently defends her own equivalent center of self against Peter Walsh's masculine assertion: "But I too, she thought, and, taking up her needle, summoned, like a Queen whose guards have fallen asleep and left her unprotected . . . so that any one can stroll in and have a look at her . . . summoned to her help the things she did; the things she liked . . . her self, in short, . . . to come about her and beat off the enemy." She plies her needle as he clasps his pocketknife in a parody of heroic "battle" (as well as of gender oppositions; 65–67).

Gender oppositions seem doubly reinforced by most conventional presentations of heroism, which polarize the sexes and isolate the heroic figure: the great hero kills the dragon single-handed, the great heroine, abandoned, dies for love, or variations to that effect.[11] Yet the "feminine" heroism of some male as well as female characters in Eliot's and Woolf's works emphasizes interrelation and gender indeterminacy, a kind of living *for* and *in* others. Considered schematically, Adam Bede might seem to represent the Peter Walsh camp in a conflict between forms of heroism: the unified, masculine subject, "something like the letter 'I' " (RO 103), quite antagonistic to the alternative, feminine heroism. Eliot does seem to have admired, in heroes like Adam, Felix Holt, and Daniel Deronda, a confident independence that would instantly be suspect in a heroine. Yet these heroes at the same time embody feminine heroism because of certain differences from the old epic type: their lack of personal vanity or fame; their class or religious marginality; and their function as representatives of the common people (Arthur Donnithorne, Harold Transome, and Grandcourt are the heroes' wealthy, vain, egotistical foils). Sympathetic, non-egotistical, often homosexual men in Woolf's novels share the honors and more of the agonies of such marginal heroism: Septimus Smith, Nicholas Pomjalovsky, or William Dodge, for example.

To say that many of these authors' male characters are subject to much the same standard for heroism as the females is not to deny that their novels, like canonical nineteenth-century fiction generally, also invoke the distinctive fetters of womanhood. Nor is it to say that female characters in this canon never verge on a "masculine" isolation of impregnable selfhood, but that interludes of independence prove,

---

[11]Joseph Campbell figures the dragon-slaying hero as ultimately transcending individualism, reaching an "essence" of selfhood without "separateness": "a realization of the All in the individual, . . . the Self in all. Centered in this hub-point, the question of selfishness or altruism disappears" (337, 386). This remains a gendered transcendence, however; the heroine has no myth whereby she and the universe become one.

like Jane Eyre's or Tess Durbeyfield's wanderings, to be nightmares ended the sooner the better. Many male characters, such as Dickens's Pip or Arthur Clennam, fail in their self-determined exploits, learning to become the opposite of the modern antiheroic loner; their lives, like those of Eliot's heroines, turn on a recognition of social bonds and fellow-feeling.

Instead of releasing their heroines for manly exploits as Meredith, Gissing (Heilbrun, *Reinventing*, 73), and authors of some "new woman" novels provisionally do, Eliot and Woolf constrain their central male characters to womanly agonies. Silas Marner, who seems to have helped Eliot to formulate the vocation of her most publicly eminent heroine, Romola, is the most feminine of heroes: poor, a secret sufferer, a domestic laborer at a craft once thought to be women's work, he becomes a surrogate mother and learns to feel the selfless love the Victorians associated with motherhood. After one more unconvincing attempt, in Felix, to portray a handsome, muscular hero of the Adam Bede sort (and he is punished for being too self-directed in his reforming zeal), Eliot in her last two novels favors the unambitious, sensitive, somewhat androgynous men who sacrifice ease for the love of a woman and social reform (Ladislaw) or the redemption of an oppressed people (Daniel). Egotists like Fred Vincy, and even the dedicated Lydgate, are schooled in their dependence on the community.

Woolf seems more skeptical than Eliot toward the hero-of-the-people, and apart from *Jacob's Room* (which dwells on the absence of the hero) and *Orlando* (which deconstructs the hero's masculinity), she never allows a male protagonist to dominate the text. Unlike Eliot, she endorses in many of her characters the privilege of solitary contemplation, but at the same time promotes a percipient selflessness such as Bernard's in *The Waves:* "There is no division between me and them. As I talked I felt, 'I am you.' This difference we make so much of, this identity we so feverishly cherish, was overcome" (377). Bernard has in a sense been chosen, like Daniel, to forge the unborn conscience of his race, or at least of the patterned voices in the novel. In the end, we see why the chosen one is male, as the paradigm of the heroic (male) quest falls into place. The conclusion of *The Waves* rouses Bernard to action like Tennyson's Ulysses: "It is death against whom I ride with my spear couched and my hair flying back like a young man's, like Percival's, when he galloped in India. I strike spurs into my horse. Against you I will fling myself, unvanquished and unyielding, O Death!" (383). A self-annihilation that would preserve from death all the selves that Bernard's voice has been able to assume does recall the sacrificial function of heroines like "many Dorotheas," but it takes here the form of a phallic fantasy, a one-on-one exploit. Once again, we see Woolf tolerating self-contemplation and defiant action more than Eliot does; resignation and social duty no longer hold their Victorian sway. The design of *The Waves* as a whole, however, adheres to Eliot's prohibition of egotism by creating permeable personae, "characters" without identity, existing only in patterns of speech.

Domestic Outsiders and History's Public and Private Spheres: *The Mill on the Floss* and *Between the Acts*

Admittedly, the problem of defining a feminine heroism that allows for "unfeminine" public action may derive from a false dichotomy between public and private life (MacKinnon 246–47). This distinction between spheres, a perennial favorite among apologists for patriarchal order, has been revived by feminists to account for the origins of oppression; some present-day feminists, like their forebears among Eliot's contemporaries, rely on this division as a source of women's superiority to male power brokers (Riley 2, 8–9, 80–83). But such superiority is affirmed as a possible counter-influence over society, immediately calling into question the distinction between private and public: such feminists propose extending the private-sphere mode throughout public life to cure social ills (Burton 33–37). The dilemma, which I have already raised in discussing Eliot's and Woolf's ideology of influence, is this: how can you preserve women's difference (and perhaps saving influence) if you challenge their isolation from the "historical" world? Thus many feminists find themselves clinging to a distinction of spheres that they know to be treacherous.

Eliot's contemporaries liked to believe that influence, women's self-effacing substitute for power, had to be reckoned with not simply behind closed doors; it insidiously reached into every area of historic life, affecting "revolutions" and "Social Reform," as Bulwer-Lytton maintained. Elizabeth Helsinger, Robin Lauterbach Sheets, and William Veeder note the irony that the Angel in the House often found her calling "out of the House," verging on power in the public sphere (xv). Woman's marginality could yield a kind of moral authority, but when this privilege was acted on, marginality could lose its edge and become simply an exclusion or censure. "How much practical energy of thought or overawing high mental power should the ideal woman have to fulfill her angelic role—before she oversteps its bounds and becomes a strong-minded woman?" (82)—such would have been the tacit Victorian question. Eliot and Woolf helped transform that insult, "strong-minded woman," into an honor, while remaining attached to feminine heroines who never overstep the bounds.

The strain of the private/public nature of feminine heroism is dramatically revealed in the portrayal of sister and brother in *The Mill on the Floss* and in *Between the Acts*. Two similar passages characterize heroines as domestic outsiders with an insider's knowledge of human history, apparently justifying the notion of separate spheres: women are bound more than men to the cyclical tasks of nurturing life in the home. Women are not therefore irrelevant to the public record, however; the texts suggest that the two histories, cyclical and teleological, form a counterpoint till gradually the women's theme must be recognized as dominant. In both texts, women submit to the cycles of devotional life, while they (more actively and less predictably) preserve the cultural heritage; men take sides in the successive violent struggles that mark a history conceived in terms of progress and mastery.

Eliot contrasts the experience of Maggie and Tom Tulliver as though they relive eternal differences:

> While Maggie's life-struggles had lain almost entirely within her own soul, one shadowy army fighting another, and the slain shadows for ever rising again, Tom was engaged in a dustier, noisier warfare, grappling with more substantial obstacles, and gaining more definite conquests. So it has been since the days of Hecuba, and of Hector, Tamer of horses: inside the gates, the women with streaming hair and uplifted hands offering prayers, watching the world's combat from afar, filling their long, empty days with memories and fears: outside, the men, in fierce struggle with things divine and human, quenching memory in the stronger light of purpose, losing the sense of dread and even of wounds in the hurrying ardour of action. (269–70)

Men enact the drama of historical progress, whereas women are doomed to look on and mimic real battle in repetitious emotional conflict. Yet the apparent disadvantage for the women is subtly discounted; in this passage as in the novel as a whole, the value lies with "memories and fears," not "conquests." The tamer of horses becomes a brute, honoring neither the divine nor the human; even his capacity to feel physical pain has been deadened. It is true that Maggie and Hecuba are in danger of solipsism, and Tom or Hector may momentarily have forgotten self, but "struggle," "purpose," and "action" lack true selflessness. Tom's economic competition renders him all mechanical forward drive, obeying only the law of evolutionary survival; he is doomed to reverse, to obey the recurring commands of the past that have compelled women all along. Thus the heroic Hecuba loses all her apparent irrelevance; while the man may shut out Hecuba, Hecuba is everything to him—the repressed that will return.

In *Between the Acts*, Woolf similarly contrasts a brother and a sister (and analogously, two portraits), alluding to age-old oppositions. We are invited to view the difference between Bart Oliver and Lucy Swithin as antedating even classical antiquity: they have attributes of Osiris and Isis. Such attributes correspond with the differentiation of public/masculine and private/feminine history that is emblematically represented by two opposing portraits in the patriarchal house, Pointz Hall: the one is a portrait of an ancestor, a squire whose name history records (though the novel does not utter it), the other simply a work of art, an unknown lady in a timeless sylvan scene. Brutish as Hector, the ancestor holds the rein of his tamed horse and seems to argue still that his "famous hound," Colin, deserved a place in the master's portrait and later his grave (there is no mention of the squire's nameless wife). For all his civilizing power to name and preserve, the hunter has confused the animal, human, and divine like any totem-worshipper (even the Christian minister who suppresses the dog-idol is himself "that skunk the Reverend Whatshisname").

The lady, in a more graceful dumb show than Hecuba's, leads "the eye up, down" into an ecstasy of colors that become verbs: "through . . . shades of silver, dun and rose into silence." She holds a decorative arrow rather than a rein, but she insinuates her own vision on all viewers, who may not be mastered by the ancestor's argument. The lady's uncanny influence leads in a spiraling dance as repetitive as Hecuba's and Maggie's agonies; the encounter of the gaze and the feminine image, reenacted at any moment, subverts the history of the male line in a gyre of negativity. "Empty, empty, empty; silent, silent, silent. The room was a shell, singing of what was before time was." The lady leads to "the heart of the house," as though her arrow points to the ultimate, domestic counter-history (BA 36–37). Primitive as the appeal of this goddess may be, it has nothing whatever to do with animality or with property.

In less extreme forms than these paintings, the brother and sister at Pointz Hall serve different histories: the public, teleological, and factual; and the private, cyclical, and visionary. Bart and Lucy replicate the relationship between Tom and Maggie, in one of Woolf's most direct transpositions of an Eliot text. They are Victorians in this modern novel; their childhood memories echo those of the Tullivers. Bart calls Lucy "Cindy," the "name that he had called her when they were children; when she had trotted after him as he fished, and had made the meadow flowers into tight little bunches" (BA 21). In their final moments, Tom utters "the old childish—'Magsie!' " and relives with his sister "the days when they had clasped their little hands in love, and roamed the daisied fields together," perhaps recalling "one of their happy mornings" when they "trotted along and sat down together" to fish, imagining "they would always live together" (MF 455–56, 37). Grown up, neither pair of siblings remains together in innocence of gender division. Bart is a tamer of animals, a conqueror of India, a "talk-producer" like the pictured ancestor (36). Lucy, like a more comic version of the pictured lady, leads to visionary oneness, as she rereads her Outline of History (which seems to reverse teleology by dwelling on "mammoths in Picadilly" [30]), or as she names the leaves on the pond "Europe. . . . India, Africa, America." With the Tullivers as with the Olivers, the women are allies of the novelists (while they are also the only genuine readers in the family); Maggie and Lucy preserve an ancient consciousness as the men drive destructively onward, albeit in the guise of heroes. Bart "would carry the torch of reason till it went out in the darkness of the cave," and he scoffs at his sister for her faith. But "every morning, kneeling, [Lucy] protected her vision," living in cycles (BA 204–6).[12]

The very qualities that exclude women from power render them expressive figures for the perennial emotions that seem, to the novelists, most characteristically human. Women might then take on the heroic function of salvaging "the treasure of human affections" while men fight the world's battles, as Eliot affirms in *Daniel Deronda* (159–60). The question remains whether the feminine and masculine heroic modes may be complementary in some redemptive design of history or merely antithetical. *The Mill on the Floss* and *Between the Acts* support a tragic response to this question: the male and female antagonists, though bound by shared memories and loyalties, will never come to an understanding that will reduce their differences. Yet the works also provide for a comic disruption of the tragic course. Ostracizing or silencing women like Maggie, Lucy, or Isa, men will propel themselves into catastrophe—heartless material progress or war—but in some

[12]For her the "slain shadows for ever rising again" are benign rather than sinister, perhaps in part because she is a forgotten old widow, not a young woman like Maggie or like Lucy's niece, Isa Oliver, who suffers agonies in silence.

transcendent realm, at the novel's end which seems to dissolve historical time, masculine and feminine reunite.

"In their death they were not divided," Eliot unpersuasively assures
us of Maggie and Tom. Rather, *only* in death could they be united; their
fond memories of childhood union distort what we have witnessed in
the opening chapters. Yet in the "Conclusion," all substantial conquests, including that of death, are proved ephemeral compared to the
cyclical order of loving, feminine nature: "Nature repairs her ravages,"
and the "two bodies that were found in close embrace" rest in a *visited*
tomb (MF 456–57). That Eliot should choose as epitaph David's lament
over Saul and Jonathan exposes the irresolution of gender difference
in this ending. The suggestion in Eliot's text of an incestuous embrace
is lent the sanctity of the supposedly gender-neutral undoing of the
law of the father in the Biblical passage: father and son are "not
divided" (II Samuel 1:23). But then the woman who divides men is
almost ecstatically excluded in the biblical passage, suggesting the
homosocial if not homosexual: David mourns for Jonathan, "Thy love
for me was wonderful, passing the love of women." Thus the epitaph
(which is also the epigraph of the novel), interposes patriarchal history
in Eliot's concluding pastoral idyl, but in effect it disconcerts that all-
too-confident history. "How are the mighty fallen in the midst of
battle!"—the echo of David's famous cry resonates in Eliot's text,
suggesting the vanity of men's endeavors. Maggie's love for Tom
surpasses her love for other men, but her rescue of him is also a foray
into the battlefield to prove her might against his; the love of women
(which Tom strangely avoids) triumphs over battle itself.

Woolf like Eliot posits no ready reconciliation between the gender
principles, and her novel's open-ended conclusion, like Eliot's, partially inverts the usual order by lending women to combat and men
to passion. Again, only outside the domain of everyday experience
can man and woman unite: "In real life they had never met, the long
lady and the man holding his horse" (BA 36). Isa and Giles, the
modern Maggie and Tom or Lucy and Bart, though united in marriage,
scarcely meet till their daily life is almost over, when they become
abstract figures in a tableau of instinctual woman and man. They will
fight "in the heart of darkness, in the fields of night" before they
embrace, perhaps to yield "another life," as the curtain rises on an
utterly new yet prehistoric or pan-historical drama (219). Men's battles
may triumph in the history that continues after the novel—World War
II will come as foreseen—but the cyclical conflicts of human emotions
have outlasted and will override public history. The next act of the

human play will be written by a woman; yet perhaps in spite of itself, it will still incorporate the homosocial, alluding not to the Bible but to Conrad's modernist dirge for imperialism.

If the antagonistic coupling of feminine and masculine principles represented in *The Mill on the Floss* and *Between the Acts* is typical of these authors' conception of men's and women's roles in history, it may seem less clear than ever how they allow for women's heroic intervention in the tragic course of the common life. The deadly embrace seems perhaps the most private of moments, having little to do with the public record—or so the conventional historian, the slave of documents, has had to assume. But the texts just considered also show the interdependence of the spheres: Eliot and Woolf furnish missing documents for a history of private experience that they assume has urgent public bearing. Maggie and Lucy, however impulsive or "batty," offer a profound reading of history by being unfit for their own times. With their passionate loyalties to the past they preserve a common faith, reviving the legends of St. Ogg's or Saint Lucy and Saint Swithin.[13] If they are martyred—ostracized or laughed at—because of their rare fidelity to passions buried in history, so be it; the heroines' influence overcomes apparent subordination.

These heroines suffer because they are misrepresented by prejudiced generalizations, but it is their own rare capacity to generalize a universal heritage that distinguishes them in the first place. Though "the world's wife" summarizes Maggie's moral conflict as a fall, and she is treated by men as though she were a common "bar-maid," *she* is singularly heroic in her "adherance to obligation, which has its roots in the past" (428–35). Similarly, Lucy is misread as a simple-minded old Christian widow in an atmosphere of prejudice, whereas she is exceptionally attuned to the novel's affirmation of collectivity amid diversity. Jews, idiots, and foreigners are "part of ourselves," we learn between the acts: "If we don't jump to conclusions . . . perhaps one day, thinking differently, we shall think the same?" (194–200). If "wide fellow-feeling" (MF 435) is the benevolent inverse of sweeping preju-

---

[13]The fictitious legend of Saint Ogg, like the epitaph in Eliot's novel, veers from its ostensible mark (MF 104–5). Maggie is perhaps the madonna rescued from the flood by the ferryman, but in the event, she is also the ferryman. Wiesenfarth traces the legend of Saint Ogg to that of Saint Christopher in Anna Jameson's *Sacred and Legendary Art* (*Notebook* 61–62, 185–86). The stress on Lucy Swithin's eyes and umbrella hints at the image of Saint Lucy bearing her eyes in a dish and the legend that Saint Swithin's day (July 15) determines the weather for the next forty days. In both cases the heroines are associated with the idea of sacred power as well as martyrdom, while both also have a darker side: Maggie is witchlike, Lucy sibylline. "Lucy," in Eliot's text, is the rival of the Magdalen, Maggie.

dice, it too can be rather hard on any single heroic figure. Characters in *Between the Acts* form constellations, none standing out like the tragic star, Maggie.

In spite of the cruelty of generalization, then, both works imply that a humanitarian ethics must affirm wide fellow-feeling and our common rootedness in the past. In full recognition of all human histories, we transcend self-love, and scarcely regret individual suffering and death. Further, we can celebrate the heroic sacrifice that promotes the common weal in subtle ways; Maggie and Lucy may not change the acts of Parliament, but they rule between the acts, as outsiders inside the gates. This is not the complete story, however; the novels also reveal the justified rage and rebellion of female individuals compressed into feminine forms.

The selfless influence and the rage don't seem to go together; what Eliot divides between her heroine's womanhood and childhood, Woolf divides between the aunt and her niece Isa (as Maggie pounds her fetish in the attic, Isa imagines the girl in the Whitehall barracks hitting the rapist with a hammer). Perhaps the division is necessary to allow for progress. Maggie's unruly potential in childhood carries forward to times of greater opportunity for women in Eliot's present and beyond, when adulthood might not mean complete self-suppression. Isa, though stifled, can be a forthright antagonist: "the age of the century" (19), she poses a more independent challenge to men than the saintly Victorian, her aunt, ever did. As though speaking to all warmongers, she silently taunts Giles: "No . . . I don't admire you. . . . Silly little boy, with blood on his boots" (111). This defiance does not assuage Isa's masochistic woe, nor does it free her from her duty to weep "all people's tears" (180). Fettered, self-sacrificing womanhood seems to instruct the patriarchal worlds of these fictions in the generalized fellow-feeling that alone can lead humanity out of brutish conflict. But angry individuals, defying the maxims of gender, threaten to break the vessel of human affections or to expose its emptiness: "A vase stood in the heart of the house, alabaster, smooth, cold, holding the still, distilled essence of emptiness, silence" (BA 36–37).

The *Antigone* and Its Moral

Eliot's and Woolf's works frequently pose feminine heroism as a means of overcoming the exaggerated division between spheres or genders, though this heroism itself paradoxically confirms the maxims of gender. Even as heroic characters work miracles of reconciliation, they raise the troubling question: can we do without the fetters that bind the feminine? Women's education for suffering has sometimes been seen as a cause for celebration, as well as a source of vengeful strength. When Adrienne Rich exalts the endurance of women under a relentless catalogue of abuse ("Compulsory Heterosexuality and Lesbian Existence"), she represents only a more Amazonian version of the division of labor between men and women that we have just seen in *The Mill on the Floss* and *Between the Acts*. Instead of dwelling on female suffering and covert resistance, others envision women's readier access to a disruptive libidinal energy. Thus Luce Irigaray sounds a familiar note when she celebrates this-sex-which-is-not-one, with its fluid, speechless, elusive currents subverting masculine discourse[14]; Rachel Vinrace's escape from heterosexual conquest into madness and death and Isa Oliver's watery poetic soliloquys take part in this subversive but still sacrificial mode. It is not certain that a miraculous abdication of patriarchal rule would eliminate the demand for such feminine heroism, which offers a diffusion of identity in a collective resistance to tyranny.

Besides the dilemma of reaffirming the maxim of selfless femininity—do we have *everything* to lose *without* our chains?—there is the other dilemma central to my redefinition of heroism, that of attributing *individual* greatness to selfless martyrs. One feature of these authors' treatment of heroism evades this second dilemma by sidestepping the common and in a sense history itself, perpetuating an aristocratic myth of archetypal individuals. In the story of Antigone both authors found their ideal heroine, a martyr to the irreconcilable difference between a private law—the obligation rooted in the past that Maggie honors—and the public law of patriarchy. Here the classic conflict is purged of the circumstantial detail that would make a modern martyr appear a selfish fool; a solitary woman directly challenges and foils the king, leaving her mark on the state as few real women ever have. Both authors mute one obvious reason for their attraction to Antigone, the fact that she is almost the only heroine of antiquity who is neither a violent egotist like Medea nor a passive victim like Alcestis, but who acts on principles that seem to her universal.

In her essay "The Antigone and Its Moral," Eliot lauds Sophocles' tragedy as an evocation of perennial human nature; the heroine, like an ancient precursor of Maggie Tulliver, dies of "the antagonism

---

[14]*Jouissance* may be less quiescent than Victorian bloom, and its theorists proclaim its nonessentialism, but it is another concept that affirms the ineffable superiority and retributive power of an ahistorical femininity (Irigaray, "This Sex Which Is Not One" and "The 'Mechanics' of Fluids," *This Sex*, 23–33, 106–18).

between valid claims," the "collision" between "the impulse of sisterly piety" and "the duties of citizenship." Eliot is peculiarly oblivious here to the dynamics of gender in the tragedy, just as she is insistently even-handed in reading its "moral":

> Wherever the strength of a man's intellect, or moral sense, or affection brings him into opposition with the rules which society has sanctioned, *there* is renewed the conflict between Antigone and Creon; such a man must not only dare to be right, he must also dare to be wrong. . . . Like Antigone, he may fall a victim to the struggle, and yet he can never earn the name of a blameless martyr any more than the society—the Creon he has defied, can be branded as a hypocritical tyrant. (265)

As Thomas Pinney points out, "There is an intense personal note" here (261), but the woman author who still respected the ideal of the female "blameless martyr" refused to specify the hypocrisy of men's tyranny over women; instead, she insists on the universal relevance of the story to the struggles of *men* of conviction. The possibilities for a modern woman's tragedy along these lines did not, however, escape Eliot. Romola poses with her father for a painting of Antigone and Oedipus, and as though petitioning Creon, she pleads with Savonarola to save her godfather (K. Chase 307, 311). Dorothea is likened to "a sort of Christian Antigone," and the novel analyzes the way in which this "new Antigone" is mismeasured and thwarted by "the rules which society has sanctioned" (M 141, 612).

Eliot cautiously adopts Antigone as a type of female heroism in the fiction but as a universal model for "man" in the essay, in striking contrast with Irigaray's conviction that the myth is "a 'feminist' fable" that undermines "the teleology of Oedipus within his own family" (Burke 300). In Irigaray's Derridean vision, the law of the father (or uncle) is indisputably a hypocritical tyrant. Though it seems true, as Gillian Beer claims, that "the myth which meant most to George Eliot was that of Antigone, resisting the authority of the king-uncle" (*Eliot* 54), Eliot no more than Sophocles sided entirely with the resistance: she did not prevent her resisting heroines from being buried alive. The sanction of the patriarch retains some of its ethical authority for Eliot, in spite of her portraits of misogynist, benevolently incompetent patriarchs like Bardo, Mr. Tulliver, Mr. Brooke, or Sir Hugo Mallinger. The author appears to share some of Dr. Kenn's nostalgia when, in comforting the fallen Maggie, he recalls that society once resembled "a family knit together by Christian brotherhood under a spiritual father" (432). What is most urgently longed for in such a dream of community is the clear function of the woman; Eliot reveals a lingering wish that "a new Antigone will spend her heroic piety in daring all for the sake of a brother's burial" (M 612). That a new Antigone might rather defy her brother for the sake of her own fulfillment, as Eliot had done, would be a personal note, not to be publicly uttered, of defiance against patriarchal tyranny.

In keeping with a twentieth-century willingness to air the defiantly personal voice, Woolf's reading of the *Antigone* is closer to Irigaray's than is Eliot's. Sophocles' portrait of Creon is an "instructive analysis of tyranny," Woolf writes; the play outlines the difference between "unreal" and "real loyalties" through "Antigone's distinction between the laws and the Law" (TG 81). Here we know whose side we are on, yet there is also an urge to universalize the myth as Eliot did, avoiding the particular grievances of the heroine's story. Woolf avows that one is "impressed . . . by heroism itself, by fidelity itself" in the *Antigone;* "the stable, the permanent, the original human being" is to be found in the Greeks, whose characters "behave in . . . the way in which everybody has always behaved" ("On Not Knowing Greek," CE 1: 4; see *VW Diary* 4: 257). Yet to revive Antigone in a contemporary context cannot simply serve the purpose of congratulating ourselves on our universal humanity; in the usual view, "the original human being" has "always behaved" according to a masculine, European norm. As Eliot shows in her story of the Christian Antigone, there is something especially poignant in the struggle of an exceptional woman faced with competing claims, when her very womanhood has been defined as a responsiveness to others' claims.

Woolf's evasive talk of "heroism itself" and Eliot's reference to the man who dares to be both right and wrong each occur in a discussion of a classic written in a language that the women had had to learn on their own; their impersonal stance as well as their learning inevitably have an aspect of making up for the difference of womanhood. Yet in *Three Guineas* even more explicitly than in *Middlemarch,* the new Antigones behave not just like "everybody," but like the nineteenth-century feminists struggling for rights: "They wanted, like Antigone, not to break the laws, but to find the law," substituting their own principles for the patriarchal rule that pretends to eternal validity (TG 138). This is as utopian as Dr. Kenn's Christian brotherhood, but unlike Dr. Kenn, the women of letters also recognize the inevitability of a clash between the woman and the patriarch. Eliot and Woolf appeal to something unchanging in woman's nature that heroically challenges the patriarchal law, an absolute that questions absolutes.

Both authors conceive this feminine heroic ideal as tragic—patriarchy appears to win—but the cumulative effect of many Antigones in the narrative of history may be a qualified comic progress.

Dorothea, buried alive in Casaubon's labyrinth like an Ariadne or Antigone, escapes to a more useful if disappointing role as the wife of a reformer of laws. It is pleasant to suppose that Eliot envisions a resurgence much like the rebirth of "Shakespeare's sister": Dorothea perhaps becomes the mother not only of the heir to Brooke's estate but also of a daughter ("two cousins" are said to visit Celia's children) who, like one of Woolf's Victorian Antigones, would "spend her heroic piety" in the women's cause in the 1860s and 1870s (M 612). Later Antigones of course also would be stifled; the captivity of a Pargiter daughter, in the "1907" episode of *The Years*, again suggests comparison with the ancient story. Sara reads her cousin's translation of "The Antigone of Sophocles" while her mind dwells on heartbreak and being "buried alive" (Y 135–37). Yet the historical outline of the modern novel registers a progressive escape from Victorian entombment, as the Pargiter women in later years find spheres of independent action undreamed of by Dorothea.

Heroines Drawn or Withdrawn from Life

If Antigone represents the heroic ideal that Eliot and Woolf are most attracted to, how can they reconcile this ideal with their pledges to portray the common life as truthfully as possible? Is the idea of a modern Antigone fantastic, given that, as Eliot puts it, "the medium in which [Antigone's and Saint Theresa's] ardent deeds took shape is forever gone" (M 612)? In fiction, the age of miracles might not be dead, but realistic heroines are meant to work miracles not by grand deeds but by spiritual resistance to a petty medium. Martyrs and tyrants in realistic narrative generally find no clearly opposing causes. Indeed, the authors postpone the benefits of women's self-sacrifice, deflating the idealistic hopes of the characters for the sake of a more realistic promise for the readers. The historical effect of fettered womanhood is portrayed as miniscule, but in Eliot's words, it is "incalculably diffusive."

When Eliot and Woolf chose to represent moderately successful heroines, they took care to moderate the success that some real women of their own day, including themselves, had achieved. Eliot and Woolf avoided direct self-portraiture in part because their own escape into artistic freedom seemed improbable if not inadmissible. To portray women who became public figures without sacrifice would have seemed the kind of wishfulness that Eliot found in "silly novels," or an evasion of "life as we have known it," in Woolf's terms. Perhaps even more important than plausibility, however, may have been the desire to represent that special efficacy earned by feminine self-denial. Thus, in two unusual instances in which heroines are drawn from life, Eliot and Woolf used as models strong-minded women near them who attempted a reconciliation of domestic and artistic demands, but they altered the terms of these women's success in favor of selfless influence. In the process of transcription, the self-assertion of the women whom Eliot or Woolf admired and loved must yield to the ideal of miracles in fetters; ambition and romance plots are severed and women are divided against each other, making them serve competing functions that might be united in life. The point is not to affirm that these novelists were captives of representationalism or to expose *romans à clef*, but to emphasize the conventions of feminine heroism that censored the models' actual self-determination. The transformations of Barbara Bodichon into Romola and of Vanessa Bell into Katharine Hilbery mark a process of effacement not unlike the development of Eliot's and Woolf's own impersonal narrative personas.

As I mentioned in Chapter 1, Eliot based her portrait of Romola on her close friend Barbara Leigh Smith, painter, educator, feminist reformer, who in effect accepted an annual, Persephone-like exile in Algiers when she became Mme. Bodichon, but who continued to enjoy considerable independence. She shared some of Marian Evans Lewes's marginality, as an illegitimate daughter, as a successor to Marian in John Chapman's dubious affections, and most importantly as an artist and a critic of the subjection of women. The fictional heroine, Romola, shares with the living model, Barbara, mainly the notable qualities of Pre-Raphaelite beauty, moderate wealth, childlessness, and a zeal for alleviating suffering (Bradbrook 6-12); Romola does not, however, share the same degree of marginality or of successful defiance of convention as Eliot and Bodichon. Romola repeatedly resists, then capitulates to patriarchal authorities whom she eventually outlives; she ultimately triumphs as long-suffering "virgin" mother, having outgrown all personal ambition. In contrast with Romola, Bodichon never gave up her art or her activism and she remained happily married, though like Romola she expressed her solidarity with a community of women, particularly those who produced *The English Woman's Journal*. Above all, Bodichon never became transfixed as a humorless, asexual madonna exemplifying the Comtean idea of "woman as moral providence of our species."

Eliot's friendship with Bodichon was all the stronger because the latter was one of the few who accepted right away the writer's deviation from the ideal of selfless chastity in living with Lewes. Eliot wrote to Bodichon in 1859,

> I will not call you a friend—I will rather call you by some name that I am not obliged to associate with evaporated professions and petty egoism. I will call you only Barbara, the name I must always associate with a true, large heart. Some mean, treacherous Barbara may come across me, but she will only be like a shadow of a vulgar woman flitting across my fresco of St. Barbara. (*GE Letters* 3: 119)

When she later traveled to Italy, Eliot admired the image of Saint Barbara by Palma Vecchio in Santa Maria Formosa at Venice: "It is an almost unique presentation of a hero-woman, standing in calm preparation for martyrdom—without . . . pietism, yet with . . . serious conviction" (Cross 2: 177). The legend of Saint Barbara that Eliot found in Jameson's *Sacred and Legendary Art* suggests elements of the narratives of Romola and of Antigone, including captivity in a tower and defiance of the father's laws and beliefs (Wiesenfarth, *Notebooks*, 63). The living Barbara undoubtedly had very little predisposition for martyrdom; she gloated over *Adam Bede:*

> 1st. That a woman should write a wise and *humourous* book which should take a place by Thackeray.
> 2nd. That YOU *that you* whom they spit at should do it!
> I am so enchanted so glad with the good and bad of me! both glad—angel and devil both triumph! (*GE Letters* 3: 56)

The wicked triumph here may be more vicarious than egotistical; Bodichon remained a wholly dedicated friend, if a friend who enjoyed Eliot's unfeminine victory. But Eliot's foreboding that her friend might be overshadowed by an egotistical double reveals that Eliot's portrait of a living model passes through an idealizing censorship. The heroine (or the pictured saint) must be clearly distinguished from a self-willed, "vulgar woman" such as one meets in everyday life. For Eliot, the common term "friend" becomes charged with treachery—most specifically that of the friends whose loyalties evaporated when Marian Evans became that vulgar woman, Lewes's mistress. Hence the intensity of Eliot's worship of "a hero-woman," the corollary of her distrust of her own egotism (Hertz 79–83).

In a similar deflection from the complex case of a living woman artist to a fictional heroine, Woolf modeled Katharine Hilbery on Vanessa Bell. She advised Janet Case to "try thinking of Katharine [Hilbery] as Vanessa, not me; and suppose her concealing a passion for painting and forced to go into society by George [Duckworth]— that was the beginning of her" (*VW Letters* 2: 109, 400). *Night and Day* appears to reconcile the heroine's passion for work with her resistance to society by ending in a promising marriage like that of the Bells (or Woolfs), but the novel withholds the more disruptive elements of the story of Woolf's sister. Katharine's secret and abstract vocation, mathematics, is a rather pale substitute for Vanessa's public, sensual experiments in art. Like a traditional heroine but unlike Vanessa, Katharine remains under her parents' roof or in "society" till marriage. In a novel deliberately faithful to conventions, there is no hint either of the liberties Vanessa took (her marriage had already expanded beyond recognition), nor of what success Vanessa had in combining the supposedly antagonistic roles of artist and mother. Katharine like Romola clearly longs for cultural achievement, not babies (Marcus, *Languages*, 26–27); like Romola, she is allowed to escape both her father, the "uncivilized male, . . . gone bellowing to his lair" (ND 500), and the fiancé he sanctions. Unlike Romola, however, she approaches the conventional heroine's end in marriage, albeit a union in which boundaries of self seem to dissolve.

Notably, Katharine is not asked to fulfill Romola's role as "visible madonna": such arduous feminine heroism is reserved for another woman. Ralph and Katharine in the end contemplate the lighted blinds of Mary Datchet's room as though *she* were the true heroine, the woman who "has her work." They imagine "something impersonal and serene in the spirit of the woman within, working out her plans far into the night—her plans for the good of a world that none of them were ever to know" (ND 505–6). Both novels end with a static portrait of the self-sacrificing, unmarried heroine who could be preparing the way for Shakespeare's sister: Romola, in a saintly fresco, instructing the coming (male) generation in the failures of great men, and Mary, a shadow framed behind the blinds, working for feminist causes. These two-dimensional images suggest how unwilling the authors were to record the well-rounded achievements of their fellow women artists. In both instances, heroines are portrayed as having outgrown personal desires (Mary herself loved Ralph, but forfeits him to Katharine), while romance and sexuality are assigned to others in the interest of a purer ideal of feminine heroism. If we compare the forceful and brilliant Cassandra (who marries Katharine's first fiancé) with Tessa, Eliot's condescending portrait of the "kept woman" as

Florentine contadina, we may suppose that Woolf is more tolerant of female sexuality, but we should recall Tito's Dionysian allure for Romola in the beginning and Katharine's apparent lack of sexual feeling throughout.

The division between heroic women and women who marry still seems very marked in Woolf's novel. Jane Marcus offers a paraphrase of Woolf's optimistic answer to patriarchy in *Night and Day:* "Let the temples to dead men be opened to living women. . . . And not only to heroic women alone, but to women with men" (*Languages* 32). The appeal is very much the same in *Romola,* and yet in neither narrative are women with men allowed heroic achievement; it is as though the conjunction of romance and ambition in one woman were an unspeakable fantasy. Later, in *Middlemarch* and *Mrs. Dalloway* and *To the Lighthouse,* both authors tried to combine heroism and womanly fulfillment, perfecting the sacrificial ideal, yet they continued to withhold the prerogative of work from Dorothea, Clarissa, and Mrs. Ramsay. The apparently irreconcilable functions—sexuality, motherhood, social influence, creative work—still tend to be assigned to diverse female characters, as they are so divisively in *Daniel Deronda* and *Between the Acts.* In spite of moments of communion between women, the functions of artists, wives, mistresses, mothers scarcely coincide in these fictions, though in real life they might be united in one person.

If Eliot and Woolf had wished to grant their heroines the full scope of the women they admired and loved in life, they might for once have shown how flimsy the barriers between men's and women's fields of endeavor could be, even when women accept the traditional duties of wife *or* mother (neither Bodichon nor Bell fulfilled both duties, any more than Eliot or Woolf did). Perhaps instead the authors were more interested in weighing women's fetters and thus enhancing the secret heroism that works miracles in spite of them.

Many Dorotheas, Jacobs, Mrs. Dalloways, and Mrs. Ramsays

As I began this chapter by suggesting, Eliot's and Woolf's conception of heroism vacillates between celebration of the rare individual and of the anonymous many, much as the heroines themselves are strained between an ideal femininity and self-fulfillment. While Eliot's and Woolf's novels single out heroines of miraculous powers, they confirm the realistic imperfection of the lives of women (that is, English ladies) in general; thus the authors generate a redemptive feminine influence on Western history by sacrificing female individuals to the multitudes, as the representative "woman" is extrapolated to "women." If "the happiest women, like the happiest nations, have no history" (MF 335), then history, these works imply, has no life but that born of unhappy women's histories. Each exceptional spirit, trapped in her general womanhood, tells a common story that becomes "part of the human gain" (TL 74). Though Lily Briscoe laughs at Mrs. Ramsay, though there are hints that Ladislaw's worship is extended narcissism and that Dorothea is quixotic, and though there is contextual justification for reading feminist protest in these texts, we should not wish away the powerful designs of desire for sacrificial "woman," for the feminine "many." Though Woolf was much more alert than Eliot to the perils of such desire, and had more reason to doubt the possibility of universal "human gain," her fiction like so many narratives before hers continues to ignite from this spark.

As we have seen, Eliot emphasizes her heroines' "common" failure, their place among "many Theresas . . . who found for themselves no epic life." Dorothea is explicitly rendered plural in Prelude and Finale as a means of clarifying her heroic role, her submission to a collective cause. Yet as I have been arguing, truly diffusive heroism is unintelligible. Thus the Prelude of *Middlemarch* opens with the story of *one* fulfilled heroine who does find "an epic life," though significantly it must be a "martyrdom," a "life beyond self."

Eliot rhetorically claims the fame of this unique story—"Who that cares much to know the history of man . . . has not dwelt, at least briefly, on the life of Saint Theresa"—as if the childhood experience of one of the few women known to history were of course a public concern (the oddity of such an opening to a novel set in Reform Era England must have been striking to first readers, most of whom, in Protestant England, had undoubtedly thought little about Saint Theresa). Secularizing hagiography, Eliot elicits the humor of childish idealism; Saint Theresa is portrayed as a happier Maggie running away from home with a dedicated, *younger* brother in a more nationalistic cause than that of joining the gypsies. We may be encouraged to "smile[] with some gentleness" at children who "toddled" toward martyrdom, but those who would laugh at all women must be severely mocked themselves. In the second paragraph, we are assured that our labors of attention to the foibles of great women have only begun: there are "many Theresas" potentially as great as the original. To reduce "blundering lives" to evidence of "the inconvenient indefiniteness" of "the natures of women," or to attempt to calculate scientifically "one level of female incompetence," is in effect to misconstrue not only women but "the history of man . . . under the varying experiments of Time." Again we encounter the criticism of generalization—look closely at the variations within women's apparent "sameness"—accompanied by the urge to generalize. If Saint Theresa were "the last of her kind," all hope would be lost. The shift from the one to the many in these two paragraphs foreshadows the shift in the course of the novel from Dorothea's role as eminent heroine with comic aspirations, to her sacrifice to Casaubon and her madonna-like rescue of Lydgate, and finally to her role as one of many Dorotheas.

Turning from the Prelude to chapter 1, we see "Miss Brooke" taking an even more commanding position than Saint Theresa. She is allowed to dominate *Middlemarch* at first, a traditional heroine as privileged as Austen's Emma. Just as the story "Miss Brooke" gave shape to the manuscript of *Middlemarch* when Eliot added it to the early chapters on Lydgate (Haight, Introduction, M xiv–xv), Dorothea herself offers reader and author an interpretive standard with which to begin. Providing both continuity and disjunction between ancient and modern, sacred and profane, she stands out like a "quotation from the Bible,—or from one of our elder poets,—in a paragraph of to-day's newspaper." Her dress, designed ostensibly to obscure herself, distinguishes her from the common run of women whose new-fashioned claims on our attention vanish into mass consumption and obsolescence like journalism. Eliot's historical art, likewise, will gain from Dorothea some of the glamor of an Italian painting of "the Blessed Virgin," accruing the unique status of a sacred text, though it also chronicles "provincial fashion" (5). The narrator later claims to choose Dorothea in emulation of Herodotus, "who also, in telling what had been, thought it well to take a woman's lot for his starting-point." Though for most purposes Rosamond would do as well (like Herodotus's Io she is "beguiled" by showy dress), we clearly must read by a subtler standard the unshowy meaning that could not have been produced by Mrs. Lemon, the provincial manufacturer of "accomplished female[s]" (71).

While the idea of the saintly, unfashionable heroine helps readers distinguish between the true lady and the bourgeois facsimile, as between the work of fine art and commercial entertainment, Dorothea is also designed to cast doubt on such distinctions, restoring faith in a collective historical life. Like the triumph of significance over indistinguishable details, like the candle that organizes the scratches on a pier-glass, Dorothea shines as heroine of Middlemarch, but on condition that she abjure such privilege. Her rare history must be absorbed into others' histories—not just Ladislaw's or Lydgate's, but all histories in our "middlemarch"—thereby (potentially) undoing the effects of privilege in a patriarchal reading of history.

Dorothea repeatedly figures as an apposite interruption of a specious historical record (today's newspaper), as well as an attractive focal point disturbing our faith in individualism. "When George the Fourth was still reigning over the privacies of Windsor, when the Duke of Wellington was Prime Minister, and Mr Vincy was mayor of the old corporation in Middlemarch, Mrs Casaubon, born Dorothea Brooke, had taken her wedding journey to Rome" (139). What could be a more poignantly comic drop in the scale of importance—king, duke, mayor, lady? What at the same time could more clearly invert the hierarchy of historical fact? The king has become a private man (in whom we have very little interest or confidence) and our heroine has taken on the importance of a public personage. Yet we have missed her over the past chapters, and resent the summary, "born Dorothea Brooke," as chilly in its way as Mrs. Ramsay's parenthetical death in "Time Passes." The heroine seems to invite such swift contractions and expansions of view, as a kind of centripetal yet centrifugal force. Her diffusive influence may influence the narrator to be diffusive, to include everything in a metonymic "particular web" (105). Yet we have seen that the woman can also function as the "make-believe of a beginning" (as the epigraph of *Daniel Deronda* puts it) and as a dwelling point for sojourners in the narrative of history.

In the Finale, at last, the heroine becomes centrifugal. The blame for missed potential no longer applies to women's "mistakes" and "bungling" but to our misperception: feminine heroism may not be "widely visible," but we should acknowledge the many "who lived faithfully a hidden life, and rest in unvisited tombs." We may deplore the loss of our favorite in her two unsatisfactory marriage plots, but should take heart that this serves a public quest. Dorothea, one of "many Dorotheas," becomes an originator like Saint Theresa, yielding "fine issues" for "the growing good of the world" (compare Mary Datchet), yet dispersed, "like that river of which Cyrus broke the strength, . . . in channels which had no great name." Such similes in this "home epic," like those in *Mrs. Dalloway,* suggest that the struggles of this commonplace Brooke *have* been as momentous (and literary) as those of the famous but unnamed river broken by the patriarchal hero. Dorothea will be as irrepressible, nameless, and diffuse as nature beneath men's desire for mastery and naming (608, 612–13).

Dorothea's very representativeness shifts her function from that of rare "cygnet" among ducklings to one of a great mass to be privately honored (by how vast a public audience for *Middlemarch!*). Eliot forfeits

Dorothea's historical prominence to show the woman's "effect" through "unhistoric acts," as well as to challenge our collusion in the social procedures that sacrifice women in general. Dorothea ostensibly ends without any more chance at a permanent public monument than the ambitious "huckster's daughter" dismissed in the first paragraph of chapter 1, but she helps Eliot's novel to earn a place in the gallery of the Masters who claim exalted subjects for art. Between them, failing heroine and triumphant author defy the limits set on "the natures of women" and their exclusion from patriarchal history (3–5, 611–12).

Less explicitly, Woolf's novels also challenge the priority of the heroic individual—"why always Dorothea?" (M 205)—and of the public sphere—"why always George the Fourth?" In the later historical narratives, the king's reign becomes entirely contingent to diverse consciousnesses, none of which can claim, even intermittently, Dorothea's rule over a text. Observers may try to single out a saintly Mrs. Ramsay, for instance, but she is always already one of many. What Eliot calls "the tragedy . . . of frequency" (M 144) emerges in Woolf's ironic treatment of heroic privilege and of common disillusionment, as well as in a stylistic diffusion that constantly reminds us of the competing relevancies impinging on any particular web.

The narrator in *Jacob's Room*, for instance, resembles the troubled historian of *Middlemarch*, though employing the absent *hero* as dubious starting and ending point:

> The observer is choked with observations. Only to prevent us from being submerged by chaos, nature and society between them have arranged a system of classification . . . stalls, boxes, amphitheatre, gallery. . . . There is no need to distinguish details. But the difficulty remains—one has to choose. For though I have no wish to be Queen of England—or only for a moment—I would willingly sit beside her. . . . And then, . . . how strange . . . to be a man of valour who has ruled the Empire. (68–69)

In spite of the hierarchy in this vision of society as a kind of opera house, the convenience of generalization must yield to the necessity of observing insubordinate detail. We could all be the heroines and heroes famed in history.

A favored organizing principle of literary discourse has been the heroic young man, but *Jacob's Room* demonstrates that no figure could be more elusive. Thus not only the indefinite variety of women's natures but also of men's defies scientific certitude. Narratives may hitherto have depended on an arbitrary choice of one exemplary being, but Woolf even more than Eliot chides us for avoiding the struggle with competing data. Even more than Eliot's heroine, Woolf's hero filters through others' judgments, threatening to disappear as he is revealed. Often the existence of Jacob seems to depend on the impressions of his female companions; he is sighted, for instance, by an unknown old lady, his fellow passenger in a train (the hero as seen from the point of view of Mrs. Brown, perhaps)[15]: "Nice, handsome, interesting, distinguished, well built, like her own boy? One must do the best one can with her report. . . . It is no use trying to sum people up" (31). With his death, Jacob leaves the narrative not as a martyr to human progress but as a missing signified; his effects are worse than incalculable. "Such confusion everywhere!" his mother cries in his abandoned room, holding out his empty shoes (176).

We need "a faithful picture of the daily life of the ordinary women" to "turn history wrong side out" ("Women and Fiction" 44), but can we get it? Gossips, like the judges of Dorothea in Middlemarch, "never come to a decision. . . . They would apply themselves to Jacob and vacillate eternally between two extremes." The narrator offers an exchange of superficial and contradictory comments on Jacob, and then facetiously gives up the whole ghost of realistic biographical history:

> So we are driven back to see what the other side means—the men in clubs and Cabinets—when they say that character-drawing is a frivolous fireside art, a matter of pins and needles, exquisite outlines enclosing vacancy, flourishes, and mere scrawls.
>
> The battleships ray out over the North Sea. . . . At a given signal all the guns are trained on a target which . . . flames into splinters. With equal nonchalance a dozen young men in the prime of life descend with composed faces into the depths of the sea; and . . . suffocate uncomplainingly together. . . .
>
> These actions . . . are the strokes which oar the world forward, they say.

Such strokes will annihilate Jacob, one of the many "tin soldiers" or "fragments of broken match-stick" "seen through field-glasses" (155–56). The trivialization of his fate, however, cannot genuinely undermine the narrator's confidence that the ladies' work of novel writing

---

[15]Mrs. Brown appears in print in 1924, after Jacob (1922). But the little old lady in the railway carriage had first insinuated herself in "An Unwritten Novel" (*London Mercury*, July 1920; *Monday or Tuesday*, 1921). She may also trace her ancestry to the widow discussed by Rachel and Richard in *The Voyage Out* (1915), as I suggested in Chapter 3.

("pins and needles") is far more crucial to the progress of human life than the mechanical, destructive drive of men's works.

It is "character-mongering," for instance, that can detect the "heroic" in a mild person like Clara Durrant, a minor figure who might warrant as much consideration as Dorothea: "What does it matter . . . that Clara . . . never yet had the chance to do anything off her own bat, and only to very observant eyes displayed deeps of feeling which were positively alarming; and would certainly throw herself away on some one unworthy of her one of these days unless . . . she had a spark of her mother's spirit in her" (154). Such hints of unwritten novels in *Jacob's Room* suggest that the heroine is familiar territory to the novelist, and that Woolf feels the greatest challenge in trying to individualize and characterize one of those remote tin soldiers in a world run by "banks, laboratories, chancellories" (156). Since Jacob like Clara eludes commodification by conventional character-mongers and prefers throwing himself away to becoming a fixed entity, he may perhaps thus attain to something like Clara's feminine heroism. Deconstructing Jacob has been one way to turn history wrong side out.

Having made the male subject relative to the perceptions of those around him, particularly women, Woolf might question the idea that the nature of *women* was their tendency to fail in their aspirations but to flourish in their incalculably diffusive influence: men too might follow this pattern. Yet Woolf cherishes the possibility that women have a privileged access to the epic life in a secret form of heroism. Mrs. Dalloway and Mrs. Ramsay disrupt today's newspaper like allusions to the sacred; like Dorothea, they are living poems. Variously interpreted, they influence moments of deeper communion because they are not great men but many women to many people. They may even extend their spirit to the suffering common man, as Woolf uneasily speculates in linking Mrs. Dalloway and Septimus Smith, or Mrs. Ramsay and Charles Tansley. If such figures appear too ignoble or inarticulate for a redemptive design, the fault may partly lie in our perceptions, as Eliot admonished in the Finale. What is Clarissa but a society hostess? It may seem "a pity that so substantive and rare a creature should have been absorbed into the life of another" (M 611), but in that sacrifice lies her heroism (Edwards 256–57).

Clarissa Dalloway begins as Dorothea ends up, feeling "invisible; unseen; unknown;" taking part in the "rather solemn progress with the rest of them" (MD 14). A less boastful version of Tennyson's Ulysses, she celebrates her diffusion: "On the ebb and flow of things, here, there, she survived, . . . she being part, she was positive, of the trees at home . . . part of people she had never met; being laid out like a mist between the people she knew best" (12). She responds to the story of Septimus Smith as a part of her whom she has never met (280); her sympathy is much like the redemptive faith that Dorothea extends to Lydgate. The latter-day, middle-aged "heart large enough for the Virgin Mary" (M 563) has become "affected" by illness (MD 4), and in fact rescues no one, but Clarissa has already given up the common yearning of womanhood for the sake of an impersonal ideal of influence.

Repeatedly Clarissa sacrifices herself to unify the dispersed consciousnesses of her circle. She exclaims to herself: "Why not risk one's one little point of view? . . . Life was that—humiliation, renunciation" (255). Her gift is the feminine gift of selflessness, "knowing people almost by instinct," and seeing beyond boundaries of self: "As we are a doomed race . . . let us, at any rate, do our part; mitigate the sufferings of our fellow-prisoners" (11, 117). Woolf grants her heroine more human failings than Eliot grants Dorothea; Clarissa, like Rosamond, is birdlike rather than statuesque, and she enjoys rank, fashion, and other fine ephemera (14). But Mrs. Dalloway at times has a goddess's gift, and she sustains the public life of her politician husband.

In *To the Lighthouse*, Woolf recurs to the troubling ideal of woman as martyr, woman as a kind of mist pervading the common life. As in *Middlemarch*, there is a rich texture of points of view on the heroine, the ironic treatment permitting glimpses of unalloyed grandeur. Lily Briscoe, who takes the place of Will Ladislaw and Peter Walsh as dominant observer of the heroine, interprets the beautiful mother and wife with resentment and awe. She witnesses Mr. Bankes's gazing at Mrs. Ramsay in "rapture," a disinterested, diffusive "love." Mrs. Ramsay's "sublime power" is disturbing to the lonely woman artist who disobeys the matriarch's commandment that all women "must marry" (73, 77). Though Lily sees that Mrs. Ramsay "completely failed to understand" the "destinies" she ruled, Lily also desires to worship this goddess. Mrs. Ramsay must possess

> some secret which certainly Lily Briscoe believed people must have for the world to go on at all. . . . She imagined how in the chambers of the mind and heart of the woman . . . were stood, like the treasures in the tombs of kings, tablets bearing sacred inscriptions, which if one could spell them out, would teach one everything, but they would never be offered openly, never made public. (78–79)

Lily's reluctant worship of Mrs. Ramsay as a biblical quotation in today's newspaper, as vessel of ancient, sacred consciousness, holder of the key to all mythologies, suggests Woolf's ambivalence toward an ideal of feminine heroism. In "Time Passes," Mrs. Ramsay has become part of people she has never met, part of trees and mists, though as an unsympathetic force unlike Dorothea and Clarissa. "The nights now are full of wind and destruction; the trees plunge and bend and their leaves fly helter skelter." Under such assault, language seems driven to imagine a providential memory of "woman," to reconstitute referentiality and intentionality. Nevertheless, as we have seen, Woolf shatters the mimetic order of gender: "No image with semblance of serving and divine promptitude comes readily to hand," just as "Mrs. Ramsay having died rather suddenly" eludes the outstretched arms of her husband (193–94). The particular story of a man seeking his abruptly absent wife, linked to an impersonal search for an "image with semblance" in the sea and wind, has much the effect of Eliot's Finale, asking us to relinquish our attachment to the one heroine in order to sense the fuller power of her diffused influence.

Death itself might be the lovely secret hidden in the breast of Mrs. Dalloway or Mrs. Ramsay, but also a feminine, undulating life.[16] We have seen that the restoration of the house and of life after death is left to the combined labors of obscure women, centering on one Mrs. McNab, whose song of universal woe becomes "the voice of witlessness, humour, persistency itself" (TL 196). Mrs. McNab seems to become many as she personifies the spirits of the house: "Like a yellow beam or the circle at the end of a telescope, a lady in a grey cloak, stooping over her flowers, went wandering over the bedroom wall. . . . It was too much for one woman, too much, too much. She creaked, she moaned" (205–6). The difference between Mrs. Ramsay and her servant becomes immaterial in this sublime perspective, unlike the cherished difference between Dorothea, the county deity, and Rosamond the manufacturer's daughter.

To determine the nature of an incalculable influence becomes the preoccupation at the end of To the Lighthouse as well as Middlemarch, and again competing versions of the heroine almost cancel each other

[16]The "nothingness" that drives the action of "Time Passes" (TL 190) might be the feminine without the personal. It resembles the emptiness and silence at the heart of Pointz Hall: "So loveliness reigned and stillness, . . . a form from which life had parted; solitary like a pool at evening, . . . scarcely robbed of its solitude, though once seen" (TL 195; compare the image of Mrs. Dalloway as queen glimpsed with her guard down). Lily almost consciously apotheosizes the mother figure (in terms recalling the feminine art of character drawing in Jacob's Room): "She called out silently, to that essence . . . that abstract. . . . Ghost, air, nothingness, . . . she had been that. . . . Suddenly, the empty drawing-room steps, . . . the whole wave and whisper of the garden became like curves and arabesques flourishing around a centre of complete emptiness" (266).

out. As Lily observes, "Fifty pairs of eyes were not enough to get round that one woman with" (294). When Mr. Ramsay expects Lily to reincarnate feminine influence and "sympathy," she feels the rage of the childish Maggie or thoroughly modern Isa. "That man took. She, on the other hand, would be forced to give. Mrs. Ramsay had given. Giving, giving, giving, she had died." Yet to some extent Lily yields to the sexual division of labor: "Surely, she could imitate from recollection the glow, the rhapsody, the self-surrender, she had seen on so many women's faces . . . evidently . . . the most supreme bliss of which human nature was capable" (223–25). This portrayal of feminine selflessness certainly gives and takes: the ecstasy is supreme, though fatal, at least fatal to one's independence and one's creative work. The memory of Mrs. Ramsay as ministering angel compels admiration: "It was her instinct to . . . turn[] to the human race, making her nest in its heart." But Lily expresses doubts about the compulsive self-sacrifice of the lady reformers: "This, like all instincts, was a little distressing to people who did not share it" (291–92).

The burden on individual women to represent the mass, to accept the feminine duty of altruism as if it were instinctual, was deadly indeed. Woolf allows a woman of a later generation to question such essentialism, and at least momentarily to resist the compulsion to give of herself. Yet like the narrator of *Middlemarch*, Lily still desires the ecstasy of feminine self-annihilation, standing in awe of the feminine heroine while deploring her loss. Her self-effacing dedication to art in effect is a reincarnation of the earlier woman's sacrifice in less deadly, gendered terms.

These fictions try to overcome the tension between the egotism of heroism and the selflessness of femininity by singling out the exceptional beings who dedicate themselves to the common life, and then by diffusing their identity. The dedication itself is sometimes figured as a female instinct, not a matter of vanity or ambition; even if the heroine's dedication was rare indeed, it must be honored to some extent in an impersonal way. The sacrifice within the text—the dispersal of the rare woman—substitutes for the authors' and other living women's sacrifices, making unapologetic individuality more permissible for many women. In a sense "the growing good of the world" may be due to novels such as *Middlemarch* and *To the Lighthouse* that offer up heroines as messianic representatives of common womanhood, much as scripture retells, and thus confirms, the substitution of ritual for human sacrifice. Admire or worship as we more or less consciously do, we gaze on Dorothea as a quaint figure already obsolete in Eliot's day of improving education for women, and Mrs. Ramsay as even more irrevocably buried in the pre-war, pre-suffrage past. Eliot and Woolf urge us to see their stories as indispensable to an understanding of human history, and they imply that these outsiders inside the gates govern our lives more profoundly than public rulers. Yet the authors cannot wholeheartedly wish to resurrect the feminine heroic ideal in practical terms, least of all to apply it to themselves. When it comes to the genuine Barbara or Vanessa, independent creative fulfillment cannot be denied. Complete selflessness seems possible only in the past, in some age of heroines.

5

Trespassing in Cultural History:
The Heroines of *Romola* and *Orlando*

Eliot and Woolf claim the significance of every element of ordinary life in a history less exclusive than *the* tradition of masterpieces or *the* pantheon of great men. In practice, however, their own narratives' claim to significance is based on high standards of exclusion; texts displaying such cultivated intelligence and discriminating artistry escape the brown pond of the commonplace. The prosaic traditionally calls out for the intervention of miraculous beings, what D. H. Lawrence in his "Study of Thomas Hardy" calls aristocrats: "The glory of mankind is not in a host of secure . . . citizens, but in the few more fine, clear lives, . . . individuals, distinct . . . from the public" (436). These aristocrats (who may or may not be literally of high rank) are often called on in novels to infuse the quotidian with the promise of the exceptional, of Eliot's "glorious possibilities" ("Amos Barton," SCL 42). Potentially, a view like Lawrence's (it is the Carlylean history of Great Men revisited) is disastrous for fellow-feeling and an enlightened common life—the almost unquestionable aims of culture as Eliot and Woolf conceived it. They would commend instead a feminine heroism, not the detached individual's appropriation of glory.[1]

Eliot later called possibilities "handsome dubious eggs" (M 61), exposing the fantasy inherent in aristocratic heroism, attributed most often to young men: the fantasy that the one might possibly escape

---

[1]Lawrence's relation to feminism is certainly more complex than has been implied in such indictments as Kate Millett's, as Carol Siegel and others have shown. Lawrence's meditation, in the "Study of Thomas Hardy," on an originary gender dichotomy—a self-creating male principle, "Will-to-Motion," vs. a passive female "Will-to-Inertia" (448)—gives due respect to the female, recalling the ideology of influence. But Eliot and Woolf could not endorse the manly individual's prerogatives.

the common lot of the many. Yet repugnant as such an exclusive fantasy ought to be for these women novelists, it is of course the fantasy they have realized in their own success. Not surprisingly, they do not seem content with feminine influence or the praise of an undifferentiated public. *Romola* and *Orlando* single out heroic figures exceptionally akin to the self-creating great women writers themselves, and to handsome, dubious aristocrats; they are unique, not one of many.

These romantic protagonists are freer from the "life of Monday or Tuesday," more removed from the authors' contexts, than most characters in the works of Eliot and Woolf. Romola, a fifteenth-century Florentine lady, while she responds to realistic conditions such as famine, preserves herself from the everyday almost as well as does Orlando, the magical English aristocrat who changes sex and who lives for centuries. This is certainly not the first time that the authors yield to the allure of high rank, of lords rather than loobies, as we note in such works as Eliot's "Mr. Gilfil's Love-Story" or Woolf's "The Duchess of Newcastle." Rachel M. Brownstein identifies the focus on the heroine in realistic fiction as in itself a holdover from "aristocratic romance" (xxi–xxii). Not only the exceptional protagonist but the cultivated author might figure as a kind of Lawrentian aristocrat, though without conspicuous will to power. Eliot's allegiance to the traditional role of the intellectual (never more manifest than in *Romola*) reflects her loyalty to an old order of landowning aristocracy, according to Deirdre David (167). Similarly, in *Orlando* Woolf hints at a biographical history of her own privileged place in a cultural aristocracy and parodies a learned gentleman in her narrator.

While Eliot and Woolf thus share with the protagonists of *Romola* and *Orlando* a detachment from the common life, the authors confront conflicting drives toward individuality and collectivity through these figures. The "visible madonna" and the immortal androgyne enjoy some of the supernatural privileges of romance as well as the aristocratic sense of embodying a *public* family history, yet like the other protagonists in these authors' works, they are schooled in some of the duties of feminine influence and fellow-feeling. Retaining their privilege, both protagonists also in a sense discover their womanhood by acknowledging their affinity for outsiders, for Lawrence's despised, undifferentiated masses.

Both novels, like their protagonists, are outsiders among the authors' works and in literary tradition. *Romola*, an historical novel or encyclopedic romance, spans the time from 1492 to the writer's present, 1863. In a lighter vein, *Orlando* too is a curious hybrid: a comic romance, mock biography, or literary history from 1553 to 1928.[2] Paralleling the central bildungsroman in each work are parables of the development of modern European culture and of the author's own vocation. Both protagonists are modeled on an eminent woman close to the author. Perhaps as a result, they have escaped being taken for the author's self-portrait.[3] In both instances, the heroines present a vocation more limited than that of the grand old women of letters. The very elaborateness of their disguises broadens the scope for the authors' anxious speculations on the place of the woman of vocation in patriarchal culture.

Romola and *Orlando* register public history as private experience: the solitary protagonist encounters great leaders and events, while absorbing the commonplaces, the manners and weather of the times. Conversely, the novels identify an individual's private history with that of an entire culture, for the moment supposing that these aristocrats have the unmediated access to the (imagined) inner sanctum of such a culture that few individuals, and far fewer women, have had. Thus the tales focus not on the struggle to become a "great" woman of letters, but on the inner metamorphosis—Romola's need for a feminine social vocation, and Orlando's discovery of his/her sexuality—that is a synecdoche for that struggle. Let's pretend, the novels seem to say, that the "letters" are there for the asking: Romola always has known Greek, Orlando has seen Shakespeare as a boy. Even the greatness, perhaps, is easy, if you are born into the right family at the right time. But the womanhood? In a sense this is the characteristic that these aristocrats first acquire and then attempt to transform into a meaningful calling.

Different as the novels are, both were written either to certify or to celebrate the authors' high rank as novelists, addressing fit audience though few. Famous for different styles of inscrutability, these works evade the censure that a broadcast appeal for women's access to cultural history would arouse. The authors prefer not to be caught trespassing, yet they are uncomfortable in the passive role of sightseer. They desire the glory of the one and the power to sway the many.

The Origins and Species of *Romola* and *Orlando*

In 1860, on Eliot's first trip to Italy—most-favored nation for Victorians in search of high culture—her longstanding wish to write an "Italian story" crystallized into a plan (*GE Letters* 2: 463; Bonaparte 6),

[2]In the manuscript of *Orlando*, the boyhood episode is headed "1553" (Hoffman 437).
[3]Woolf seems partly justified in grouping Romola with Janet, Dinah, Maggie, and Dorothea as a "disguised," self-conscious version of George Eliot herself ("GE" [1919]

somewhere between grave cultural study and the liberty of romance. Writing to her publishers, she took the stand of an enthusiastic scholar: "Florence, from its relation to the history of modern art, . . . has stimulated me to entertain rather an ambitious project" (*GE Letters* 3: 300). The work would focus on "Savonarola's career and martyrdom. Mr. Lewes has encouraged me . . . , saying that I should probably do something in historical romance rather different in character from what has been done before" (*GE Letters* 3: 339; the subject appears to have been Lewes's suggestion [3: 295]). Under these austere auspices, however, lay that common British enthusiasm for passionate southern climes, for the Italy of gothic, of *Corinne: or Italy*. Perhaps there Maggie Tulliver (who could not bear to finish *Corinne*) would not have had to drown.[4]

Eliot was not one to wallow in Italian indolence, however, beginning to collect historical material on this very first visit. Back in England, she interrupted her daunting project to write "another English story," *Silas Marner*. She and Lewes later returned to Florence for more extensive research. Again and again she despaired from what she called "too egoistic a dread of failure" (Haight 348). The excitement of challenging the old prohibitions—in the spirit of Woolf's later call for writers to "trespass at once" ("The Leaning Tower," CE 2: 181)—was stifled for Eliot as she dutifully read through countless sources in the original (Haight 349–50; Bonaparte). Repeatedly, Lewes described her as "buried in musty old antiquities, which she will have to vivify"; he was dispatched to track down these "unreadabilities" while she labored at home like a subservient translator (or at best, a positivist historian) hoping for a spark of the novelist's genius. Lewes, believing that the great writer must master his material, enlisted John Blackwood's help "to discountenance the idea of a Romance being the product of an Encyclopaedia." The remote age and locale seem to have exaggerated her desire for accuracy; details pertaining to the most cherished traditions of modern Europe seemed less easily domesticated than the commonplaces of nineteenth-century rural England (*GE Letters* 3: 430, 457, 420, 474; Haight 353).

Eliot suffered more than the usual difficulties with *Romola*, difficulties only partly due to obdurate historical material. The undertaking raised doubts about her vocation: she was expected to deliver home truths rather than historical panoramas. She thought of publishing

---

157). Woolf linked *Romola* with her favorite, *Middlemarch*, as an innovation in the English novel that demonstrates "that men and women think as well as feel" ("GE" [1921]).

[4]Stephen claims that "Romola was . . . a cousin of Maggie Tulliver," "loftier" and learned. Instead of having her boat land safely, "she clearly ought to have been drowned, like Maggie" (*George Eliot* 136, 138).

Silas Marner ahead of the Italian story, which could be serialized anonymously to avoid the predictable public complaints about an author's change of heart (*GE Letters* 3: 339). Her escape from the domestic novel entailed a kind of desertion of ordinary readers: "I myself have never expected—I might rather say *intended*—that the book should be as 'popular' . . . as the others. If one is to have freedom to write out one's own varying unfolding self, and not be a machine always . . . spinning the same sort of web, one cannot always write for the same public" (*GE Letters* 4: 49). Abandoning English subjects, her loyal publisher, and her accustomed public all at once may have seemed necessary for her to gain the privilege of variable genius rather than the duty of womanly reproductive labor.

Besides this challenge to her vocation, Eliot was faced with perhaps unconscious misgivings about her ideal of feminine self-sacrifice. Romola, unlike Maggie, survives her escape from "The Valley of Humiliation," her honor and independent selfhood intact, but she still must serve woman's mission. The less troubling English fable, *Silas Marner*, was at once closer to home and more impersonal. Silas like all Eliot heroines must learn the lesson of self-denying affection; like Romola he is reborn when he finds the lesson easy to learn. Both Romola and Silas, however, are removed from the Victorian woman's predicament: what question of individual rights, still less of women's rights, can there be for an antiquated common man or a lady in a Renaissance city-state? Apparently the common man yields his individuality more readily than the lady. The gold Romola is to forfeit—her pride, ambition, sexual love—may be a more doubtful price to pay, may even be, as Ruby Redinger claims, Eliot's "means of self-flagellation" to enforce the selflessness that she had been unable to attain (454).

The implied author's anxieties and the heroine's strain between aristocratic and feminine heroism undoubtedly contribute to readers' mixed impressions of the novel. Most often, criticism is directed at generic or historical crossbreeding instead of at the underlying gender conflict.[5] Leslie Stephen articulated the common objection to *Romola*: "The 'historical novel' is a literary hybrid. . . . Either the historian condemns it for its inaccuracy, or the novel-reader complains of its dulness" (*Eliot* 126; cf. Levine, " 'Romola,' " 82). Whereas the George Eliot of *Adam Bede* was able to "become a contemporary" of early nineteenth-century English rustics, Stephen continues, she could not

[5]Early reviewers for the most part received *Romola* with praise, believing it "as faithful as history, as it is great as romance" ([R.H. Hutton], *The Spectator*, 18 July 1863, in Lerner and Holmstrom 62). Yet most later readers have sensed a conflict in the author's aims, the accurate historical detail and cultural argument stifling the romance.

as naturally become a quattrocento Florentine, given the unladylike brutality of the age. Stephen, like many critics of the novel, wishes to set aside "the historical paraphernalia" that fail to disguise the Victorian "spiritual history" in *Romola* (128–41; cf. Robinson 31–32). Thus Stephen reflects the very presupposition—that women must not trespass in men's history—that the novel exists to challenge.[6] Yet though Renaissance Florence may not be essential to the tale, a substantial, tumultuous historical milieu at some remove from the novel-reader is absolutely indispensable to this revision of history as the biography of a great woman.

Critics have often explained the perceived disunity of the novel in biographical terms, citing Eliot's unusually personal defense of it (Greenstein 489; Sanders 9). To those who deplored a departure from domestic realism, she explained that "the 'Drifting away' and the Village with the Plague belonged to my earliest vision . . . as romantic and symbolical elements," yet she conceded that the attempt to mythologize cultural history may have led to "a more ideal treatment of Romola than I had foreseen" (*GE Letters* 4: 104). Against the contrary complaints about excessive historical detail, she explained that she simply may have gone too far in her usual quest for "as full a vision of the medium in which a character moves as of the character itself" (*GE Letters* 4: 97). Had readers not praised the substantial setting in *The Mill on the Floss* and *Silas Marner*? Were readers not themselves failing to follow the author's vision of the dependence of handsome dubious possibilities on determining social circumstances?

Romola was, finally, the test of her greatness: the one work she could defend "as having been written with my best blood, such as it is" (*GE Letters* 6: 335–36). According to John Cross, "The writing of 'Romola' ploughed into her more than any of her other books. She told me she could put her finger on it as marking a well-defined transition in her life. In her own words, 'I began it a young woman,—I finished it an old woman' " (Cross 2: 255). Andrew Sanders emphasizes what is often overlooked in this passage, that *Romola* was a formative as well as an arduous task; the "old woman" went on to the greater achievements of her later career (8–10). I would add that these images of personal transformation alert us to the autobiographical nature of

[6]Whether critics have found in the novel a rather bald Comtean or Feuerbachian allegory (Paris 214–22; Peterson 49–52; Bullen 425) or an artful work of historical criticism (Poston 356; Wiesenfarth, *Eliot's Mythmaking*, 146–47; Ronald; Hurley), they agree that the fifteenth and the nineteenth centuries meet in the work. Fleishman contends that the "application of . . . realism to the historical novel" failed to produce convincing links between character and background; the same actions could take place in any period (*Historical Novel* 159–60).

the project: she remade herself, writing with her "best blood," as an heroic, self-sacrificing woman author. With *Romola*, she confirmed her standing as the Grand Old Woman of English Letters.

Orlando, like *Romola*, was conceived as "something rather different" in a genre never before broached by the author, and it too reveals the stress of the author's ambition and sense of failure. Even more than Eliot's novel, Woolf's has been read biographically, as an index to a personal transformation. Much as *Silas Marner* seems to have rescued Eliot from doubts that she would ever do anything worthwhile again, *Orlando* lifted Woolf out of a characteristic depression following publication of *To the Lighthouse*. Like the laborious *Romola*, however, the more reassuring work for Woolf raised questions of vocational and generic intention that were closely related to uncertainties about feminine heroism and the common life.

In 1927 Woolf toyed with a series of factual and fantastic projects: first "a new kind of play"; then "memoirs; have a plan already to get historical manuscripts & write Lives of the Obscure" (compare Eliot's initial search among old books for the life of a great man); soon the project became "a Defoe narrative" yet a "fantasy" about two poor old women dreaming of Constantinople, with hints of sapphism. "My own lyric vein is to be satirized. Everything mocked. And it is to end in three dots . . . so. For the truth is I feel the need of an escapade after these serious poetic experimental books. . . . I want to kick up my heels & be off" (*VW Diary* 3: 128–31). Eliot, similarly torn between realism and romance (and between high and low art), also had moments of rebellion ("and suddenly burst my bonds, saying, I will not think of writing" [Haight 350]), but after an escapade in "lives of the obscure," Eliot fulfilled, in *Romola*, her duty to a history of the great. *Orlando* itself was the undutiful escapade—hence perhaps Woolf's flirtation with the little-old-lady alternative to the great tradition. Woolf fled not only the obligation to live up to high modernism but also a promise to write a critical history of the novel—"that bloody book which Dadie and Leonard extort, drop by drop, from my breast" (this became "Phases of Fiction"). If she could not yield to them sentences written in her best blood, she could "dip[ ] [her] pen in the ink" and write "as if automatically, on a clean sheet: Orlando: A Biography" (*VW Letters* 3: 428). This might be a new kind of romance-encyclopedia; it could be history inverted, it could be a "life" beyond one finite self.

According to Leon Edel, it was Lytton Strachey who had first prompted Woolf's project; that innovator in the art of biography had suggested " 'something wilder and more fantastic . . . like Tristram

Shandy' " (138–39; Moore 304). Strachey's instigation echoes Lewes's prompting of a new form of historical romance; the men of letters seem to train the women for the role of cultural challenger. Whether harnessed or unleashed, each woman must have felt that the stakes were high: her own right to the inherited genre she was told to transform. The men sanctioned what was also for both authors an independent impulse: to Vita Sackville-West, Woolf declared, "It sprung upon me how I could revolutionise biography in a night" (*VW Letters* 3: 429; Sackville-West, "Woolf and 'Orlando,' " 157), much as Eliot testified that Florence itself had inspired her.

Taking a holiday from tradition, Woolf felt she might also give the common reader a break; *Orlando* would be "very clear & plain, so that people will understand every word"—"the one popular book!" (*VW Diary* 3: 162, 198). Perhaps accessibility would be a sign that the work was not one of her bids for the honors of high art. Ironically, Woolf succeeded in creating a popular work that remains a kind of private joke attesting to her intimacy with an aristocrat. Whereas Eliot defended a work excessively civilized, Woolf denied responsibility for a work run wild, "extraordinarily unwilled by me" (*VW Diary* 3: 168). Yet her playful revolution had become a torment reminiscent of Eliot's struggles with *Romola:* "I am rather depressed. Orlando so bad"; *he,* her protagonist, has become an incubus, "an old man of the sea"; "worse in his death than in his life" (*VW Letters* 3: 475, 471, 510). These complaints appear in letters to the living, female model of the protagonist, as though the usual dread of failure became mixed with her feelings toward her threateningly independent lover and toward powers she associated with masculinity.

Her fears were somewhat confirmed by the initial slow response when the book was published, though she claimed to have cheerfully put behind her a book *not* written with her best blood.[7] Although Woolf subtitled the book "A Biography," "for the fun of" it, she immediately encountered the confusion of booksellers and reviewers as to how it should be classified (*VW Diary* 3: 198).[8] More recently,

---

[7]Like *Romola, Orlando* brought its author unaccustomed prosperity, appeasing some of the authors' anxieties about public reception. Smith Elder offered £10,000 for *Romola,* an unprecedented sum; due to Eliot's scrupulosity, the final terms were £7,000 (Haight 355–56). According to Quentin Bell, "*Orlando* sold 8,104 copies in the first six months. Financial anxieties were at an end" (Bell 2: 140).

[8]The labels ranged from Desmond McCarthy's praise—"a wonderful phantasmagoria"—to Arnold Bennett's dismissal—a "novel, which is a play of fancy, a wild fantasia, a romance, a high-brow lark." It has also been called "an allegory," "an autobiography," "a spirited prose epic of intellectual adventure," "her most elaborate love-letter," and an " 'anti-novel' " (Majumdar and McLaurin 225–37; Nicolson 3: xxii; Wilson 173).

with the amplification of the biographical study of Woolf, the subtitle has been taken more seriously; *Orlando* is "about" Woolf's affair with Vita Sackville-West (Hawkes 53; Love), while it contributes to Blooms-bury experiments in biography.[9] Woolf wrote of biography: "On the one hand there is truth; on the other there is personality. And if we think of truth as something of granite-like solidity and of personality as something of rainbow-like intangibility and reflect that the aim of biography is to weld these two into one seamless whole, we shall admit that the problem is a stiff one" ("The New Biography," CE 4: 229). The polarity is obviously gendered here, like the contrast in *To the Lighthouse* between "this delicious fecundity, this fountain and spray of life," and "the fatal sterility of the male . . . like a beak of brass" (TL 58). Eliot's loyalties to the masculine granite and Woolf's celebration of the feminine rainbow do not obscure their shared desire to weld the two in a narrative of the feminine in history.

Both *Orlando* and *Romola*, then, support a "personal" reading *because* as well as in spite of the authors' display of technical fireworks beyond gendered expectations for women's writing. Both works arose in re-sponse to a monumental task, the duty of the great woman of letters to explicate a dominant tradition, whether Renaissance history or the novel. *Romola*, Eliot's fourth full-length fiction, and *Orlando*, Woolf's sixth, come after each author had attained recognition and now wished to extend her range, in a deliberate swerve from what was expected. Both disguised autobiographies of the woman writer were conceived after the authors had delved into the family romance of their child-hoods. In *The Mill on the Floss* and *To the Lighthouse*, conflicts between the genders had been resolved into momentary fluidity in the drown-ing of Maggie and Tom and the belated voyage to the lighthouse, with apparently lasting benefit to the authors (Beer, *Past*, 128; Knoepfl-macher, "Genre," 97, 115; Redinger 33, 49; Schlack, "Fathers," 55–57; DiBattista, *Woolf's Major Novels*, 110; Gordon 202). *Romola* and *Orlando* brave the question of sexual difference with greater freedom, escaping the home setting to enter the new territory of their later works, particu-larly anticipating the historical breadth of *Daniel Deronda* and *Between the Acts*. In equally ambitious departures, Eliot and Woolf trespassed in forbidding forms, moving back in time, far afield, incorporating a lifetime's study of Western tradition in a revisionary guide to patriar-chal history.

[9]For example, Harold Nicolson's *Some People* (1926) and *The Development of English Biography* (1927), Strachey's *Elizabeth and Essex* (1928) and other works, Vita Sackville-West's *Knole and the Sackvilles* (1922), and Woolf's own essay "The New Biography" (1927), reviewing *Some People* (CE 4: 229–35; see Naremore 190–218; Philipson).

The Quest of the Woman of Genius

How does the exceptional woman earn the right to trespass in cultural history? Like Romola and Orlando, the implied authors become sojourners in other times and strange lands, as though they had adapted the Grand Tour to a woman's purposes, always with the final return to the home. While training their aristocrats to side with the "others" in history, the authors preserve the privileges of high culture and the leeway of romance. Each protagonist is the darling of authorial Fortune, handsome and talented, innocently thrust into the public arena of history yet remaining reclusive and impressionable, more observer than agent.[10] Such is the pattern of the preeminent instance of the Victorian woman writer in Italy. Woolf's response to *Romola* was mediated by her "reading," as well as Eliot's, of Elizabeth Barrett Browning.

When Eliot ventured into Italy and Florence, she followed Elizabeth Barrett Browning, whose famous escape from Victorian domestication bore the fruit of *Aurora Leigh*, the first fictional work in English on the development of a woman writer.[11] *Orlando*, more venturesome, is another female *künstlerroman* following after the voyages of Barrett Browning (and Mary Shelley) as well as George Eliot (Knoepflmacher, "Exile," 112–15). Later, in *Flush* (1933), Woolf deflects reverence for female as well as male precursors toward that most obscure domestic outsider, the household pet.[12] Flush, like the Victorian lady his mistress, is an innocent captive; in suppressing his nature to gain affection, he develops neurotic sensitivity. Both the woman poet and her dog come alive in Italy, beyond Victorian chained walks, much as Orlando changes sex in Turkey and unleashes her poetry after the Victorian age. The dog's perception of the glories of Florence is ren-

[10]Eliot had written a fable about a male Lady of Shalott, though Silas is reborn when love enters his room rather than dying by going out to seek it. (Although Jennifer Gribble does not refer to *Silas Marner*, she traces the figures of the solitary, the web, and the mirror in the works of Eliot and Woolf, among others.) Both *Romola* and *Orlando* could be further versions of the fable. The Italian lady descends from the tower, sees through the tirra-lirra knight, disembarks from her boat alive, and reascends the tower voluntarily, now free to pass judgment on events outside. Like Silas Marner, Orlando overcomes appropriative manhood and takes on the abilities of womanhood; like Silas, his transformations come about in trancelike states simulating the "deaths" of the Lady and Romola. Only when "he" becomes a lady is she able to ascend the artist's tower and weave her best poetry.

[11]On Eliot's response to *Aurora Leigh*, see Haight 185; Barrett Browning observed Eliot on the famous novelist's first visit to Rome (Haight 324). See Cooper; Woolf, "Aurora Leigh," CE 1: 209–18.

[12]Flush was the gift of Mary Russell Mitford to Elizabeth Barrett Browning (Moers 54) and hence a kind of mascot for the female literary tradition.

dered in mock-Paterian tone: "Form and colour were smell; music and architecture, law, politics and science were smell." Flush outdoes the Victorians: "He knew Florence as no human being has ever known it; as Ruskin never knew it or George Eliot either" (138–40). Excluded from the culture that brings these pilgrims to Florence as a Mecca, endowed with heightened susceptibilities and a privileged but partial knowledge of the lives of poets, Flush is an apt persona for Woolf as outsider and literary descendant. At the same time, Barrett Browning's rise from chronic illness to artistic achievement, fame, and love has obvious significance for Woolf.

As Woolf presents it, Barrett Browning dictated both Eliot's enterprise in *Romola* and her own in *Flush:* " 'Savonarola's martyrdom here in Florence,' wrote Mrs. Browning, 'is scarcely worse than Flush's in the summer.'. . .The fleas of Florence are red and virile." The two English poets can only cure the spaniel by shaving off his coat, the sign of his "pedigree," till he feels "emasculated." But the humiliation frees him: "To be nothing— . . . To caricature the pomposity of those who claim that they are something—was that not in its way a career?" (141–43). Like the women writers, like Romola as well as Aurora Leigh, Flush reaches an acceptance of a feminine career in the "virile" climate of Italy, where the Victorians felt they could unite an ethics of work and self-sacrifice with a sense of play and physical immediacy ("religion itself was smell" [138]).

Like *Flush,* both *Romola* and *Orlando* dramatize the transaction between a creature of refined sensibility and the spirit of an age; with varying degrees of seriousness each woman writer shows that biographical history has mistakenly centered on great men. The human protagonists cannot remain as passive as the pet with his involuntary sense of smell, whatever may be expected of the passivity of women.[13] The authors to an extent master the cultural encounter; these works record the authors' efforts to overcome a Flush-like misery before the spectacle of culture, while Romola and Orlando never appear to doubt that their quests are part of that spectacle. Though in each work the interest seems divided between the protagonist and cultural history, this division is instructive, as it suggests a refusal to accept the woman novelist's portion. Seizing the world for women, these works are preoccupied with historical figures and events, with the buildings and artifacts that give texture to a period, and above all with the "spirit of the age" that molds character.

[13]Flush "was violently sick" upon meeting Carlyle, whose own dog, Nero, seemingly attempted suicide—a facetious comment on a "dog's relation to the spirit of the age" (*Flush* 147, 151, 183–84) and on Woolf's relation to the Victorians.

Savonarola in Florence, the Sackvilles at Knole: the authors recreate figures who enacted history in an age-old setting. The Duomo and St. Paul's still stand to mark the changing spirit of the ages since they were new. Like Eliot or Woolf, anyone might visit Florence or Knole and see many of the same frescoes or portraits. Yet both authors wrote a kind of guidebook to a sight no tourist would see unaided: Florence just beginning to decline from the Medici era, Knole just as Thomas Sackville was writing *Gorboduc*. They seemed eager to distinguish themselves from ordinary tourists. Whereas in inventing Cheverel Manor in "Mr. Gilfil's Love-Story" Eliot had been able to draw on memories of Arbury House, where her father had worked, she had to rely on research to construct a setting for the Florentine elite. Lewes was delegated to study the interior of Savonarola's monastery, which was off limits to women (*GE Letters* 3: 417; Haight 345); with Romola, we are allowed to visit the rebellious martyr inside. Woolf was intimate with someone who had been raised on the noble estate, and herself frequented such houses, but she both reveled in and resented a sense of being excluded from the libraries if not the luncheons of Oxbridge, as Eliot had been excluded from the monastery.

With all the air of being to the manor born, the narrators of both works take up the conventional personas of masculine writers of fact-finding forms, history and biography. After *Adam Bede*, *Romola* and *Orlando* are the only works of fiction by either author to be narrated in a predominantly masculine manner. Though the convention of narrative history allows Eliot's narrator to know "What Florence Was Thinking Of" (chapter 35), he does not insist on his own absolute authority. Indeed, he emphasizes changing perspective and selective evidence, conceding the interpretive accidents of historiography without questioning the reality of a "universal history" to which all histories refer (White, "Interpretation in History," 281–87; Mink, "Narrative Form," 140–41).[14] Woolf's personified narrator, the narrator who claims to be in charge (though much of the text appears to have been designed by another, impersonal voice, that of a subtle modernist), not only presumes a universal history but the possibility of a uniquely true account of it; with his nostalgia for positivism, he unconsciously parodies the objective mask Eliot respectfully dons. Even by his own

---

[14]Eliot meticulously displays successive frames of historical reference, from that of the modern visitor (reader) to that of Romola's contemporaries: to us the "buildings" in the Via de' Bardi are "quaint," to them, they are "too modern." Indeed, "historical memory" (the narrator's?) recalls "the famous houses of the Bardi family, destroyed by popular rage in the middle of the fourteenth century," the earlier version of history erased by a hostile audience, as it were (90).

standards Woolf's narrator does a poor job: he is unequal to analysis and unable to criticize his sources, and he shuns "metahistorical" questions. His positivist claims founder before the text of someone else's life, which seems to spell the death of the author: "The first duty of the biographer . . . is to plod, without looking to right or left, in the indelible footprints of truth . . . till we fall plump into the grave and write *finis* on the tombstone above our heads"(65). Not only the inchoate truth of life but the polyphony of tradition overwhelm this narrator, who mouths classic authors pell-mell.[15]

The comic strife of this narrator suggests that Eliot could have "been saved all that nonsense" (*VW Letters* 2: 322), as the attempt at a serious, encyclopedic work must yield to the romance of any quest for knowledge or memory. The very documents themselves are squirming with bizarre life. Even Woolf's naive narrator shows, as Eliot's does, how history shifts according to the perspective of the observers, and he becomes increasingly defiant of authority and precedent: "The true length of a person's life, whatever the *Dictionary of National Biography* may say, is always a matter of dispute" (305–6). In spite (or under cover) of masculine narrators, both implied authors defy the exclusion of women and "others" from contemporary historiography. Even in taking liberties with the accepted facts, however, Woolf retains the conventional sequence of periods in English history. Instead of Eliot's citation of historical authorities, Woolf offers playful acknowledgments and an index.[16] Moreover, though much of *Orlando* might be called modernist lyric aimed over the head of the witless biographer, the narrative as a whole displays what Woolf considered old-fashioned confidence in its referential transparency. In spite of some opaque embellishment, language here seems comparatively at ease with its mission of mirroring reality ("reality" itself generates the distortion).

While the authors adapt and modify the conventions of historiography, they also take on the matter of high culture, as we have seen in their association with Barrett Browning's Italy. No doubt about it, these novels are artsy, laden with cultural prestige. But of course there *is* doubt about it—doubt of the observers' authority, context,

---

[15]Among the allusions are those to Sir Thomas Browne (O 72–73, 81), Austen (139), Carlyle (78), Pater and Swinburne (47), Vita Sackville-West (109; in the ms., Sackville-West's poem "The Land" and Thomas Sackville's "Induction to the Mirror for Magistrates" are quoted [Moore 322–31]), Virginia Woolf (98, passim), while Shakespeare, Pope, Shelley, and others appear in person and as consultants, in effect, on the spirit of the age (Schlack, *Presences*, 145–50).

[16]The dedication, "to V. S-W," the Sackville family portraits and allusions to their works, the resemblance of Orlando's house to Knole, and other details (Moore) establish a perhaps closer relation to factual history than in Eliot's text.

reverence. The implied authors pose at times as art critics, docents, or even anthropologists. Both *Romola* and *Orlando* became the authors' only novels originally to be published with illustrations, images that seemingly would substantiate their historical fictions while inviting the reader to supply the context of contemporary versions of art history.[17] Eliot invents prominent works of art, like di Cosimo's triptych, and Woolf playfully misidentifies the portraits of the Sackvilles: "Orlando as a Boy," "Orlando as Ambassador." Like anthropologists, they witness ritual spectacles: the quaint twirling towers and the new-fangled "triumphal car like a pyramidal catafalque" (R 139), or the "pyramid, hecatomb, or trophy" of "ill-assorted objects . . . where the statue of Queen Victoria now stands!" (O 232). Both displays seem fantastic yet true, though Eliot's image is documented and Woolf's is an invented metaphysical conceit. The awe-inspiring cultural history that oppresses the heroines (Romola must be protected at home from the carnival of the streets, while Orlando's sense of feminine lack arises with that Victorian pyramid of objects) is made to serve the authors' designs. I would like now to sample passages in each novel that typify these designs, as the narrators refashion high culture and history to encompass the quest of the woman of genius.

Although there are more dramatized scenes in *Romola* than critics such as Barbara Hardy have allowed (58, 185), the general perception that this is a discursive rather than dramatic work seems correct. In *Romola* we receive the already received; often we are placed in the role of critic of an historic event or work of art presented to us as a palimpsest, with the political implications somewhat obscured. In one key scene-painting, Tito enters the Church of the Nunziata during a festival celebrating the Eve of the Nativity of the Blessed Virgin. Eliot has characterized the peasants, coming into Florence "like a way-worn ancestry returning from a pilgrimage on which they had set out a century ago" (193), as predominantly female; inside the church, this feminine crowd bows beneath the images of generations of dead men struggling for a place in history. Tito belongs in his androgynous way

---

[17]Eliot consulted with Frederic Leighton on the period details in his illustrations for *Romola* (Haight 360); it was standard for fiction published in the *Cornhill* to be illustrated. The spirit of Ruskin haunts this novel, whereas the spirit of Roger Fry haunts *Orlando*; as Witemeyer reminds us, Eliot was not a "formalist" or "forerunner of Roger Fry or Clive Bell" (171). Woolf asked Vita for photographs of Sackville portraits, and included pictures of her friend (*VW Letters* 3: 434–35). *Three Guineas* and *Roger Fry* were also published with photographs, which confirms the association of *Orlando* with biographical history more than with modernist poetics, though it burns with an aestheticist flame.

neither to the common worshipers nor to the fathers-in-effigy. Tito
sees the church

> filled with peasant-women . . . the coarse bronzed skins, and the
> dingy clothing of the rougher dwellers on the mountains, contrasting
> with the softer-lined faces and white or red head-drapery of the well-
> to-do dwellers in the valley, who were scattered in irregular groups.
> And spreading high and far over the walls and ceiling there was
> another multitude . . . the crowd of votive wax images, the effigies
> of great personages, clothed in their habit as they lived: . . . popes,
> emperors, kings, cardinals . . . some of them with faces blackened
> and robes tattered by the corroding breath of centuries, others fresh
> and bright in new red mantle . . . the exact doubles of the living. . . .
> It was a perfect resurrection-swarm of remote mortals and fragments
> of mortals, reflecting . . . the somber dinginess and sprinkled bright-
> ness of the crowd below. (199–200)

Here is a narrator who has been to school to Ruskin; such passages,
like ecphrases or narratives of paintings, are frequent in *Romola* (Stein
17–18; Stange, "Art Criticism"; Witemeyer 32, 157–73). Buried in a
novel full of such bizarre antiquities, the passage may lose some of its
force as social and historical commentary, and appear merely as a
fleeting effect of chiaroscuro. But the spectacle of replicas of great men
vying for a place "nearer the potent Virgin," in a grotesque simulation
of their struggle for survival in life, is no benign reflection of the
crowd below. The peasant women, in their hopeless devotion to the
Madonna who might intercede for them with the Father, are figures
of the collective human past that opportunists like Tito will tread down
in their rise to power. The "resurrection-swarm" of damnable men of
all eras foretells Tito's doom; a mob of political men will try to tear
him limb from limb. Class, gender, and two orders of history, that of
great men and that of the common life, are diagrammed in this tableau.
As in the episode of the Great Frost in *Orlando*, extremes of the social
order appear grotesquely fixed in a kind of cross-section, as though
illustrating the platitude that high and low share the same fate. In
both instances, however, the divisions are made only more obvious.

Though clearly operating under a broader license than the historian
of *Romola*, the biographer of *Orlando* appeals to much the same sense
of estrangement from a social order once considered natural. Any
history or biography is a lark, a romance, because nothing could be
more outrageous than the human past. Orlando's biographer cannot
perceive this, even when evidence disintegrates before his eyes: "Just

when we thought to elucidate a secret that has puzzled historians for a hundred years, there was a hole in the manuscript big enough to put your finger through" (119). To narrate the celebrations and riots in Constantinople when Orlando becomes Duke, the narrator must resort to the testimony of an officer's Defoe-style journal and a lady's Richardsonian letter, competing accounts biased toward either political maneuvers or the politics of the ballroom. Woolf's crowd scene "at the end of the great fast of Ramadan" closely resembles Eliot's at the festival of the Nativity, with the cultural hierarchy of imperialism added to the hierarchies of class and gender.

An English naval officer, John Fenner Brigge, records having climbed into a "Judas tree" to avoid the promiscuously mixed crowd roused by fireworks at the British Embassy. Brigge writes (the ellipses mark the holes in the manuscript), "There was considerable uneasiness among us lest the native population . . . fraught with unpleasant consequences to all, . . . English ladies in the company." But when no uprising occurs, Brigge experiences a moment of imperialist pride: the fireworks have "impressed upon" the natives the "superiority of the British. . . ." Brigge himself admires the superiority of the aristocrats inside the palace, though deploring the "conduct of Lady ———— which was of a nature to fasten the eyes of all upon her, and to bring discredit upon her sex and country," whereupon Brigge falls out of his tree and is injured (127–28).

Brigge is an opportunistic observer like Tito, a social climber who enforces with his saber-rattling the oppression of the populace and of women of all classes, as he worships all signs of rank. He does not belong, and he has a fall—but it is the pratfall of a minor fool, whereas Woolf's mock hero continues for some hours to rise, very much like Meredith's Sir Willoughby Patterne ("Such a leg! Such a countenance!!" [O 129]) crossed with Byron ("adored of many women and some men," "he formed no attachments" [O 125]). As the hero continues to flourish, the task of scene painting is taken up, after Brigge's fall, by Miss Penelope Hartopp, whose epistolary effusions would have been breathless even without the effacement of the manuscript. Fragments of luxury remain: "candelabras . . . negroes in plush breeches . . . pyramids of ice . . . [. . .] jellies made to represent His Majesty's ships." Miss Penelope subscribes implicitly to the same scale of values as Brigge, gazing on "negroes" and "Lady Betty" as part of the delectable feast while presuming that His Majesty's forces will protect all ladies from all natives. Like Eliot's novel, Woolf's exposes the tensions in such hierarchical relations while exploiting the picturesque contrasts.

The downtrodden crowd does revolt in both novels; when Orlando receives his coronet, order disintegrates and Turks burst into the Embassy. This preliminary outbreak, easily quelled by the British, heralds Orlando's transformation, suggesting a massive return of the repressed. First Orlando, having discarded "the insignia of his rank" (131), marries a gypsy woman by unofficial deed (much like Tito's alliance with Tessa), before falling into a trance. Then, the "terrible and bloody" Turkish rebellion breaks out in earnest, but Orlando's abdication of his role as statesman spares him the revenge of the rioters, whereas Tito is the chosen prey of the Florentine mob. In mockery of the entire code of honor and privilege that makes "the gentlemen of the British Embassy" choose "to die in defence of their red boxes" (133), Orlando sleeps till he is reborn as a woman, and then runs away to the gypsies. He has chosen to opt out like Romola or the childhood Maggie rather than to accept the masquerade of Western patriarchy, the swarm of men fighting for precedence over the mass of women and "natives" in mute subjection below.

Both the reliable and unreliable historians, as we may characterize the narrators of *Romola* and *Orlando*, suggest that the only enduring narrative is the private yet collective history of women such as the female peasantry. The biography of the public man, like the wax effigies, will become fragmentary and vain. Though in retraction from patriarchal history, however, both novels compromise with the conventions of aristocratic romance, as I have suggested, not limiting themselves to peasant-like realistic detail. Eliot deliberately recalls the tradition of romance with her errant protagonist's name. Although "Romola" is the name of an actual village near Florence (Haight 351), it also implies the feminine form of "Romulus," the founder of an empire. The only novel Eliot entitled after the heroine thus in effect feminizes the heroic or epic, much as Woolf was to do. Not incidentally, in preparation for *Romola* Eliot studied both Boiardo's *Orlando Innamorato* and Ariosto's *Orlando Furioso* (Bonaparte 20–24, 32), as though drawn to the repeated reincarnations of the romantic hero. In her early essay proscribing the errors of lady novelists, Eliot had offered a glimpse of the possibilities for comic updating that Woolf was later to exploit: "The Orlando of Evangelical literature is the young curate, looked at from the point of view of the middle class, where cambric bands are understood to have as thrilling an effect on the hearts of young ladies as epaulettes have in the classes above and below it" (318).

The romantic hero who changes with the chances of fashion, class, and the conventional desires of his female counterparts is certainly material for farce. At the same time, both Eliot and Woolf appear to have considered the idea of recurring heroic models as a serious reflection on possible designs for the self: some exceptional beings might be immortal or ahistorical, escaping the prescriptions of gender; *or* some types are inescapable, prescribed by timeless fate.[18] It is one form of the question of rebellion or duty that *Romola* repeatedly poses: is the individual capable of fashioning unforeseen destinies, or must she or he relive the old stories of the race? In both romances, we follow the career of a dutiful descendant who unwittingly becomes a rebel and an exemplar of what Ellen Moers calls "traveling heroism," the "feminine substitute for the picaresque" (126–27). Orlando, allowed to dominate the text like no other character in Woolf's or Eliot's novels, is more strictly a picaresque figure than Romola, whose prowess is mostly exerted in confinement, the equivalent of a gothic castle. Both protagonists are emphatically bereft of "normal" family ties. Orphaned and disillusioned by the successive avatars of romance, doctrine, or letters, they attain a kind of self-determination extremely rare for women. Romola is provided with several father figures as a kind of insurance, whereas Orlando has only remote ancestors or senior poets toward whom he feels little anxiety of influence; in both works, paternal figures tend to die off, leaving the heroine, without the usual female foils, to devise her own lot.

Eliot and Woolf resist the easy cure for such solitude in the usual romantic plot. As a woman, Orlando resembles Romola in her choice of an androgynous counterpart, but her marriage to Shelmerdine is thoroughly open (she has her "career"), while Romola declares her legal subjection to Tito null and void well before his death (she is perhaps the least scandalous precursor of the divorcée). In the end, the protagonists arrive at a timeless present of feminine procreation that is also a retrospective on gendered destinations in patriarchal narrative. Though both novels end in a "scene" rather than an "overview," to apply Marianna Torgovnick's terms, a self-conscious "*circularity*" as well as a concluding formal and temporal distance from the

---

[18]Along with historic figures such as Francesco Cei, Eliot presents archetypes: Tito as resurrected Greek god (Dahl 83); Savonarola as Christ; Romola as the Madonna. See Karen Chase (304). Bardo the Stoic, Tito the Epicurean, Bernardo the Roman statesman, Dino the medieval Catholic, and Savonarola the spirit of the Reformation all influence Romola as she progresses toward the positivistic outlook. Disregarding the realistic limits of the lifespan, Woolf gives Orlando an eternal housekeeper, for a few hundred years a Mrs. Grimsditch, then a Mrs. Bartholomew (233–34). Shakespeare or Sasha, alive in memory, or Nick Greene, a man of letters in every age, reflect Woolf's playful literalization of typological metaphor; the romantic hero *is* for all time. As Vita writes of her Sackville ancestors, "Each [is] the prototype of his age," while "carry[ing] on . . . the tradition . . . [and] his race" (*Knole* 28).

main action function as a kind of "epilogue" in each novel, a framing commentary on the role of the feminine in history (11–15). Whereas Romola merely stands in as a kind of fatherly mother to Tessa and the children (much as Aurora Leigh claims to be a second mother to Marian Erle's son to replace the missing father), Orlando is directly the mother of sons (no father seems necessary) and creator of a poem, "The Oak Tree." In both cases, the heroines nod to their forefathers' tradition, while expunging from that tradition the masculine penchant for ambition and violence. In a final tableau (whether Pre-Raphaelite or surreal), an admiring man approaches the woman whose reign is at last uncontested, though in the context of patriarchal tradition: Piero di Cosimo brings flowers for Romola's shrine to the martyr, Savonarola; Shelmerdine descends from clouds with the wild goose of Orlando's chase.

In spite of a liberating departure from familiar territory in both works, the ideology of influence is ultimately enforced: women should enjoy the fullest access to a privileged tradition without forfeiting their redeeming difference from men. Indeed, Romola learns to transpose her biological burden into a moral mission, while Orlando perhaps learns the inverse, to acquire the biological burden that corresponds with his/her moral mission. Yet conservative as Romola and Orlando may be, they belong in a feminist context. On the one hand, Romola appeared during the decade when women in Eliot's circle began to agitate for the vote, and Eliot subscribed £50 "from the author of Romola" for the foundation of Girton, as I have noted. On the other hand, Orlando appeared during the post-war and post-suffrage decade of expanding opportunities for women, and in the same month in which it was published (October 1928), Woolf presented at Newnham and Girton the two lectures that were to become A Room of One's Own. In that manifesto she confronted the issues of tradition, education, and independence for women of creative ambition that had been raised in both Romola and her own Orlando. I turn now to follow more closely in each of these tales the steps whereby the trespasser inherits the property. A woman's education and vocation magically coincide with the fulfillment of tradition; history becomes the biographies of great women as well as men.

Romola as a Woman's History

As we have come to expect, Eliot's novel dramatizes a declaration of independence less for the heroine than for the author. There are many textual deflections from the female protagonist; the Proem, ostensibly symmetrical with the Epilogue, actually obliterates the feminine domestic sphere that presides in the end. With an interest in historical synchronicity that anticipates *Orlando*, the Proem declares "the broad sameness of the human lot" and overlooks difference. To support this broad humanism, Eliot resurrects a Florentine (d. 1492) in order to trace his impressions of Florence in 1863. The spirit was both a man who left a waxen image of himself in the Church of the Nunziata, and one of many in the carnival crowd below; an oppressor yet a reveler like both Orlando and Tito, he belongs in the "busy humming Piazze where he inherited the eager life of his fathers"—a zone alien to ladies. Though solidly bourgeois, the "Spirit" could make an amusing Orlando, alive across centuries and full of contradictory qualities: "of Epicurean levity and fetichistic dread; of pedantic impossible ethics . . . and crude passions." But imagining such cultural dialectic within one representative being does not lead Eliot, as it does Woolf, into a rhapsody on androgynous indeterminacy. Rather her narrator insists that "human conscience" binds "self-indulgent paganism" to public duty: "Public spirit can never be wholly immoral, since its essence is care for a common good" (44–48). About to chronicle the disastrous effects of opportunistic "public spirit," the narrator here protests too much, but he also anticipates Romola's eventual ethics of domesticated public spirit.

Eliot's narrative proceeds to detail the decadence of public men and the ascent of one heroine to supplant the Spirit of the Proem. Eliot's Florentine heroine is not Everywoman, however; she is a kind of fairy-tale princess sealed up in an ancient house with a blind father, the impoverished scholar Bardo. He lives among his fragments of antiquity as though communing "with the great dead" themselves (91–96). Like Casaubon—who also bears an ironic resemblance to the blind, daughter-exploiting Milton—Bardo has failed to complete his "great work"; he blames the desertion of his son, Dino. No daughter, he claims, can be "a fitting coadjutor," given "the wandering, vagrant propensity of the feminine mind . . . [and] the feeble powers of the feminine body" (97). Denied the freedom of her father's library, Romola later must resign herself to "delicious influence" (170) and "the ready maternal instinct which was one hidden source of her passionate tenderness" (543). That hidden source may be something she can't help, but she is willing enough to stifle it at first: "I will try and be as useful to you as if I had been a boy," she tells her father. Bardo grants that she is remarkably learned for a woman and has "a man's nobility of soul," unlike her dead mother. He has kept her "aloof from the debasing influence" of women, a dubious advantage that leaves Romola unschooled in her lot in life (100). She is not allowed to escape into acquired manliness; she must be a fit nurse for her father, and ultimately she must extend this function in public life. She is unable to replace her father's son except by marrying Tito, the young Greek scholar. As husband, he usurps the father's place and robs his wife and Florence of the classical scholar's collection of ancient relics.[19]

Romola begins in much the same position in the patriarchal structure as that other exotic aristocrat, Leonora Charisi, whose rage makes Romola's capitulation all the more striking. Daniel Deronda's mother insists on the ineluctable difference of sex even as she suggests that gender is acquired: "You are not a woman. You . . . can never imagine what it is to have a man's force of genius in you, and yet to suffer the slavery of being a girl. . . . [My father] wished I had been a son; he cared for me as a makeshift link" (DD 694). Eliot's narrator in Romola seems not to imagine fully Romola's consciousness of manly powers and female slavery; this docile heroine ultimately approves her role as patriarchal link (though I will argue that she has the last word on her failed fathers and mentors).

The contrast between Romola's manly "nobility of soul" and Tito's self-indulgent pusillanimity disturbs the sexual stereotypes that Eliot will not abandon outright. Tito "could easily be made to shrink and turn pale like a maiden" (164).[20] Might Tito not be an incarnation of narcissism rendered poisonous by ambition, a forerunner of Gwendolen Harleth? (Daniel is certainly a male Romola: beautiful, sensitive, a bearer of a people's moral burden.) Although Tito offers Romola a life of luxuriant pleasure such as Maggie Tulliver glimpses in the boat with Stephen Guest, the Florentine couple soon confront their irreconcilable temperaments, like Maggie and her brother Tom. As in the earlier novel, in Romola the socially enforced division of labor exaggerates difference where there could be childlike union. Instead, Tito and Romola endure a nightmare of the Victorian bourgeois family, he utterly corrupted by public life, she imprisoned in the home without the consolations of wifely influence or motherhood. The male and female players have been miscast. Behind his armor of egotism, Tito is beyond influence (his literal armor is donned to ward off the rejected patriarch's revenge), while Romola appears incapable of Tessa's cozy

---

[19]See Emery on Romola's and Tito's efforts to replace Dino (85). Eliot's repudiation of the father figure is doubly accomplished by Tito.

[20]Woolf's father asserted, "Tito is thoroughly and to his fingers' end a woman" (139). Tito has the Protean as well as Dionysian qualities associated with effeminacy (Gilbert, "Costumes," 405): he changes costumes and roles with Orlando's freedom, whereas Romola cannot run away from her wifehood disguised in a nun's habit.

devotion to husband and children. If Romola is perhaps too manly (for the gender stereotype), Tito is not man enough; like the ungendered Bacchus, he plays as though he will always be granted another life, and so he must die twice, first drowned by his "fellow-men" and then strangled by his stepfather, a fellow-demon (637–39). Romola in contrast overcomes egotism and so is granted another life after death-by-water, achieving sainthood without self-annihilation because the patriarchs die in her stead.

Though this tale appears to affirm the compensations of "moral evolution" for those who are misfits in the "worse share" of woman-hood, it also exposes the failings of the father's law and allows the woman to resist it to a surprising degree. This rebellion is hidden under historical material apparently too weighty to be moved by one woman's desire for change. The objects that especially speak for patri-archal law seem at times to have more life in them, more agency than the heroine herself. The most frequently discussed symbolic objects, Dino's cross and Tito's triptych, make concrete the brother's and husband's attempts to steer Romola into different paths of devotion. The hyperactive jewelry and gems likewise perform as the will of tradition or the return of the past in this novel, as they do in romance generally (Wiesenfarth, "Antique Gems"; Levine, " 'Romola,' " 86–88), but here the treasures tend to subvert the law of the father. For example, the necklace Tito gives to Tessa leads Romola to rescue her, thus affirming a bond between wife and mistress in spite of the man. Yet Eliot makes certain we see Romola's reluctance to resist the ex-change of women; when Romola removes her betrothal ring, she seems to be "rending her life in two" (391). In contrast, Tito supports his life of pleasure by selling the gems that could ransom his stepfather out of slavery; he cannot in the end rend his life in two, as his origins return by means of the gems to destroy him. Gems, valued for their rarity and the narrative of the past that they retain, also elicit an aesthetic response that for Eliot rouses anxiety (and for Woolf, delight): such pleasure invites "self-indulgent paganism."

Eliot tries to persuade her readers that public spirit, or collective historical progress, controls the egotistical designs of the individual: "As in the tree . . . each single bud with its fruit is dependent on the primary circulation of the sap, so the fortunes of Tito and Romola were dependent on certain grand political and social conditions which made an epoch in the history of Italy" (267). But this history of Italy is dead to us without our desire for the heroine's fulfillment and for the dreadful end of the hero's brilliant career: the tree depends on the buds and fruit. We have seen how the organic or horticultural image could be used to endorse "natural" gender difference; here it endorses as well the subordination of individuals to the collective growth. But Eliot's deterministic realism and fidelity to patriarchal tradition yield to rebellious romantic wishes. Romola, surrounded by archival commonplaces, serving as a disciple of a great historical personage, nevertheless seems one of the least historical of Eliot's heroines, fed by some nectar other than ordinary sap. She is exempt from women's domestic servitude: she has no chores, no children, and no trivializing ignorance. Eliot had praised great women who never neglected their domestic duties, but she invented a heroine who for a time is freed from such duties.

In what sense, then, does this oddly free yet dutiful heroine find her vocation as a woman? First, she does so by falling out of her domestic niche: once, "tenderness and keen fellow-feeling for the near and the loved . . . had made the religion of her life" (391), but her father dies and Tito betrays her. Then, just as she strikes out on her own to become a scholar, a new father intervenes who instructs her in the tenets of womanly influence. From Savonarola she learns "sympathy with the general life," though she lacks an "innate taste for tending the sick and clothing the ragged" (463). It is a strange instinct that must be acquired—as Orlando discovers when she becomes a woman, feminine "graces" are "only attain[ed] . . . by the most tedious discipline," not "by nature" (O 157)—but it gives her something to do that would have just suited a Victorian lady like Dorothea Brooke. Indeed, fulfilling her resemblance to certain Victorian reformers, she becomes a public nurse. Savonarola seems to have Florence Nightingale in mind when he defines Romola's vocation: she is to "labour for the suffering and the hungry . . . as a daughter of Florence. . . . I desire to behold you among the feebler and more ignorant sisters as the apple-tree among the trees of the forest, . . . as a lamp through which the Divine light shines the more purely" (438).[21] Like the mythic Nightingale, Romola is to domesticate public space, thereby framing rebellion as a duty in the manner of many Victorian ladies. Even the myth of the lady with the lamp was a quiet retort against patriarchal mismanagement, proving what a lady could do.

Romola as powerless daughter and wife experiences the wrongs that Bodichon and others campaigned against in the 1840s–60s, particularly

[21]In both instances the quasi-divine leader of a sisterhood of mercy is not apparently much suited for domesticity. Nightingale spent much of her life as a bedridden invalid spurning her own family but consulted by statesmen. Mary Poovey has most recently illuminated the contradictions in this eminent Victorian (164–98), contradictions very much like the man-womanly Romola's.

the injustice of the education system and property laws, but Eliot's novel stands apart from the very causes it makes a case for. Instead of pursuing her scholarship, reclaiming her father's property, or confronting her husband's double standards, Romola abandons the political crisis and puts out to sea in an alienated trance rather like Orlando's. She is reborn as the "Holy Mother" (641–44) for the plague-ridden village, a community unlike the gypsies that honors the heroine more than her native society ever would. Like Nightingale, then, Romola is apotheosized after one spectacular foreign campaign of nursing, whereupon she retires to her home—but not to administer imperial affairs. It is not that Romola can *only* take things personally, like a woman. She does take the downfall of her mentor Savonarola as a calamity more personal than political, but she has long since lost the narrow domestic feeling that would grieve at Tito's infidelity or death. Rather, her selfless politics are confined to personal strategies. In the end she makes it her business to tend Tito's home and to keep sacred the personal memory of Savonarola. Like a Renaissance Josephine Butler, who crusaded against the Contagious Diseases Acts (which authorized the policing of women in military districts to make prostitution safe for men) and who founded a home for prostitutes, Romola subverts the effects of the double standard by uniting with the other woman, while at the same time retaining the forms of paternalistic faith. But unlike either Butler or Nightingale, she never campaigns for public power.

In her quest, Romola has learned to be an earthly madonna— that is, "woman" in Victorian terms—but she has also triumphed over the patriarchs, as the last scenes of the novel make clear. Savonarola's execution takes place in the final chapter before the Epilogue, titled "The Last Silence." The heroine inevitably imagines herself in the place of the martyr, but he takes this part in her stead. Still withholding her sympathy for the masses, she witnesses the spectacle as a lady at a window high above the crowd—"the baser part of the multitude delight in degradations," but not she. She repeatedly covers her eyes as Savonarola is brought out, but at the last "she only saw what he was seeing . . . only heard what *he* was hearing. . . . The moment was past. Her face was covered again, and she only knew that Savonarola's voice had passed into eternal silence" (670–71). Thus ends the action of the novel in 1498. Yet the witness survives, because what really matters is not his suffering or his death, but his silence. No longer is it his voice that holds her within the city of her fathers, but her own.

Why is the ensuing portion of the novel not narrated from the point of view of a male bourgeois Spirit of 1509, like the Spirit of 1492 in the

Proem? Why alternatively does the narrator himself not have the last word in person? Because the novel needs the asymmetry of a woman's speech against the voices that have predominated since the Proem. Like the highest ranking survivor in a tragedy, Romola has the last word. As the title of the novel reminds us and the Epilogue quietly insists, the great man's story is not the whole story. The Epilogue is a tableau that pays decorous tribute to the patriarchs while foregrounding Romola's authority.

First, we see that Savonarola has been reduced to a small portrait over a wreathed altar. Then we focus on the other women: first Tito's clever daughter, who like Maggie "toss[es] her . . . hair out of her eyes"; then Tessa, "not very clever," plump with "childish content"; then Romola's inadequate mother-surrogate, cousin Monna Brigida, sleeping her life away.[22] The rather scornful image of women here sets Romola apart from them, closer to the men, yet triangularly facing both ("Romola sat nearly opposite Lillo," both of them "farther off" from the women). Romola, though she has gained "placidity," is still beautiful and very much awake; from the beginning she has rejected parasitical idleness. She seems to turn her back on history, gazing "absently on the distant mountains."

A dialogue begins when Lillo, tired of memorizing a poem addressed to the ideal future statesman (a poem by Petrarch, one of Bardo's approved poets), asks Romola what he should be when he grows up. "Mamma Romola" suggests that he emulate Bardo, who is *not* in fact Lillo's grandfather but only the second foster father whom Lillo's father betrayed. Lillo, the raw material of another Tito, says he would rather not die a defeated old scholar; he wants to be "a great man, and very happy besides." Romola, in a voice suspiciously like George Eliot's, admonishes him that the "highest happiness," enjoyed by the "great man," comes of "having wide thoughts, and much feeling for the rest of the world as well as ourselves. . . . We can only tell [this sort of happiness] from pain . . . because our souls see it is good. . . . No man can be great—he can hardly keep himself from wickedness—unless he gives up thinking much about pleasure or rewards." This doctrine grants a painful sort of happiness only to those who do not think of themselves as Bardo always did; to reflect on one's greatness is to fall into wickedness. Romola summarizes Tito's career as an illustration of "calamity falling on a base mind."

[22]In these childish, dozing figures, it is tempting to see Eliot's judgment of her "husband's" very plump other wife, Agnes Lewes, whom she may not have forgiven as readily as Romola does Tessa.

According to Romola's definition, the only great man in the book—
the only figure who has abandoned self-interest in a grand cause—is
Romola herself. She "never for a moment told herself that it was
heroism or exalted charity" (656) to rescue her base husband's "other
wife" and children.

It is helpful to return a little to consider Savonarola's egotism, the
besetting sin of the heroically great. Romola, in the chapter before the
frate's execution, was a critical reader of his confession: his entire
career (the doubtfully authentic document states) was designed to
make him "for ever famous." He always claimed that "the cause . . .
should triumph by his voice, by his work, by his blood. In moments
of ecstatic contemplation, doubtless, the sense of self melted in the
sense of the Unspeakable." But unlike Romola, and perhaps more
like Eliot herself, he cannot sustain self-abasement; he desires "preeminence" (664–65). Eliot too strives in this novel for preeminence,
serving the cause in her own voice, writing with her best blood.
Romola is more fortunate than great egoists like Savonarola and Eliot,
because she can be great without knowing it. For though she is not to
be grouped with the feeble women in her domestic circle, she has that
dedication to others which seems more readily imagined in woman
than man. If Romola had ignored Savonarola's instructions on how to
become the lady with the lamp, if she instead had made her way to
Venice on her first venture to compete with great learned men, her
martyrdom (like the Alcharisi's) would have been most severe. Having
given a thought to her own greatness, she would have forfeited its
purest rewards.

In the Epilogue, Romola neither mentions her own lost ambition
nor tells Lillo of his parentage or his father's crimes. Romola's little
matriarchy is founded on the secret of illegitimacy and the lie that
Romola has no desires. Thus what may look like the praise of famous
men is rather a refusal to condemn the fathers' glaring failures. Filial
piety has been a very unreliable principle throughout the book, not
only because every father has been an egotist more or less hostile to
his child's life, but also because the fathers have died in shame,
Savonarola the last among them. Moreover, along with filial piety, the
novel has preached a competing doctrine: "The law was sacred. Yes,
but the rebellion might be sacred too" (552). Romola sees that she, like
Savonarola, faces a call to "the duty of resistance" (540). Antigone's
confrontation with two incompatible goods is reenacted here. The
child who wishes to grow to the father's stature in patriarchy must
rebel, but the female child seldom succeeds in replacing the patriarch.

The futility of women's rebellion lends them an appearance of selfless obedience, of moral superiority, though like men they may desire preeminence. But why should the fathers, the proponents of sacred law, be honored by the daughters who obey that law better than they? So asked the Victorian women's movement, so implicitly asks Romola.

In a curious acknowledgment of the patriarchal construction of gender, Eliot shows that Romola needs a man to teach her a woman's supposedly natural "fellowship with suffering" (396), her part in the "common life" (433). But when her instructor vainly identifies his cause with God's, she protests: "God's kingdom is something wider— else, let me stand outside it with the beings that I love" (578). This rare moment of outspoken confrontation exposes her competing egoism, which must be washed away before the heroine can pose as a truly great woman in the Epilogue. Yet in her last words we sense that she is still carrying out her duty of rebellion, standing outside the patriarch's kingdom in her own domestic paradise; here she may forgive men because they are absent. Savonarola has become an image as fixed as any madonna; the artist Piero di Cosimo and another man approach outside, bringing flowers to the shrine, far more in honor of Romola than of the martyr.

Romola herself admits, in the final speech to the boy, that Savonarola is only to be worshiped through the medium of love, not through the fathers' doctrine. "Perhaps I should never have learned to love him if he had not helped me when I was in great need" (676). The greatest help he offered was to teach her the failings of the law of the father. He is sacrificed to wash away the sins of Romola's, and perhaps of the author's, own rebellious ambition. In the Epilogue, the great woman has become the link she might have been if she had been a son, teaching Lillo as her father taught her, but the tradition has been subtly modified by her influence.

Orlando and the Quest for Womanhood

If Romola's greatness lies in her having outgrown what Woolf calls "romantic . . . individuality" ("GE" [1919] 154), Orlando's greatness surely lies in refusing to grow up (in several ways Orlando is a high-brow Peter Pan).[23] Unlike Eliot or Romola, unlike Woolf herself, this

---

[23]In an unpublished paper, Ellen Barber has traced many fascinating parallels between *Orlando* and *Alice in Wonderland*—another parable of the anxieties of growing up. Paul West briefly links Woolf's epistomological play in *Orlando* to Lewis Carroll (99).

romantic individualist never has to face opposing duties of obedience and rebellion, never has to play Antigone or Oedipus to fatherly prohibitions. Yet in the transformation from man to woman, the heroic type does temper romantic individuality; this is the story of a moral progress not unlike Romola's, in spite of the delightfully amoral by-play. Along with the deconstruction of gender and identity, there is the development of a woman's mission originating in the biography of the questing woman writer. In its "personal" relevance, as I have suggested, *Orlando* may be taken seriously, at the risk of playing the straight man, like the narrator who never gets the joke.

Woolf herself, like Romola, was raised in her father's library as in "the heart" of one of Eliot's novels, "cloistered like a place of worship, but that she no longer knows to whom to pray" ("GE" [1919] 159); whereas Romola's husband dismantles the library, Woolf inherited it intact (Silver, Introduction, *Notebooks*, 26). Though his was a more tolerant age, Leslie Stephen could be a kind of Bardo toward his talented daughters. In autobiographical writing, Woolf charges that such oppressors were indulged because everyone accepted two precepts, that "men of genius are very ill to live with" and that "the woman was his slave" ("Sketch" 124–26). If there is a duty to rebel against such precepts, Woolf nevertheless venerates the father's library and pays tribute, even in her most playful fiction, to shades of her father (rather as Romola honors Savonarola's portrait). *Orlando* can be seen as a woman's effort to be as useful to the father as if she had been a boy, though in an inversion of the academic manner that Stephen criticized in *Romola*.

At the outset Orlando's biographer, like the narrator of the Proem, affirms the "sameness" of a masculine norm of humanity. Yet Woolf's narrator is more elitist than humanist, subscribing to the chivalric code as he introduces Orlando practicing his swordsmanship on the "head of a Moor" that resembles a "football." Vowing to emulate his forefathers, Orlando "would steal away from his mother" to abuse this adversary, "fastening [the skull] with some chivalry almost out of reach so that his enemy grinned at him through shrunk, black lips triumphantly." The author may invite our laughter at such brutal and racist chivalry, but the narrator blindly adores the hero. He rhapsodizes, "Happy the mother who bears, happier still the biographer who records the life of such a one! Never need she vex herself, nor he invoke the help of novelist or poet." That the male biographer should outdo the female creator—the mother or the author—of the hero is a fine commentary on the presumption of patriarchal authority (and Orlando's mother and Woolf the woman novelist are both effaced).

This biographer anxiously suppresses any sign of non-exploitive hero-ism—that personal "riot and confusion . . . which every good biogra-pher detests" (13–16).

Woolf's hero enjoys the advantages not only of Romola's beauty, intellect, and transcendence of the petty conditions of history, but also of wealth and manhood, and hence a freedom denied to heroines (and the woman author). Even in the age of a powerful queen, Orlando's potency is derived from his Turk-slaying forebears and his identity as male heir. His sister, like Shakespeare's, would not have been allowed to act the heroic part. With more than 365 rooms of his own (Sackville-West, *Knole*, 4), he is free to choose the literary life. Woolf romantically softens certain features in this portrait of Vita and waffles between the "nature" and "nurture" accounts of difference. The real descendant of the Sackvilles, although there could be some doubt of her sex, was barred from the inheritance of Knole. In the fiction, Orlando is able to inherit her estate in a vision of legalized androgyny. Although the narrator (in his or her more open-minded phase) declares that "in every human being a vacillation from one sex to the other takes place," and speculates that gender is only superficially signaled by customary dress, he or she also insists, "The difference between the sexes is, happily, one of great profundity" (188–89).

The difference between Orlando and you and me is profound in-deed. He enjoys the charms of an elaborately preserved history with-out sensing its burdens, and he can commit every social transgres-sion—even crossing class boundaries—without a troubled conscience. An instance of Orlando's privilege is his relation to romantic objects, the fragments of overdetermined narrative resembling the triptych, cross, and gems in *Romola*. Queen Mary's prayerbook and the tapes-tries and relics at Knole follow Orlando through the centuries, but they condone rather than restrain his every whim. Gems, the correlatives of characters' rarity, beauty, and connection to the past, here celebrate a Paterian *jouissance*, though always appropriate to the social code. At first Orlando burns with as gemlike a flame as Tito, squandering a patrimony in such indulgences as "illicit love in a treasure ship," among bags of rubies (30). Becoming a woman, Orlando retains her hedonism, bartering the "emeralds and pearls . . . of her ambassado-rial wardrobe" to play gypsy; at the same time the gypsies destroy her pride in property and rank ("a Duke . . . was nothing but a profiteer or robber" [140, 147–48]), and they prove hostile to a woman's (or Romantic poet's) contemplative love of nature.[24]

[24]Opening the Byron that Carlyle ordered closed, Woolf makes her Byronic hero take on the marginality of women and the orient more permanently than Don Juan does in the harem. Her mock-epic is to the moment, like Joyce's, but with an exotic difference

Orlando remains at heart an English aristocrat, and with the shifting moods of history she rededicates herself to traditional hierarchies. She wears Queen Elizabeth's gift of a "vast solitary emerald" as a stamp of rank and independence until the nineteenth century, when she feels "a ring of quivering sensibility about the second finger of the left hand"; at last sharing Romola's mores, she feels she is only half a woman without a wedding band (239–41). Yet she cannot subject herself to a chivalrous wooer like the Archduke. Only a fellow romantic venturer, Shelmerdine, can fulfill Orlando's "womanly" need for romance without suppressing her "manly" ambition; in this extraordinary marriage, she may release the youthful gemlike passion that more responsible ages had dimmed. In the end she greets her husband with ready love: "Her pearls burnt like a phosphorescent flare in the darkness" (329; Sackville-West, "Woolf and 'Orlando,' " 157; Fleishman, *Woolf,* 140–45).

The narrative that these gems tell in miniature is highly ambivalent toward its own disruption of traditional order. This apparently freewheeling romance also implies a *progress* in English cultural history and in the development of a representative individual (albeit with some nostalgia for the blades and wits of early periods), with preference for the mature woman of the present day. At the same time, Woolf's romantic world is more rebellious than obedient, taking liberties with determinacy that Eliot's narrator cannot allow. Indolence, sexuality, defiance have no victims like Baldassarre or Tessa, and meet no punishment; the past plays along rather than tracking anyone down, and all commonplaces are gemlike exotics. Only in the nineteenth century are the pressures of the double standard and of feminine duties brought to bear, but like Romola, Orlando sidesteps domestic slavery.

With every reason to prolong those moments of alienation in Whitehall (RO 101), Orlando instead creates a sanctum within the old order from which to contemplate the errors of patriarchy. This feat is the hero/heroine's greatest achievement: by becoming a woman, Orlando fulfills the duties of feminine heroism, serving a collective destiny and preserving an ancestral home. The ideology of influence has been partially restored after a day of misrule. The misrule is genuine, and manly heroism will never be the same, but a lingering mystique of feminine and aristocratic charm remains. How does this wayward pilgrim's progress arrive at a destination so like its beginning, and rather like Romola's ending?

(de Almeida 61; DiBattista, "Joyce, Woolf," 111). Unlike Maggie Tulliver, and unlike her boyish former self, Orlando has no desire to master these pagans (a woman does not wish "to make an Englishwoman" of every "negress" [RO 52]), though continuing to regard them as Other (Stimpson 136).

Much as Romola awakens from the sea as a madonna in a strange land, Orlando is transformed during a trance in foreign parts, attended by three madonna figures representing "Purity," "Chastity," and "Modesty." Yet instead of blessing the heroine's rebirth, these ladies strive to veil some obscenity and must be driven away by trumpet blasts of "TRUTH" (one of the male "Gods" [136–37]). The old fairy tales must give way, it seems—very liberating for the abject female figure in such tales, but still not a guarantee of free agency, since a patriarchal reality principle can do the work of a stepmother's curse. Orlando will not have to be a daughter asleep in a tower, but she must give up swashbuckling and learn how to be rescued. There are compensations for such passivity, she thinks on her voyage toward eighteenth-century England. Anticipating *Three Guineas*, she meditates on the advantages of woman's "poverty and ignorance" and the privilege of forgoing exploits for the sake of "contemplation, solitude, love" (160). Such outsider's pride is fragile, and Woolf can only preserve it apart from the frustrations of everyday domestic life. Orlando unlike Romola never holds still for an Epilogue, and constantly reverts to "manly" desires; her life continues to be a vacillation between contemplative solitude and immersion in city turmoil.

Back in London three charges are brought against her: "(1) that she was dead, and therefore could not hold any property whatsoever; (2) that she was a woman, which amounts to much the same thing; (3) that she was an English Duke who had married one Rosina Pepita," whose three sons declared the Duke dead and claimed their inheritance. Her indefinable identity in itself deemed a crime, she retires "incognito or incognita" to the country (168), like Romola evading the power plays of the state in a quest for her own vocation. Yet Orlando's vocation is to be heir and poet without the belittling suffix "ess" on either title, and to find "life and a lover" (185). For all this, she must venture out into the spirit of the age and make the most of her freakish indeterminacy. She bemoans the artifice of "Society," romps with the men of letters in the salons, quarrels with their misogyny, and for relief dresses as a man to gain the freedom of the back streets, where she befriends the whores.

When the fog of the nineteenth century settles, however, she feels she must cease cross-dressing, adopt the crinoline, and "take a husband" (243). Gender has come to be more insistently defined, but she and the Shelleyan Shelmerdine are able to strike a compromise with the marital spirit of the age. They unite the woman-manly adventurer and the man-womanly poet (RO 108), each blending aristocratic and feminine heroism; to each lover it is "such a revelation that a woman could be as tolerant and free-spoken as a man, and a man as strange and subtle as a woman" (258).[25] Yet there is a distinct division of labor: Shelmerdine "had explored the East" (251) and compulsively rounds Cape Horn—in other words, he is an agent of the Empire—whereas Orlando waits at home, her ambassadorial ventures behind her.

Since the protagonist has ceased to play an "important part in the public life of his country" (119), she has increasingly viewed herself as object ("becoming a little more modest . . . of her brains, and a little more vain . . . of her person" [187]), while the naive biographer-narrator has increasingly doubted his command of his subject. What could be more ineffable, more absent, than the woman and the *writer?* In a triumph of impersonality, Orlando fulfills a woman's mission by marrying, thereby becoming reconciled with "the spirit of the age"; this reconciliation promotes her mission as writer: "She could write, and write she did" (266). These acts stun the patriarchal biographer, the rival writer who wants to define "life" in terms of action and external fact.

He resorts to gender convention: "When we are writing the life of a woman, we may, it is agreed, waive our demand for action, and substitute love instead" (268).[26] Yet, in spite of her claim that woman-hood entails contemplation and love rather than action, Orlando foils the biographer's old love plot, declining to slip off her petticoat for a gamekeeper as D. H. Lawrence would have her do (269). With this, as Orlando's opus nears completion, the old biographer is completely overcome by the woman writer's wiles: "Let us go, then, exploring, this summer morning, when all are adoring the plum blossom and the bee" (270). Like the protagonist, the narrator in a kind of trance changes sex, and begins to develop what might be called the lyrical epic combining collective history and private emotion (in the wake, not incidentally, of Aurora Leigh, Barrett Browning, and Woolf herself).[27]

Orlando has borne her poem, "The Oak Tree," much like Romola's pursuit of a higher good, through successive cultural phases, and has disguised "something highly contraband"—her freethinking ambi-tion—by "dexterous deference" to the bourgeois Victorian definition

[25]The lovers are curious and enthusiastic—"they had to put the matter [of each other's sex] to the proof at once" (258)—diverging from conventional romantic, appropriative love. This brush with the erotic is unusual in Woolf's fiction, but as in the union of Esther Lyon and Felix Holt, it displays the innocence of children and angels.
[26]"The truth is that when we write of a woman, everything is out of place . . . the accent never falls where it does with a man" (O 312).
[27]Woolf wrote in her diary as she finished the manuscript of *Orlando,* "I feel more & more sure that I will never write a novel again. Little bits of rhyme come in" (*VW Diary* 3: 177).

of the lady and the writer (265–66). How to carry manly assurance over into the womanly sphere of contemplation without losing an aristocratic *sprezzatura* would be a challenge, Woolf suggests, for any writer in a professionalized, self-conscious age, but particularly for a rarity like Orlando, a lady who can recall being a pageboy for Queen Elizabeth when writers were servants to the great. Orlando will always be "out of it"; her art for art's sake will always be a throwback, a distillation of a precious history but never quite the full Woolfian articulation of the common life. Woolf adores and condones this privileged withdrawal from the thoroughfares of history, but as her own work concludes she dedicates Orlando's inner life, if not Orlando's art, to a kind of public service.

As Orlando approaches the present she perfects her understanding of a tumultuous common life within us all. She tries to marshal her "more than two thousand" selves under "the Captain self, the Key self," recognizing the insubordination of identities and the synchronicity of all times in biographical history (310–14, 305). The narrator still strives for a more definite order: "The reader can judge from overhearing her talk as she drove (and if it is rambling talk, disconnected, trivial, dull, and sometimes unintelligible, it is the reader's fault for listening to a lady talking to herself; we only copy her words as she spoke them, adding in brackets which self in our opinion is speaking, but in this we may well be wrong)" (310). The modern woman writer insists on her own style of interior monologue. Though the narrator still clings to chivalrous notions of a lady's privilege, Orlando has (like a truly great woman or man?) become permeable to other identities and the pulsing ordinary life beyond such privilege. She recognizes that she may be a spoiled snob, though she likes "peasants" and rural life; she drives through a "crowd of market people" unnoticed in spite of her fame and rank (310–12). Like Flush shorn of pedigree, Orlando might make a career out of being "nothing," mocking those who claim to be "something"; she might become part of everything she has met. But like Romola posing for the portrait of a great woman, Orlando still has too much romantic individuality to commit herself wholly to an influential disappearing act.

The Heroine's Progress

In her concluding retirement, Orlando has achieved more in her own right than Romola can claim to have done; she has inherited her ancestral home, she has remained a happy wife and has become a mother (though without giving these roles much thought), she still has plenty of fun, and she is a well-known poet, winner of the Burdett Coutts prize. There is a covert social comment in this last detail, since the rise of female reformers like Angela Burdett Coutts (the great philanthropist and friend of Dickens) coincided with the feminist movement, and Orlando's independence marks a great social reform. Yet whereas Eliot's aristocrat was driven by the *noblesse oblige* of a Burdett Coutts, Orlando has never made bandages or dispensed soup; she is the spirit, not the conscience, of a female literary tradition. Like Romola, Orlando retreats to rest on her laurels and pass on the patriarchal heritage: "With my guineas I'll buy flowering trees, flowering trees, flowering trees and walk among my flowering trees and tell my sons what fame is" (312). The suggestion that both protagonists reign over a flowery domestic world in which they define fame or greatness for male successors seems to dampen hopes for further female quests. What women might emulate their example, might trespass so far? Yet both heroines have fulfilled their aristocratic destinies in spite of being daughters. In the final pages, Orlando welcomes the return of Queen Elizabeth's ghost *and* Shelmerdine, as though in 1928 (a far cry from 1509), the woman's heritage and desire may both be fulfilled.

The implausibilities and longueurs of *Romola*, the raucousness and lacunae of *Orlando* reflect conflicting impulses toward affirming a providential process or a miraculous heroine. Seizing more license than Eliot, Woolf still relies on readers' shared sense of "real" history. Against a deterministic sequence of change, in which the common people serve as material sculpted into history, Eliot and Woolf offer the rare instance of escape from the predictable (Beer, *Past*, 117–37). Romola and Orlando are heroic anomalies, aristocrats who earn their inheritance in spite of patriarchal law. In womanly ways, they gain their place among "lives of the obscure," almost as much a part of the medium of racial memory as are the old-fashioned peasants near Florence or Knole; but they remain like their authors keenly aware of their difference from the masses. Outliving the men who have their political day, Romola and Orlando serve as vessels for the spirit of the age and all ages, subtly influencing "the growing good" (though the good is more indulgently construed in Woolf's text). These heroines escape temporal definition, like the relics that have survived into the reader's present, and as a result they beg the question of female vocation: not only the tradition, but the greatness *and* finally the womanhood are compatible givens in these make-believe worlds.

The authors, implied and actual, stand above the circumscribed achievements of their characters. Whereas Romola consecrated herself to future generations, George Eliot gratified her own ambitions of learning (few novels have been as learned), success, recognition, and—for the living woman—domestic happiness outside patriarchal marriage laws. Perhaps Eliot's emphasis on serving the common people in *Romola* and in the next novel, *Felix Holt*, is offered as atonement for her freedom as outsider, as well as an expression of resentment of the price the public had exacted from her. In all honesty, the salt of the earth could be quite tasteless, and she was glad to dine, as it were, with ladies and gentlemen. When she returned to the English midlands in her next works her persona had gained a more assured, cosmopolitan perspective, as though she claimed the artistic equivalents of Romola's inherited advantages as well as the prerogatives that any English gentleman could take for granted. The strain of *Romola* paid off.

Similarly, Woolf had more to show for herself, to those who knew her from her works or in person, than Orlando's "The Oak Tree" and " 'The Burdett Coutts' Memorial Prize" (312).[28] The epic poem seems almost the natural offspring of tradition; certainly it is no experiment of high modernism, though for the implied author if not for Orlando it opens new generic territory. *Orlando* itself, of course, encompasses "The Oak Tree," synthesizing elements of the entire history of English literature as the poem could not. The author, whom we know as a child of literary criticism, raised among famous writers, must be amused by Orlando's dismay at the human failings of literati and the decline of patronage. Always in the vanguard as her protagonist brings up the rear, Woolf seems to recall with some indulgence her own development toward literary independence, from the early absorption of her father's library, through an apprenticeship in the nineteenth-century novel, to the new voices and forms from *Jacob's Room* onward.

This literary progress also enacts a shift in forms of heroism. It is as though the hero, like Jacob (whose name recalls the patriarchal thief of the birthright), had become the mock hero in Orlando, only to be supplanted, in a trance, by the true feminine heir. In *The Waves* six personae divide between them the "many different people . . . all having lodgment at one time or another in the human spirit" (O 308). Thus the feminine heroism of renunciation that Eliot celebrates becomes the selflessness of the magnanimous creature who is all ages

[28]Sackville-West's "The Land" and the Hawthornden Prize are the patent parallels. Woolf, while she admired Sackville-West's talent, also said she had a "pen of brass" (Nicolson 3: xx–xxii) and viewed the Hawthornden award ceremony as a display of literary philistinism (*VW Diary* 3: 139).

and sexes at once—with a twist of aristocratic egoism. The privilege of illimitable personality beyond gender was seized by this trickster in a book no one was to take seriously, so that the author's next experiments would be received as emanating from the grand old woman of English letters—with a playful difference.

Orlando has all the charm that *Romola* lacks. And yet we can see that the erudite historical romance and the belletristic *jeu d'esprit* alike devise a role for the great woman, reconciling romantic individuality and a collective tradition, rebellion and duty. While "the movement" of Eliot's "mind" may have been "too slow" for humor ("GE" [1919] 155), the escapade Woolf allowed herself in *Orlando* may have been too mercurial; the tendency to be pedantic or to be arch is part of each writer's response to an entire cultural history. Perhaps feeling that they had begun like Flush—awed, puzzled, bound by a leash to the masters or mistresses they loved—they had overcome the dutiful role of sightseer and had learned to trespass. At the same time, in each work the author raises a monument to the dominant cultural heritage; even the iconoclastic *Orlando* suggests that radical changes—of sex, perception, style—are mere intensifications of what went before. As Orlando says to the dead queen returning to the ancestral home in the moonlight, "Nothing has been changed. The dead Lord, my father, shall lead you in" (328).

6

"God was cruel when he made women": *Felix Holt* and *The Years*

Once having made a name for themselves, Eliot and Woolf were in a position to instruct their audience but were also expected to dazzle it. Overt preaching or propaganda was taboo; a novel by a woman would be extremely vulnerable to charges of special pleading if it explicitly presented the feminist cause. In *Felix Holt* (1866) and *The Years* (1937) the authors disguised their arguments about gender and class in apparently impartial histories of everyday life, adding more explicit political statements as nonfictional appendices: "Address to Working Men, by Felix Holt" (1867) and *Three Guineas* (1938). Both novels are clearly serious social histories, whether of class conflict in a Midlands town in the Reform Era, or of the day-to-day impressions of an upper middle-class family in London from 1880 to 1937; as achievements, they appear more admirable than lovable, and neither is a particular favorite with readers or critics. Yet these become extraordinary—and curiously allied—works when considered as women writers' attempts to forge art from political argument.

In response to an immediate political threat—the second Reform Bill or the rise of fascism—each novel advocates gradual amelioration of private life, above all of women's lot. As though keeping up a calm debate in the midst of an air raid, both narrators appear to distract us with an unsettling mixture of historical panorama and domestic vignette, avoiding any direct call to arms. Like so many of their contemporaries, Eliot and Woolf perceived an affinity between women and the "lower" classes, but viewed the bonds of the common life as uneasy at best.[1] The feminism of *Felix Holt* and *The Years* for the most

---

[1] Woolf's pacifism and her belief that "improvement of one's own moral state" was the "answer" to fascist "horror and violence" are signs, for Quentin Bell, of her spinsterish, Victorian sensibility, linked to popular feeling. At a Labour Party meeting, she steered

part is sealed off from the public political action of committees or votes, while ladies are perceived as under siege not only by patriarchs but by the masses.

Eliot more than Woolf openly begs her social questions: Which misogynist is Esther Lyon to marry? Which fate is better for the workers in the short run, brute subjection or brute rebellion? But Eliot seeks to appease the classes and the sexes within the tradition of the novel of manners, through a slightly eccentric marriage in which the heiress marries the poor man (forfeiting her wealth) and seems prepared to help him run a kind of workers' institute. Woolf only hints at the threats to the old order—the Jew in Sara's bath, the futuristic song of the caretaker's children, for example—and offers, as a stay against chaos, the eccentric modes of communion in Sara's friendship with the homosexual Nicholas or in Eleanor's fleeting ecstasies.

Felix Holt may be seen as an attempt to subsume the agitation for women's suffrage in the 1860s under scenes of masculine political life from the 1830s, in the locale and period of Eliot's youth, working within literary and social traditions (Zimmerman, *"Felix Holt,"* 432–37). In *The Years*, Woolf in effect wrote a sequel to *Felix Holt*, a twentieth-century version of the feminist political novel. She purposefully returned in this novel to literary territory dominated by George Eliot. *The Years* begins in 1880, the year of Eliot's death. The novel proceeds to span a period in which Woolf herself grew up (she read *Felix Holt* in 1897 [DeSalvo 221]) and in which Eliot's reputation declined, then rose once more with the help of Woolf's centenary revaluation. Finally, "Present Day," the concluding segment of *The Years*, brings the tradition of Eliot's art of fiction up to the date of publication, in 1937.

As a Study of Cultivated Life, *The Years* resembles *Middlemarch*, which grew out of *Felix Holt* as another biographical history of the English Midlands in the 1830s. Woolf famously acknowledged *Middlemarch* as "one of the few English novels written for grown-up people" ("GE" [1919] 156), but never mentioned *Felix Holt* in her published statements on her predecessor. This disparity in Woolf's recognition of the two works undoubtedly is due to the enormous difference between them in power and design. Yet many of the elements of the acknowledged masterpiece are already present in the preceding work, though with an almost inverted emphasis. Such inversion makes *Felix Holt* the more revealing counterpart to Woolf's effort to proclaim a political statement in silence. Eliot's earlier novel leaves the political issues of class and gender surprisingly exposed and unresolved,

---

the debate toward local gossip, while her nephew, a committed socialist, watched in dismay: "She was much nearer to the feelings of the masses . . . than I was. I wanted to talk politics, the masses wanted to talk about the vicar's wife" (Bell 2: 186–87).

whereas in her "greater" novel, scenes of political life and feminist protest are marginalized. Is it partly the dictum that great art is not political that has devalued *Felix Holt*, and that hampered Eliot as she wrote it?[2] *The Years* is also, but more guardedly, a political novel—as though taking the lesson of *Felix Holt* to heart. Instead of avoiding charges of propaganda by marginalizing the political while historicizing the personal (as in *Middlemarch*), *The Years* marginalizes both personal and political elements almost equally, resisting the appetite for a hero, a heroine, and even the much-favored device of a concluding marriage. Woolf carries on Eliot's attempt in *Middlemarch* to convey the illusion of the passage of time in the lives of many people. She subtly integrates imagery and allusion almost on the grand scale of *Middlemarch*, but with a new skepticism toward metaphor and symbol (though not toward myth): sometimes a walrus-brush is just a walrus-brush. In *The Years*, collective history and moments of being are now the protagonists. Unanswered protests have gone underground.

Though *The Years* seems to me a more balanced success as a novel than *Felix Holt*, the balance is largely due to Woolf's more rigorous suppression of her political "message."[3] *Felix Holt*, almost in spite of Eliot, seems *overtly* the more radical text: it could be said to render the evidence, unassimilated, for the kind of feminist case Woolf makes in *Three Guineas*. It is as though Woolf, after "the years" of agitation since Eliot's day, could face the full implications of the analogy Eliot drew between all injustice and the suppression of the feminine, but perhaps as a result she had to mask the rage Eliot portrayed in Mrs. Transome. That ailing woman, before being put to bed and "soothe[d] . . . with a daughter's tendance" by Esther, says, "Men are selfish . . . and cruel. What they care for is their own pleasure and their own pride." "Not all," is Esther's rather inadequate response to these "painful" words (597–98).

In *Three Guineas*, Woolf continues the "fight that our mothers and grandmothers fought" (TG 102); as I have indicated, she pays a daughter's homage to the feminist associates of Eliot. *The Years* instead disguises its heritage while invoking the Angel in the House, a creature that haunts Eliot's novels, only to slay it. The murder goes almost undetected; the novel begins as the mother, Rose Pargiter, a sweet-

[2]Obviously, many "great" novels have political themes, and many even stage battle or election scenes (*War and Peace*, *The Red and the Black*, *Waverley*, *Vanity Fair*, *Middlemarch* come to mind). But it seems that the arbiters of the canon prefer not to be reminded that literature is politically situated.

[3]My reservations about *Felix Holt* have little to do with the presence of political themes, but rather are based on the implied author's retreat from their implications. I am not suggesting that *The Years* is in any sense more "art" because less "politics."

tempered Mrs. Transome tended by her daughters, slowly passes
away in an upstairs bedroom, never charging her husband with the
selfish cruelty of his adultery.

As in their other writings, in *Felix Holt* and *The Years* the authors
strive to reconcile the gendered public and private spheres. Eliot's
narrator announces the attempt to "understand ourselves," in Woolf's
words, in political context: "This history is chiefly concerned with the
private lot of a few men and women; but there is no private life which
has not been determined by a wider public life" (FH 129). *The Years*
likewise concerns a few representative lives formed by historical
change—a family over a few generations. The Pargiters are not as
"rooted in the common earth" as Eliot's characters, but lead the upper
middle-class "conservatory existence" that still depends on "a nether
apparatus of hot-water pipes liable to cool down on a strike of the
gardeners or a scarcity of coal," as Eliot reminds us (FH 129). Hothouse
flowers (like readers) should be deeply concerned with conditions at
the mines. Woolf presumes this interconnection much as Forster,
in *Howards End*, presumes that the Schlegel sisters must face the
inscrutable facts of Leonard Bast and the Porphyrion Fire Insurance
Company. Like Forster, Woolf holds less faith than Eliot in widespread
fellow-feeling and more in the epiphanic connections drawn by refined
beings like the Schlegels. Woolf would reverse Eliot's emphasis, insisting that there is no public life that has not been determined by a
wider private life.

Fact and Vision, Politics and Art:
The Development of the Novels

Given these ambitions to integrate masculine and feminine spheres
of political history, it is not surprising that *Felix Holt* and *The Years*
have seldom been read as unified achievements. These novels occupy
similar places in the authors' developments and reflect similar struggles to reconcile elements that have often been read as antagonistic—
though Woolf deliberately reflected this antagonism in formal *di*sunity.
Eliot and Woolf returned, after *Romola* and *The Waves*, to the realistic
portrayal of their own milieus within their lifetimes, in works reminiscent of their early novels yet animated by more acute concern for the
lot of women and the threat of untrammeled mass movements, as
well as by the more elaborated conception of their vocations derived
from their most recently published works. *Felix Holt* borrows its setting
and some characterization from *Adam Bede* (in both novels, an edu-

cated artisan has a rich, egotistical rival), while its political intrigue and mob action develop out of *Romola*. *The Years* was designed to combine "facts, as well as the vision. . . . The Waves going on simultaneously with Night & Day"; Woolf sought a relief from modernist stringency after "20 years—since Jacob's Room" (*VW Diary* 4: 129, 151–52, 133, 233).

Each author attempted to confine her argument within a popular, realistic mode, as though wishing to cement her hold on the public. *Felix Holt* has been read as a political novel in the genre of Disraeli's *Sybil* (Williams 103; Bodenheimer 208–10, 222–23). At the same time, Eliot's novel incorporates the Dickensian model, particularly the treatment of legalistic inhumanity and of the embittered matriarchs in *Bleak House* and *Little Dorrit*. More than either of these models, Eliot's novel attempts an aura of historical authenticity—*Felix Holt* is one of her heavily researched novels—and her Author's Introduction assumes the testimonial authority of the sages Carlyle and Ruskin. *The Years*, similarly, relies on the authoritative convention of the impersonal chronicler. Woolf had in mind contemporary family chronicles such as *The Forsyte Saga*.[4] It is almost as though she set out to conquer the territory she had dismissively relinquished to Bennett, Wells, and Galsworthy in "Mr. Bennett and Mrs. Brown," the territory of matter-of-fact that Eliot had helped to clear. Woolf would add to such materialists the greater intimacy with the facts of the "ordinary mind on an ordinary day," as well as the more detached perspective of the searchlight that sweeps the first overture in *The Years*.

Both Eliot and Woolf suffered more than the usual birthpains in delivering a novel from the union of fact and vision (Zimmerman, " 'Mother's History,' " 84–85; Rose, *Parallel*, 221; *VW Diary* 5: 31). *Felix Holt* originated in a low period after Lewes had taken the foundering verse drama *The Spanish Gypsy* out of Eliot's hands; much as *Silas Marner* interrupted *Romola*, *Felix Holt* at first offered a refreshing return to English territory (Haight 381). Eliot might once again rely on her own memory, while the story could be as remote from autobiography as her earlier stories of a carpenter or a weaver. But the labor on *Felix Holt* was little easier than that on *Romola*; she struggled with the novel, suffering "ill health . . . dreadful nervousness and depression," according to Lewes (Haight 385–86). In addition to the pressures on

---

[4]James Hafley compares *The Years*, "possibly the best" of Woolf's novels, to *The Forsyte Saga* (132, 142). Fleishman deplores the resemblance to such popular fiction (*Woolf* 172). Almost alone, Daiches praises *The Years* as an advance on the experiments in *Mrs. Dalloway* and *The Waves*, not another *Forsyte Saga* (111–13). See Lipking 141.

the established woman of letters, there may have been the anxiety induced by her first near approach in fiction to current political conflicts.

Most critics of this novel appear to take it less "personally" or biographically than *Romola*. For one thing, Eliot issued no statements about its embodying her endeavors as grand old woman, and for another it is not as radical a departure from the Austen sphere. Instead, critics discuss disjunctive political and "personal" plots or conflicting generic intentions without acknowledging their assumptions about gender difference. Eliot does seem to have been doubly concerned with the accuracy of a historical-political novel on the Reform Era and with the effectiveness of a tragedy in novel form.[5] As Fred C. Thomson reads it, *Felix Holt* originated in Eliot's study of classical tragedy as she worked on *The Spanish Gypsy*, but she later worked up an interest in electioneering politics ("Classic Tragedy" 47; "Genesis"; Introduction). Like the tendency to suppress the subtitle, "the Radical," this belief in the priority of the Transome story reflects a formalist bias toward "apolitical" art. Yet one does not have to be a dedicated formalist to find, as I do, that the greatest energy in the book is sparked by Mrs. Transome rather than by election politics (Vance 119–20). Conversely, critics with a bias toward political art maintain that Mrs. Transome's story is the afterthought. Arnold Kettle represents the view that the novel is not political enough. Reversing Thomson's account of the composition, he claims that the original study of two kinds of radical was deflected by Eliot's interest in "the position of woman"; her "failure" entails a refusal to face "the realities of the social situation . . . the nature of the common people and their problems" (106–9). A personal (feminist) bias interferes with the social historian's work.[6]

Thus critics resist the idea that the plots centering on Mrs. Transome, Esther, Felix, and Harold might be more than incidentally related; men's politics and women's relationships hardly appear to speak the same language. In spite of the manifest analogies in the novel between the politics of the drawing room and of the hustings, the accounts of Eliot's having been distracted from one sphere into the other persist, partly justified because it *is* impossible to make a fully

---

[5]Early critics, while generally admiring, laid out two lines of attack: against the political novel and against the moral drama (Carroll, *Critical Heritage*, 251–70; Sandler 137); *Felix Holt* was more a critical than a popular success (Haight 387).

[6]Though Carroll does not insist that the "spheres of love, politics, and religion" are separate, he claims that Esther has "usurped Felix's central position" ("*Felix Holt*,"134, 140). See also Wiesenfarth, *Eliot's Mythmaking*, 170–85.

coherent novel out of *Felix Holt*. There is, especially, a surplus of feminist protest, surplus because narrator, characters, and plot largely ignore it.

The tragedy of Mrs. Transome is that of a woman who is unable to renounce her personal desires and who finds no wider calling; she is a pettier prototype of the Alcharisi, the dark double of the grand old woman of letters. Female ambition without voluntary self-sacrifice is always a disturbing force in Eliot's work. As though to contain this force, the novel shows the results of conscientious research into things as they were: the history of the Reform Era as it opened and quickly closed the possibility of extending political rights to workers and women (Haight 381; Thomson, "Genesis," 577–83). The Comtean lawyer Frederic Harrison and John Blackwood praised the "politics" of the first two volumes, dispelling her "depression as to [the novel's] practical effectiveness," though she remained in her accustomed "state of utter distrust and anxiety about my work" (*GE Letters* 4: 247–48, 256, 300).

Like *Felix Holt*, *The Years* first arose as a relief from the author's sense of defeat. Woolf had begun *The Common Reader, Second Series* and *Flush* in order to offset her habitual panic on publishing a novel, in this case *The Waves*; this relief characteristically took the form of critical essays, in which she was confident of excelling, and of a playful biography in the line of *Orlando*, immortalizing Barrett Browning's dog as a very tame precursor. But both works had become drudgery that stood in the way of an ambitious project first conceived back in 1931 (*VW Diary* 4: 142). This was to have been an "Essay-Novel," alternating essays on the condition of women with selected chapters from an "unwritten" novel about the Pargiter family. As the difficulties of sustaining this double form hit home, Woolf later divided the two elements into the "1880" section of *The Years* and the germ of *Three Guineas*. Much as Thomson and others view Eliot as having shifted intentions in the face of incompatible elements, Mitchell Leaska believes that in February 1933 Woolf compacted the essay "interchapters" into the novel because she recognized the inevitable failure of the " 'marriage of granite and rainbow' " (Introduction, *The Pargiters*, xvii).

Yet two months later she was still hoping "to give the whole of the present society— . . . facts, as well as the vision" (*VW Diary* 4: 151–52). After tediously revising the first, nine-hundred-page draft, she sent the last typescript to be printed in galley proofs before Leonard had read it, so hopeless was she about this novel. Like Eliot, she was ill and tormented by "a feeling of complete despair & failure" (*VW*

Diary 5: 24; Bell 2: 191–96). Virginia seized on Leonard's possibly forced approval of the revised proofs much as Eliot depended on Lewes's, Harrison's, and John Blackwood's praise. Woolf immediately took refuge in writing *Three Guineas*, which like *The Years* grew out of a speech to the National Society for Women's Service (*VW Diary* 4: 6); her historical research, unlike Eliot's, was published complete with footnotes. Woolf had advised herself to postpone writing "On Being Despised," as *Three Guineas* was then called: "This fiction is dangerously near propaganda" (*VW Diary* 4: 300).

Though this warning to herself might seem to confirm Leaska's claim that the novel was distinguished from the essays as non-didactic *art*, Woolf like Eliot clothed historical argument in private experience without accepting a conventional separation of spheres: the art of personality *was* political. Both projects claimed a place in traditional high art; much as Eliot attempted a prose fiction tragedy, Woolf wove a texture of allusion and image in the Dantean and Miltonic tradition, but with a subversive emphasis on matriarchal cults. The mysterious patterns of red and gold and recurring objects distract us from any traces of polemic, while the lacunae in the work—much of Woolf's labor on the novel consisted of cutting—disguise her original design of a feminist history, wrong side out, of two hundred years (Radin, " 'Two enormous chunks,' " 221–27).

The response to *The Years* was largely favorable but mixed (Majumdar and McLaurin 371–99), much like the response to *Felix Holt*, though sales were relatively brisk for Woolf—*The Years* was a bestseller in the United States. Beginning with Leonard Woolf, many readers have felt that *The Years* is overburdened with historical fact, a kind of admirable but dull study like *Romola*, perhaps. Jean Guiget, for example, sees the externality of fact in *The Years* as alien to the visionary who had written *The Waves*, and reads the later work biographically: *The Years* is a "novel *manqué*, whose failure is perhaps the most significant symptom we have of the disequilibrium that made Virginia Woolf's originality and greatness—and which led to her undoing" (309, 317–18).[7] Since the more sympathetic revival of Woolf in the 1970s, the biographical author is usually granted more control over her fate and more command over the public sphere; with the publication in 1977 of *The Pargiters* and of the revaluation of *The Years* in the *Bulletin of the New York Public Library*, critics more commonly affirm that the amalgamation of fact and vision was successful (e.g.,

---

[7]Schaefer attributes such a disequilibrium to the incompatible spheres of gender, and traces the sadness of the novel to Woolf's own discomfort with the "masculine world" of fact (135).

Radin, *Woolf's "The Years"*). Recently it appears that this realistic novel demands exegesis on a Joycean scale (Marcus, *Languages*, 36–74), while its anti-fascism on private and public fronts must be retraced as well (Comstock). For all the careful patterning in the novel, the "drive[ ] toward disjunction" seems purposeful (Middleton 160); Woolf herself wrote, "Its failure is deliberate" (*VW Diary* 5: 65; Lipking 144). It remains a puzzle, best pieced together by readers who have absorbed the kind of feminist argument that is exposed in *Felix Holt* and thoroughly explicated in *Three Guineas*.

Both *Felix Holt* and *The Years*, then, suggest that the grand old women of letters felt called on to teach their public unwelcome social truths while at the same time advancing artistic tradition, and both have been read as examples of an inevitable clash between such aims, particularly for the woman writer. The authors acknowledged the risk they had taken in attempting political art. After the publication of *Felix Holt*, Eliot reminded Harrison that "aesthetic teaching . . . if it lapses anywhere from the picture to the diagram . . . becomes the most offensive of all teaching" (*GE Letters* 4: 300). Woolf too saw the perils of a plan to incorporate "millions of ideas but no preaching." The challenge, as she stated it, was to "get the round, not only the flat. . . . I mean intellectual argument in the form of art: I mean how give ordinary waking Arnold Bennett life the form of art?" (*VW Diary* 4: 152, 161). Indeed this was the difficulty: the artful worlds of *Felix Holt* and *The Years* at times do seem reduced to two-dimensional tracts. Yet the ambition to unite "intellectual argument" as well as "ordinary waking Arnold Bennett life" with "art" was inherent in the vocation of these historical writers. Mitchell Leaska sees Woolf as a "pargeter" in *The Years*, that is, "one who glosses and smoothes over" the "chasms" between "historic fact" and "immediate feeling."[8] Eliot, too, might be seen as a pargeter in her effort to meld Reform Era politics and domestic drama. Yet those "chasms" between history and experience would have seemed, to Woolf and Eliot, only another aspect of the questionable division between public and private spheres. The gap to be closed between fact and vision was more an aesthetic than an epistemological one: how to write a novel and not a tract out of their insight into the history of the common life.

That politics are personal, that reform depends on private more than public change, is the argument not only of *Felix Holt* and *The Years*, but also of their appendices, "Address to Working Men, by

---

[8]Leaska, Introduction, *The Pargiters*, xiv–xv. Leaska acknowledges Marcus's suggestion that the word would appear in the *English Dialect Dictionary* edited by Joseph Wright, the model for Mr. Robson in "1880."

Felix Holt," and *Three Guineas*. The latter works seem to preach inaction even as they brandish weapons borrowed from activists. In an essay written for the cultivated audience of *Blackwood's Magazine*, Eliot adopts Felix's name and homiletic style to admonish an almost preindustrial working class to recognize their common cause with their masters, improve themselves, and consider the greater good of gradual change. Felix seems to view the class order as an ahistorical given, and tacitly excludes all consideration of women, inviting respect for the great men who have added to the common stock of humanity. In *Three Guineas*, a far more sophisticated and compelling work, Woolf's persona writes to a gentleman of her circle, deferentially explaining why educated men's daughters cannot subscribe to anti-war causes; they must, like Eliot's working men, improve themselves first. The letters gather fascinating historical detail concerning the great lady reformers to show that women do not share a common interest with men of power and that they should mock all symbols of eminence. Eliot's ventriloquism dissociates her from both speaker and implied audience; she places herself among the educated men. Woolf speaks as though she herself belongs to the underprivileged class, yet she is the sister, not the employee, of the men in power. She rephrases Eliot's appeal on behalf of Arnoldian culture, a collective human development that makes demands for individual rights or expression seem impertinent and self-centered. While Eliot's and Woolf's polemical essays release from the novels unruly challenges to powerful men, they do not promise a radical break with traditions of class and gender, though Woolf's separatist critique of patriarchy has transformative potential.

The arguments of both novels and tracts appear politically conservative, resting hope on the influence of the enlightened few. The Tory John Blackwood wrote to Eliot, "How good your politics are. . . . I suspect I am a radical of the Felix Holt breed" (*GE Letters* 4: 246; Pinney 415). The righteous eponymous hero, generally seen as "too good to be true" (Lerner 49), has been condemned as a spokesman for Eliot's dread of an enfranchised mob, in line with Arnold's response to the Hyde Park Riots in *Culture and Anarchy* (1869).[9] Woolf is similarly reproached from the left for class insensitivity, but unlike Eliot she

[9]Myers, *"Felix Holt,"* 15. Raymond Williams and David Craig deplore Eliot's fear of the mob, which led her to wish to defer political reform till education counteracted the effects of poverty (Williams 104–9; Craig 67–74; Perkin 126–29). Linda Bamber instead praises Eliot's anti-deterministic, non-pragmatic insistence on improving human nature. Catherine Gallagher places *Felix Holt* alongside *Culture and Anarchy* in an excellent analysis of the crisis in liberal thought in the 1860s (*Industrial Reformation* 228–37).

was censured by contemporaries for her feminist polemic as well. Q. D. Leavis, reviewing *Three Guineas* in 1938, rebuked the author for being "quite insulated by class" and for indulging in a "release of sex hostility" in the mode of "Nazi dialect without Nazi convictions." Leavis's own extreme hostility did not prevent her from seeing the Victorian roots of Woolf's feminist politics: "What respectable ideas inform this book belong to the ethos of John Stuart Mill" (382–85).

In spite of their obvious conservatism in some respects, both novels offer a radical insight into the correspondence between the lots of women and the fate of European civilization, between historical events and moments in the domestic interior. Mrs. Transome's battle with her son is more than coincidentally linked with the battle between ancient right and the rioting rabble on election day. In the same way, the question of education and professions for women is raised by the ritual of afternoon tea in a Victorian drawing room. Almost defiantly out of step with their times, the novels are set well before the crises of the 1860s or the 1930s, in order to dramatize the gradual change in obscure lives. In addition to this careful historical scale, the novels also suggest a timeless aspect of human relations. Mrs. Transome's and Esther's complementary stories have a mythical quality, as though like Demeter and Persephone they enact the recurring seasons; the generations of Pargiter women similarly enact their seasonal rituals of death and rebirth, while Eleanor and Delia, like Mrs. Transome, recognize that home is a Dantesque hell. The complex structures of these novels—shifting between plots, households, times, points of view—draw analogies between the private choices of women and men and the transitional epochs in which they live. What cannot be put asunder, according to the outlook of these novels, cannot be joined without masking the rough margins; the authors are pargeting before our eyes.

Holding by the Roots, Pargeting the Spheres

What do we see if we read these novels as being *about* their own disjunctions, *about* the imbalance between inseparable spheres and elements? As the biographer of Orlando confesses, "When we write of a woman, everything is out of place" (O 312); when a woman writes of personalized politics, perhaps, the emphasis falls unexpectedly. Before interpreting the gender politics in detail, I want to remark on some of the strange first impressions presented by these emphatically public, impersonal novels, novels asserting control over detail. Harold Transome claims for men the prerogative of participation in historical change: "Women keep to the notions in which they have been brought up. It doesn't signify what they think—they are not called upon to judge or to act" (FH 117). But if feminine domestic details *do* have a mind and a development of their own, do signify in history, the patriarchal interpreter is seriously mistaken. Neither novel, however, shouts the voice of Harold down.

The usual interpretive guidelines as to what does signify appear to be missing from both novels. As they wrote and revised, both authors deflected attention from female characters onto male, and deployed impersonal descriptive passages and titles that subordinate the domestic, particular perspective of the women. Mrs. Transome and Transome Court are only part of the story of 1832, and a less timely part; Esther, similarly, remains outside public life, more like Maggie Tulliver than Romola. The struggles of the men, Harold, Jermyn, Rufus, and Felix, on the other hand, appear almost identical with the historical crisis of the novel. Yet as Eliot's two Radicals are brought to express their feelings for the ladies of the house, so her heroine is allowed to demonstrate her influence on a public stage. Woolf's primary female characters, unlike the women in *Felix Holt*, resemble Romola in their ultimate independence from men and in their more constant though subtle involvement with public life. Whereas in *The Pargiters*, the first version of "1880," the women predominate, in the finished novel men have an almost equal share; "1880" opens from Abel Pargiter's point of view, and the novel continues with extensive studies of men interspersed throughout.

Both novels encourage us to know ourselves as one of many, as parts of a general pattern that foils our egotistical plans; hence the impersonal overview of the narrators. The Author's Introduction and epigraphs to each chapter, added late to *Felix Holt*, are transformed into the overtures to each "year" in *The Years*, inserted in proof (Thomson, Introduction, xviii, xxviii; Radin, " 'Enormous chunks,' " 226). The narrators seem at once intimately acquainted with and pityingly remote from past "weather." The Proem of *Romola* and the overtures in *The Waves* were precedents for such signposts of formal unity and authorial impersonality. The overtures in *The Years*, however, frustrate the reader's search for intelligible pattern. After these diachronic preliminaries, both Eliot's first chapter and Woolf's open on a certain afternoon in a specific year, centering on an unhappy parent who waits for a delayed change in the family. Women are restless in their drawing rooms; men return from their affairs in the world and impose their authority. Both novels, then, open with a wide-circling bird's-eye view, only to perch in a gilded cage.

Eliot's narrator is kin to De Quincey ("The English Mail-Coach"), Thackeray's showman (chapter 7, *Vanity Fair*), and the future Theophrastus Such: "Five-and-thirty years ago the glory had not yet departed from the old coach roads." He warns that when "Posterity" travels "like a bullet through a tube," the picturesque "stories of English life" garnered on a coach ride will be lost. Instead, this slow drive through the Midlands will trace a chronological history, "from one phase of English life to another," from pastoral harmony to market towns to manufacturing districts. Our narrator, like the coachman another "Virgil," will lead us into the inferno of hereditary tragedies lurking on estates like Transome Court that try to resist social change (FH 75–84). Thus we pass through changing social conditions to enter Mrs. Transome's hell in chapter 1, when expected good fortune—the return of her son—merely confirms her enslavement to her past and her womanhood. Two chapters later the novel reverses this move, and examines those surrounding conditions in the light of her tragedy.

The action of *Felix Holt* is compressed into the nine months from Harold's arrival to Esther's wedding. This compression, while it hastens Esther's metamorphosis from a creature of Byronic sensibility to one of Wordsworthian duty, calls attention to the design of tragedy as Eliot viewed it; each of the main characters faces an "irreparable collision between the individual and the general." In "Notes on *The Spanish Gypsy*," she particularly illustrates the individual's needs as those of a woman born with "inherited" disability, like the worse biological share of womanhood ("she may be lame . . . she may be a negress"). Such an individual can only find "well-being . . . through large resignation," but "happily, we are not left to that. Love, pity, constituting sympathy . . . with . . . the lot of our fellow-men . . . become . . . willing submission and heroic Promethean effort" (Cross 3: 33–34; Thomson, "Classic Tragedy," 48–49). Though such sacrifice appears triumphant, Eliot means to affirm as well the triumph of general conditions over those unluckily born to subjection.

The compensatory lesson of selflessness is taught in *Felix Holt* partly through repeated deflections from what appears to be the center of interest, the favored individual. When we abandon Mrs. Transome or Felix for long passages until Esther comes to them in their prisons, we should perceive the pattern in a larger web than the fate of one hero or heroine. After meeting Harold, Mrs. Transome, and Matthew Jermyn, we must turn to their equally self-important analogues, Felix,

Mrs. Holt, and Rufus Lyon, accepting the pattern of the frustration of personal desire. "And the lives we are about to look back upon . . . are rooted in the common earth, having to endure all the ordinary chances of past and present weather. As to the weather of 1832, the Zadkiel of that time had predicted . . . unusual perturbations in organic existence . . . that mutual influence of dissimilar destinies which we shall see unfolding itself" (129). The cue for Woolf's weather interludes is sounded here. Social history evolves catastrophically, regardless of individual will or perspective.

Less the endearing raconteur or prophet, Woolf's narrator in the first paragraphs describes "uncertain" weather as a kind of epochal element uniting all England, farmers and Londoners. Instead of a coach ride through the Midlands, we have a survey of London districts filled with "processions" of different sorts of people, carriages, birds. Between sentences we leap the hours of a presumed day in 1880, and then to the passage of all time: "Slowly wheeling, like the rays of a searchlight, the days, the weeks, the years passed one after another across the sky" (3–4). Here is a novel to be read not with the "pity and terror" of passenger and coachman (FH 83), but with the unpersonified inquiry of a searchlight.

The Years emulates Felix Holt in unfolding interdependent lots in the medium of changeable public "weather." In another typical overture, the narrator travels like a bullet through a tube from the spirit of the age to far-flung scenes, then to a particular character's point of view:

> Money was in brisk circulation. The streets were crowded. . . . The wind ruffled the channel, tossed the grapes in Provence, and made the lazy fisher boy, who was lying on his back in his boat in the Mediterranean, roll over and snatch a rope.
>
>   But in England, in the North, . . . Kitty, Lady Lasswade, . . . drew the cloak round her shoulders. (89)

Simultaneity binds the fisher boy to Kitty, just as it connects Job Tudge and Mrs. Transome, or Jo the crossing sweeper and Lady Dedlock in Bleak House. Here, however, the "mutual influence of dissimilar destinies" appears less tragic than sublimely incidental—or rather, the recognition that there is only an incidental link between individuals lends a sublime sense of the tragedy of human life.

Woolf's chapters or segments represent not so much the conjunction as the dispersion of dissimilar destinies, even more effectively challenging the egocentrism of narrative focused on individuals, but without affirming a redemptive resignation. In the "First Essay" of The

Pargiters, ostensibly a speech on professions for women, Woolf argues that "we cannot understand the present if we isolate it from the past. . . . We must become the people that we were two or three generations ago." (The essay expresses more confidence than the taciturn novel about the power of sympathy to overcome difference.) To perceive the collision of the individual with the general, Woolf will read "chapters from an unpublished novel" tracing the Pargiter family from 1800 to 2032, "to represent English life at its most normal." Such a utopian "novel of fact" would be truer than the "clumsy" history that declares, " 'In the year 1842 Lord John Russell brought in the Second Reform Bill' and so on" (8–9). Woolf here stakes a claim in Eliot's historical territory: *Felix Holt* is the novel of two Reform Bills, fleshing out representative English life and casting the chronology of the history books in the background. Woolf's history indeed casts so much in the background, including any individual Promethean struggle, that it risks being a blur of boring fact, yet it offers glimpses of heroic myth and everyday tragedy.

In such novels mixing tragedy and fact, the customary narrative drive can seem lost. In *Felix Holt* there are dark family secrets, musty wills, lovers' lockets, but nothing more sensational arises than an anticlimactic riot. To most readers, Mrs. Transome and Matthew Jermyn broadcast their secret affair long before Harold knows of it, while the legal dispute between the Transomes, Durfeys, and Bycliffes remains hardly more than it appears to Esther, a muddle of prerogatives magically invoked to change lives.[10] Even the title raises doubts, not only as to the sense in which "Radical" applies to a man who opposes what would become the Chartist program, but also as to the centrality of the fortunate and faith-upholding Felix Holt to the moral drama of the novel. Happy is he who holds by the roots, the title seems to say, yet Felix must undo his father's errors and Esther must escape her inheritance (Wiesenfarth, *Eliot's Mythmaking,* 177–80). E. S. Dallas observed in 1866 that a male author would have named the book after Esther (Carroll, *Critical Heritage,* 267; Rosenman, "Women's Speech," 237). Indeed, most of the novel centers on the metamorphoses of the heroine, whose namesakes, Dickens's Esther Summerson and Queen Esther, are likewise poor foster daughters who find favor with powerful men. Eliot's Esther earns her moral crown by refusing a luxurious place as chief concubine, but she uses her influence to help her lover and her father, as Queen Esther saves Mordecai. The

[10]The Lyons receive the news of Esther's inheritance as "magic"; Felix says her fitness for ladyship gives "sanction to that musty law . . . the appropriate conditions are come at last" (FH 557).

tragic Vashti, a famous actress in *Villette* (1853), in this novel has become the defeated Mrs. Transome, almost as though Eliot, like another King Ahasuerus, wished to make an example of the rebellious woman.[11] Precedent and tradition are subtly modified but without avowed challenge to patriarchal order.

The Years similarly sends contradictory signals. With its sequence of dated segments, its details of dress and household objects, its family of characters, it seems to offer a chronicle of the English educated class from 1880 to 1937. Yet Woolf fails to supply the genealogy, and she leaps across "precipices from 1880 to here & now," seemingly at random (she considered adding "an appendix of dates" reminiscent of Galsworthy [*VW Diary* 4: 129, 146]). There are only one dramatized death and an anticlimactic funeral, no lovers' vows or weddings, no great achievements or crises, while the historical events of those years are shunted offstage. A street crier announces, "The King's dead!" at the end of "1910"; in "1911" the men "discuss the situation in the Balkans" while "Eleanor's attention wandered" (Y 191, 201).

Only Eleanor approaches the role of heroine through her endurance and growing insight. In early drafts of *The Years*, Woolf perceived "Elvira" becoming too much the "dominant" heroine. Much as Eliot had intertwined "Miss Brooke" with Lydgate's story, Woolf determined that her heroine must "be seen only in relation to other things" (*VW Diary* 4: 152). She divided Elvira's role between Eleanor and Sara, finally deleting long passages of Eleanor's development in galley proofs and suppressing the feminist political argument of the original essays (Middleton 163–64; Squier 200; Radin, " 'Enormous chunks,' " 234). As published, the narrative shifts for long passages to Kitty's, Martin's, North's, and others' points of view, while between the years figures like Eugénie have unceremoniously ceased to exist in the manner of Mrs. Ramsay. The title suggests this impartial succession of collective experience.[12] Time passes, Woolf declares, and ordinary people are the medium of its passage; life consists mostly of detail. Women here do outgrow their upbringing, but no one is "called upon to judge or to act."

[11]The Book of Esther sets the context of *Felix Holt*, but the heroine's role as political savior of her people has been privatized. Lawyer Jermyn is Haman the villainous minister; Felix, like Mordecai, is an unruly outsider yet a guide for Esther inside the palace. See Zimmerman, "*Felix Holt*," 441n.11. Charlotte Brontë's "Vashti" is judged as a woman rather than as an artist, suggesting a precedent for Eliot's defiant Alcharisi in *Daniel Deronda*.

[12]Woolf's list of possible titles confirms her intention to narrate a collective experience of time: The Pargiters, Here and Now (chosen because it would "not compete with the Herries Saga, the Forsyte Saga & so on" [*VW Diary* 4: 176]), Music, Dawn, Sons and

As though avoiding the unpersuasive electioneering scenes of *Felix Holt*, Woolf's narrator ignores such drama as the General Strike altogether and abbreviates the suffragette or Irish agitation as an anecdote in the life of Rose or Delia. Eliot, on the other hand, ignores the implications of the domestic drama that *The Years* was to reenact and that the essays of *The Pargiters* and the letters of *Three Guineas* were to interpret. Significantly, Eliot made no public statement on the sexual politics of *Felix Holt*, as though unaware that her novel alluded to any current issue besides the second Reform Bill of 1867, yet she was closely allied with agitators for female education and enfranchisement. Woolf similarly glosses over the class issue her predecessor sought to settle, even though Virginia shared with Leonard Woolf a commitment to a kind of socialism.[13]

In the novels themselves, political activity is shown to be corrupt, idealistic, ineffectual, or worse, the cause of social chaos; Felix gives a fine speech, Rose joins a committee, and both are jailed for their part in civil disorder, but these enthusiasms are shown to breed further violence. Whereas Felix, wounded and imprisoned, endures an ordeal of the passive femininity he initially despised, Rose remains fixed in a martial fantasy as "Pargiter of Pargiter's Horse!" "Force is always wrong," says Kitty in "Present Day"; "still . . . Rose had the courage of her convictions. Rose went to prison." Martin denounces the suffragettes because they led the mob into the Great War; their means, like those of Felix, spelled disastrous ends: "She smashed his window . . . and then she helped him to smash other people's windows. Where's your decoration, Rose?" (Y 420).

The fate of these political activists alerts us to a set of convictions that the novels are *not* reluctant to teach. You cannot evade the claims of the past (you self-making men!); force is always wrong; politics must accommodate the inner common life. At odd moments, these principles are revealed. Lawyer Jermyn, trying to blackmail the opportunist Scaddon, incriminates himself as well to the reader: as he says, "There may indeed be claims which can't assert themselves—a—legally, which are yet molesting to a man of some reputation" (315). The lawyer is one of the devious masculine "radicals" who profit by their changeability, but who in the end must recognize the rule of consequences that women seldom defy; he might complain that " 'tis grievous, that with all amplification of travel . . . a man can never

---

Daughters, Daughters and Sons, Ordinary People, The Caravan, The Years (Leaska, Introduction, *The Pargiters*, xv n.4).

   [13]Leonard Woolf called himself "a heretical socialist," not quite in harmony with the "true-red socialist nor even the pinkish trade unionist" (*Downhill All the Way* 85).

separate himself from his past history" (epigraph, chapter 21, 310). There are no shortcuts in moral life, the perhaps-Tory, perhaps-female narrator tells us; "the slow old-fashioned way of getting from one end of our country [or life] to the other is the better thing to have in the memory" (75). Jermyn has become a gentlemanly villain by a slow, coach-ride process, "led on through the years by the gradual demands of a selfishness." Like the egotist Jason abandoning the woman he believes he is "not at all obliged to," Jermyn will meet his Medea's vengeance (513).

In the world of Woolf's novel there is no coherent vengeance. The "dead hand" of the past has relaxed; memory recurs not as a matter of ethical responsibility but as a matter of self-knowledge. As in *Felix Holt*, in *The Years* your enemy is always your *semblable*, but no "plots" undo you. One cryptic scene, when Sara and Martin lunch together in a City chophouse, might be a later version of Eliot's study of "the market dinner at 'the Marquis' " in Treby Magna: both mark the changes in traditional hierarchy when outsiders enter the elite male world of commerce and politics, with its "many gradations of dignity"; like the effigies in the Florentine church of the Nunziata, many vie for access to "the secret of the highest affairs" (chapter 20, FH 299). Woolf's scene confronts martial Martin, who is beginning to question orders, with his poor, spinsterish cousin Sara, a kind of Antigone. This educated man's daughter will never sell herself to men's prosperity (TG 93); she is a true radical in a sense only hinted at, in Eliot's novel, by the rebellious Mrs. Transome (who is consciously Tory). In one oracular outburst, Sara denounces war and all hegemony:

> " 'Roll up the map of Europe,' said the man to the flunkey. 'I don't
> believe in force'!" She brought down her fork. A plumstone jumped.
> Martin looked round. People were listening. (232)[14]

Martin is still trapped in his patriarchal role, the notions in which he was brought up; he laughs at being treated like "God" by the old servant Crosby, yet he is enraged, just as his father would have been, when the waiter tries to cheat him.

[14]All responses to institutionalized violence seem subtly implicated in that violence. Sara seems to attack the lunch table, while the man repudiating force seems to command not only his flunkey but all of Europe. Compare the motto on the statue of Nurse Cavell: "Patriotism is not enough." Eleanor calls this "the only fine thing that was said in the war," though the statue honors Nurse Cavell's contribution to the war effort. Eleanor curses the "bully" Mussolini and tears up his picture in the paper (Y 336, 330–31; Marcus, *Languages*, 42).

In Woolf's novel, a community of outsiders arrives at a vision of personalized politics only dimly foreseen by Felix and Esther. In "1917," Eleanor encounters a discussion between a Frenchman, her cousin Maggie's husband, and their Polish friend Nicholas, concerning Napoleon and "the psychology of great men"—Carlylean subjects Eleanor at first assumes to be beyond her "reach" (281). As though Felix were to ask Esther's opinion on corrupt electioneering practices, however, Eleanor is brought into the political discourse; the demarcations between spheres have disintegrated—"the war, perhaps, removing barriers" (284). The men are themselves outsiders, in exile; instead of hero worship, they propose a history of common experience. Nicholas explains to Eleanor, "I was saying we do not know ourselves, ordinary people . . ., how then can we make religions, laws, that—"; Eleanor completes the thought: "that fit—that fit." Eleanor is surprised that his thought so closely fits hers, but Nicholas observes, "We all think the same things; only we do not say them" (281–82). Eleanor the Victorian is slowly catching up, realizing that Nicholas the homosexual and Sara can love each other without romance, realizing that her squeamishness about homosexuality is obsolete.

Eliot would have been as slow to catch up, perhaps, as Eleanor. The Victorian author cannot consciously declare all battles ignoble, all decorations spurious; she must still rely on the revelatory plot and the clearly ordered progression of individual enlightenment. The modern perspective unravels teleological narrative, makes change less intelligible, and doubts, for example, that in nine months (the span of *Felix Holt*) men can learn feeling and women can learn responsibility. Yet both Victorian and modern meditations on social difference vacillate between liberal dreams of consensus—we all think alike—and visions of dissolution and miscommunication. The interrupted monologues of the eccentric Rufus Lyon and Nicholas Pomjalovsky both suggest that the preacher must be a kind of outsider. No one succeeds in commanding a sympathetic, discerning audience in either novel; the sheltered circles addressed by *Romola* and *Orlando* are no longer so comfortably entertained. If art is a means of extending our sympathy for the common life, why are most common figures so repugnant here? The human animals of the Sproxton mines or the streets around Sara and Maggie's flat are noted but scarcely particularized, and they manifestly threaten educated ladies. What has become of the progressive social vision that I have argued Eliot and Woolf share with Victorian lady reformers? Where are the positive effects of feminine influence?

It seems that in *Felix Holt* and *The Years* the hopes of the ideology of influence are more difficult to abandon *because* they are so obviously hopeless; the schisms within the traditional social order have never before gaped so wide in these authors' works. Feminine difference cannot be directly questioned if there is to be any escape from a pattern of patriarchal fatality. Thus, while the injustices of class and gender are barely "pargeted" over, the wall of civilization, as Woolf figures it in *Between the Acts*, still stands, supported by the personal feelings, the moments of sympathy, in which women have specialized for so long. Meanwhile, the women's desperation, their lack of something to do outside the world of love, is finely delineated but neither judged nor acted upon.

Many moments in *The Years* suggest that Woolf in effect is summarizing and extracting many *Felix Holt*s, many unwritten Victorian novels, as they repeat themselves over the years. A scene in "1880," for instance, proposes what might have been the story of *Felix Holt* from Esther's point of view: Kitty meets an educated worker, Jo Robson, the self-made scholar's son, fresh from carpentry work in the garden (is he another Adam Bede?). Mr. Robson, whose original, Joseph Wright, provided the dictionary definition of "the Pargiters," might have played a role like that of Rufus Lyon (or Caleb Garth). In the humble setting, Kitty is ashamed of her fine clothes and manners, and the muscular hero appeals to her. However, like Dorothea Brooke's sister Celia (dubbed "Kitty"), she later marries the eligible, titled suitor, whereas Esther adapts herself to her romantic hero of the working classes. Like most elliptical moments in *The Years*, Kitty's encounter is the road not taken, the Victorian memory of yet another memory, as though nostalgia for the unrefined passion of youth or for the un-bourgeois classes were an inherent condition of the gentlewoman's oppressive liberty.

If the gentlewomen are captives in both novels, they (and a few rare sympathetic men) nevertheless have an insight into the perpetual emotions that offer the only recourse as institutions fail to meet human needs (and both novels project a universal humanity from the English middle class). Fellow-feeling is no magic remedy in either historical crisis. The double standard weighs heavily on both men and women, and there is little to alleviate the ache of loveless family bonds; generations will continue to suffer unless they can come to know themselves. Yet there is a glimmer of hope in a harmony of the sexes, figured here in the concluding wedding of Felix and Esther or the arrival of a couple in a taxi at dawn. Historically, Woolf's redaction inscribes the failure of Eliot's rainbow of promise; the granddaughters of Esther and Felix would still struggle between domestic oblivion and public achievement as the Pargiters do. Successive generations have to work out for themselves the terms of compromise between men and women. The crisis of one year becomes the same old story, repeated over many. A sense of closure has given way to an uneasy segue.

How Those Details Signify

Simply to note the trivial matters of lives of the obscure may be a form of protest. If women have been consigned to lives of domestic detail, it is time the history of such particulars were related. No details of women's lives should be dismissed as "small airs and small notions," as Felix calls them. On the contrary, these novels maintain that such matters are of determining importance: the key to the history of nineteenth-century parliamentary reform or of twentieth-century world wars was kept in the workbaskets and writing tables of mothers, daughters, wives. Yet when women cross the boundary of their sphere, the consequences are not pretty: Mrs. Transome's cold lust for power, Rose's militarism, and the doctor Peggy's lonely rationalism provide monitory examples. Instead, the influence of Esther, the freedom and innocence of Eleanor and Sara are presented as the feminine alternative to the corruption of masculine power and ownership; Esther's testimony is the forthright Victorian counterpart to the modern spinsters' trancelike prophecies. Several male characters are brought in the end to acknowledge women's claims on them. As Harold must accept his dependence on others, and Felix must accommodate his idealism to the fact of a wife, Martin and North must question their own relation to authority and the patriarchal family.

The boundaries of English ladies' lives remain essentially the same in 1832 and in 1880, when *The Years* begins; even in 1937, "Present Day," the past lives on in such figures as Eleanor, whom Peggy sees as a "portrait of a Victorian spinster" (Y 333). In both novels, these limits are defined by the threshold of the home: women are depicted indoors, looking out; home becomes sanctuary or prison, while life outside beckons as well as threatens. At Transome Court, Esther opens the blinds to see the river and the trees: "She wanted the largeness of the world to help her thought." To Mrs. Transome, the same vista only reflects "boundary" and "line," "the loneliness and monotony of her life" (590, 596). (Compare Dorothea's view from the boudoir at Lowick.) In the end, Esther rejects "a silken bondage" as a lady at the manor in favor of "the dim life of the back street, the contact with sordid vulgarity" (591–92), much as Eleanor decides, in the repressed drawing room of "1880," that "the poor enjoy themselves more than we do," and her sister suspects her of wanting to "go and live" with them in the back streets (30–31). The younger Pargiter girls, not allowed to occupy themselves with charity, peep out the window at the young man arriving next door ("Don't be caught looking" [19]), while Kitty, trapped in the Lodge of an Oxford college, stares out at the tormenting tree that leans but never falls. It appears that the social order itself is founded on the clear demarcation of spheres and on the liminal status of women who, like little Rose, must pay if they cross the boundary.

In 1832, ladies depend on gentlemen's protection; during the riot, Felix reassures Esther in her home before he tries to lead the mob, only to find himself swept along in its rampage toward Treby Manor. There, as earlier in an inn, his knightly impulse is to rescue the women, but ironically he is forced to pose as the aggressor, brandishing his "sabre" in a lighted window before "a group of women clinging together in terror," frightened as much by him as by the pillagers he is trying to turn away. The soldiers shoot him as though he were the leader of the rabble, wounding "the shoulder of the arm that held the naked weapon which shone in the light from the window." The phallic image of the man who has entered the women's interior incriminates him, though his intentions were chivalrous indeed (431–32).

The Pargiter girls in 1880 are still captives, while they restlessly vie for male attention; they compete for invitations to dinner and talk only of marriage. The Pargiters do escape in time, though the threat of sexual assault has lurked beyond the door; in their sorties, they destroy the old ideal of the lady. Eleanor must deal man-to-man with the contractor for the housing she has had built. Maggie and Sara in their poor lodgings must live by the rhythms of the street; criers, musicians, drunks, trucks invade their once enforced privacy, making a city flat seem like a primitive cave (189). Yet Eleanor progresses from being the spinster servant of her father to being an Athena-like seer (Marcus, *Languages*, 61), pursuing youthful adventure in increasingly exotic places with a gypsy's freedom. Woolf seems to be redefining women's sphere and influence; in the end Eleanor has her own flat with a newly installed shower-bath, as though the "goddess" (14) were at last able to appoint her own shrine and font.

Female characters in both novels are represented in relation to household trappings.[15] Esther is first introduced as the minister's

---

[15]Compare the use of certain objects to trace the history of the characters and family relations in both novels: Bycliffe's locket and notebook; the Pargiters' ink-stained walrus-brush; the "crimson chair with gilt claws" (see Leaska, "Woolf, the Pargeter," 184–85; and Marcus, *Languages*, 58).

daughter who objects to the smell of ale and tallow candles. Her fastidiousness sets her apart from the vulgar, "weak sisters" who pester their minister Rufus (133), yet she herself threatens her father's and Felix's vocations. Felix sneers at Esther's indulgence in wax candles: "I thank Heaven I am not a mouse to have a nose that takes note of wax or tallow" (140). Catherine Gallagher points out here the conflict of Felix's contempt for such material "signs" and the narrator's realistic method (*Industrial Reformation* 237–43); misogyny and contempt for detail coincide in Felix with an egotistical denial of interdependence. Felix declares: "A fine lady is a squirrel-headed thing, with small airs and small notions, about as applicable to the business of life as a pair of tweezers to the clearing of a forest" (153). He will have to refine his sense of scale, to learn how the sexes might collaborate in domestic and public life, whereas Esther must recognize that the doll-madonna is a captive, and that wax candles may come at the price of a woman's freedom.

As though her wish for refinement were granted, Esther is invited to choose a new home with all the amenities lacking in Malthouse Yard. Transome Court seems like "Paradise" until she recognizes the role of the woman in it; it is "haunted by an Eve gone grey with bitter memories of an Adam who had complained, 'The woman . . . she gave me of the tree, and I did eat' " (585). In contrast with Felix, Harold prefers the decoration to the life, asking Esther to pose in finery like one of the Transome portraits. She refuses, however, to adopt a fixed, false image (498). The portrait of Mrs. Transome in young and hopeful days seems to admonish her to "put out the wax lights that she might get rid of the oppressive urgency of walls and upholstery," thus rejecting her first vanity for a higher vision (586; Coveney 47).

Although Esther's choice, like that of so many heroines, is personified by two lovers, it is clearly prompted by a dread of powerlessness. Both the man who sneers at domestic detail and the man who wants to pile it up around his women are dangerous suitors for a woman who likes self-definition, just as these men are distressing sons to their willful mothers.[16] Eliot seems to be defining radicalism as masculine independence from hereditary authority; both Harold and Felix eagerly replace the father and repudiate the mother and all feminine influence. Harold's "busy thoughts were imperiously determined by habits which had no reference to any woman's feeling" (93). The man

[16]Felix rejects the dishonest occupation of his dead, mountebank father, thus distressing his mother; Harold repudiates his Tory lineage, neglects his imbecile "father," and almost kills Jermyn, his real father, all in a contest of wills with his mother.

uprooted from the past, the man who cannot be domesticated, is the man trying to his mother's will; thus Mrs. Holt and Mrs. Transome, "women who appear . . . to have a masculine . . . force of mind," have "come into severe collision with sons arrived at the masterful stage" (535).

Whereas Felix is a kind of hippie (his mother grieves that he wears no stock), Harold is no genuine radical, but a composite of all the prejudices of the privileged European male: he is imperialist, racist, classist, and sexist. As Esther senses, "to Harold Transome, Felix Holt was one of the common people who could come into question in no other than a public light. She had a native capability for discerning that the sense of ranks and degrees has its repulsions corresponding to the repulsions dependent on difference of race and colour" (522–23). Thus she shrinks from telling Harold that she has been intimate with Felix—that she has privately shared in the common life. Yet she is horrified to hear that Harold's first wife "had been a slave—was bought, in fact" (541). Esther's "native" discernment has everything to do with her having been conditioned as a woman; she may play along with ranks and degrees, but she begins to find them repulsive in themselves, since race and gender remain, like class, the registers on which the patriarch marks his supremacy.

Somewhat like Gwendolen in *Daniel Deronda*, Esther resists the surrender implied in accepting a man: "The homage of a man may be delightful until he asks straight for love, by which a woman renders homage." Harold's love "seemed to threaten her with a stifling oppression" (592), almost as though she intuits the opinion he declared when he first returned from Smyrna as a widower: "I hate English wives; they want to give their opinion about everything" (94). Perhaps less ominously, after having kissed Felix "she felt as if she had vowed herself away, as if memory lay on her lips like a seal of possession" (592); he at least has taken the trouble to argue with her opinions. Crudely, she must choose between the radical who sees women as useless delights and the radical who sees women as temptations unless useful. With more conscience and foresight than Mrs. Transome, Esther chooses duty rather than pleasure, the man who scolds her rather than the man who flatters.

In outline, Eliot's novel promises little for women. While Esther seemingly must submit to Felix in the end, Mrs. Transome must endure a living hell for her adultery. Yet as to the necessity for such sacrifices, the narrator offers contradictory commentary, generated especially by the figure of Mrs. Transome. Having married an imbecile, chosen a lover, and with him managed her failing estate, Mrs. Transome is now told she must become "grandmamma on satin cushions" (95). Her power has not gained her love, and now she is powerless; the narrator can only advise resigned silence: "Half the sorrows of women would be averted if they could repress the speech they know to be useless" (117). It is advice that Eliot herself, in the powerful voice of the narrator, does not follow. Observing Harold's bulldozing egotism, the narrator offers this rebuke:

> It is a fact kept a little too much in the background, that mothers have a self larger than their maternity, and that when their sons have become taller than themselves, and are gone from them to college or into the world, there are wide spaces of their time which are not filled with praying for their boys, reading old letters, and envying yet blessing those who are attending to their shirt-buttons. Mrs. Transome was certainly not one of those bland, adoring, and gently tearful women. (198)

Those bland women seem to be relegated to the world of unrealistic fiction. Esther, too, is not one of the quiescent type; at least in the beginning she appears self-sufficient, working as a tutor of French and setting herself up as judge of men's taste and behavior. But faced with the long-range prospects for women, she knows her best hope is to find a man who will appreciate her taste and behavior, her mind as well as her beauty. She complains to Felix: "It is difficult for a woman ever to try to be anything good . . . when it is always supposed that she must be contemptible." Men may choose a "hard" and "great" lot, but "women, unless they are Saint Theresas," "must take meaner things, because only meaner things are within [their] reach" (364–67). Esther's growing desire to dedicate herself as helpmeet to noble reform seems to excuse this early egoistic complaining, but nothing in the novel suggests that she does not complain of a real injustice.

For some time it seems likely that Esther will take Harold, who is within her reach. Mrs. Transome predicts Esther's sacrifice to Harold with the bitterness of one of the damned. "This girl has a fine spirit— plenty of fire and pride and wit. Men like such captives, as they like horses that champ the bit. . . . What is the use of a woman's will?— if she tries she doesn't get it, and she ceases to be loved. God was cruel when he made women" (488). The servant Denner replies that she is used to being a woman, and as Mrs. Transome later says, "the misery of being a woman" is preferable to "the baseness of a man" (519). Denner's view is the comic relief to her mistress's tragedy: "I shouldn't like to be a man—to cough so loud, and stand straddling about on a wet day, and be so wasteful with meat and drink. They're a coarse lot, I think" (488). Censure of men may be warranted to some degree, but the novel cannot recommend it. In complaints or reproaches, "poor women, whose power lies solely in their influence, make themselves like music out of tune, and only move men to run away" (437). To point out in this way the selfish, cowardly response of men may not be the surest way to recommend women's submission, but it does appear to exalt the strategies of influence on the premise of feminine superiority.

As a chivalrous gentleman, Harold never appears to "straddle about," but the narrator, like Mrs. Transome and eventually Esther, detects the flaws of egotism beneath his veneer: " 'A woman ought never to have any trouble. There should always be a man to guard her from it.' (Harold Transome was masculine and fallible; he had incautiously sat down this morning to pay his addresses by talk about nothing in particular; and, clever experienced man as he was, he fell into nonsense)" (499–500). The corollary of Harold's gallantry is that women should protect men from wounded vanity. Thus Harold is uneasy when he suspects that Esther has a mind as well as a beautiful face: "She was clearly a woman that could be governed. . . . Yet there was a lightning that shot out of her now and then, which seemed the sign of a dangerous judgment; as if she inwardly saw something more admirable than Harold Transome. Now, to be perfectly charming, a woman should not see this" (525). The final caustic comment belongs, in spite of the counsel of resignation, to a feminist narrator rather like Austen's in *Northanger Abbey*.

Esther has what Eliot maintains are womanly flaws: "She was intensely of the feminine type, verging neither towards the saint nor the angel. She was 'a fair divided excellence, whose fulness of perfection' must be in marriage" (551). Characteristically, Eliot presents feminine independence as the exception to the common order, a possibility for rare spirits like Saint Theresa or Romola. Yet an inert and ignorant Angel in the House will spread a curse as much as any demonic Mrs. Transome. Esther must retain her will and aspiration. At her great moment, she assumes the role of a heroine of history:

When a woman feels purely and nobly, that ardour of hers which breaks through formulas too rigorously urged on men by daily practical needs, makes one of her most precious influences. . . . Her inspired ignorance gives a sublimity to actions . . . that otherwise . . . would make men smile. Some of that ardour which has . . . illuminated all poetry and history was burning to-day in the bosom of sweet Esther Lyon. In this, at least, her woman's lot was perfect: that the man she loved was her hero; that her woman's passion and her reverence for rarest goodness rushed together in an undivided current. (571)

There could hardly be a more explicit image of the compensations of influence, yet Esther does not consume her life in obeisance to her manly hero. Like another Elizabeth Bennet, she could only be happy with a man "greater and nobler than I am," but she reserves a little of her wealth and, playfully, of her power: "You don't know how clever I am. I mean to go on teaching a great many things"—including Felix— "and you will not attribute stupid thoughts to me before I've uttered them." She will enjoy the "retribution" of demanding that he be worthy of her sacrifice (602–3).[17] Eliot would later present a more convincing portrait of such a relationship in that of Mary Garth and Fred Vincy. Felix unlike Fred must play the part of mentor, but it is a role Esther creates and makes him worthy of.

As in most positive images of marriage in these authors' novels, the final union in *Felix Holt* is cleansed of any hint of sexual mastery. Felix and Esther unite rather as though Maggie and Tom Tulliver were able to prolong their last moment outside of gender difference, like children or angels: "He smiled, and took her two hands between his, pressed together as children hold them up in prayer. Both of them felt too solemnly to be bashful. They looked straight into each other's eyes, as angels do when they tell some truth" (556). The fusion of male and female lots at the end belies the instructive disunity of the novel. Felix and Esther leap out of history and gendered sexuality into the vanguard of an idealized common life. Yet as with Orlando and Shelmerdine, for all practical purposes their future will retain the division of labor and separation of spheres; Esther can look forward to no professorship, no career of public lectures in the "Cause."

In *The Years*, women's choices no longer have to be personified by men. Nonetheless, the young women in "1880" confront their domestic heritage in objective forms strikingly similar to those in *Felix Holt*. The Pargiter daughters, trapped in the drawing room of Abercorn Terrace—midway, it might be said, between Malthouse Yard and Transome Court—fuss as Esther did, not about cheap candles but

---

[17]Coveney points out that Esther's "laugh as sweet as the morning thrush" in this concluding scene echoes the scene in prison when Esther, "like a thrush . . . a messenger of darkness," warns Felix of failure (chap. 45, n.1, chap. 51, n.2).

about an "old-fashioned" kettle decorated with "a design of roses that was almost obliterated." Whereas Esther's mother is a romantic memory, Rose Pargiter lies almost obliterated on her deathbed, like the kettle that won't boil. Once again, the matron haunts the drawing room in a portrait of her lost youthful purity: "The portrait of a red-haired young woman in white muslin holding a basket of flowers . . . smiled down on" Milly and Delia (10). Like Esther with her little luxuries and the volume of Byron in her workbasket, these girls furtively adorn their barren world with romantic aspirations.

In later years, the younger Pargiter women choose, like Esther, not to repeat the decorative captivity of the ladies in the portraits. Yet the teakettle and the portrait persist like timepieces to clock changes in the family. To Martin, who like Felix has always resisted things feminine, the painting in 1908 "had ceased to be his mother" under its film of dirt, while the hateful kettle seems worse than obsolete now (149, 152). In 1910, the second Rose relates memories of the portrait and kettle as traces of ancient history (166). At last, in "Present Day," Peggy notices "the picture of her grandmother" over her aunt Eleanor's, formerly the grandmother's, writing table. The portrait has been cleaned, so that the flower on the grass, which Martin missed in 1908, has reappeared, but Eleanor doubts the portrait's likeness to the real Rose or to the granddaughter Peggy, said to resemble her. Records of the past are inevitably distorted, while present interpreters, faithful as they try to be, can only see through new eyes: "One thing seemed good to one generation, another to another" (325–26). Abercorn Terrace "was Hell!" Delia repeatedly declares to the present generation (417), much as Esther recognizes hell in the seeming paradise of Transome Court. The entire novel suggests an alternative to a revision of myth like *The Waste Land*, as the women ritually tend vessels such as the teakettle (Marcus, *Languages*, 43), in honor of the dying goddess of the portrait, reborn in each generation.[18]

In contrast with *Felix Holt*, *The Years* revises the tragic plots of the adulteress or the stifled wife, inventing new plots with succeeding generations. Kitty, although she cannot emulate her spinster tutor, Lucy Craddock, finds moments as Lady Lasswade when she masters

---

[18]For example, Eleanor "descend[s]" the stairs (apparently "carrying a . . . pitcher on her head") as though descending into hell, passing the sulphur in the dog's bowl and stepping over this domestic Cerberus (43). Marcus observes that the house suggests the unburied dead, "abier" meaning dead but unburied in Wright's dialect dictionary: "With 'corn' and 'terrace' it suggests the ritual of the death and rebirth of the Year-Spirit and Antigone's burial of her brother" (*Languages* 40).

a vast domain. In the present day, Peggy has her career as a doctor. Women no longer must choose meaner things; everything is within their reach, even, rarely, being "happy in this world—happy with living people" (Y 387). Back in "1880," Eleanor observes her sisters' malaise: "They stay at home too much, she thought. . . . Here they are cooped up, day after day. . . . Again she stopped herself. She must wait till she was alone" (32). Her critique of the drawing room captivity of middle-class women seems a guilty thought in that drawing room—a stifled protest, like Esther's unvoiced doubts about Harold's chivalry, from a woman who shares the point of view of the poor.

The women's self-suppression is complemented and enforced by the compulsive egotism of men. Over the years women begin to break free as they frankly observe this compulsion at work. After the death of the unchallenged patriarch, Colonel Pargiter, Eleanor half-listens, with some lingering admiration, to the imperialist adventures of Sir William Whatney, a man who might have been her husband: "stories that sailed serenely to his own advantage" (202). But it is Maggie's husband Renny, a skeptic about war and the psychology of great men, whom Eleanor would have liked to have married. (Notably, Woolf's radicals are non-domineering men who, along with a few visionary women, recognize the claims of women and the past.) Whereas Esther confined her criticism of Harold or Felix to occasional sallies, in the new century Peggy never wavers in her self-assertion; she yields neither her attention nor her respect to a young man's hammering "I, I, I." "But he couldn't help it, not with that nerve-drawn egotist's face. . . . He had to expose, had to exhibit. But why let him?" Deliberately, she in turn says "I" to drive him away (361). As Eliot observes in *Felix Holt*, men run away from women's self-assertion.

In the present, men too are becoming critical of the old sexual code. Peggy's brother North, like Felix an outsider who dreads domestication, mocks the bonding customs: "The men shot, and the women . . . broke off into innumerable babies" (375). Like the two "radicals" Harold and Felix, North expresses the misogyny of those threatened by women's independence, but he responds with Felix's hostility rather than Harold's flattery: "Damn women, he thought, they're so hard; so unimaginative. Curse their little inquisitive minds. What did their 'education' amount to? It only made her [Peggy] critical, censorious" (395–96). As in *Felix Holt*, the denigration of women is mirrored by their abuse of men. Peggy counters North's unspoken insult: "The vanity of men was immeasurable. . . . He'll tie himself up with a red-lipped girl, and become a drudge. He must, and I can't.

I shall pay for it, I shall pay for it" (396). Women like Mrs. Transome and Peggy who deliberately oppose men will lose the comforts of love.

In Woolf's later version of sexual politics, the possible fusions of gender seem to multiply. Throughout the tormented party in "Present Day," Eleanor keeps discovering miracles: Sara and Nicholas's new kind of love (370); the change "for the better" in human nature exemplified by Renny and Maggie, "two people out of all those millions [who] are 'happy' " (386–88). The novel concludes with images of a perpetual sexual mystery. Two children of the caretaker, the "younger generation," their sex unidentified, sing nonsense both ancient and futuristic; even this nightmarish chant of the other can be heard without terror in the new day. Eleanor witnesses the arrival of unknown newlyweds by taxi at a neighboring house, promising that the ritual will continue, each time a little different, each time perhaps a little better if we gradually come to know ourselves.

The "Progress" of Political Art

Woolf's continuation of the history of the common life, although it represents progress since the compromise of the heroine of 1832, displays skepticism about such apparent advance, as though insisting that the inherent divisions in society that Eliot exposed ought to undermine the teleology of the novel itself in an unending ritual of return. In both *Felix Holt* and *The Years*, the social divisions are conceived in terms of class as well as gender. As in *Romola* and *Orlando*, Eliot and Woolf represent the common people ambiguously, as both the medium of continuity and a volatile force for change; common people and upper-class women are implicitly linked in their shared exclusion from corrupt modes of power. As before, the novels exalt less the crowd or the suffering masses than individual obscure beings, the Bartons and Browns. Educated, independent men or women of the people such as Felix Holt, Rufus Lyon, Lucy Craddock, or the workingclass don, Mr. Robson, exhibit the selfless virtues that will influence the growing good of the world (though Felix and Rufus both have egotistical failings that Woolf's obscure saints apparently do not). Their influence may be narrow and unsteady, but it is the ingredient heretofore missing from public life. Ladies at times are able to collaborate with them. Esther rises in court in defense of Felix, "break[ing] through" the rigid systems of men (571) very much in the spirit of *Three Guineas*. Eleanor eagerly petitions her brother Edward, the Oxford don, on behalf of Runcorn the porter's son, who "wants to go to college," to rise on his merits; Edward grudgingly accepts his duty to help bring about such rises (410–11).

In the twentieth century, it is no longer an article of faith, as it still was for Felix, that "there's some dignity and happiness for a man other than changing his station" (FH 557). The Pargiters are living out the effects of the challenge to inherited station that in 1832 jarred the Treby Magnas of England out of a slumber of centuries; the family witnesses the decline of empire and the loss of the power and prosperity of the upper middle class in Britain. Eliot tries to dramatize the political crisis of her times, but public events are upstaged by the skirmishes between men and women, which in her view more profoundly determine the course of human history. Woolf seems at once more confident that the history of the common life takes precedence over the public record, and more cautious in writing a political novel, where propaganda may defeat art. Her aim is to revise the history of the people that "we" were, to fight her literary predecessor's fight, at a time when many of the barriers that had constrained Marian Evans had at last broken down. Woolf implicitly honors "radicals" of any gender: social experimenters who do not try to lay down the law and who are not afraid to think back through their mothers. Yet from a certain perspective, neither author radically questions sexual difference, which they rely on to outlast historical change; genders will continue to find only temporary fusion, and the feminine must temper the masculine.

In the different Victorian and modern contexts, we are shown a radical disjunction between those interlocked spheres, private and public life. Through the guidance of women, Eliot and Woolf seem to say, the business of the world may be conducted less deceptively, so that signs of authority are not mistaken for signs of virtue or merit. Indeed, if women and other outsiders can teach us to know ourselves, ordinary people may become more an honor to our species, though never all alike. Women such as Mrs. Transome should be allowed to lead by "virtue of acknowledged superiority" (91), once they have been truly educated; instead they have been cultivated for "bloom and beauty" without regard for "things not personal" or for "what is . . . good for mankind" (105). Women such as Peggy should be allowed to become doctors without forfeiting Eleanor's beauty or selfless sympathy, and without losing the possibility of marrying a man like Renny. Such things should be, but Eliot and Woolf are not so crude as to preach them in so many words. Still less do they condone the anger of Mrs. Transome and of Peggy because these ideals have so far proved impossible. God was cruel when he made women—perhaps;

but should he have created men? The mitigating art of love practiced by Esther and by Eleanor would be too great a loss, Eliot and Woolf seem to say, if a bomb were dropped on the hell of home, leaving male and female alike. Meanwhile, might the misery of being a woman be preferable to being a base egotist, whether radical or tyrant? Are these the only alternatives defining "man"?

7

"The Ancient Consciousness of Woman": A Feminist Archaeology of *Daniel Deronda* and *Between the Acts*

As the last acts of their careers as novelists, Eliot and Woolf both present perhaps the darkest, most equivocal and open-ended of their works. *Daniel Deronda* and *Between the Acts* raise the ominous question of what comes next for a civilization rotting from within, yet both works find sources of energy in that decay. And now? "I shall live," cries Gwendolen, who once meant not only to live but to lead, whereas the dying Hebrew prophet assures Daniel, the future leader, "Is it not begun? . . . We shall live together" (DD 879, 882). "Then the curtain rose. They spoke," writes Miss La Trobe of her archetypal man and woman, who fight to the death like animals; the fruit of their differences may be a child or a play that shall live (BA 219). The doubtful promise of these endings emerges from a covert but violent warfare that has shaken the foundations of the patriarchal family and religion.

The heart of the darkness in these novels is gender conflict, which I will approach on two fronts, on the one hand the networks of sacred allusions and themes, and on the other, characterization and action. Like the "separate spheres" I have frequently considered, these fronts are inseparable, of course. To me the most remarkable aspect of both novels—and what gives these different works most in common—is the daring conjunction of religious and cultural history with the private theatricals of the novel of manners. In both final novels, the stress between patriarchal culture and women of vocation has become impossible to ease. It is no longer a question of extending to the rare, aristocratic woman a special license to trespass, as in *Romola* and *Orlando*; it is no longer possible to pursue a social history of metonymic detail and interdependent spheres, as in *Felix Holt* and *The Years*. Here the fiction that calls women nature, men culture, women the personal or particular, men the public or universal, has become an excruciating delusion. Who would buy the patriarchal lie that founds modern European civilization? Who could bear the truths that would destroy it?

Feminist tactics for unearthing such truths have often taken the two approaches I follow here, which for simplicity I term vocational and archaeological. The vocational feminist analysis has been the basis for most feminist literary criticism (and it has set the pattern for much of my own study); it may focus on the vocation of female characters in line with biographical readings of women of letters, and it may consider genre and plot, social convention, or the historical conditioning of authorship and readership, among other rewarding concerns. Yet the vocational front can become narrow without an engagement on the archaeological front as well. Thus many feminist theorists and critics have insisted that the struggle of heroines and women writers to break silence must be placed in deeper and more far-reaching contexts: beyond the modern European middle class; beyond phallogocentrism; or *Beyond God the Father* with Mary Daly or Merlin Stone. From this perspective, there is no articulate voice proper to woman in Western civilization, whatever the women of letters and their female characters may strive for or achieve. Only the triumphant laughter of Demeter, of Medusa, of the hysteric or priestess of *jouissance* (Cixous and Clément 33–39) promises a different story.

In this discussion of the last novels I set out by a less explored archaeological route, which often intersects with the vocational path. The authors delve into cultural memory in order to reveal primitive tensions behind the more immediate question of what women are to do. As we have seen, the novels of Eliot and Woolf generally answer that immediate question negatively: women cannot hope for perfection both of the art and of the life, cannot, as heroines or as living women, figure in both ambitious and erotic plots without paying a great price of suffering.[1] What happens when the novels defy this "thou-shalt-not" without relying, as in *Romola* and *Orlando*, on the excuses of historical remoteness or aristocratic privilege? Instead of an array of happily adjusted, successful women, we find eruptions of frustration and rage exceeding Mrs. Transome's, and we find strange labyrinths of primitive imagery and hints of alien rites exceeding those in *The Years*.

---

[1]Aurora Leigh postpones the erotic plot till she has become an eminent poet, at which time she concedes: "No perfect artist is developed here / From any imperfect woman. . . . / Art is much, but love is more" (Book 9, 341). None of Eliot's or Woolf's characters manages to "have it all" in this way.

Surely there is a familiar logic to the rage—you beat me, I fight back—and feminist critics have been quick to locate such textual revenge of the oppressed (Eliot's Alcharisi is a star in feminist criticism; see Pell; Gallagher, "The Prostitute," 54–55; Rosenman, "Women's Speech"). But are we as familiar with the archaic forms of the return of the repressed in these novels? To me it is a haunting question why Eliot and Woolf should frame their vocational feminism in such bizarre archaeological fragments, and the fragments themselves have a startling freshness and antiquity when brought to light. Lily Briscoe "imagined how in the chambers of the mind and heart of the woman . . . were stood, like the treasures in the tombs of kings, tablets bearing sacred inscriptions" that would always remain secret. But Lily the archaeologist has a desire not so much to decipher the code as to enter those chambers and stay there: "It was not knowledge but unity that she desired . . . nothing that could be written in any language known to men, but intimacy itself, which is knowledge" (TL 79). In my readings of these novels, I will try to return alive out of the underworld, bearing signs of what Eliot calls "the treasure of human affections" (DD 160)—an intimate knowledge of primitive beliefs, of a feminine unconscious—without seeking unity with the deadly myths of sacred womanhood.

A novel completed during World War II inevitably takes a different view of cultural origins, the design of history, and narrative generally than one published in the 1870s. *Between the Acts* seems to revel in the irresolution that *Daniel Deronda* laments, drawing recreative energies out of the primitive mud that threatens to swallow civilization in both novels.[2] Yet both novels strive to shore up tradition, whether a restored Judaism or English literary history; the first turns to inherited law and religion, the second to a collective, spontaneously restored spirit: "We're the oracles . . . a foretaste of our own religion" (BA 198). Woolf's modern question, prompted by the nightmares of nationalism and anti-Semitism that Eliot's novel warned of, could well be asked in both works: *"How's . . . the great wall, which we call, perhaps miscall, civilization, to be built by . . . orts, scraps and fragments like ourselves?"* (BA 188). In the figures of Mordecai and Daniel, however, Eliot seems to reconstitute the humanist individual under the authority of a teleo-

---

[2]Although it is unlikely that Woolf had *Daniel Deronda* in view as a specific precedent among Eliot's novels—she scarcely referred to this novel except as evidence of Eliot's final decline ("GE" [1921])—in effect *Between the Acts* extends and develops the speculation in *Daniel Deronda* on the resurgence of the primitive common life alongside contemporary redefinitions of women's vocation.

logical monotheism, rising above all modern dissolution. Why should these women writers have strained so hard to preserve a tradition that they largely condemned? Before entering the labyrinths of the pagan and Judeo-Christian, the primitive and civilized in these novels, I take a "vocational" detour to consider the novelists' responses to their historical moment and cultural mission. At the end of this chapter I return to the vocational preoccupations of these novels, with their proliferation of women artists, including the most powerful and enraged artist figures in Eliot's or Woolf's oeuvres, the Alcharisi and Miss La Trobe.

The Last Novels in Context:
Authors and Audience, History and Form

Both final novels appear to have been formed under pressure of political upheaval, of the loss of an assured public, and of a craving for generic innovation. In both works the authors have constructed time scales at once more expansive and more immediate than usual. *Daniel Deronda*, unlike Eliot's earlier novels, occurs within a decade or so before the date of publication in 1876; it registers the international impact of such events as the American Civil War and the Franco-Prussian War, while it prepares for the restoration of a Jewish homeland that had been prophesied in ancient scripture. The title itself subscribes to the Judaic cyclical model of history; the hero's name invokes both the princely exile reared as advisor in the gentile king's house and a rounding out of the history of the Jews (The Book of Daniel 4:8–9). *Between the Acts* suggests a more doubtful relation between prophetic pretexts and fulfillment.[3] Set in 1939, during the "present" of composition (1938–41), it is an idyll of a few hours bounded by war (like the first and last parts of *To the Lighthouse*), while it follows the same span of English literary history as *Orlando*. Like several of Woolf's novels and like only *Daniel Deronda* among Eliot's, *Between the Acts* ends "here and now," facing a terrifying future; its first readers were in the midst of the cataclysm anticipated in the novel. Rather than

[3]Eliot's use of Judeo-Christian heritage would seem to affirm a teleological model of history, but her narrator at the outset announces, "No retrospect will take us to the true beginning"—or project a certain end (35). Woolf rather adverts to a myth of eternal return, suggesting the pagan or Viconian model of historical cycles; repetition is the most striking aspect of the book (Hartman 74, 80–81). J. Hillis Miller notes in *Between the Acts* the combination of repetitive "musical, architectural form" with realistic "social notations" like "those of Austen or Eliot" and a chronological plotline of history (*Fiction* 206–9).

closing a circle, it divides what it also connects: the two World Wars; the sexual acts of Isa and Giles; the acts of the pageant and of the disjointed novel-play that encloses it; and the beginning and end of human history.[4]

The stress laid on the form of history in each of these novels underscores similar arguments about the impossibility of continuing on the present course, particularly because of the abuses of patriarchal and nationalistic power. This is not to say that these works blame all contemporary suffering on the bourgeois family or the British nation or even national spirit itself. The intolerance of the tribe for difference within and without is to blame, not the social bonds themselves, which perhaps prevent the worse tortures of a state of nature. British imperialism and European fascism are harshly satirized, but both novels mount last-ditch defenses of a more worthy nationalism— the shared historic achievement of the chosen people or the chosen literature. Eliot's Theophrastus Such calls for a nationalism without xenophobia; the English must recognize the right of all peoples (including the Jews) to a homeland if they themselves are to "resist conquest with the very breasts of their women" ("The Modern Hep! Hep! Hep!" TS 189–90). *Between the Acts* confronts not only the threat of foreign domination, but also the incompatible desires to defend the homeland *and* to liberate the women while opening the borders to the alien or suppressed. "And what about the Jews?" exclaims a nameless member of the audience. "People like ourselves, beginning life again" (121). National survival depends on tolerating the full diversity of "people like ourselves," both novels say. In the later novel, Klesmer's and Deronda's tolerant cosmopolitanism has become the ineffectual sympathy of Lucy Swithin, who disbelieves in history and its subdivisions of ages and nations (174–75), or the comparative detachment of Cobbet of Cobb's Corner, who sees sexual vitality as the same in East and West (110).

It is difficult to sustain pluralism without relativism or indifference, without abandoning worthy tradition or yielding to the status quo, and many forces lurk ready to destroy the balance. The fragile values and the disruptive impulses together contribute to a metamorphosis of genres in these novels, as the old forms break down with the old order. Both final novels challenge the ranks, rules, and realism of the novel of manners and of English society with the more communal or fantastical powers of drama, music, or poetry. Both *Daniel Deronda*

---

[4]Daniel's true surname is "Charisi," an appellation for exile and for "promised redemption" (Fleishman, "Charisi," 102–4). Since each self is an acted part, an "act," Woolf's title also says "only connect." See Naremore 228–39; Fussell 267–68.

and *Between the Acts* aspire to the condition of theater, especially in its more ancient forms. Almost all the female characters in these novels are actresses, amateur or professional, and plays-within-the-play are repeatedly staged, from Gwendolen's theatricals to the female Prospero's pageant in *Between the Acts*. Expanding the idea of theater held by drawing-room or village audiences, however, the authors introduce a forgotten mode of the drama often "undramatic" in the modern sense. Such drama more closely resembles the ancient communal rites of sacrifice and rebirth, and it plays down individual action in favor of collective manifestations.[5] In contrast with the solitary endeavors of the painter, novelist, or poet, both drama and music can unite performers and audience in shared social ritual, inviting a return to "unpersonified feelings" in an affirmation of the "common weal."[6]

Woolf appears to have been drawn to the theory, expressed by her friend Jane Harrison in *Ancient Art and Ritual*, that drama originated in rituals in which everyone participated; later, the rite ("*dromenon*, 'a thing done' ") was distanced from practical consequences, as actors were distinguished from spectators (124–27, 35).[7] Like drama, music might long predate interest in individual expression, deriving from original instincts and the creations of "Anon," the unknown minstrel Woolf imagined for a projected book on English literary history begun in 1940 (Silver, " 'Anon,' " 382). Both novels are drawn to an ideal of

[5] A. V. Dicey complained of the substitution of "a chorus of moralists" for dramatic action in *Daniel Deronda* (Carroll, *Critical Heritage*, 399); indeed, the narrator resembles the chorus of Greek drama, while there are repeated monologues or soliloquies. Similarly, Malcolm Cowley noted that *Between the Acts* had "no plot . . . no sense of drama or dialectic." Instead, Woolf substituted the chorus, the collective "we" for the "I," the ritual act for the plot (Majumdar and McLaurin 448; *VW Diary* 5: 135).

[6] The terms are Jane Harrison's (233, 246). Marcus compares *Between the Acts* to *The Years*, with its similar Greek chorus, reference to a benefit pageant, and operatic subtext. In a review of 1909, Woolf wrote on a performance of Wagner in Bayreuth where the audience came out to view the landscape between the acts (Marcus, "Sources," 1–2; *Languages*, 16–17, 36–39).

[7] See Maika 7–9. Harrison shares much of Nietzsche's vision of the origins of tragedy and of the artistic creator who becomes "at once poet, actor, and spectator" (Maika 68; Nietzsche, *Tragedy*, 36–42, 52). Eliot's views have some Carlylean elements in common with Nietzsche, in spite of his distaste for Eliot's moralism (Myers, *Teaching*, 119–24; Beer, *Past*, 76–77). Brockett entertains theories that theater originated in storytelling or in dance alongside the still-viable theory that it originated in ritual (6–7). Harrison seems to incite Woolf to write *Between the Acts* in her account of ancient origins of theater: "The whole body of worshippers would gather, just as now-a-days the whole community will assemble on a village green. . . . All are actors. . . . It is in the common act, . . . or collective emotion, that ritual starts" (126). Hoff attacks Cuddy-Keane for ignoring the role Harrison assigns to the leader of the dithyramb or spring festival, but I agree with Cuddy-Keane ("Reply") that Harrison distinguishes this form of transferable and impersonal leadership from the individualistic artist-as-originator, without imagining a purely nonhierarchical community.

nonindividualistic art. The composer Klesmer, though a Romantic believer in individual genius, nevertheless perceives the artist's vocation as one of self-sacrifice and willingness to die anonymous and poor. For Eliot, music helps us "to escape the limitations" of self, and the true genius lives more "for the next age . . . than for his own" (Baker, Introduction, 31–35; Harrison 233–34; Eliot, "Liszt, Wagner, and Weimar," 98); liturgical music can lend a "sense of communion" with "long generations of struggling fellow-men" (DD 416). Miss La Trobe never poses as a genius, but sweats with her actors behind the scenes. She enlists the help, for her pageant, of "Bach, Handel, Beethoven, Mozart or nobody famous" (BA 188), as well as the incidental music of cows, rain, or airplanes, precisely for the sake of such liturgical communion. Instead of the single, signed, and formally staged play, drama like music becomes the history of a people in microcosm.[8]

The generic experimentation in these last works served the critique of modern deracinated civilization, but it also helped the women of letters in their continuing effort to escape the woman's sphere of the novel. Eliot had turned repeatedly to poetry (with drama, still the privileged literary form), and she had successfully published several long poems, including one, *The Spanish Gypsy*, that had originated as a play (Eliot abandoned it to work on the "tragedy" of Mrs. Transome).[9] Yet her desire to write a play remained unsatisfied. In June 1873 she told Lewes her plan for *"novel and play* Deronda" (Haight 471). For Woolf as well, a leaning toward poetry joined with an interest in the most public literary form, the drama. Since the 1920s, Woolf had been resisting the designation "novel" for what she wrote, and had incorporated the lyric, the elegy, and the essay in her fictional forms. Her one play, *Freshwater*, privately performed in 1935, anticipated her last novel by recreating the cultivated circle of her great-aunt Julia Cameron at a country retreat (Bell 2: 189).[10] She conceived *Between the Acts* as a "Play" or a "medley," to include "poems (in metre)" to channel her "prose lyric vein, which . . . I overdo" (*VW*

---

[8]Daniel reads a passage from Leopold Zunz on the "National Tragedy" of the Jews "lasting for fifteen hundred years, in which the poets and the actors were also the heroes" (575).

[9]The notebooks containing Eliot's research on Jewish subjects also show her continuing study of poetry and prosody (Baker, Introduction, 11–13). In the 1860s and 1870s, Eliot wrote the poetry that was collected in *The Legend of Jubal and Other Poems* (1874) (Haight 406).

[10]The impulse to preserve a "fortress of civilization" and the memory of such figures as Tennyson (played by Julian Bell, killed in the Spanish Civil War) carried over from this play to *Between the Acts*.

Diary 5: 139, 193, 200). Isa's private verse and Eliot's epigraphs in *Daniel Deronda* in different ways give vent to the lyric, with its evident temptations to personality, whereas the novels take the larger, impersonal scope of public drama.

In both works, the once quiet territory of the English novel of manners has been conquered not only by a generic medley but also by international strife.[11] Austen's stock in trade—the three or four families in a country village, the flirtatious theatricals, the misplaced affections and trusts, and the comic resolution in marriage—was transformed when Eliot added scenes of Jewish life, and then again when Woolf interpolated the drama of English literature itself. Both amplifications of domestic fiction prove the interpenetration of provincial family life and international politics. Daniel's search for family fulfills his promise as political leader, while through him the history of the Jews intersects with Gwendolen's marriage plot. Miss La Trobe, outside the family, creates a pageant that challenges social and artistic class systems;[12] ordinary people play historical leaders, and everyone unknowingly participates in a kind of allegory linking the family romance and world politics. In neither *Daniel Deronda* nor *Between the Acts*, however, are genteel hierarchies altogether discarded. Daniel will continue to behave like a proper English gentleman in the East, and vulgar Jews and unruly women will be left behind (Edgar Rosenberg notes that Eliot still relies on stereotypes of the Jews [161–84]). The canonical texture of Woolf's pageant is still best deciphered by the cultivated few, and after a day of carnival the elite family circle closes once more. Indeed, both works borrow the closure of comedy, though readers can hardly be happy about the union of the couples given all those loose ends—Gwendolen, Miss La Trobe, the horror. Is the price of peace a restoration of sexual and social hierarchy, and is such restoration even possible (Little 4–7, 92–98)?

The authors satirize contemporary society yet cling to certain vestiges of order, and they do so more urgently than ever, reflecting a change in their relations to the public. They seem to have increasingly figured themselves as outsiders within a shrinking coterie; there was no happy democracy of readers. Eliot "expected" her choice of subject to arouse "resistance and even repulsion" in the general public, but her aim was to awaken "the imagination of men and women to a vision of human claims in those races of their fellow-men who most

---

[11]On the political contexts of these novels, see, for example, Hester 115–18; Sudrann 436–39; Zwerdling 302–23; Sears 212–35.
[12]Pageants were frequently used for suffragette as well as Marxist propaganda (Marcus, "Sources," 2).

244 Greatness Engendered

differ from them in customs and beliefs." She waged war on "the stupidity . . . of our culture," which promoted imperialistic "dictatorialness" and a "deadness to the history which has prepared half our world for us" (*GE Letters* 6: 301–2). Although she aimed to instill a sense of common humanity in her public, she also displayed the antagonism of a prophet among the Philistines.

Woolf extended Eliot's challenge to the English public, yet at the same time longed for the understood right to chastise that public. She too saw a self-loving complacency, vulgarity, and xenophobia that would lunge into self-destructive war.[13] Like Eliot, she anticipated that her novel "wont please anyone, if anyone should ever read it" (*VW Diary* 5: 160). Her sense of being an outsider increased: "The war— our waiting while the knives sharpen for the operation—has taken away the outer wall of security. No echo comes back. . . . I have so little sense of a public" (*VW Diary* 5: 299). This was an ominous lack: when the reader's "attention is distracted, in times of public crisis," she wrote, "the writer exclaims: I can write no more" (Silver, " 'Anon,' " 428). Eliot's dismay over her inability to correct contemporary dissolution and prejudice cannot have been as acute as Woolf's fear of the planes over Sussex, but similar vocational doubts influenced both works.

These open-ended novels have an insistent finality: Eliot completed no other novel, and Woolf committed suicide before *Between the Acts* was published. After the monumental success of *Middlemarch*, Eliot had feared a falling off, while she felt the need to preserve her "reputation" as a kind of "eminent clergyman[ ]" (Redinger 472; *GE Letters* 6: 75–76). Perhaps more urgently, she felt that only a more stringent form of writing could touch the "egoism" and "moral stupidity" of a decadent empire (*GE Letters* 6: 99). As though like Felix Holt she had found herself unable to steer the mob, she retreated in her next work to the essay form.[14] In "How We Encourage Research" it is tempting to read a bitter satire directed at her own public as a latter-day horde offering human sacrifices. Scholars become water monsters hurling "fountains of acrid mud . . . over the fresh wounds" of the noncon-

---

[13]Note the village verdict on the idiot and on savages (BA 194–99), and Bart Oliver's memories of India (17–18). Woolf writes of being "bored & appalled by the readymade commonplaces" of village Women's Institute plays: "the minds so cheap, . . . like a bad novel" (*VW Diary* 5: 288).

[14]Stange, in "The Voices of the Essayist," observes Eliot's return to the voice of "an experienced masculine commentator" in "the declining genre of the moral essay" (317, 322, 329–30). See "Poetry and Prose from the Notebook of an Eccentric" (1846–47) in Pinney 13–26; Haight 61; Collins 385–405.

forming author, Merman (TS 40–46).[15] This violent imagery anticipates the subtler satire in *Between the Acts*, which likewise stages present-day pagan rites and likens humans to animals in a malign inversion of evolution.

The reception of *Daniel Deronda* would not in itself justify the disillusionment Eliot expressed: "the painful impression that we write for a public which has no discernment of good and evil." Among some Jewish readers, at least, the response was all that she could wish (*GE Letters* 6: 379), and some English reviewers found much to praise (Carroll, *Critical Heritage*, 365–447; Perkin 67–74); good American and English sales seemed "an unmistakable guarantee that the public has been touched" (*GE Letters* 6: 314). But Eliot no more than Woolf could rest assured of such an anonymous "guarantee." Although before her death she did begin a novel on the Napoleonic era, it is likely that George Eliot the novelist would have had great difficulty appearing before the public after Lewes's death in 1878, given his role in fostering her persona.[16]

Woolf in her last years seems to have adopted a Theophrastus-like stance toward the conventionalized oppression that binds any society, but particularly her own English educated class. At the same time, she evolved the inspiriting idea of the anonymous traditional voice. Perhaps the return of the collective madness of war and of her own madness confirmed her worst fears that history consisted of relentless repetition that no outsiders could disrupt, in spite of her hopes in *Three Guineas*. Her sense of vulnerability when facing publication of a novel must have seemed unendurable when the work might face no "public" at all. Just as Woolf viewed Eliot's last novel as a falling off, many reviewers accounted for Woolf's posthumously published novel as a work of declining power or as an unfinished piece, though some praised it highly (Majumdar and McLaurin 436–52). With deep misgivings and to a mixed reception, then, the women of letters strove in these unresolved works to defuse the friction between diverse cultures

[15]The more usual "mer*maid*" comes to mind, linking this essay to the images, discussed below, of Gwendolen and the Alcharisi as Lamia-like or serpentine. Eliot defends the "genius" Liszt (a model for Klesmer) concerning his apparent licentiousness: "Even an ordinary man has to pass through so many 'mud baths' before he reaches his fortieth year. . . . But, take him all in all, he is . . . one of those men whom the ancients would have imagined the son of a god or goddess" ("Liszt, Wagner, and Weimar" 98). In Eliot's imagination, vocational struggles figure as mythological dramas expressing primitive drives.

[16]Baker, "New Eliot Manuscript." Redinger represents Eliot's marriage with Cross, and the resulting reconciliation with her brother Isaac, as reducing "her motivation to write" (483).

and spirits that threatened to explode like the components of some inconceivable bomb. These bleak visions avoid becoming suicide notes for humanity, I believe, because of the ancient powers brought to light through the archaeological labors I have spoken of. The revelations were not so much reassuring as tentatively promising of women's power to redesign history.

Ancient Consciousness and
the Designs of History

Now I set the stage for the role of the unconscious and the feminine in history as these novels similarly present it, before plotting, in the two following sections, the different reenactments of ancient narratives in each novel. Eliot offers a justification for *Daniel Deronda*'s double scale—holding a woman's life and a civilization in the same balance—that applies almost equally to the cubistic *Between the Acts*. "Could there be a slenderer, more insignificant thread in human history," runs the famous passage,

> than this consciousness of a girl . . .?—in a time, too, when ideas were with fresh vigour making armies of themselves, and the universal kinship was declaring itself fiercely: when women on the other side of the world would not mourn for the husbands and sons who died bravely in a common cause, and men stinted of bread on our side of the world heard of that willing loss and were patient: a time when the soul of man was waking to pulses which had for centuries been beating in him unheard, until their full sum made a new life of terror or of joy.
>
> What in the midst of that mighty drama are girls and their blind visions? They are the Yea and Nay of that good for which men are enduring and fighting. In these delicate vessels is borne onward through the ages the treasure of human affections. (159–60)

This might be a pageant celebrating the sexual division of labor, the different fates of Hector and Hecuba, Tom and Maggie Tulliver, or Bart and Lucy Oliver. But a universal kinship might spell universal terror, as was repeatedly affirmed from the 1870s to the 1930s in such concepts as the herd instinct; the treasure of human affections, as

Eliot's novel already demonstrates, may be a Pandora's box.[17] Gwendolen is indeed blind to the mighty drama beyond her immediate desires, and her store of affections is nearly empty. If history is guided by the disregarded "pulses" or "affections" of a collective unconscious, then Gwendolen's condition does have historical significance (this is no trivial marriage plot). But is she a benign influence, as the pageantry would suggest: is she some crusader's muse, or is she a Helen or a Medea?[18] It is no secret in Eliot's text that a young girl might have the drives of a conqueror (when women refuse to mourn their men for whatever cause, I see a flaw in the image of the passive vessels of affection).

Gwendolen, creature of the marriage market, is fighting the world's battles in her own spirit, and the conflict reveals a gothic version of the unconscious. The epigraph of the novel is thus more revealing of the bitter effects of sexual oppression and emotional repression than the above pageantry of influence:

Let thy chief terror be of thine own soul:
There, 'mid the throng of hurrying desires
That trample o'er the dead to seize their spoil,
Lurks vengeance.

Here we encounter the modern anxiety that each "soul" harbors a mob in miniature, like the "thousands of emotions . . . in astonishing disorder" within the Woolfian representative mind ("Bennett and Brown," CE 1: 336). The self becomes a nightmare state of nature in which the repressed turn oppressors. This epigraph invites us to focus on Gwendolen, with her phobias, her accursed spoil of diamonds, and her magical vengeance on Grandcourt. She "would not mourn" her husband, who stands for the universal tyrant. But the crimes and retributions of the unconscious are also implicated in the logic of prophecy that Daniel's story fulfills. His desire to affiliate himself with the Jews coincides with his rescue of a Jewess and his discovery that

[17]Eliot would have known that "the mighty drama" of the American Civil War was less noble than here represented: the War between the States divided families, while the British government, if not the millworkers, stood by the slave states for much of the war.
[18]One of the figures Gwendolen considers representing in her tableaux vivants is Briseis, a woman sacrificed between men, a "Yea or Nay" of war in *The Iliad*. Such roles are drawn up from "Greek wickedness" or "Christian wickedness" to remind us of the woman's cultural destiny, and that these dramas are not, as Rex suggests, "all gone by and done with" (90).

he was born a Jew; these correspondences seem to point to the function of a racial destiny regardless of individual will.

Like many of her contemporaries, Eliot was eager to locate a medium of cultural transmission beyond conscious action by individuals. The concept of racial memory as such a medium took different forms in the writings of Pater and Yeats, for example, as well as in Samuel Butler's *Unconscious Memory* (1880), which was particularly influential on the modernists (I. Bell 181, 191–95). In a late essay, Eliot denies that actual transmission through "tradition or identity of descent" is necessary to explain analogies between cultures; human nature, or a racial unconscious, is the common element (Collins 387–90). Accordingly, Deronda responds to the story of his mother's effort to obscure his Jewish origins with "a latent obstinacy of race"; she, in contrast, acted on the belief that one can design oneself regardless of origin: "I was not like a brute, obliged to go with my own herd" (698). Yet the law of the father forces her to complete the original narrative: "Events come upon us," she says, "like evil enchantments; and thoughts, feelings, apparitions in the darkness are events. . . . I don't consent. . . . I obey something tyrannic" (693). The tyrannic events of her unconscious, the "spots of memory" (699), compel her to fulfill the collective destiny of her people, not her own ambition.

For Woolf, in the age of Freud, the throng of desires trampling the dead has gained uncanny familiarity. Woolf and her friends in Bloomsbury alternatively viewed the potential for "group consciousness" as a positive unanimism or a sinister herd instinct (McLaurin, "Consciousness," 36–38). In "The Leaning Tower" (1940), Woolf places Eliot and the Victorians (rather implausibly) in an age of faith, when the classes of society resembled motionless, unconscious herds in "separate fields." But 1914 changed all that, and writers were compelled "to tell . . . the unpleasant truth," "analysing themselves honestly, with help from Dr. Freud" (CE 2: 164–66, 177–78); the war raised more alarming visions of herd instinct as a force, in Nietzsche's terms, to "wreck the . . . faith [of the community] in itself" (*Good and Evil* 113). In the pastoral setting of Pointz Hall, Freudian analysis is under way, though the herd instinct is still contained in separate fields by a lingering feudal order. The Olivers and their guests seem able to hear each other's thoughts, as they become members in an ancient yet avant-garde chorus composed by an anonymous author in collaboration with a herd of cows.[19] Dreamlike fragments of overdetermined

[19]Woolf's longtime interest in interpersonal consciousness intensified in late years, informed by a reading of Freud's *Group Psychology* during 1939–40, in connection with "The Leaning Tower," "Thoughts on Peace in an Air Raid," and "Anon" and "The

narrative—"Papa's beard," "Mama's knitting," "how Mira's slipper got lost in the mud"—could alert the community to the psychopathology of everyday life, and indeed Miss La Trobe has instigated some self-analysis in the audience: "Did she mean . . . the unconscious as they call it? But why always drag in sex" (159, 174, 199).

In both novels the ominous romantic comedy of English upper-class society appears to be guided by unconscious desires and racial destiny; a customary separation of the spheres—men fight, women suffer—and a lingering social hierarchy mask a fierce universal kinship. The "megaphonic, anonymous" narrator of the pageant warns, "*A tyrant, remember, is half a slave*"; someone in the audience concurs, "We all, I admit, are savages still" (BA 187, 199). But this negative common life is irredeemable without some vestige of hierarchical difference. Who but a messiah or goddess could restore life after bloodshed? The redemptive influence will come, as legend has it, from among outsiders. Perhaps "the ancient consciousness of woman . . . for so many ages dumb" ("GE" [1919] 159), the collective history of the oppressed, will be able to repair the social web, mitigating harsh conditions in the spirit of Victorian reform.[20] But can outsiders be trusted to treasure the same goods as their oppressors? Women, like the masses, are reputed to encompass the best and worst of human impulse, the power to create new life and the urge to trample the dead in vengeance. What will happen if the marginalized are permitted to act?

A resurgence of the feminine common life, instead of preventing holocaust, might smash every structure in sight. Culture requires boundaries as speech requires silence, and Woolf almost as much as Eliot admits the need for certain traditional boundaries. "A few were chosen; the many passed in the background," as the sentimental Rev. Streatfield puts it (BA 192). In *To the Lighthouse*, Mr. Ramsay poses the riddle of the relation between the elite and the *unchosen*:

Reader" (Silver, *Notebooks*, 115–16). In "The Leaning Tower," she sides with her audience of workers: Arnoldian culture would soon topple, she argued; writers must now "write the common speech . . . share the emotions of their kind" ("The Leaning Tower," CE 2: 169–76).

[20]That Woolf is still intrigued by Eliot's vision of feminine reforming influence is suggested by a passage in "Notes for Reading at Random" (a projected literary history written concurrently with *Between the Acts*): "The song making instinct. The map of London. Alfred Tennyson, Mrs GH Lewes had suggested: a meeting was held in March . . . in Gower St. at 8. This is continuity—the [*extension*] certain emotions always in being: felt by people always" (Woolf's ellipses; Silver, " 'Anon,' " 373–74). Here Eliot (in her guise as Victorian lady reformer) might be getting up a committee to restore the music of humanity. These cryptic notes condense several elements of Woolf's vision at this time: first, the origin of art in instinctive song or ritual; then spatial history (such as a map of London or a country house near the Roman road); then nostalgia for Victorian faith in fellow-feeling.

Does the progress of civilisation depend upon great men? Is the lot
of the average human being better now than in the time of the
Pharaohs? Is the lot of the average human being . . . the measure of
civilisation? Possibly not. Possibly the greatest good requires the
existence of a slave class. The liftman in the Tube was an eternal
necessity. The thought was distasteful. . . . He would argue that the
world exists for the average human being; that the arts are merely a
decoration imposed on the top of human life. (67)

The very hierarchy that uplifts art must oppress those who are left
underground, and Eliot and Woolf cannot naively accept Mr. Ramsay's democratic solution to the riddle: there remain tensions between
the chosen passengers and particular liftmen. Yet they would only
have agreed up to a point with Nietzsche's claim that cultural advance
"needs slavery" (*Good and Evil* 201); Western civilization and myriad
forms of oppression have evolved in tandem, but such guilty "progress" must be, *will* be arrested whatever the loss.

Both novels strike an uneasy compromise between the cultivated
characters and the "people." Daniel, for example, can only redeem
his people by abandoning Gwendolen and Leonora Charisi as prin-
cesses in exile; he must reject the godforsaken European present much
as the author spurns readers unwilling to follow an arid argument on
Zionism. Similarly, Miss La Trobe can revive English literature for the
people only by staging a kind of *Reader's Digest* literary history that
ironically repels and scatters the audience, holding up mirrors to their
isolation and puzzlement. Further, the characterization in these works
reflects little love of ordinary people, who are often vulgar like the
Cohens and Mrs. Manresa, or snobbishly parasitical like Vandernoodt
or Mrs. Parker. To accept humanity must be to welcome all these
to one's estate, though heroism, greatness, the very foundations of
civilization may have depended on selectively closing the gates. Deronda's uneasy condescension to the Cohens resembles that of the
Olivers to the villagers at the tea ceremony ("few, it is to be hoped,
will be offended to learn" that "the entire Cohen family" were invited
to Daniel's wedding [880]). The Jewish people Daniel sets out to lead,
however, like the costumed laborers whose song is wafted away from
the audience of the pageant, form a soft-focus ideal of a common
humanity.

If culture must necessarily exclude in order to survive, it does so at
the peril of its own self-understanding, which in turn is essential for
survival. The final novels would like to affirm that art promotes such
self-understanding in the average human being, whether tyrant or

slave; from this perspective, "we" are allied (in spite of lingering racism and classism) with the anonymous liftman as collaborators, instead of being "great men" served by a slave class (thus Miss La Trobe, "a slave to her audience," "worked like a nigger" to produce the Victorian age [94, 150], yet the audience and actors are her minions, in a sense distributing her authorship). "We" are dispersed the moment we speak this desire for unity; some must be chosen to lift our common brutality toward divinity. Vain as such aspirations can be in these novels, both works implicitly concur with J. S. Mill's belief that, "in a good and a bad sense, the English are farther from a state of nature than any other modern people" (124). It is a question of salvaging the virtues of this advancement—through the pan-culturalism of aliens like Daniel or Miss La Trobe—while braving a return to forgotten origins in order to prepare for the next act.

Besides invoking the ritualistic origins of art, these novels retrieve forgotten beliefs from a collective pantheon; ancient religion becomes another means of sustaining meaningful continuity. Woolf's novel is characteristically more varied and elusive than Eliot's in its deployment of a sacred heritage, and it implies more heterogeneous historical *narratives*. Incorporating prehistory, Woolf also alludes to archaic Christianity alongside Egyptian and Greek mythology, constructing an elaborate analogical machinery in the modern style, as though *Between the Acts* were a *Ulysses* with a bias toward matriarchal myths. Eliot also draws on pagan mythology and Christian hagiography, without conspicuously preferring female deities; these allusions might appear to be a matter of cultivated habit rather than subversive design. Yet at the same time, Eliot engages Judaism as a living religion, not just a convenient source of imagery for the secular cosmopolitan. Even the apparently casual association of characters with sacred legends, such as the comparison of Gwendolen to Calypso, reveals an earnest intent, an argument about women's destiny. Woolf plays with typological characterization even more earnestly, turning similitude into surreal identity: her ladies and gentlemen *are* pagan deities or Christian saints, just as her villagers claim to be figures from English history.

Corresponding to this difference in characterization between Eliot's intelligible metaphors and Woolf's perverse allegories, different modes of interpretation are invited by these works according to their favored systems of belief. *Daniel Deronda* replicates the Mishnah and the Gemara of the Talmud, overlaid parallel commentaries denoting a history of response to a text nevertheless affirmed to have been revealed for all time. In contrast, the segments of *Between the Acts* might be the broken panels of an Egyptian monument, an edifice that calls for a kind of three-dimensional hermeneutics: it must be entered and lived in before the inscriptions yield their meaning (Brockett 13). To our Western minds, the Hebrew text remains comparatively decipherable, whereas the ancient matter of Egypt has no continuous tradition of commentary. Yet the collaborative exegesis of Miss La Trobe's pageant, itself a form of literary criticism, resembles the Rabbis' polyphonic commentaries, which have never known any detail to be insignificant or any reading to have the last word.[21]

Why should the women of letters have been attracted to the ancients and to alien forms of thought and belief? Certainly this attraction was common enough in literary and intellectual circles throughout their lifetimes (Jenkyns; Vickery). Evelyn Haller, to whom I am indebted for an understanding of Isiac mythology in *Between the Acts*, maintains that Woolf adopted the Egyptian myth of Isis because "Egyptology" "undermined the Victorian world view" and because Egyptian mythology subverted "imperialism, Christianity, and patriarchy" ("Isis" 109–10). But Egyptology was an expanding horizon in the worldview of many Victorians, including Eliot, and for many it was an extension of the British empire of reason as well as imagination (Paden). Woolf owed her acquaintance with things Egyptian to explorations begun by Victorians.[22] In her attraction to a civilization more alien than the early Christian or classical Greek, Woolf was very Victorian as well as modern: "Neither one thing nor the other; neither Victorians nor themselves," says the audience in an Arnoldian mood (BA 178; see "The Leaning Tower," CE 2: 176).

The drive to coordinate alien mythologies in a universal cultural history was well under way when Eliot came to intellectual maturity (she satirized that drive in her portrait of Casaubon), and it survived the growing doubts about the foundations of the self, of knowledge, and of empire. Works such as Harrison's *Ancient Art and Ritual* and Frazer's *The Golden Bough* grew out of the Victorian quest for origins and cultural consensus, and influenced younger generations of writers in turn.[23] Thus Woolf became intrigued by the Egyptian cult of Isis,

---

[21]Like biblical narrative, Woolf's is laconic, "fraught with background," as Erich Auerbach would have it (12); her last novel exhibits the repetition of words and action, the stress on dialogue, and the absent narrator of biblical texts as described by Robert Alter (21, 178–85). Eliot more nearly approximates the surface elaboration of Homer than the spare action of the Bible (Handelman 29–33).

[22]As Haller herself points out, the Egypt Exploration Fund was established in 1882, the year of Woolf's birth (Haller, "Isis," 109–10); an eminently Victorian enterprise, it began only two years after Eliot's death.

[23]See Vickery. Eliot would have recognized Harrison's assumption that present-day rituals among European folk or exotic tribes could be "read" as historical records (Harrison 126). See "The Natural History of German Life" (1856) 274–75. Woolf read

which had already attracted Eliot's speculations (her notebooks for *Daniel Deronda* record references to that cult [Baker, *Eliot Notebooks*, 1: 156–60]). Eliot appears more interested in the Hellenic myth of Persephone, a narrative that downplays the questing role of Isis, but that implies the mother's power in the Eleusinian mysteries; Woolf repeatedly draws on the Demeter-Persephone narrative, particularly in *To the Lighthouse* (Pratt 150–53), and it resurfaces at times in her last novel.

Woolf's innovation on Eliot's use of ancient belief, then, lies not in the direction but in the extent. Woolf undertakes the kind of excavation that Freud performed in *Moses and Monotheism* (published by Hogarth Press in 1939, during the writing of *Between the Acts* [Beer, *Past*, 164]). Not only is your Christianity founded on Judaism, she seems to say with Eliot, but that Judaism itself grows out of Egyptian cults, she seems to add with Freud. Yet Woolf has not left Eliot's perspective far behind. No evidence that we could present of the historical layering of beliefs would have surprised Eliot. In light of German historical criticism ("Evangelical Teaching" 171), without nostalgic faith, the biblical scriptures become "simply the history and literature of a barbarous tribe that gradually rose from fetichism to a ferocious polytheism, offering human sacrifices, and ultimately, through the guidance of their best men, and contact with more civilised nations, to Jehovistic monotheism" ("Introduction to Genesis" 257–58). Her last novel would add another clause here: "Through contact with English humanism, it will finally rise to an enlightened Zionism." Judaism cannot claim a unique providential progress if it is repeatedly influenced by "more civilised nations," not only the British but the Egyptians long before. The notebooks for *Daniel Deronda* suggest that Eliot wished to impart to the English a sense of all time-honored beliefs, not just Judaism, including the matter of Egypt that Woolf was to emphasize in *Between the Acts*.[24]

---

subsequent anthropology, including Ruth Benedict's *Patterns of Culture* in 1940 (*VW Diary* 5: 306). Harrison emphasizes Isiac ritual and the kinship of dying god myths as well as totemistic beast-dances (15–20, 46).

[24]Eliot noted, as Freud later did, that "Moses" was an Egyptian name meaning child, suggesting that the Jewish leader (not unlike Daniel) might have been Egyptian by birth and religion as well as upbringing (Baker, *Eliot Notebooks*, 3: 51); Eliot may have derived this fact from a guidebook for a possible journey to Egypt in 1874 (Baker, *Notebooks* 3: 196–97n.1); Haight 473–74. See Freud, *Moses and Monotheism*, 5. Freud kept a statue of Isis as well as Athena on his desk. Eliot's commonplace book probably dating from 1868–69 quotes the Egyptian Book of the Dead, as well as European and English poets and Hebrew scripture on the lasting fame of the prophet or poet (Waley). Another notebook records numerous entries on the role of Egyptian women, who were better off than women in other ancient societies (Wiesenfarth, *Notebook*, 6–7).

Neither author is plundering ancient myths merely out of scholarly curiosity, of course. For them this is an archaeology of the self and its gendering in contemporary civilization. In spite of the thunder of Jehovah in Eliot's text, mythology and saints' legends can be heard murmuring of an ancient consciousness of women's suffering. Similarly, though Woolf, like male modernists such as Yeats and T. S. Eliot, recalls the myth of a dying god (Vickery 230, 256), she does so to revise the heroic archetypes that subject women, and subtly honors female divinity.[25] Instead of the myth of Persephone, who like Gwendolen is the mother's periodic hostage to a male power, Woolf engages the myth of Isis (or Isa), a life-giving goddess, consort of the dying god, who gathers the limbs sundered by his monstrous male rival and restores him in the seasonal rebirth of the Nile, their son. The myth of Isis offers an alternative to, though not a complete escape from, the woman's tale of rape and captivity; it incorporates female agency in what is nevertheless a succession from father to son. And as Isa's meditation on rape and the recurring refrain of "sister swallow" suggest, violation and silence are ever-present threats in narratives about women or goddesses.[26]

The dramatis personae of these novels are types drawn from many of the same myths and legendary histories. Characters in both novels discover within them an "unacted part," the original type "lost-in-the-mists-of-antiquity" (BA 153, 190).[27] Whereas Eliot relies on the messianic hero and counterbalances the worlds of Daniel and Gwendolen as "equivalent centre[s] of self" (M 157), Woolf multiplies such centers in an unheroic group. The results of these authors' archaeological labors should be displayed in the context of each novel to suggest

[25]According to Freud, the earliest traces of religion suppress not only the murder of the patriarch by sons wishing to possess the mother but also a matriarchal phase that succeeded that murderous rebellion; the worship of a ritually slain animal-totem commemorates the slain patriarch (and is one source for the myth of a dying god [*Moses and Monotheism* 104–11]).

[26]"Isis becomes a swallow to search for her . . . husband," as Haller notes ("Anti-Madonna" 104), but the swallow is also Philomela, the sister of Tereus's wife Procne, who is tricked into marrying Tereus (a rape); when Philomela threatens to tell, he cuts out her tongue, and she weaves a tapestry of the tale for Procne to see. In revenge, Procne kills Tereus's son, and the sisters escape; the raped and mutilated sister (creator of a text) becomes the swallow, and the murderous wife becomes the nightingale, able to sing (Hamilton 270–71).

[27]See Frye on the use of typology to lend "meaning and point to history" (*Code* 80–81). Landow distinguishes Eliot's "allusive literary iconography" from biblical typology (3, 107). Yet there is secular typology in these final novels. If Moses is the type of Christ, he is the antitype of Osiris, and Daniel himself can be introduced in this series. Eliot discounts the privileging of Christ as the one messiah, the one typological meaning: Daniel is both antitype (a second Moses) and type of the messiah still to come (Pykett 68).

their implications for a feminist revision of history. The overlaid types and cultural histories in these works uncover contemporary versions of an ancient sexual division of labor. While webs of allusion surround the male characters, the women seem endowed with the most ancient consciousness, the most "unacted" parts.

Sexual War and Unconscious History
in *Daniel Deronda*

When Eliot encrusted the figure of Dorothea Brooke with such gems as "Saint Theresa" and "Ariadne," or that of Gwendolen Harleth with "Saint Cecilia" or "Lamia," she was not just displaying knowledge or adorning a tale. She was both exalting her unknown women as historical "types" and challenging the unique truth of modern accounts of civilized society. Allusions to saints' legends and mythology pervade English literature, of course, but Eliot brought to English fiction a new level of learned encoding, outdoing her contemporaries as at times Woolf would outdo hers.[28] For the women writers, an encyclopedic display of "all mythologies" might lend superhuman powers to a heroine or it might reveal recurring patterns of female sacrifice and expose depths of delusion in empiricist versions of contemporary reality. The pavement underfoot, the foundation of knowledge, is porous, as Dorothea realizes in visiting the necropolis of "visible history," Rome (M 143); this heroine might be sharing in one of Woolf's moments of alienation in Whitehall, or one of Lucy Swithin's visions of mammoths in Piccadilly. The forms of polite society disguise the resemblance of a husband to a minotaur; indeed, you and I might be grotesque metamorphoses of the divine and base. Hence Eliot's mythological subtexts in *Daniel Deronda* reveal unseemly intimacies and conjunctions beneath a Victorian faith in the differences that ground social order and progress. The confident distinctions between such enterprises as sports, courtship, and international conquest, like those between Englishmen and animals or Englishmen and Jews, break down as characters reveal thronging multitudes within them.

---

[28] Anna Jameson, the famous Victorian woman of letters and feminist, popularized art history and added to the repertoire of heroic female parts (e.g., Shakespeare's heroines as role models). Her *Sacred and Legendary Art* furnished Eliot with saints' legends and iconography for her heroines in *Romola, Middlemarch,* and *Daniel Deronda* (see Wiesenfarth, *Notebooks,* 58–68, 183–88). The Brontës and Christina Rossetti exploited the subversive power of fairy tales in much the same way, but without claiming learned authority.

The focus of many of the superstitious distinctions of society is the young English lady, whose profession is to enact her difference from a raw female and from a man. Like Isa Oliver, Gwendolen Harleth is especially burdened with a fateful repertoire of roles; very up-to-date, she is full of rebellious desires that unconsciously hark back to primitive practices. Gwendolen appears as a "young witch" (127) of "demon ancestry" (99), with prophetic dreams and phobias, and an uncanny malevolence toward suitors; she is also "a perfect Diana" (199) transformed into a Persephone (824, 831): from huntress to victim.

Unlike Dorothea Brooke, Gwendolen deliberately poses as a saint—and the vain posing mocks the likeness. When she sits at the organ in their new house and cries, "Someone shall paint me as Saint Cecilia" (the patroness of music credited with inventing the organ [55]), she seems to be displaying her accomplishments, but she also reveals her ignorance and profanity. In her mother's "black and yellow bedroom," where she has a "pretty little white couch . . . by the side of the black and yellow catafalque known as the 'best bed' " (the colors of death, marriage [and jealousy], and purity respectively, Anna Jameson tells us [1: 36–37]), Gwendolen poses before the mirror and says, "I should make a tolerable Saint Cecilia with some white roses on my head . . . only, how about my nose, mamma? I think saints' noses never in the least turn up" (56–57). She is right at least that she misrepresents the saint, who according to Jameson should be shown in an aesthetic rapture, with "an expression of *listening* rather than *looking*," and her crown of heavenly roses "should be *red* and *white*, symbolical of love and purity" (her emphases; 2: 594–96). Loving only her mother (who has shown that marriage is a kind of death) and the image in her own mirror, Gwendolen lacks precisely the loving devotion to music of the saint or of Herr Klesmer. Her association with white ("Gwen" means white) will be threatened by a deadly and jealous marriage, but she will continue to desire her own chastity and freedom like Gwendolen, the Welsh Diana (the "Lady of the bow" and goddess of the moon).[29]

This sort of subtle criticism of the heroine's egotism and sexual subjection is carried on throughout the novel. Gwendolen parades before the company at Leubronn like a "Nereid in seagreen robes" or

[29]The goddess Gwendolen corresponds with Venus as well as Diana, and her story shares the pattern of Greek myths. She was a queen deserted by her husband for another woman; she made war on her husband and killed him, and she drowned his mistress and their daughter. Eliot's source here is another contemporary woman of letters like Jameson, Charlotte M. Yonge; Wiesenfarth, *Notebooks*, xxxvi; Baker, *Eliot Notebooks*, 1: 101–2; Introduction 36–37.

a "Lamia" (40–41)—suggesting a blend of the animal and divine that endangers men. Indeed, she seems to tempt a "revival of serpent-worship" as though all desired women invite idolatry. These images implicate sexual politics: "Why should not a woman have . . . supremacy" like a man (39, 47)? This is Gwendolen's question as well as the slimy Mr. Vandernoodt's, and thus implicitly a misguided one, but we find the narrator also questioning the idea that only men rule supreme. Gwendolen's greater likeness to a pagan goddess than a Christian martyr parallels her endeavor to be a ruler rather than a subject.

Many critics of the novel have recognized currents of political metaphor as well as animal imagery in Gwendolen's relations with Grandcourt; both clusters of allusion add to the heroine's goddess-like function as a primitive resistance to patriarchal tyranny, while they challenge the civilized pretensions of modern England. Gwendolen is a "princess in exile" ruling a "domestic empire" because of "her inborn energy of egoistic desire" that commands others' fear; in this respect she is exactly like "a very common sort of men." "Who is so much cajoled and served with trembling by the weak females of a household as the unscrupulous male . . . ?" (71). Though the narrator thus places Gwendolen in the father's position as pinnacle of the household pyramid, this placement does not render the issue of egotism identical for both sexes; in the end, all the women of Offendene become Grandcourt's subjects. He exercises "triumphal diplomacy" such as could "govern a difficult colony" (645, 655) to compel his wife to act her part. The supreme imperialist, he makes the world his cheerless home (whereas the women and the Jews all experience exile); he has none of the fear of doing harm that ultimately saves Gwendolen from the hell of egotism ruled by this plutonic gentleman (71, 509).

In spite of parading as huntress ("My arrow will pierce him before he has time for thought," she imagines before meeting Grandcourt [127]), Gwendolen unconsciously understands her role as huntsman's prey or explorer's prize. In her first conversation with Grandcourt, she even echoes the horticultural imagery of the Victorian debate on women's education, and neatly links it to imperialism *and* Egyptology: "We women can't go in search of adventures—to find out the North-West Passage or the source of the Nile, or to hunt tigers in the East. We must stay where we grow, or where the gardeners like to transplant us. . . . That is my notion about the plants: they are often bored, and that is the reason why some of them have got poisonous." At this moment, though Gwendolen flatters herself that she is a powerful huntress, Grandcourt's "lotos-eater's stupor" has begun to poison her, turning her into a "statue" gripping "the handle of her whip"—an *inanimate* figure of vain desire for power. She can only try to escape by pretending to drop her weapon (171–72). Gwendolen's bloom, her ignorance, is indeed deadly, as it subjects her to a predator almost as ignorant yet wholly without bloom, and all the more deadly because he appears to be the English heroic type.

In the savage sport of courtship, females fight as hard as males, and perhaps with more conviction. If slaughter bores Grandcourt, Gwendolen has a zest for the kill. For instance, she thrives at the archery meet, itself a disguised marriage market:

> The time-honoured British resource of "killing something" is no longer carried on with bow and quiver; bands defending their passes against an invading nation fight under another sort of shade than a cloud of arrows; and poisoned darts are harmless survivals either in rhetoric or in regions comfortably remote. Archery has no ugly smell of brimstone; breaks nobody's shins, breeds no athletic monsters. (134)

Maidens may take part in archery (though they should not fox-hunt) because of a conspiracy of forgetfulness, yet Gwendolen, lady of the bow, is half aware of her warlike desires. Though men objectify her either as an animal to be tamed ("a high-mettled racer") or a creature who turns men to animals—a "Calypso" (134)—she figures herself as masterful subject: she "wished to mount the chariot and drive the plunging horses herself, with a spouse by her side who would fold his arms" (173). Grandcourt, however, is more successful in turning humans to brutes: he torments his dog Fetch as he would a jealous woman, and treats his factotum Lush like a superior pet whom "he might kick . . . only he never did choose to kick any animal" (161, 164). He hunts a spirited woman "worth his mastering" (195) and soon manages "his wife with bit and bridle" (744; Hardy 226–29). Grandcourt's perfect demeanor and respectability mask the misogynist brutality condoned by genteel practices.

Eliot insistently associates this agent of civilization with primitive stages of evolution and with the underworld. In the opening scene of *Daniel Deronda*, Gwendolen has fled this suitor to enter a "gas-poisoned" gambling hall full of "human dross" with "crab-like hand[s]" or heads like "a slight metamorphosis of the vulture," all "specimen[s] of a lower order" to which Gwendolen, though decked out like a "serpent," believes herself superior (36–40). Grandcourt himself is another throwback: his "sudden impulses . . . have a false air of daemonic strength . . . though perhaps their secret lies merely in the want of regulated channels for the soul to move in— . . . ducts of habit without which our nature easily turns to a mere ooze and mud" (194). What is civilization if it is ruled by a creature of the primeval slime or a "handsome lizard of some hitherto unknown species" (173–74)?

Clearly it is hell for Gwendolen, who in widowhood imagines a return to her mother's bucolic home as a return to paradise "after following a lure through a long Satanic masquerade . . . end[ing] . . . in shrieking fear lest she herself had become one of the evil spirits who were dropping their human mummery and hissing around her with serpent tongues" (831).[30] In spite of her "human mummery" of innocent beauty, she has proved as satanic as her husband, king of the underworld; she may have too high a voice for tragedy, as she once playfully observed, but in her soul lurks vengeance.[31] Her wish for Grandcourt's death is magically realized; forced to be passive, she nevertheless can *feel* simultaneously "the outlash of a murderous thought and the sharp backward stroke of repentance" (72), between the acts, as it were. Gwendolen becomes a vessel of women's ancient, demonic rage against their abductors.

Leonora Charisi also reenacts a perpetual animosity toward ruling men. Feminist readings of *Daniel Deronda* readily point to this woman artist's resemblance to Eliot herself, but her similarity to Gwendolen is less obvious. Neither Gwendolen nor the Alcharisi has "felt exactly what other women feel—or say they feel" (691); their ambition belies the enforced selflessness of womanhood. In a passage that in many details recapitulates the opening encounter between Daniel and Gwendolen, Eliot introduces the mother as a mysterious creature of appearances (her son might again ask, "Was she beautiful or not beautiful?"); she is likened to Melusina, another enchanted, half-serpentine woman like Lamia. Leonora is more august than seductive, a figure of royalty capable of encompassing "myriad lives in one," appearing to Deronda like "a mysterious Fate" or "a sorceress" (687–

---

[30]The home of Grandcourt's mistress, which he vindictively wills to his wife, is "purgatorial," though it "would be a paradise" if one were in the coal business (830–31). Not only is Persephone's return to a green world suggested here, but also Dante's pilgrimage. Deronda seems a Miltonic archangel to Gwendolen, and Milton presides over the novel at the last: the final words of the novel, from the ending of *Samson Agonistes*, bless the death of Mordecai.

[31]Gwendolen frequently wants to play-act; she compares herself favorably to the tragic Jewish actress, Rachel: "The more feminine a woman is, the more tragic it seems when she does desperate actions. . . . As if all the great poetic criminals were not women! I think the men are poor cautious creatures" (84–85).

89, 723). The epigraph to chapter 51 fittingly presents the Greek poet Erinna, figured here as a Lady of Shalott who must spin unintelligibly and repetitively "while the throng / Of gods and men wrought deeds that poets wrought in song." Left out of the advancing tradition like another Maggie (or Hecuba), the woman is denied original authorship (Rosenman, "Women's Speech," 238, 244–46). Leonora has sought revenge in a career of deeds and song that defies male authority (and the epigraph to chapter 53 links her to Shakespeare's Cleopatra). She claims that "a great singer and actress is a queen," but her power is only temporary, as patrilineal descent restores order: "She gives no royalty to her son" (697). Instead, she can only become a princess by marriage, fulfilling the obscure tasks of the domestic woman. She ends with a blasphemous will to die that contrasts with Gwendolen's frail but devout willingness to live.

Daniel must fulfill his destiny as an exiled prince who founds his own country, at the cost of abandoning these two imperious goddesses, as though they represent the idolatry that the chosen people must spurn, the goddess-worship that patriarchal monotheism historically supplanted. Yet Eliot portrays Daniel as deserving to lead because, unlike Grandcourt, he cares for the suffering of women and other underlings and he wants to know history; he is *not* the English Philistine, xenophobe, and misogynist. Daniel stands apart from the Grandcourts' malingering British materialism, a kind of polytheism without the creed. On a tour of the abbey, for example, Gwendolen and Grandcourt weigh the value of their future possessions, whereas Daniel senses a history of belief recorded in such features as the old choir turned into a stable; here Daniel unconsciously bares his head. " 'Do you take off your hat to the horses?' said Grandcourt, with a slight sneer" (473–74). The well-bred Englishman, Grandcourt participates in a cult of horseflesh, but he has no trace of genuine reverence and has forgotten history.

Daniel's polymorphous reverence saves him from Grandcourt's ruthless egotism, but it also presents a danger: he too might lack the channels that prevent a reversion to ooze and mud. Full of suffering and sensibility, Daniel takes a kind of historical interest in saving women, but he must resist the barbaric practices subtly associated with them. Until properly schooled by Mordecai, Daniel confuses the allure of the past with decadence and idolatry: "the heaping of cat-mummies and the expensive cult of enshrined putrefactions" (414). This is a strange necrophiliac temptation, and it coincides with his fascination with self-destructive women (both Gwendolen and Mirah catch his attention as spectacles of doom, but Mirah is attempting to drown herself, whereas Gwendolen will later "drown" her husband). Mr. Vandernoodt teases Daniel for being more interested in an "ante-deluvian . . . scandal about Semiramis"[32] or "a lady [with] a rag face and skeleton toes" (488) than in the gossip about Grandcourt's aban-doned Medea, Mrs. Glasher. Such allusions point to the sexual be-trayal of women (a very old story), but also suggest that Daniel more readily desires a victim with a long history than a full-blooded woman with a future. He joins a male apostolic succession, with a helpmeet who does not stand for a competing deity.[33]

If it is possible to construe Daniel's vocation—which the author appears to take very seriously—as a means to elude a threatening suitor, Gwendolen (who has made her own escape to Leubronn), it appears that Gwendolen's power to determine the Yea or Nay is great indeed. Gwendolen's flight from Grandcourt is futile, leading to hell, whereas Daniel's escape from her is said to lead to a new paradise. The contest of wills between heroine and hero at the end appears like a battle of titans, a test of the ultimate force of patriarchy. When Daniel announces his plan to found a Jewish homeland, Gwendolen's fear of horizons and her superstition are confronted with the historical world and religious duty. The passage, recalling the more famous depiction of girls as vessels of human affection in the midst of men's battles, implies that all the violence of age-old myth and contemporary war lurks within the imagination of the woman suddenly forced to aban-don her egotistical hopes.

The world seemed getting larger round poor Gwendolen, and she more solitary and helpless. . . . There comes a terrible moment to many souls when . . . the larger destinies of mankind, which have lain aloof in newspapers . . . enter like an earthquake into their own lives—when the slow urgency of growing generations turns into the tread of an invading army or the dire clash of civil war, and grey fathers know nothing to seek for but the corpses of their blooming

[32]In "Notes for Reading at Random," Woolf refers to "Semiramis— . . . Aspasia— witches & fairies," that is, ancient women of power and learning; Silver links this reference to Woolf's observation that anonymous poets were often accused witches (RO 50–51; Silver, " 'Anon,' " 371, 374).

[33]Daniel's mission is distinguished from that of a woman like Fedalma, who is chosen to renew her race in *The Spanish Gypsy,* by the fact that it does not entail a forfeiture of family life: a man may combine ambition and romance plots, but clearly only a chastened romance with a sisterly, self-effacing woman. Egyptian mummies are dangerous to one who would reconstitute Judaism.

sons, and girls forget all vanity to make lint and bandages which may serve for the shattered limbs of their betrothed husbands. Then it is as if the Invisible Power that has been the object of lip-worship and lip-resignation became visible, according to the imagery of the Hebrew poet, making the flames his chariot and riding on the wings of the wind. . . . Often the good cause seems to lie prostrate . . . the martyrs live reviled, they die, and no angel is seen holding forth the crown and the palm branch. (875)

From one point of view this passage recollects biblical rhetoric chastising those who see with "the eyes of frivolity" (876), rebuking women as well as nations for imputed wantonness; they must be taught the true religion of selflessness and racial destiny. From another angle, this is a passage of indirect interior monologue; the imagery of carnage seems drawn from the racial unconscious as it emerges in Gwendolen. The fathers and girls seem to enact myths of the dying god (as Isis rebinds the shattered limbs of her husband, and Osiris recovers his son Horus); as in those myths it is never clear that the mourners are not also the murderers.

The passage unleashes rage against man, the prostrated good cause; it suggests that Gwendolen's murderous wish turns now from Grandcourt to her unresponsive mentor. No angel relieves Gwendolen's torment in this final encounter, but none is sent by her to relieve Daniel's: his "anguish was intolerable. He could not help himself. He seized her outstretched hands . . . and kneeled at her feet. She was the victim of his happiness." Like so many heroes before him he must abandon the victim that he appears to worship, and she must join the suppressed ancient consciousness of woman. She has become a seated Fate like his mother; she acts her emotions—like the Alcharisi's, the repetitions of tyrannical memory: "A great wave of remembrance passed through Gwendolen and spread as a deep, painful flush over face and neck." Her covertly resistant words indicate the cost of the suppression. " 'Don't let me be harm to *you*. It shall be better for me—' She could not finish. . . . The burthen of that difficult rectitude towards him was a weight her frame tottered under." (Daniel's mother commanded, "I shall have done you no harm" [727].) Gwendolen's insistent claim that she "will live" may be less obedient than defiant, since she has been condemned to the deadly emotional repetition of a woman's life, to become "a mere speck" in the wide perspective of public history. She will not go gently into that oblivion: "Through the day and half the night she fell continually into fits of shrieking" (875–79).

We learn, in the ensuing chapter, of the "blessed protectiveness" of Daniel's love for Mirah; his wife will be a "flower in the warm sunlight," like a plant unaware of its greenhouse, and he will soothe her "memories of privation and suffering" with "the sweetest fountains of joy." In this fairy-tale life, she worships him as a "rescuing angel"— the angel that does not come to those awakened to the nightmare of history—and she explains away those who are left out (the abandoned Hans and Gwendolen; 879–80). Though Mirah does have a past, and is said to harbor "fervid emotion . . . supposed to require the bulk of a Cleopatra" in her tiny "Psyche-mould" (801), she somehow has nothing to do with cat-mummies. She will reincarnate the biblical matriarchs without recalling any of their affiliations with suppressed deities. The sinister energies that have resurfaced in recent excavations in the East are forgotten when the Derondas depart on their missionary campaign, outfitted with the most modern equipment as though they were only more life-affirming tourists than the Grandcourts.

In spite of this rosy prospect, other forces in the novel do not allow us to forget a past marked by wrongs against women, and hence the threat of revenge. One final example of such a haunting reminder particularly anticipates *Between the Acts;* it is one of the more prominent of the nightmarish scenes that pursue Gwendolen: the episode of the Whispering Stones. Before this episode we have seen, in Gwendolen's response to the picture of the dead face and fleeing figure, that she shares a gothic heroine's suspicion that civilization itself is haunted. At the archery meet she seems to discover who it is that haunts it: the figure of the wronged woman. The arcadian setting, "an extemporised 'As you like it,' " is a perfect disguise for an encounter between rival women; everyone else but Lush believes the play is about Grandcourt's pastoral chase of Gwendolen. The rendezvous between the hunter's past and present prey takes place at "the Whispering Stones, two tall conical blocks that leaned towards each other like gigantic grey-mantled figures," ominous enough to make "good ghosts on a starlit night" (188). Hearing Mrs. Glasher's claim that *she* should be Grandcourt's wife, Gwendolen "felt a sort of terror: it was as if some ghastly vision had come to her in a dream and said, 'I am a woman's life' " (190). This is yet another prophecy that she must end in witchlike cursing as other women do. A horrifying return of the repressed is suggested by a pagan worship of stones and ghosts, embodying the unappeased power of abandoned women. Woolf similarly plays with the uncanny potential of the primitive in a domesticated pastoral. In the final scene of her novel, the Olivers' armchairs become huge nameless rocks at nightfall, like the Whispering Stones by starlight, on the threshold of dreams.

Between the Acts of Sexual War
in Modern Memory

Much of the historical drama of sexual conflict and primitive beliefs in *Between the Acts* coincides with that in *Daniel Deronda*, as I have suggested. But Woolf's webs of intercultural allusion are even more extraordinary than Eliot's, weaving in surreal detail a magnified image of the underside of English society. The idea that individuals simultaneously play disparate historical parts has become the core of the action, and the question of possible female supremacy is more emphatically raised. Adultery, rape, and the double standard can be named without melodramatic secrecy—in the newspapers, not behind the Whispering Stones. Yet though Isa is no longer under the heavy guard that surrounds Gwendolen's purity, English upper-class civilization appears much the same tissue of lies that it was; it still channels instincts into sports, it still shores up class and gender hierarchy as well as empire. Many skirmishes in the ancient war between the sexes in the earlier novel are repeated in the later.

As if emulating Eliot's allusions to Saint Theresa or Saint Cecilia, Woolf dresses her characters, particularly the older generation at Pointz Hall, as saints; at the same time, each of the central characters plays a part in the Egyptian myth of Isis and Osiris, disrupting any religious unanimity with compulsive and redundant rites. Lucy Swithin, the most religious figure of the day, is a devout Christian in the guise of an ordinary old widow wearing a cross. But William Dodge wonders, "How could she weight herself down by that sleek symbol?" (73). There is something madly inclusive about "Batty," as the servants call her; her favorite reading is the "Outline of History," about "rhododendron forests in Piccadilly" and "the mammoth, and the mastodon; from whom presumably, . . . we descend" (8–9).[34] Her sense of the common origins of all life coincides with her unconscious

---

[34]Compare Rachel's vision in *The Voyage Out* (67), and Bernard's in *The Waves:* "The growl of traffic might be any uproar—forest trees or the roar of wild beasts" (W 253); see also Jinny's comment (W 310–11). Woolf supplies Lucy with her own version of H. G. Wells's *The Outline of History* and *A Short History of the World* (Beer, *Past*, 174), but also incorporates Trevelyan's prehistory (see my Chap. 3 above).

function as a composite saint. The morning of the pageant, she gazes at the sky for signs of any covenant between the weather and humanity, and her "eyes glaze[ ]" from superstitious dread of rain; she prays and "finger[s] her crucifix" while her brother blasphemously suggests providing umbrellas (23).

Details of such a passage can be partly accounted for by the kind of search for origins that epitomizes *Between the Acts*. Saint Lucy, an early Sicilian Christian who met martyrdom by stabbing, is associated with light and the eyes; she is the type of wisdom, represented carrying a knife, a lamp, or her eyes in a dish (Jameson 2: 613–20)—hence the frequent mention of Lucy's eyes. Saint Swithin's feast day (July 15) is believed to determine good or bad weather for the next forty days (roughly the time till the Second World War breaks out) and hence is one source of the preoccupation with rain. Lucy's sainthood readily slips into paganism, as in the odd "consolidating" ritual of cutting bread for sandwiches (the eucharist for the later mass in the Barn?), during which she "held the knife up" and "skipped . . . from yeast to alcohol; so to fermentation; so to inebriation; so to Bacchus; and lay under purple lamps in a vineyard in Italy" (34). The worship of saints is intertwined with pagan superstition, and any village festival descends from the Bacchanal.[35] The alleged spirituality and childish fancy of women, as well as the supposed lack of appetite in old widows, are made into a kind of literal joke by this multitudinous characterization. Lucy is both as grand and as silly as all folk belief, and she is an influential priestess of the pageant in spite of Bart's mockery.

We have seen that Lucy struggles with her brother in a conflict like that of Maggie and Tom Tulliver, but we are never allowed to identify with Lucy as a heroic martyr like Maggie. If Mrs. Swithin resembles the prophet Mordecai, her heritage is a hodgepodge of symbols and associations. Her one disciple is the homosexual artist-clerk, William, whom she initiates into the household pantheistic faith; she shows him the books like "pan pipes" representing "the poets from whom we descend by way of the mind," and later the nursery, "the cradle of our race," where an image of a dog seems to be worshiped (68–71). But "Old Flimsy" cannot be a Saxon Ezra, it would seem, because she is a woman; even the superfluous Rev. Streatfield has more authority, though his message could be a Swithinian doctrine: "We act different parts; but are the same" (192). Her faith cannot survive in public

[35] Lucy's mind may revert to native Sicily here. Her name harks back to Wordsworth's Lucy, "rolled round in earth's diurnal course," much as Gwendolen recalls the indigenous Celtic goddess; the heroines seem to recall a pantheistic faith in natural cycles. Both also affirm feminine purity (as "Lucy" means light, "Gwen" means white).

discourse, but only in orts and scraps of nature and time like Lily Briscoe's "little daily miracles" (TL 240):

> Fish had faith, she reasoned. They trust us because we've never caught 'em. But her brother would reply: "That's greed!" "Their beauty!" she protested. "Sex," he would say. "Who makes sex susceptible to beauty?" she would argue. He shrugged who? Why? Silenced, she returned to her private vision, of beauty which was goodness. (205)

Bart's Darwinian and Freudian counter-argument defeats Lucy's Paleyan argument from design, silencing her natural supernaturalism as a threat to patriarchal distinctions.[36] Lucy is Our Lady of Cycles: "Every morning, kneeling, she protected her vision. Every night she opened the window and looked at the leaves against the sky. Then slept. Then the random ribbons of birds' voices woke her" (206).

If Mrs. Swithin functions primarily as a vestige of primitive Christianity and nature worship, her niece Isa Oliver serves as the goddess Isis, though all central women in the book share the goddess's attributes and none are fixed in a single role.[37] Just as the first scene of *Daniel Deronda*, in the hellish gambling salon haunted by human beasts, introduces the heroine as a sinister goddess, the first scene of *Between the Acts* introduces a modern Isis in a drawing room peopled with beasts and infiltrated by subterranean memories and desires. Mrs. Haines, "goosefaced" and gobbling, objects to discussing "the cesspool . . . to bring water to the village," but readily brings up her buried ancestors. As though participating in the conversation, "a cow cough[s]"; a "bird chuckle[s]" as it devours "worms, snails"; then Mr. Oliver adds his own kind of excavation to those of the diggers of the cesspool, the worshiper of ancestors, and the humanoid animals: a mental archaeology of the "scars made" on the landscape "by the Britons; by the Romans;" and by farmers "in the Napoleonic wars."

---

[36]*Between the Acts* in many ways recapitulates *In Memoriam*, as an elegy defying scientific assaults on faith, building up echoing fragments, and concluding with the promise of offspring of a representative couple. Its collective voice is Tennysonian (running into Swinburne): "There's a poem, *Tears, tears, tears*, it begins. And goes on, *O then the unloosened ocean*" (BA 200). The recurring songs to the swallow misquote Swinburne's "Itylus" (Maika 29) and recall a song in Part IV of *The Princess*.

[37]If Isa owes something to Saint Isabel of Portugal, a self-sacrificing peacemaker between son and husband (Attwater), she may also recall James's Isabel Archer (and perhaps Gwendolen and other heroines of the archery match): she aims arrows of jealousy at Giles, whose patron saint's emblem is the arrow (208). On names, see Maika 18–19.

The layers of consciousness, of belief, of history can be stripped away at any moment.

Isa enters ceremoniously, less grotesque than Mrs. Haines, more fluid than earthy, herself a confluence of images for Venus, Juno, and Isis: "like a swan swimming," wearing "pigtails" and "a dressing-gown with faded peacocks on it," she comes from tending her ailing son. She desires her guest Mr. Haines, the gentleman farmer, and she imagines moonlit romance with him, floating "like two swans down stream" (3–5); Mrs. Haines is jealous. As a romantic plot sketch, this scene may be clear enough, but its bizarre details can be traced to various myths and rites. The vocation of Isis is to "bring water to the village"; she is associated not only with water, but with the moon and cows (as well as the fish pond, the lotus [or water lily], and the swallow), all of which ritualistically resound in *Between the Acts*.[38] In this scene, the swan of Venus, the peacock of Juno, the pigtails and "three-cornered chair" (5) of a seated Egyptian deity, and even the nightingale of Procne form a deliberate mythological confusion mimicking the "astonishing disorder" of our deeply superstitious minds.

Isis is compelled to search (sometimes in the form of a swallow) for her husband-brother Osiris (a kind of gentleman farmer) who has been slain and torn apart each year; she finds him (sometimes in the form of a fish) and restores him to life as her son, Horus (or Isa's son George), representing the waters of the Nile that she has nursed. Haines has given Isa the attributes of Isis, the situla and sistrum, in the form of a cup and a racquet, as Haller points out ("Isis" 119). Throughout the novel, Isa (like others in the family) harps on fish and longs for the inundation at the New Year or summer solstice (as Swithin would bring rain; Haller 116). As "the primeval voice" of cows once saves the pageant from "death . . . when illusion fails," so again Miss La Trobe's work is revived when Isa weeps "all people's tears" in a rain "sudden and universal" (140, 180).

Readers can accept the dream logic of such details without tracing their origins (some would say because we share Jungian archetypes), yet this poetically compressed novel makes new sense when we recall forgotten mythology. Like Gwendolen, Isa plays a woman's age-old

---

[38]See Haule and Smith. Maika's *Virginia Woolf's "Between the Acts" and Jane Harrison's Con/spiracy* (1987) explicates the symbolism of names and iconography in this novel almost to the limits possible. It appeared after I had completed my original investigation of these patterns (including unprecedented consideration of saints' legends), and it frequently corroborates or extends what I had found; it is a very useful key to the many mythologies in this novel. Maika does not refer to Haller, though Haller's studies appeared before 1984, Maika's first copyright. Who should try to claim originality when we all are thinking in common?

roles in patriarchal narrative and can be either Persephone (155) or
"Venus . . . to her prey" (208), victim or huntress, though Isa is more
closely allied than Gwendolen to the primitive violence and natural
cycles encoded in these myths. Whereas Eliot's heroine generally
follows a progression from huntress to victim, Woolf's heroine (always
one of many, unlike the star, Gwendolen) performs her multiple parts
again and again, more spatially than temporally. The posing for Saint
Cecilia or Hermione no longer halts the flow of "real" life; Isa's very
existence is a layering of poses and emblematic props.

Still there is a temporal sequence to this narrative: small incidents
on the day of an annual festival. The disjointed details look innocent
enough. Yet the family at Pointz Hall unconsciously compose medleys
on their own roles as deities, Egyptian and Christian. When Isa asks
whether the fish ordered for lunch will be fresh coming so far from
the sea, Mrs. Swithin breaks in, " 'Once there was no sea . . . at all
between us and the continent.' . . . 'When we were savages,' said
Isa." In the ensuing chatter on fish, false teeth, and the incestuous
marriages of the Egyptians who invented them, the family uncovers
its origins. Bart observes, "The Olivers couldn't trace their descent for
more than two or three hundred years. But the Swithins could. The
Swithins were there before the Conquest" (28–31). Displaying his own
false teeth, Bart shows his resemblance to the fragmented Osiris, while
Isa characteristically longs for the fish of Osiris and the waters of
Horus; Lucy as usual joins land and sea, like the present and prehistory, and she reflexively recalls the pharaohs, incarnations of these
sibling gods. Worship of the male god (here incarnated as the Normans
or Olivers) is more recent than matriarchal worship (represented here
by the Saxons or Swithins). Certainly Bart lives more in the post-
Victorian present than Lucy, with his passion for historicist distinctions; "she belonged to the unifiers; he to the separatists" (118).

Every page of this text proliferates more meaning than can be con-
templated here. Woolf may have felt an archaeologist's pleasure in
constructing a (Joycean?) dig to keep the mythologically minded in-
definitely busy. But for Woolf as well as for Eliot, these embedded
narratives contribute subtly to an argument about women's fate in
history. Isa's longing for the sea is not unlike Gwendolen's wish to
set out for "the North Pole" rather than to "do as other women do"
(DD 101). In person more cautious than Gwendolen, in imagination
Isa is a daring adventurer: "To what dark antre of the unvisited earth,
or wind-brushed forest, shall we go now? Or spin from star to star"
(51). But Isa no more than Gwendolen has a goddess's power to drive
the horses herself. As though replicating Gwendolen standing like

a statue with a whip and speaking of greenhouse plants with her implacable wooer, Isa stands like a "statu[e] in a greenhouse" beside the hydrangea (or water-vessel), holding a knife as her admirer William Dodge looks on. She continues the play: " 'And from her bosom's snowy antre drew the gleaming blade. "Plunge blade!" she said. And struck. "Faithless!" she cried. Knife too. It broke. So too my heart,' she said." These heroines must self-destructively repeat old romantic plots; whether the ineffectual gestures with whip or knife are aimed at themselves or at the faithless men who would master them, the effect is the same.

Such scenes indicate the remarkably similar sexual theater of these novels, but in the later novel there are some striking variations in the depiction of men as well as women, and a newly explicit attack on phallocentrism. It is no accident that Isa confides in the greenhouse with William Dodge, the homosexual, from whom women "had nothing to fear, nothing to hope" (113). The woman and the gay man may be conspirators, but he does idealize her in her feminine sacrificial role, and he worships the phallus as she no longer does. The legend, according to John Lemprière, recalls that Isis "recovered the mangled pieces of her husband's body, one part only excepted, which the murderer had thrown into the sea" (754), and which, according to Sir James Frazer, had been eaten by fish (2: 10). This part, Frazer is unashamed to explain, was "the genital member," later commemorated in phallus worship (Frazer 10; Lemprière 754), which appears to be revived in William's and Mrs. Manresa's as well as Isa's desire for Giles. Isa's husband is frequently accompanied by a popular song to the phallic hero: "Armed and valiant, bold and blatant, firm elatant" (110); and Mrs. Manresa, "the wild child . . . Queen of the festival" (79), "goddess-like, buoyant, abundant" (119), chooses him as her counterpart.

Giles rightly perceives William, the man-raiser's mercurial sidekick, as a threat to that firm ideal; he reviles him as a "toady; a lickspittle . . . not a man to have straightforward love for a woman" (60)—the kind of inversion he will later trample. "And the fingers of William's left hand closed firmly, surreptitiously, as the hero approached." Giles's homophobia detects William as one who commits the crime that has no name: Giles "knew not his name; but what his left hand was doing. It was a bit of luck—that he could despise him, not himself" (110–11). The homosocial network of animosity is much like that between Grandcourt and Lush as well as Daniel, but Woolf treats sexual practice more suggestively than Eliot would have dared to do. In context, however, only Giles and the alert reader notice that William is masturbating.

Even Isa, who now dissents from the worship of Giles, was once susceptible to phallus worship. As in *Daniel Deronda*, courtship figures in this novel as a predatory sport, but the myth of Isis seems to determine that the sport be fishing. The young Olivers "had met first in Scotland, fishing. . . . Her line had got tangled; she had given over, and had watched him with the stream rushing between his legs, casting, casting—until like a thick ingot of silver bent in the middle, the salmon had leapt, had been caught, and she had loved him" (48). Although Giles is fisherman, not fish, in this memory, he seems to be Osiris (pictured carrying a stick) retrieving his own phallus from the water; the syntax suggests it may be the salmon whom Isa loves. A memory of fishing also binds the sister and brother household gods, Lucy and Bart; we recall their Wordsworthian childhood like the Tullivers', "when she had trotted after him as he fished." Though Lucy and Isa are femininely "shocked" by the "blood" of this sport (21), Isa like Gwendolen has predatory impulses equivalent to a man's. Isa cannibalistically serves fish for lunch; Giles, coming home to dine, feels "held . . . fast, like a fish in water" by his work in the City (47), but hurriedly eats his fillet of sole (soul?).

Though Giles can be victim, he remains the most empowered object of patriarchal desire; at Pointz Hall, only Isa and Lucy resist this sexual, economic, and political aggressor. His father loves and searches for him, for the good reason that they are aspects of the same principle. Whether as Christian saints or as phases of Osiris, they are credited with a kind of missionary imperialism. As king of Egypt, Osiris instilled morals, instituted laws, and improved the agriculture of his people before spreading enlightened religion through Arabia, Asia, and Europe (Lemprière 754). Saint Bartholomew is credited with spreading the gospel in India and elsewhere; Bart, retired from the Indian Civil Service, dreams of cowing savages in the parched desert (17).[39] Bart is always accompanied by his Afghan hound, Sohrab, like the wild beast often carved at the feet of a saint to signify that "he cleared wasteland, cut down forests, and substituted Christian culture and civilisation for paganism and the lawless hunter's life" (Jameson 1: 28).[40]

In every respect, the son seems less the accomplished ruler and

[39]Bartholomew is the apostle "in whom there is no guile," according to the Gospel of John (Attwater; Jameson 1: 244–45). Like his sister Lucy's patron saint, Bart's is associated with the instrument of his martyrdom, the knife.

[40]The hound's name alludes to Arnold's "Sohrab and Rustum," the blank-verse tale of a battle that ends in peace when the long-lost father, Rustum, unknowingly kills his disguised son, Sohrab—a strange reversal of the Oedipal conflict fittingly associated with the Victorian Bart.

more the combative quester. The dream of empire has become a nightmare, and Giles can only dress as a cricketer and fulminate against the coming assault from Europe (46). Like Grandcourt stifling his wife-colony and his sidekick Lush, Giles intimidates his wife and the "halfbreed" Dodge as though they are less civilized than he. Yet the stockbroker resents the system by which he himself has been civilized, forced to spend his life, according to Lucy, "buying and selling—ploughs? glass beads was it? or stocks and shares?—to savages who wished most oddly—for were they not beautiful naked?—to dress and live like the English?" (47). The legend of Saint Giles is that of the nature-loving outsider rather than the colonizer: Giles was a hermit whose pet hind was slain by an arrow of the king's hunting party (his emblem is the arrow). As saint he became the patron of cripples and the indigent, but Woolf's Giles would discipline any deviation from an upright norm. (As though to anticipate Foucault, "Cripplegate, St. Giles's, Whitechapel" are invoked by the Victorian policeman in the pageant; they are more madhouses or prisons than churches, in which workers must labor to pay "the price of Empire" [163].)

The young English gentleman is further characterized by more primitive narratives of the elements; loosely, he is the earth to Isa's water, Bart's sun or fire (17), and Lucy's air. If Grandcourt has turned to slime, Giles is the hard dry earth of action that Isa must water.[41] Giles gravitates away from his ethereal aunt, who has "nothing in her to weight a man like Giles to the earth," toward the magnetic Mrs. Manresa: he "would keep his orbit so long as she weighted him to the earth" (116–19). Both father and son feel renewed by Mrs. Manresa, the phallic goddess associated with mud, or earth made fertile by water.

Besides the inferred sex act with Mrs. Manresa in the greenhouse, Giles commits only one overt "act" before the end: an instinctive assault on the feminine, the homosexual, and the cycle of birth and death that encompasses him. It is also a declaration of war that commemorates Saint George's victory over the dragon as well as countless similar legends founded on the ancient conflict between the patriarchal thunder god and the serpent of the goddess (Stone 67–68, 204–10; Frye 187–91):

[41]Bart consults "Lemprière" on the origin of the superstition "Touch wood; touch earth; Antaeus" (25), unconsciously alluding to his son; Hercules stifles Antaeus in the air because, like Giles, Antaeus draws "new strength" from the earth (Lemprière 677). Miss La Trobe and those who gaze into the lily pond find new life in the mud, but Giles resists such contemplation.

This dry summer the path was strewn with stones. He kicked—a flinty yellow stone . . . as if cut by a savage for an arrow. A barbaric stone; a pre-historic. Stone-kicking was a child's game. He remembered the rules. . . . The gate was a goal; to be reached in ten. The first kick was Manresa (lust). The second, Dodge (perversion). The third, himself (coward). . . . He reached it in ten. There, couched in the grass, curled in an olive green ring, was a snake. Dead? No, choked with a toad in its mouth. . . . It was birth the wrong way round—a monstrous inversion. So, raising his foot, he stamped on them. . . . Action relieved him. (98–99)

The arrow of Saint Giles becomes part of a child's game expressing unconscious prehistory; what once were sins ("lust") are now called drives. Combat once thought heroic now seems merely the lesser of two evils, like putting an animal out of its misery, and it brings him no glory ("Silly little boy, with blood on his boots," Isa later silently taunts him [111]). Giles is a less hypocritical tyrant than Grandcourt, at least, in that he does his kicking himself; he may "pose [as] one who bears the burden of the world's woe, making money for [Isa] to spend" (111), and he may impose the double standard, but he acts on his appetites as crudely as a child. Isa in contrast must act in the other sense; like Gwendolen she must perform a marital "cliché conveniently provided by fiction" (14), that of the loving, obedient wife.

Yet in spite of old gender conventions, the goddesses in *Between the Acts* have far more say in the course of events than the two female "Fates" in *Daniel Deronda*. Isa, Lucy, Miss La Trobe, even Mrs. Manresa participate in an often exuberant colloquy of folklore without always having to compete, like females in a romantic comedy, for the scarce commodity of male sanction. Much of the ancient consciousness of womanhood that they share seems to center on the lily pond, a vessel of perpetual emotions complementing the alabaster vase at the core of the house. "It was in that deep centre, in that black heart, that the lady had drowned herself. Ten years since the pool had been dredged and a thigh bone recovered. Alas, it was a sheep's, not a lady's. . . . But, the servants insisted, they must have a ghost; the ghost must be a lady's; who had drowned herself for love"(44). The common version of the past holds more lasting power than historical fact, though it tells a tale of feminine undoing. Mrs. Manresa openly sides with such power as no lady in an Eliot novel may. If servants "must have their drowned lady," "so must I!" she cries, in a sense refusing to grow up and become civilized. Her association with the freedom of the unconscious is explicit: "A spring of feeling bubbled up through her mud. They had laid theirs with blocks of marble" (44–45). This barbaric power also entails the kind of prophecy of the warring man's death that is attributed to Gwendolen. Mrs. Manresa claims she "*knew . . . that Ralph, when he was at the war, couldn't have been killed without her seeing him*—'wherever I was, whatever I was doing,' she added, waving her hands so that the diamonds flashed in the sun" (44). These diamonds, not unlike Mrs. Grandcourt's jewelry, have a guilty history (they were "dug out of the earth with his own hands by a 'husband' who was not Ralph Manresa"), but the modern woman can ignore past scandal and enjoy herself (39–40).

In contrast with Mrs. Manresa, Isa more closely resembles the martyred Lady Ermyntrude than the servants, though she serves the common life. She murmurs, "How am I burdened with what they drew from the earth; memories; possessions. . . . 'Kneel down,' said the past. 'Fill your pannier from our tree. Rise up, donkey. Go your way till your heels blister. . . .' That was the burden . . . laid on me in the cradle; murmured by the waves; . . . crooned by singing women; what we must remember; what we would forget" (155). Isa figures as history's obedient beast of burden, but she also has the privilege of preserving the song (burden) of buried collective memory. The nursery tales of crooning women have a subliminal power, though they record oppression.[42] The king is in his counting house; rich man, poor man, beggar man, thief—such is the hierarchy. Although Eliot and Woolf suggest that a trance may keep the "queen" in her parlor, eating bread and honey as war breaks out outside, they do not imply that she is powerless in her separate sphere. She can summon a vast history in which war is just a recurring fit, part of a cycle of love, hate, peace.

If love and war are just the same old story over and over, art promises to retrieve some sense from the senseless repetition. Indeed art has become the inviting vocation for women in both novels as though to channel the rhythmic waves. Miss La Trobe's pageant becomes, in the present day, an Isiac ritual, the jerking mirrors shattering the mimetic order of difference (Haller, "Isis," 116–17), insisting through nonsensical repetition, "*O we're all the same*"—alike brutal and vile. Yet with a few affirmative qualifications, the ensuing music gathers "the whole population of the mind's immeasurable profundity" to unite "us," drawing "from chaos and cacophony measure" (187–89). Such would be the ambition of the pageant itself and the

[42]Arthurian romance and fairy tales lurk in each novel like popular memories. Were we each chosen or cursed in the cradle; are we each, like Guinevere or Sleeping Beauty, a pawn of national or sexual destiny?

novel as a whole: through art to unite the community in spite of its monstrous nature, moving beyond the masquerade of gender.

Thus the drawing room in the evening dissolves to expose natural appetites: "There in that hollow of the sun-baked field were congregated the grasshopper, the ant, and the beetle. . . . Bartholomew, Giles and Lucy polished and nibbled and broke off crumbs" (216). This is no domesticated green world for an *As You Like It*, but a zone of terror such as Gwendolen encounters behind the Whispering Stones. At the last, Isa and Giles face each other in silence:

> Before they slept, they must fight; after they had fought, they would embrace. From that embrace another life might be born. But first they must fight, as the dog fox fights with the vixen, in the heart of darkness, in the fields of night.
>
> The great hooded chairs had become enormous. . . . The house had lost its shelter. It was night before roads were made, or houses. It was the night that dwellers in caves had watched from some high place among rocks.
>
> Then the curtain rose. They spoke. (219)

This timeless sexual battle dissolves the individual in the species as it levels male and female; before property and boundary, the fight seems more equal. This scene, further, has been set by a collaboration of crooning women. Miss La Trobe is answering Isa's earlier unspoken wish: "Surely it was time someone invented a new plot, or that the author came out of the bushes . . . " (Woolf's ellipses; 215). But Isa's wish itself was an answer to Miss La Trobe's even earlier vision as she drank in the smoky pub in a ritual reminiscent of Isis: "Words rose above the intolerably laden dumb oxen plodding through the mud. Words without meaning—wonderful words. . . . There was the high ground at midnight; there the rock; and two scarcely perceptible figures. Suddenly the tree was pelted with starlings. She set down her glass. She heard the first words" (212). War and literary history fade as we enter the world of the collective unconscious. Cruelty and exploitation would not vanish in a return of the beasts (like a return of the Jews); the allusion to Conrad's heart of darkness should chasten our millenarian hopes. Yet just as language might begin to lose its patriarchal loyalties in a return to semiotic origins, Miss La Trobe might flourish, though she is nobody famous, as the medium for a new life, a kind of natural art, fertilized by mud and birds and oxen, by the almost indistinguishable dog fox and vixen.

Artistic Vocation and the
Great Women of Letters

The archaeological quest, started so long ago, does not return quite to its beginning; at least we have retrieved some sense of the demonic power of feminine ancient consciousness. But the quest was launched by the question of vocation, and should return to that point, as vocational difficulties still remain. These novels have not shown us the way to reconcile women's ambitions and history as men have made it. Why, to put a recurring feminist question most plainly, why are there no flourishing women artists in the works of either author? As Woolf observed, Eliot's heroines present "the incomplete version of the story of George Eliot herself" ("GE" [1919] 160). A degree of incompleteness affects Woolf's heroines as well, though one may cite the achievements of Lily Briscoe, Orlando, and Miss La Trobe. If the woman artist in these authors' oeuvres betrays some lack when compared to the grand old woman of English letters, why—and here is the second question to be entertained in this section—why do Eliot's and Woolf's most archaeological novels seem so crowded with women artists? (I will return later to the question of why criticism focuses so much on women authors' female characters.)

As we have seen, Eliot's novels never resolve the clash of women's ambition and erotic plots, and at last in *Daniel Deronda* the tendency to divide (while interweaving) the gendered public and private narratives, which first became marked in *Felix Holt,* has reached such extremes that many have been tempted to sever the hostile parts from each other.[43] Though incapable of forming a stable, "organic" whole (Shuttleworth 201), the Gwendolen and Daniel stories reveal a fundamental interdependence in the need of the latter to silence the former. Though Woolf has broken the silencing effect of the romantic plot, and though she creates independent artists such as Orlando and Lily Briscoe, she as much as Eliot confirms Carolyn Heilbrun's observation that "women writers do not imagine women characters with even the autonomy they themselves have achieved" (*Reinventing* 71). Women of vocation in Woolf's fiction must espouse some measure of obscurity, in keeping with the lingering ideology of influence.

In the final novels, however, both Eliot and Woolf seem to question more than ever the enforced noble failure of creative female characters.

---

[43]Henry James, in *"Daniel Deronda:* A Conversation" (1876), was one of the first to advocate the division of a novel excellent in parts; see Fleishman, "Charisi," 86–87; Lerner and Holmstrom 138–43, 153–55.

Daniel Deronda and *Between the Acts* repeat the female artist figure as they repeat images of goddesses, and they center women's artistic endeavor in the communal ritual of theater. As performers, the women enact their resistance to the law of fathers and husbands, but they tend to conceive of their art as depending on male judgment, and ultimately they give it up. Only Miss La Trobe, purged of self-regard and feminine modesty, defies her audience and launches her own creation yet again. Her remarkable temerity—she may *become* great— is the exception to the rule of these novels, and a heavy price is paid for it in the prior history of women's silent submission. The Alcharisi has *been* great, but has given it up—and unlike Dorothea, she does not like giving up. I wish to survey briefly the vocational options for women in the last novels before attending most closely to the two figures who are publicly recognized as artists in their own right—the Alcharisi and Miss La Trobe (whose names, not incidentally, imply the recurring patterns or tropes of history).[44]

In these final novels the authors subvert the commandment of domestic sacrifice by the portrayal of so many cygnets in the brown pond, and no suitable outlets in family life. The usual alternatives for women, marriage and motherhood, are given little genuine appeal; the widow Mrs. Davilow tells her daughter, "Marriage is the only happy state for a woman," miserable as her own marriages have been (DD 58). Certainly, the young heroines discover no happiness in that state, but only a bitter contest of wills. Motherhood has been presented throughout Eliot's and Woolf's novels more as a woman's estrangement from herself than as her proper vocation (Zimmerman, " 'Mother's History,' " 82–84; N. Auerbach, *Imprisonment*, 171–83); it generally happens after the heroine's story is over, as in the Finale of *Middlemarch*. *Between the Acts*, for the first time in either Eliot's or Woolf's novels, represents a young heroine, Isa, as a mother. It is easier for dead mothers, like those of Mirah and Mordecai and of Lucy and Bart, to become "objects of universal veneration" like Mrs. Ramsay (81). Living mothers are almost always presented as more flawed, either overindulgent (like Mrs. Davilow) or unloving (like the Alcharisi, who openly resents motherhood as a poor substitute for her career). The egotists Gwendolen and Mrs. Manresa and the artist Miss La Trobe (like Lily Briscoe) logically remain childless, whereas Mrs.

---

[44]I call her "the Alcharisi" as many critics have done, though doubling the definite article, because it suits English usage. "Charisi" refers to return from exile. Haller ("Isis" 124–25) and Maika (11–12) offer plausible derivations for La Trobe's name, but it is also an allusion to the tropism that guides the germinating seed: a *direction* of life. And I think her honorific, "Miss," becomes a pun.

Swithin, long ago a wife and mother of two, has left such definitive roles behind; she might be a celibate priestess (rather like an aged Mrs. Dalloway). Gwendolen and Isa, caught within the heterosexual hothouse, still wish to preserve a *self* from maternity: Gwendolen dreads having a child, and Isa escapes the nursery in her imagination.

If marriage appears to be the exchange of women, if romantic love entails a rivalry between women, if motherhood devours the woman's identity, what has become of the English lady's "mission" to spread the influence of fellow-feeling? The demand "what can I do?" has become a clamorous mob of desires and impulses. Though Gwendolen and Isa must carry the burden of ancient consciousness and lose themselves in worldwide feelings, their thought-arrows will hit their mark. Simply by reenacting a counter-history of emotions always in being, women may undermine the public history of wars and conquests, acting as a kind of feminine universality dissolving the claims of a universalizing civilization. If this myth is not always so far-reaching in Eliot's and Woolf's novels, often "the ancient consciousness of woman, charged with suffering and sensibility, . . . seems in [their heroines] to have . . . overflowed and uttered a demand for something" ("GE" [1919] 159) through artistic expression, curtailed as that expression is shown to be.

For several of the female characters in *Daniel Deronda* and *Between the Acts,* performing is a livelihood (for which they are paid directly or indirectly).[45] Theater seems to focus the genteel woman's captivity—she must act her part—as well as her secret freedom to act any part, while it stresses communal ritual, as we have seen. Historically, theater had been one of the few dignified (if not wholly respectable) vocations open to women; the alternatives of teaching or the Meyricks' ladylike handiwork would humiliate Gwendolen. It is never suggested that Gwendolen might write for a living. Eliot allows no lady novelists in her fiction until the last novel, and then only the wealthy, "ridiculous" Mrs. Arrowpoint whose "literary tendencies" certainly yield silly results (Gwendolen makes fun of her: "Home-made books must be so nice" [74–75]). The lady novelist could retain her respectability as a lady but hardly win honor as a novelist, at least not in an ambitious novel by a Victorian woman, since the risk of autobiography would be too great.

Eliot allots professional artistic talent only to Jews, Klesmer and Daniel's mother and wife-to-be. The latter women artists emphatically

---

[45]Nina Auerbach depicts "George Eliot as an actress for whom the role of Great Author is merely the culmination of a life of continual self-creation," and she notes the insistent theatricality of the characters in *Daniel Deronda* (*Imprisonment* 255–56).

are not English ladies, hence their freedom in public; yet they are allowed only the precarious fame of performers, not originating power. In an essay written when she was about to make her first bid for recognition as a great author, Eliot had warned that lasting fame and greatness, or "the sympathy of mankind with individual genius," is awarded only to "the great poet or the great composer," not the performer.[46] Moreover, for women the theatrical profession was generally open more to beauty than talent, and thus it could figure as another market for the physical charms that are notoriously short-lived; this fact is part of the warning and protest in the story of the Alcharisi. The actress may seem to rule supreme, but she generally cannot control the form of her career, which vanishes like the bride's power after marriage. The woman novelist, however homely to begin with, may appear to be judged on the substance of her work, not her womanhood; but the woman of letters, too, seems forced into embodiment by a critical public, as we have seen.

The difficulty of reconciling the woman and the artist in the theater of European society is a repeating theme in Eliot's novel. Mirah, though she is a gifted professional singer and actress, abhors public life and is only too grateful to vanish in Daniel's monumental shadow. Gwendolen is Mirah's opposite, an amateur "stunner" of great ambition; she hopes to go on the stage, but learns that her person will only sell on the marriage market. With options closed, the most frankly egotistical of Eliot's young heroines is thus blocked in both ambition and romance plots. The only ambitious professional woman artist in Eliot's fiction is the Alcharisi (Heller 38), the famous diva who combines Mirah's gifts and Gwendolen's will to power. As though to punish her egotism, Eliot has the Alcharisi's public career founder (as Eliot's certainly did not) when, thinking she is losing her talent, she flees into the refuge of marriage and motherhood.[47] She must assume the roles of daughter, wife, and mother that she had sought to obliterate in her invented persona. Thus for Daniel's wife, lover, and mother, private life triumphs over the artistic career, but not without unresolved tensions.

In *Between the Acts*, Woolf creates a similar array of frustrated female

[46]See Gallagher, "The Prostitute," 55. Eliot expresses warm admiration for "musical and dramatic artists," but they cannot live into the "next age"; "the memory of the *prima donna* scarcely survives the flowers that are flung at her feet on her farewell night" ("Liszt, Wagner, and Weimar" 98–99)—the actress as Persephone?

[47]Eliot did fear a loss of command over her public after *Middlemarch*, as I have noted, and she did, after *Daniel Deronda*, belatedly marry. The anxiety of the woman artist to continue to meet her own standard of greatness is figured also in Armgart, the opera singer in the poem of that name (1870).

talent, this time consisting not only of the powers of performance but also the powers of literary creation; in each instance, the woman succeeds in securing a certain independence from male judgment or domination, and there are signs of alliance between women—a kind of alliance conspicuously absent in Eliot's last novel. Lucy stage-manages the rites at Pointz Hall and shares "a common effort to bring a common meaning to birth" with Miss La Trobe, whom she thanks for rousing her "unacted part," Cleopatra (152–53). Mrs. Manresa, a kind of amateur diva, plays Giles Oliver's fantasy of the earth mother without ever yielding to the role of wife, mother, or mistress. Like the Alcharisi, the Manresa gains notoriety and freedom because she is somehow beyond the pale (born in Tasmania, married to a Jew)—like Eliot, both divas are great favorites with the gentlemen but not quite suitable company for the ladies. Mrs. Manresa resembles Leonora Charisi in being massive and queenly, a performer at heart ("she acted her own emotions"), with the power to sway men (DD 691); their presumed licentiousness is part of their fascination. Yet Woolf's portrait of the man's woman is if anything more damning than Eliot's; whereas Leonora insists that "nature gave [her] a charter"—"the voice and the genius matched the face" (728)—Mrs. Manresa has no pretensions to beauty, spouts the clichés of a hedonistic "barbarian" (176), and knows no feminist theory.

It may have become easier in Woolf's fiction for women to escape the hothouse as the Alcharisi strove to do, but somehow the more accessible "strange bright fruits of art and knowledge" ("GE" [1919] 160) lose the flavor of desire; as Isa ignores old books, Mrs. Manresa flaunts her ignorance. Woolf's novel appears to favor the less self-advertising, less happy Isa over Mrs. Manresa (like Mirah, Isa is a kind of small-voiced singer liable to drown herself); Mrs. Oliver performs the parts of "Sir Richard's daughter" (16), a mother, jealous wife, and potential adulteress, while her most independent act is that of a poet. In contrast with Gwendolen, Isa has a genuine if minor talent that she keeps entirely hidden, though she collaborates with the authors of pageant and novel (Mrs. Manresa even accuses "Mrs. Giles" of having written the pageant [61]).

Finally, Miss La Trobe not only combines the talent and the dedication of the spinster Lily Briscoe, but is also a writer who reshapes the English tradition more radically than Orlando does. Although behind the scenes and excluded from the inner circle of Pointz Hall, the playwright is the most nearly omnipresent character in the book and governs the actions of most of the players; her artistry is both the core of the book, the pageant, and its frame, the new play at the end. Like "the Alcharisi," La Trobe's foreign name with its definite article seems to announce her essential difference from the common woman: "Nature had somehow set her apart from her kind" (BA 211). Yet Miss La Trobe has none of the Alcharisi's magical fame and success. She struggles with her unruly audience and material, and is popularly laughed at as "Bossy"; she herself despises the notion of unique authorship or the honors paid to genius (she hides in the bushes, though sometimes behaving like a dictator). Without acclaim, she is nevertheless more artist than woman. Unlike the grand "Princess," Miss La Trobe lacks all the traditional signs of feminine excellence: she is "swarthy, sturdy and thick set," neither "altogether a lady" nor "pure English" (BA 57–58; she bears some resemblance to the "squat," "harsh" lady writer, Mrs. Arrowpoint, or her antecedents, the bluestocking and the strong-minded woman [DD 74]). This lack of charm may be the secret of her continuing artistic license. Daniel's mother, in contrast, is brought briefly before the reader's eyes as she is forced to pay for her charm as well as license; it is like watching a genie forced back into its bottle, a mortal woman's body. Her career is long since dead and her body is dying as the facts of her family bondage enforce their consequences. Was she too much "woman" to be an enduring artist, or must she fail because "the woman [was] lacking in her" (723)?

Miss La Trobe avoids the capitulation to heterosexual "womanhood" of each of the other talented women in the final novels. Though Woolf seems to endorse the playwright's vocation, she holds some gifts in reserve. Miss La Trobe's art is a refreshing departure from high modernism and an ambitious redaction of drama through the millennia. But the novel does not risk taking the pageant too seriously; it is on the surface an abortive, provincial performance by an unknown, not *received* as the work of a grand old woman of English letters. The playwright moreover lacks her creator's charm, social standing, and lifelong helpmeet: she lives in lonely poverty, deserted by her actress-lover. These gifts may be withheld to avoid autobiography, to avoid implausible wish-fulfillment, or—and this is the most telling motive—to retain the obscurity of "one who seethes wandering bodies . . . in a cauldron" (153). The witch-artist, "Anon.," thus exemplifies feminine heroism and defies old notions of greatness.

With varying degrees of talent and ambition, then, the primary female characters in these final novels yearn to triumph in art but either give it up or fail in life, or both. Eliot and Woolf themselves escaped the same old story of the talented woman's tragedy by retelling that story—their own artistic success bought at the price of their heroines' apparent failure or covert greatness. Their full-fledged authorship defied the boundaries of woman's sphere, even as their texts to some degree retained an ideal of feminine self-effacement. At the same time, there is a subtle triumph over the exclusive aesthetic standards that denigrate women's art. Though, for example, Gwendolen is an amateur, no one has ever performed more powerfully under more duress the part of charming English lady. Similarly, an ephemeral village pageant, a labor of the folk, becomes a contender for the worthiest prize of modernism: being so old, indigenous, and authentic that it is truly new.

The extent of Miss La Trobe's command of a collective heritage bears further remark, as only Orlando among these authors' artist figures can match it (the Alcharisi must be silenced in order to contribute to her racial destiny). Miss La Trobe seems to take charge of a female literary tradition when she produces the Victorian scene in the pageant, signaling the women novelists' need to escape the marriage plot and the heroine's fate. Here Miss La Trobe displays the kind of metacritical command that Eliot and Woolf sought in their essays, and she braves the juxtaposition of "reality" and artifice as no novelist may (can "real swallows" cross a page as they do the "painted" set?[BA 164]). The Victorian scene in the pageant is a pastiche of the canonical Victorian novel that might be called wooing in the missionary position. In a bourgeois picnic party distilling scenes from a range of novels, from *Emma* and *Jane Eyre* to *The Voyage Out* and *A Passage to India*, Edgar Thorold, another St. John Rivers, woos Eleanor Hardcastle to choose "a lifetime in the African desert among the heathens" (166). Mrs. Hardcastle and the chorus mimic Mrs. Bennet in *Pride and Prejudice* (as well as the effusive ramblings of Miss Bates in *Emma*): "O has Mr. Sibthorp a wife?" (168–69). Novels had to ask other questions than who would marry the eligible newcomer, the Darcy or Grandcourt, as Eliot and Woolf show. Further, La Trobe's pageant, like Eliot's and Woolf's novels, reveals the political and cultural exploitation behind the seemingly innocent pleasures of fiction: as love sweetens the submission of the wife, religion gilds the domination of the empire.

Although Miss La Trobe commands much of the grand authorial powers and the Alcharisi *has been* an eminent artist, it is clear that they suffer deeply, that their lives are loveless, their glory fleeting. Genius is conventionally tormented, of course, as though a happy artist were an oxymoron; a maternal, domestic artist is conventionally an even more monstrous contradiction in terms. But though these female artist figures suffer conventional constraints, they participate indirectly in the genuine sufferings of their creators.

And now I come to a question that may concern readers of the preceding comparison of artist heroines and their authors. Why do we ask women writers to represent themselves in fiction? Are women writers less capable than men of distancing themselves from their creations? We must challenge the automatic comparison of female author and heroine (just as we should examine the habit of biographical criticism in which text and female author are especially liable to be confused). Because women's writings are so generally read for access to much-touted feminine privacy, I believe Eliot and Woolf sensed danger in textual self-revelation. Perhaps to complete the artist heroine's story would have seemed to reduce the actual authors' artistic freedom, binding them too closely to the plausibly limited destinies of their female characters and exposing the feminist argument so elegantly presented in more archaeological than vocational terms. Grand old women of English letters should have had the right to disguise in fiction their own ambition plots, as much as they had the right to adopt the point of view of male characters and masculine or androgynous narrators.[48] But at the same time that they asserted their own claim to the public life of ambition and history, they afforded readers access to an anterior feminine privacy not simply shaped by the individual's heterosexual desire, but by ancient, collective "pulses" of revenge, remorse, fear, and hatred, as well as sexual passion.

Some readers will wonder why I emphasize the incompleteness of Lily, Orlando, Miss La Trobe—don't they flourish in an "other" way? Yes indeed: in the later age, Woolf imagines not only a wider scope for female talent, but also a different model of success without need of patriarchal laurels. As Susan Gubar observes, Woolf and other modernist-feminists placed fewer handicaps on their female artist characters, in part owing to a new valuation of domestic arts (consider Mrs. Ramsay's *boeuf en daube*) and a new articulation of a silenced "woman's language." Yet these women writers still held their female characters at a remove from their own careers, because, Gubar argues, their own self-assertion had been an inadmissible rejection of their mothers and the "natural and distinct sphere" of womanhood that the feminist-modernists continued to believe in ("Birth of the Artist" 39, 49–50). I would add that Woolf came closer to creating an autobiographical portrait of the artist not only because of a new outlook on female creativity, but also because of the modern fashion for self-referential art. Moreover, Woolf was able to draw on a tradition that

---

[48]Carolyn Heilbrun restates the difficulty of escaping the feminine plot of subordination to some "other" and of fulfilling a powerful ambition plot: in female biographies, "the public and private lives cannot be linked, as in male narratives" (*Woman's Life* 24–25).

was only beginning in Eliot's day, that of fictional autobiographies of the woman writer, from *Aurora Leigh* to Dorothy Richardson's *Pilgrimage*. Yet Woolf's portraits of the woman artist, like Eliot's, carefully distance and contain feminist protest, and perhaps as a result have found a steadier canonical perch than more transparent and permissive autobiographical writings.

While Eliot and Woolf protect their own "impersonal" standing, they also muster greater force in their works by engaging the services of suffering women. Their heroines' fulfillment in both art and life would lessen the archaeological force of their works. What would be the call for unburying the ancient consciousness of woman if the diverse vitality of women today were free to find expression in both vocation and love? And such freedom might only be won—it has yet to be realized for more than a few rare women—by a costly release of repressed, primitive feeling, the human store believed to be guarded by women through the ages. According to the writings of Eliot and Woolf, at least, certain ladies, selfless ones among many, may achieve a greatness engendered by their *failed* resistance to silence and obscurity.

The Alcharisi and Miss La Trobe, however, are not great martyrs in this sense. Terrifying in their refusal to become "many," part of the herd, in different ways they personify both feminine heroism and the heroism of "man's force." The Alcharisi's life is an operatic performance, the tragedy of the heroic woman that demands a dying aria. Miss La Trobe has harnessed the folk opera of crooning women, and can make a Lady Ermyntrude out of a sheep's thighbone (or Queen Elizabeth's silver cape out of "swabs used to scour saucepans" [83]). Women do not have to replay the dying parts forever; their labors can transform everyday detail into art. At the same time these artists violate the gender code with the rage and hubris of warriors (Miss La Trobe is "an Admiral on his quarter-deck" [62], and the Alcharisi declares, like a Cleopatra, "Men have been subject to me" [730]). This will to dominate reduces, perhaps unfairly, most readers' sympathy for these manly leaders and assures their distance from the implied authors, figures of the most profound consideration of others.

Still, some likeness with the living women authors remains. The Alcharisi seems to confess to Eliot's own defiance of her father's religion and of patriarchal law in her union with Lewes, and perhaps more importantly to her ambition and love of success. Yet the great opera singer, a beautiful Jewess with "masculine" ruthlessness, is not to be mistaken for George Eliot. Miss La Trobe bespeaks Woolf's dedicated struggle with her medium and her audience, her sense of isolation as well as her lesbianism. But no one surely would mistake the plain village bohemian for the beautiful lady of Bloomsbury, still less for a "great" woman of letters in traditional terms. It is tempting, however, to imagine Miss La Trobe as in some sense Woolf's reincarnation of Eliot. In her published writings on Eliot, Woolf dwelt on her manliness and ugliness, her lower-class background, her scandalous private life and her seclusion. Naturally, this incarnation is the incomplete story of the Grand Old Woman of Letters. All women artists in these oeuvres are doomed to a degree of failure, however magnificent has been their demand for "art and knowledge" beyond a captive woman's reach. Woolf more than Eliot could dispute the interdependence of artistry, authority, and masculine identity. The later woman author could reach, but she would not unquestioningly grasp. Yet as Woolf uttered her demand for something incompatible with the "facts" of European civilization, in a sense she strove to complete, as her heroines were unable to do, the story of George Eliot herself.

Works Cited

Abel, Elizabeth. *Virginia Woolf and the Fictions of Psychoanalysis.* Chicago: University of Chicago Press, 1989.

Albright, Daniel. *Personality and Impersonality: Lawrence, Woolf, and Mann.* Chicago: University of Chicago Press, 1978.

Alter, Robert. *The Art of Biblical Narrative.* New York: Basic Books, 1981.

Altick, Richard D. *The English Common Reader: A Social History of the Mass Reading Public, 1800–1900.* Chicago: University of Chicago Press, 1957.

Anderson, Nancy F. "Autobiographical Fantasies of a Female Anti-Feminist: Eliza Lynn Linton as Christopher Kirkland and Theodora Desanges." *Dickens Studies Annual: Essays on Victorian Fiction* 14 (1985): 287–301. Ed. Michael Timko, Fred Kaplan, and Edward Guiliano. New York: AMS, 1985.

Annan, Noel Gilroy. *Leslie Stephen: The Godless Victorian.* New York: Random House, 1984.

Armstrong, Nancy. *Desire and Domestic Fiction: A Political History of the Novel.* New York: Oxford University Press, 1987.

Arnold, Matthew. "The Function of Criticism at the Present Time." 1864. *Prose and Poetry.* Ed. Archibald L. Bouton. New York: Scribner's, 1927. 20–51.

Attwater, Donald, ed. *The Penguin Dictionary of Saints.* Harmondsworth, Eng.: Penguin, 1983.

Auerbach, Erich. *Mimesis.* Trans. Willard R. Trask. Princeton: Princeton University Press, 1953.

Auerbach, Nina. *Romantic Imprisonment: Women and Other Glorified Outcasts.* New York: Columbia University Press, 1986.

——. *Woman and the Demon: The Life of a Victorian Myth.* Cambridge: Harvard University Press, 1982.

Austen, Jane. *Emma.* Oxford: Oxford University Press, 1971.

——. *Northanger Abbey, Lady Susan, The Watsons, and Sanditon.* Ed. John Davie. The World's Classics. Oxford: Oxford University Press, 1980.

——. *Persuasion.* Harmondsworth, Eng.: Penguin, 1965.

Austen, Zelda. "Why Feminist Critics Are Angry with George Eliot." *College English* 37 (1976): 549–61.

Baker, William. *The Libraries of George Eliot and George Henry Lewes*. Victoria, B.C.: University of Victoria Press, 1981.

——. "A New George Eliot Manuscript." *George Eliot: Centenary Essays and an Unpublished Fragment*. Ed. Anne Smith. London: Vision, 1980. 9–20.

——, ed. Introduction. *Some George Eliot Notebooks: An Edition of the Carl H. Pforzheimer Library's George Eliot Holograph Notebooks*. 4 vols. Vol. 1 (Ms. 707); Vol. 3 (Ms. 711). Salzburg: Universitat Salzburg, 1976.

Bamber, Linda. "Self-Defeating Politics in George Eliot's *Felix Holt*." *Victorian Studies* 18 (1975): 419–35.

Banks, Olive. *The Biographical Dictionary of British Feminists*. Vol. 1: *1800–1930*. Brighton, Sussex: Wheatsheaf/Harvester, 1985.

Barrett, Dorothea. *Vocation and Desire: George Eliot's Heroines*. London: Routledge, 1989.

Barrett, Michèle. "Ideology and the Cultural Production of Gender." *Feminist Criticism and Social Change: Sex, Class, and Race in Literature and Culture*. Ed. Judith Newton and Deborah Rosenfelt. New York: Methuen, 1985. 65–85.

——, ed. Introduction. *Women and Writing*, by Virginia Woolf. New York: Harcourt Brace Jovanovich, 1979. 1–39.

Bauer, Carol, and Lawrence Ritt. *Free and Ennobled: Source Readings in the Development of Victorian Feminism*. Oxford: Pergamon, 1979.

Beer, Gillian. *Arguing with the Past: Essays in Narrative from Woolf to Sidney*. London: Routledge, 1989.

——. *Darwin's Plots*. London: Routledge & Kegan Paul, 1983.

——. *George Eliot*. Key Women Writers. Brighton: Harvester, 1986.

Bell, Barbara Currier, and Carol Ohmann. "Virginia Woolf's Criticism: A Polemical Preface." *Feminist Literary Criticism: Explorations in Theory*. Ed. Josephine Donovan. Lexington: University Press of Kentucky, 1975. 48–60.

Bell, Clive. *Civilization*. London: Chatto & Windus, 1928.

Bell, Ian F. A. *Critic as Scientist: The Modernist Poetics of Ezra Pound*. London: Methuen, 1981.

Bell, Quentin. "Reply to Jane Marcus." *Critical Inquiry* 11 (1985): 498–501.

Benstock, Shari. *Women of the Left Bank: Paris, 1900–1940*. Austin: University of Texas Press, 1986.

Bentley, Eric. *The Importance of Scrutiny: Selections from "Scrutiny," a Quarterly Review, 1932–1948*. New York: Stewart, 1948.

Black, Naomi. "Virginia Woolf and the Women's Movement." *Virginia Woolf: A Feminist Slant*. Ed. Jane Marcus. Lincoln: University of Nebraska Press, 1983. 180–97.

——. "Virginia Woolf: The Life of Natural Happiness." *Feminist Theorists: Three Centuries of Key Women Thinkers*. Ed. Dale Spender. New York: Pantheon, 1983. 296–313.

Blain, Virginia. "Narrative Voice and the Female Perspective in Virginia Woolf's Early Novels." *Virginia Woolf: New Critical Essays*. Ed. Patricia Clements and Isobel Grundy. New York: Barnes & Noble, 1983. 115–36.

Blake, Kathleen. "*Middlemarch*: Vocation, Love, and the Woman Question." *Love and the Woman Question in Victorian Literature: The Art of Self-Postponement*. Totowa, N.J.: Barnes & Noble, 1983. 26–55.

Blind, Mathilde. *George Eliot*. Famous Women Series. Boston: Roberts, 1883.

Bodenheimer, Rosemarie. *The Politics of Story in Victorian Social Fiction.* Ithaca: Cornell University Press, 1988.

Bonaparte, Felicia. *The Triptych and the Cross: The Central Myths of George Eliot's Poetic Imagination.* New York: New York University Press, 1979.

Booth, Wayne C. *The Company We Keep.* Berkeley: University of California Press, 1989.

Bowlby, Rachel. *Virginia Woolf: Feminist Destinations.* Oxford: Basil Blackwell, 1988.

Bradbrook, M. C. *Barbara Bodichon, George Eliot, and the Limits of Feminism.* James Bryce Memorial Lecture, Somerville College, Oxford, 6 March 1975. Oxford: Holywell, n.d.

Brantlinger, Patrick. *The Spirit of Reform: British Literature and Politics, 1832–1867.* Cambridge: Harvard University Press, 1977.

Brockett, Oscar G. *History of the Theatre.* 3d ed. Boston: Allyn & Bacon, 1978.

Broe, Mary Lynn, and Angela Ingram, eds. *Women's Writing in Exile.* Chapel Hill: University of North Carolina Press, 1989.

Browning, Elizabeth Barrett. *Aurora Leigh.* Chicago: Academy Chicago, 1979.

Brownstein, Rachel M. *Becoming a Heroine: Reading about Women in Novels.* New York: Viking, 1982.

Buckley, Jerome H. *The Triumph of Time.* Cambridge: Harvard University Press, 1966.

Bullen, J. B. "George Eliot's *Romola* as a Positivist Allegory." *Review of English Studies* 26 (1975): 425–35.

Burke, Carolyn. "Irigaray through the Looking Glass." *Feminist Studies* 7 (1981): 288–306.

Burton, Clare. *Subordination: Feminism and Social Theory.* Sydney: George Allen & Unwin, 1985.

Butler, Marilyn. *Jane Austen and the War of Ideas.* 1975. Oxford: Clarendon, 1987.

Campbell, Joseph. *The Hero with a Thousand Faces.* 1949. Cleveland: Meridian, 1964.

Caramagno, Thomas C. "Manic-Depressive Psychosis and Critical Approaches to Virginia Woolf's Life and Work." *PMLA* 103 (1988): 10–23.

Carby, Hazel. *Reconstructing Womanhood: The Emergence of the Afro-American Novelist.* New York: Oxford University Press, 1987.

Carlyle, Thomas. *On Heroes, Hero-Worship, and the Heroic in History.* Ed. Carl Niemeyer. Lincoln: University of Nebraska Press, 1966.

——. "On History." *Critical and Miscellaneous Essays.* 5 vols. 2: 83–95. Vol. 27. *The Works of Thomas Carlyle.* 30 vols. London: Chapman & Hall, 1899.

——. "Signs of the Times." *Critical and Miscellaneous Essays.* 5 vols. 2: 56–82. Vol. 27. *The Works of Thomas Carlyle.* 30 vols. London: Chapman & Hall, 1899.

Carr, Edward Hallett. *What Is History?* The George Macaulay Trevelyan Lectures, University of Cambridge, January–March 1961. New York: Vintage, 1961.

Carroll, David R. "*Felix Holt:* Society as Protagonist." *George Eliot: A Collection of Critical Essays.* Ed. George R. Creeger. Englewood Cliffs, N.J.: Prentice-Hall, 1970. 124–40.

------. Introduction. *George Eliot: The Critical Heritage*. London: Routledge & Kegan Paul, 1971. 1–48.

------. "The Sibyl of Mercia." *Studies in the Novel* 15 (1983): 10–25.

Chase, Cynthia. "The Decomposition of the Elephants: Double-Reading *Daniel Deronda*." *PMLA* 93 (1978): 215–27.

Chase, Karen. "The Modern Family and the Ancient Image in *Romola*." *Dickens Studies Annual: Essays on Victorian Fiction* 14 (1985): 303–26. Ed. Michael Timko, Fred Kaplan, and Edward Guiliano. New York: AMS, 1985.

Christian, Barbara. "The Race for Theory." 1987. *Feminist Studies* 14 (1988): 67–79.

Cixous, Hélène. "The Laugh of the Medusa." Trans. Keith Cohen and Paula Cohen. *The Signs Reader: Women, Gender, and Scholarship*. Ed. Elizabeth Abel and Emily K. Abel. Chicago: University of Chicago Press, 1983. 279–97.

Cixous, Hélène and Catherine Clément. *The Newly Born Woman*. 1975. Trans. Betsy Wing. Foreword by Sandra M. Gilbert. Theory and History of Literature, vol. 24. Minneapolis: University of Minnesota Press, 1986.

Collingwood, R. G. *The Idea of History*. Oxford: Clarendon, 1946.

Collins, K. K. "Questions of Method: Some Unpublished Late Essays." *Nineteenth-Century Fiction* 35 (1980): 385–405.

Comstock, Margaret. "The Loudspeaker and the Human Voice: Politics and the Form of *The Years*." *Bulletin of the New York Public Library* 80 (1977): 252–75.

Comte, Auguste. *Auguste Comte and Positivism: The Essential Writings*. Ed. Gertrud Lenzer. New York: Harper & Row, 1975.

------. *The Catechism of Positive Religion*. Trans. Richard Congreve. London: John Chapman, 1858.

Cook, Blanche Wiesen. " 'Women Alone Stir My Imagination': Lesbianism and the Cultural Tradition." *Signs* 4 (1979): 718–39.

Cooper, Helen. "Mrs. Browning and Miss Evans." *Nineteenth-Century Fiction* 35 (1980): 257–59.

Cottom, Daniel. *Social Figures: George Eliot, Social History, and Literary Representation*. Foreword by Terry Eagleton. Theory and History of Literature, vol. 44. Minneapolis: University of Minnesota Press, 1987.

Coveney, Peter. Introduction. *Felix Holt*. Harmondsworth, Eng.: Penguin, 1972. 7–65.

Craig, David. "Fiction and the Rising Industrial Classes." *Essays in Criticism* 17 (1967): 64–74.

Cross, John W., ed. *George Eliot's Life as Related in Her Letters and Journals*. 3 vols. New York: Harper & Bros., n.d.

Cuddy-Keane, Melba. "The Politics of Comic Modes in Virginia Woolf's *Between the Acts*." *PMLA* 105 (1990): 273–85.

------. "Virginia Woolf and the Greek Chorus: Reply." "Forum." *PMLA* 106 (1991): 123–24.

Dahl, Curtis. "When the Deity Returns: *The Marble Faun* and *Romola*." *Papers on Language and Literature* 5 (1969): Supplement: Studies in American Literature in Honor of Robert D. Faner. Ed. Robert Partlow. 82–99.

Daiches, David. *Virginia Woolf*. Norfolk, Conn.: New Directions, 1942.

Daly, Mary. *Beyond God the Father: Toward a Philosophy of Women's Liberation*. Boston: Beacon, 1973.

David, Deirdre. *Intellectual Women and Victorian Patriarchy: Harriet Martineau, Elizabeth Barrett Browning, George Eliot*. Ithaca: Cornell University Press, 1987.

Davis, Lennard J. *Factual Fictions: The Origins of the English Novel*. New York: Columbia University Press, 1983.

de Almeida, Hermione. *Byron and Joyce through Homer*. New York: Columbia University Press, 1981.

DeSalvo, Louise. *Virginia Woolf: The Impact of Childhood Sexual Abuse on Her Life and Work*. Boston: Beacon, 1989.

DiBattista, Maria. "Joyce, Woolf, and the Modern Mind." *Virginia Woolf: New Critical Essays*. Ed. Patricia Clements and Isobel Grundy. New York: Barnes & Noble, 1983. 96–114.

———. *Virginia Woolf's Major Novels: The Fables of Anon*. New Haven: Yale University Press, 1980.

Doody, Margaret Anne. "George Eliot and the Eighteenth-Century Novel." *Nineteenth-Century Fiction* 35 (1980): 260–91.

Eagleton, Terry. *The Rape of Clarissa: Writing, Sexuality, and Class Struggle in Samuel Richardson*. Oxford: Basil Blackwell, 1982.

Edel, Leon. *Literary Biography*. 1959. Bloomington: Indiana University Press, 1973.

Edwards, Lee R. *Psyche as Hero: Female Heroism and Fictional Form*. Middletown, Conn.: Wesleyan University Press, 1984.

Eliot, George. "The Grammar of Ornament." *Essays and Reviews of George Eliot*. Ed. Mrs. S. B. Herrick. Boston: Aldine, 1887. 184–92.

———. *Wit and Wisdom of George Eliot*. Boston: Roberts, 1873.

Eliot, T. S. "Virginia Woolf I." *Horizon: A Review of Literature and Art* 3 (1941): 313–16.

Ellis, Sarah. *The Women of England*. N.p., n.d. [1839].

Ellmann, Mary. *Thinking about Women*. New York: Harcourt Brace Jovanovich, 1968.

Emery, Laura Comer. *George Eliot's Creative Conflict: The Other Side of Silence*. Berkeley: University of California Press, 1976.

Ermarth, Elizabeth Deeds. *Realism and Consensus in the English Novel*. Princeton: Princeton University Press, 1983.

Evans, Mary. "Introduction: What Is to Be Done?" *The Woman Question: Readings on the Subordination of Women*. Oxford: Fontana, 1982. 13–23.

Faris, Wendy B. "The Squirrel's Heart Beat and the Death of the Moth." *Virginia Woolf: Centennial Essays*. Ed. Elaine K. Ginsberg and Laura Moss Gottleib. Troy, N.Y.: Whitston, 1983. 81–91.

Feltes, N. N. *Modes of Production of Victorian Novels*. University of Chicago Press, 1986.

Fisher, Philip. *Making Up Society: The Novels of George Eliot*. Pittsburgh: University of Pittsburgh Press, 1981.

Fleishman, Avrom. "Daniel Charisi." *Fiction and the Ways of Knowing*. Austin: University of Texas Press, 1978. 86–109.

———. *The English Historical Novel: Walter Scott to Virginia Woolf*. Baltimore: Johns Hopkins University Press, 1971.

———. *Virginia Woolf: A Critical Reading*. Baltimore: Johns Hopkins University Press, 1975.

Fogel, Daniel Mark. *Covert Relations: James Joyce, Virginia Woolf, and Henry James*. Charlottesville: University Press of Virginia, 1990.

Forster, E. M. *Virginia Woolf*. New York: Harcourt Brace, 1942.

Frazer, Sir James George. *The Golden Bough: A Study in Magic and Religion. Part IV: Adonis Attis Osiris: Studies in the History of Oriental Religion*. 2 vols. 3d ed. New York: Macmillan, 1935.

Freedman, Ralph, ed. "Introduction: Virginia Woolf, the Novel, and a Chorus of Voices." *Virginia Woolf: Revaluation and Continuity*. Berkeley: University of California Press, 1980. 3–12.

Freud, Sigmund. *Group Psychology and the Analysis of the Ego*. Trans. James Strachey. 2d ed. London: Hogarth, 1922.

——. *Moses and Monotheism*. 1939. Trans. Katherine Jones. New York: Vintage, 1967.

Friedman, Susan Stanford. "Women's Autobiographical Selves: Theory and Practice." *The Private Self: Theory and Practice of Women's Autobiographical Writings*. Ed. Shari Benstock. Chapel Hill: University of North Carolina Press, 1988. 34–62.

Frye, Northrop. *The Great Code*. New York: Harcourt Brace Jovanovich, 1983.

Fussell, B. H. "Woolf's Peculiar Comic World: *Between the Acts*." *Virginia Woolf: Revaluation and Continuity*. Ed. Ralph Freedman. Berkeley: University of California Press, 1980. 263–83.

Gallagher, Catherine. "George Eliot and *Daniel Deronda*: The Prostitute and the Jewish Question." *Sex, Politics, and Science in the Nineteenth-Century Novel*. Ed. Ruth Bernard Yeazell. Baltimore: Johns Hopkins University Press, 1986. 39–62.

——. *The Industrial Reformation of English Fiction: Social Discourse and Narrative Form 1832–1867*. Chicago: University of Chicago Press, 1985.

Gallop, Jane. *The Daughter's Seduction: Feminism and Psychoanalysis*. Ithaca: Cornell University Press, 1982.

Gardiner, Judith Kegan, Elly Bulkin, Rena Grasso Patterson, and Annette Kolodny. "An Interchange on Feminist Criticism: On 'Dancing through the Minefield.' " *Feminist Studies* 8 (1982): 629–75.

Gaskell, Elizabeth. *The Life of Charlotte Brontë*. 1857. Harmondsworth, Eng.: Penguin, 1975.

Gilbert, Sandra M. "The Battle of the Books / The Battle of the Sexes: Virginia Woolf's *Vita Nuova*." *Michigan Quarterly Review* 23 (1984): 171–95.

——. "Costumes of the Mind: Transvestism as Metaphor in Modern Literature." *Critical Inquiry* 7 (1980): 391–417.

——. "Introduction: A Tarantella of Theory." *The Newly Born Woman*. By Hélène Cixous and Catherine Clément. Trans. Betsy Wing. Theory and History of Literature, vol. 24. Minneapolis: University of Minnesota Press, 1986.

Gilbert, Sandra M., and Susan Gubar. *The Madwoman in the Attic*. New Haven: Yale University Press, 1979.

——. *The War of the Words*. Vol. 1: *No Man's Land: The Place of the Woman Writer in the Twentieth Century*. New Haven: Yale University Press, 1988.

Gordon, Lyndall. *Virginia Woolf: A Writer's Life*. Oxford: Oxford University Press, 1984.

Graver, Suzanne. *George Eliot and Community: A Study in Social Theory and Fictional Form*. Berkeley: University of California Press, 1984.

Greenstein, Susan M. "The Question of Vocation: From *Romola* to *Middlemarch*." *Nineteenth-Century Fiction* 35 (1981): 487–505.

Gribble, Jennifer. *The Lady of Shalott in the Victorian Novel*. London: Macmillan, 1983.

Gubar, Susan. "The Birth of the Artist as Heroine: (Re)production, the *Kunstlerroman* Tradition, and the Fiction of Katherine Mansfield." *The Representation of Women in Fiction*. Ed. Carolyn G. Heilbrun and Margaret R. Higonnet. Baltimore: Johns Hopkins University Press, 1983. 19–59.

——. " 'The Blank Page' and the Issues of Female Creativity." *The New Feminist Criticism*. Ed. Elaine Showalter. New York: Pantheon, 1985. 292–313.

Guiget, Jean. *Virginia Woolf and Her Works*. Trans. Jean Stewart. London: Hogarth, 1965.

Hafley, James. *The Glass Roof: Virginia Woolf as Novelist*. Berkeley: University of California Press, 1954.

Haight, Gordon S. *Selections from George Eliot's Letters*. New Haven: Yale University Press, 1985.

Haller, Evelyn. "The Anti-Madonna in the Work and Thought of Virginia Woolf." *Virginia Woolf: Centennial Essays*. Ed. Elaine K. Ginsberg and Laura Moss Gottleib. Troy, N.Y.: Whitston, 1983. 93–109.

——. "Isis Unveiled: Virginia Woolf's Use of Egyptian Myth." *Virginia Woolf: A Feminist Slant*. Ed. Jane Marcus. Lincoln: University of Nebraska Press, 1983. 109–31.

Hamilton, Edith. *Mythology: Timeless Tales of Gods and Heroes*. New York: Mentor, 1969.

Handelman, Susan A. *The Slayers of Moses: The Emergence of Rabbinic Interpretation in Modern Literary Theory*. Albany: State University of New York Press, 1982.

Handley, Graham. Introduction. *Daniel Deronda*, by George Eliot. Oxford: Clarendon, 1984. xiii–xxxii.

Harding, Sandra. *The Science Question in Feminism*. Ithaca: Cornell University Press, 1986.

Hardwick, Elizabeth. *Seduction and Betrayal: Women and Literature*. New York: Random, 1974.

Hardy, Barbara. *The Novels of George Eliot: A Study in Form*. London: Athlone, 1959.

Harrison, Jane. *Ancient Art and Ritual*. New York: Henry Holt, 1913.

Hartman, Geoffrey H. "Virginia's Web." *Beyond Formalism*. New Haven: Yale University Press, 1970. 71–84.

Hartmann, Heidi. "Capitalism, Patriarchy, and Job Segregation by Sex." *The Signs Reader: Women, Gender, and Scholarship*. Ed. Elizabeth Abel and Emily K. Abel. Chicago: University of Chicago Press, 1983. 193–225.

Haule, James M., and Philip H. Smith, eds. *A Concordance to "Between the Acts" by Virginia Woolf*. Oxford: Oxford Microform, 1982.

Hawkes, Ellen. "Woolf's 'Magical Garden of Women.' " *New Feminist Essays on Virginia Woolf*. Ed. Jane Marcus. Lincoln: University of Nebraska Press, 1981. 31–60.

Heilbrun, Carolyn G. *Reinventing Womanhood*. New York: Norton, 1979.
——. *Toward a Recognition of Androgyny*. New York: Knopf, 1973.
——. *Writing a Woman's Life*. New York: Ballantine, 1988.
Heller, Deborah. "George Eliot's Jewish Feminist." *Atlantis* 8 (1983): 37–43.
Helsinger, Elizabeth K., Robin Lauterbach Sheets, and William Veeder. *The Woman Question: Literary Issues 1837–1883*. Vol. 3 of *The Woman Question: Society and Literature in Britain and America, 1837–1883*. 3 vols. New York: Garland, 1983.
Herrick, Mrs. S. B., ed. *Essays and Reviews of George Eliot*. Boston: Aldine, 1887.
Herstein, Sheila R. *A Mid-Victorian Feminist, Barbara Leigh Smith Bodichon*. New Haven: Yale University Press, 1985.
Hertz, Neil. "Recognizing Casaubon." *The End of the Line*. New York: Columbia University Press, 1985. 75–96.
Hester, Erwin. "George Eliot's Use of Historical Events in *Daniel Deronda*." *English Language Notes* 4 (1966): 115–18.
Hill, Katherine C. "Virginia Woolf and Leslie Stephen: History and Literary Revolution." *PMLA* 96 (1981): 351–62.
Hirsch, E. D. *Validity in Interpretation*. New Haven: Yale University Press, 1967.
Hoff, Molly. "Virginia Woolf and the Greek Chorus." "Forum." *PMLA* 106 (1991): 122–23.
Hoffman, Charles G. "Fact and Fantasy in *Orlando*: Virginia Woolf's Manuscript Revisions." *Texas Studies in Literature and Language* 10 (1968): 435–44.
Hollis, Patricia, ed. *Women in Public 1850–1900: Documents of the Victorian Women's Movement*. London: Allen & Unwin, 1979.
Holtby, Winifred. *Women and a Changing Civilization*. 1935. Cassandra Editions. Chicago: Academy Chicago, 1978.
Homans, Margaret. *Bearing the Word: Language and Female Experience in Nineteenth-Century Women's Writing*. Chicago: University of Chicago Press, 1986.
Hurley, Edward T. "Piero di Cosimo: An Alternate Analogy for George Eliot's Realism." *Victorian Newsletter* 31 (1967): 54–56.
Huyssen, Andreas. "Mass Culture as Woman: Modernism's Other." *After the Great Divide: Modernism, Mass Culture, Postmodernism*. Bloomington: Indiana University Press, 1986. 44–62.
Irigaray, Luce. *Speculum of the Other Woman*. 1974. Trans. Gillian C. Gill. Ithaca: Cornell University Press, 1985.
——. *This Sex Which Is Not One*. Trans. Catherine Porter and Carolyn Burke. Ithaca: Cornell University Press, 1985.
Jacobus, Mary. "Is There a Woman in This Text?" *New Literary History* 14 (1982): 117–41.
——. *Reading Woman: Essays in Feminist Criticism*. New York: Columbia University Press, 1986.
James, Henry. "*Daniel Deronda*: A Conversation." *George Eliot: A Collection of Critical Essays*. Ed. George R. Creeger. Englewood Cliffs, N.J.: Prentice-Hall, 1970. 161–76.
Jameson, Anna Brownell. *Sacred and Legendary Art*. 2 vols. 1848. London: Longmans, Green, 1870.
——. *Sisters of Charity: Catholic and Protestant, Abroad and at Home*. London: Longman, Brown, Green, & Longmans, 1855.

Jardine, Alice A. *Gynesis: Configurations of Woman and Modernity.* Ithaca: Cornell University Press, 1985.

Jenkyns, Richard. *The Victorians and Ancient Greece.* Oxford: Basil Blackwell, 1980.

Johnson, Claudia. *Jane Austen: Women, Politics, and the Novel.* Chicago: University of Chicago Press, 1988.

Jones, Ann Rosalind. "Writing the Body: Toward an Understanding of *l'Ecriture feminine.*" *The New Feminist Criticism.* Ed. Elaine Showalter. New York: Pantheon, 1985. 361–77.

Jordan, Ellen. "The Christening of the New Woman: May 1894." *The Victorian Newsletter* 63 (1983): 19–21.

Kaminsky, Alice R., ed. *Literary Criticism of George Henry Lewes.* Regents Critics Series. Lincoln: University of Nebraska Press, 1964.

Kamuf, Peggy. "Replacing Feminist Criticism." *Diacritics* 12 (1982): 42–47.

Kennard, Jean E. "Personally Speaking: Feminist Critics and the Community of Readers." *College English* 43 (1981): 140–45.

Kenner, Hugh. *A Sinking Island: The Modern English Writers.* New York: Knopf, 1988.

Kermode, Frank. *The Sense of an Ending: Studies in the Theory of Fiction.* New York: Oxford University Press, 1967.

Kern, Stephen. *The Culture of Time and Space 1880–1918.* Cambridge: Harvard University Press, 1983.

Kettle, Arnold. " 'Felix Holt the Radical.' " *Critical Essays on George Eliot.* Ed. Barbara Hardy. New York: Barnes & Noble, 1970. 99–115.

Killham, John. *Tennyson and "The Princess": Reflections of an Age.* London: University of London / Athlone, 1958.

Kirkham, Margaret. *Jane Austen, Feminism, and Fiction.* New York: Methuen, 1986.

Knoepflmacher, U. C. "Genre and the Integration of Gender: From Wordsworth to George Eliot to Virginia Woolf." *Victorian Literature and Society* (1984): 94–118.

——. *George Eliot's Early Novels.* Berkeley: University of California Press, 1968.

——. "On Exile and Fiction: The Leweses and the Shelleys." *Mothering the Mind: Twelve Studies of Writers and Their Silent Partners.* Ed. Ruth Perry and Martine Watson Brownley. New York: Holmes & Meier, 1984. 102–21.

——. *Religious Humanism and the Victorian Novel: George Eliot, Walter Pater, and Samuel Butler.* Princeton: Princeton University Press, 1965.

Kolodny, Annette. "Dancing through the Minefield: Some Observations on the Theory, Practice, and Politics of a Feminist Literary Criticism." *The New Feminist Criticism.* Ed. Elaine Showalter. New York: Pantheon, 1985. 144–67.

Lacey, Candida Ann, ed. *Barbara Leigh Smith Bodichon and the Langham Place Group.* New York: Routledge & Kegan Paul, 1987.

Landow, George P. *Victorian Types, Victorian Shadows: Biblical Typology in Victorian Literature, Art, and Thought.* Boston: Routledge & Kegan Paul, 1980.

Langbauer, Laurie. *Women and Romance: The Consolations of Gender in the English Novel.* Ithaca: Cornell University Press, 1990.

Lawrence, D. H. "Study of Thomas Hardy." *Phoenix: The Posthumous Papers, 1936.* Ed. and intro. Edward D. McDonald. Harmondsworth, Eng.: Penguin, 1978. 398–516.

Leaska, Mitchell A. "Virginia Woolf, the Pargeter: A Reading of *The Years.*" *Bulletin of the New York Public Library* 80 (1977): 172–210.

——, ed. *The Pargiters by Virginia Woolf: The Novel-Essay Portion of "The Years."* New York: The New York Public Library, 1977.

Leavis, Q. D. "Caterpillars of the Commonwealth Unite!" *The Importance of Scrutiny: Selections from "Scrutiny," a Quarterly Review, 1932–1948.* Ed. Eric Bentley. New York: Stewart, 1948. 382–91.

Lemprière, John. *Bibliotheca Classica.* Ed. Lorenzo L. Da Ponte and John D. Ogilby. Philadelphia: Lippincott, 1860.

Lerner, Laurence. *The Truthtellers: Jane Austen, George Eliot, D. H. Lawrence.* New York: Schocken, 1967.

Lerner, Laurence, and John Holmstrom, eds. *George Eliot and Her Readers.* New York: Barnes & Noble, 1966.

Levine, George. "George Eliot's Hypothesis of Reality." *Nineteenth-Century Fiction* 35 (1980): 1–28.

——. " 'Romola' as Fable." *Critical Essays on George Eliot.* Ed. Barbara Hardy. London: Routledge & Kegan Paul, 1970. 78–98.

Lewes, George Henry. "The Lady Novelists." *Essays and Reviews of George Eliot.* Ed. Mrs. S. B. Herrick. Boston: Aldine, 1887. 7–24.

——. *The Principles of Success in Literature.* 1865. Ed. Fred N. Scott. Boston: Allyn & Bacon, n.d. [1894].

Lewis, Sarah. *Woman's Mission.* Philadelphia: Hazard, 1854.

Lipking, Joanna. "Looking at the Monuments: Woolf's Satiric Eye." *Bulletin of the New York Public Library* 80 (1977): 141–45.

Little, Judy. *Comedy and the Woman Writer: Woolf, Spark, and Feminism.* Lincoln: University of Nebraska Press, 1983.

Love, Jean O. "*Orlando* and Its Genesis: Venturing and Experimenting in Art, Love, and Sex." *Virginia Woolf: Revaluation and Continuity.* Ed. Ralph Freedman. Berkeley: University of California Press, 1980. 189–218.

Lukacs, Georg. *The Historical Novel.* Trans. Hannah and Stanley Mitchell. Lincoln: University of Nebraska Press, 1983.

Macaulay, Rose. "Virginia Woolf, II." *Horizon: A Review of Literature and Art* 3 (1941): 316–18.

Macaulay, Thomas Babington. *The History of England from the Accession of James II.* 2 vols. New York: Harper & Bros., 1849.

——. *Lays of Ancient Rome.* 1842. Intro. George Macaulay Trevelyan. London: Longmans, Green, 1928.

MacKinnon, Catharine A. "Feminism, Marxism, Method, and the State: An Agenda for Theory." *The Signs Reader: Women, Gender, and Scholarship.* Ed. Elizabeth Abel and Emily K. Abel. Chicago: University of Chicago Press, 1983. 227–56.

Maika, Patricia. *Virginia Woolf's "Between the Acts" and Jane Harrison's Con/spiracy.* Studies in Modern Literature, no. 78. Ed. A. Walton Litz. Ann Arbor, Mich.: University Microfilms Inc. Research Press, 1987.

Majumdar, Robin, and Allen McLaurin, eds. *Virginia Woolf: The Critical Heritage.* Boston: Routledge & Kegan Paul, 1975.

Marcus, Jane. Introduction. *New Feminist Essays on Virginia Woolf.* Ed. Jane Marcus. Lincoln: University of Nebraska Press, 1981. xiii–xx.

——. "Lycanthropy: Woolf Studies Now." *Tulsa Studies in Women's Literature* 8 (1989): 101–10.

——. "Quentin's Bogey." *Critical Inquiry* 11 (1985): 486–97.

——. "Some Sources for *Between the Acts.*" *Virginia Woolf Miscellany* 6 (1977): 1–3.

——. *Virginia Woolf and the Languages of Patriarchy.* Bloomington: Indiana University Press, 1987.

Marder, Herbert. *Feminism and Art: A Study of Virginia Woolf.* Chicago: University of Chicago Press, 1968.

Marshall, Paule. Speech. Women Artists and Scholars Series, University of Virginia, Charlottesville, 9 April 1987.

Martin, Carol A. "George Eliot: Feminist Critic." *The Victorian Newsletter* 65 (1984): 22–25.

Martineau, Harriet. *Harriet Martineau on Women.* Ed. Gayle Graham Yates. New Brunswick, N.J.: Rutgers University Press, 1985.

McGann, Jerome. Introduction. *Historical Studies and Literary Criticism.* Madison: University of Wisconsin Press, 1985. 3–21.

McGowan, John P. "The Turn of George Eliot's Realism." *Nineteenth-Century Fiction* 35 (1980): 171–92.

McLaurin, Allen. "Consciousness and Group Consciousness in Virginia Woolf." *Virginia Woolf: A Centenary Perspective.* Ed. Eric Warner. London: Macmillan, 1984. 28–40.

——. *Virginia Woolf: The Echoes Enslaved.* Cambridge: Cambridge University Press, 1973.

McKee, Patricia. *Heroic Commitment in Richardson, Eliot, and James.* Princeton: Princeton University Press, 1986.

Meisel, Perry. *The Absent Father: Virginia Woolf and Walter Pater.* New Haven: Yale University Press, 1980.

Meredith, George. *The Egoist.* 1879. Ed. Robert M. Adams. New York: Norton, 1979.

Middleton, Victoria S. "*The Years:* 'A Deliberate Failure.' " *Bulletin of the New York Public Library* 80 (1977): 158–71.

Mill, John Stuart. *The Subjection of Women.* New York: Appleton, 1870.

Miller, J. Hillis. *The Ethics of Reading: Kant, de Man, Eliot, Trollope, James, and Benjamin.* New York: Columbia University Press, 1987.

——. *Fiction and Repetition.* Cambridge: Harvard University Press, 1982.

Miller, Nancy K. "Changing the Subject: Authorship, Writing, and the Reader." *Feminist Studies/Critical Studies.* Ed. Teresa de Lauretis. Bloomington: Indiana University Press, 1986. 102–20.

——. "Emphasis Added: Plots and Plausibilities in Women's Fiction." *The New Feminist Criticism.* Ed. Elaine Showalter. New York: Pantheon, 1985. 339–60.

——. *Getting Personal: Feminist Occasions and Other Autobiographical Acts.* New York: Routledge, 1991.

——. *Subject to Change: Reading Feminist Writing.* New York: Columbia University Press, 1988.

——. "The Text's Heroine: A Feminist Critic and Her Fictions." *Diacritics* 12 (1982): 48–53.

Mink, Louis O. "History and Fiction as Modes of Comprehension." *New Literary History* 1 (1970): 541–58.

——. "Narrative Form as a Cognitive Instrument." *The Writing of History: Literary Form and Historical Understanding.* Ed. Robert H. Canary and Henry Kozicki. Madison: University of Wisconsin Press, 1978. 129–49.

Minow-Pinkney, Makiko. *Virginia Woolf and the Problem of the Subject.* New Brunswick, N.J.: Rutgers University Press, 1987.

Moers, Ellen. *Literary Women: The Great Writers.* New York: Oxford University Press, 1985.

Moi, Toril. *Sexual/Textual Politics: Feminist Literary Theory.* New York: Methuen, 1985.

Moore, Madeline. "*Orlando:* An Edition of the Manuscript." *Twentieth Century Literature* 25 (1979): 303–55.

Morgan, Susan. *Sisters in Time: Imagining Gender in Nineteenth-Century British Fiction.* New York: Oxford University Press, 1989.

Mudge, Bradford K. "Exiled as Exiler: Sara Coleridge, Virginia Woolf, and the Politics of Literary Revision." *Women's Writing in Exile.* Ed. Mary Lynn Broe and Angela Ingram. Chapel Hill: University of North Carolina Press, 1989. 199–223.

Murray, Janet Horowitz. *Strong-Minded Women and Other Lost Voices from Nineteenth-Century England.* New York: Pantheon, 1982.

Myers, William. "George Eliot: Politics and Personality." *Literature and Politics in the Nineteenth Century.* Ed. John Lucas. London: Methuen, 1971. 105–29.

——. "Politics and Personality in *Felix Holt.*" *Renaissance and Modern Studies* 10 (1966): 5–33.

——. *The Teaching of George Eliot.* Leicester, Eng.: Leicester University Press, 1984.

Naremore, James. *The World without a Self.* New Haven: Yale University Press, 1973.

Newton, Judith Lowder. *Women, Power, and Subversion: Social Strategies in British Fiction, 1778–1860.* New York: Methuen, 1985.

Nicholson, Linda. "Feminism and Marx: Integrating Kinship with the Economic." *Feminism as Critique: On the Politics of Gender.* Ed. Seyla Benhabib and Drucilla Cornell. Minneapolis: University of Minnesota Press, 1987. 16–30.

Nicolson, Nigel. Introduction. *The Letters of Virginia Woolf.* Ed. Nigel Nicolson and Joanne Trautmann. New York: Harcourt Brace Jovanovich, 1977. 3: xi–xxii.

Nietzsche, Friedrich. *Beyond Good and Evil.* Trans. Walter Kaufmann. New York: Vintage, 1966.

——. *The Birth of Tragedy and The Case of Wagner.* Trans. Walter Kaufmann. New York: Vintage, 1967.

Oldfield, Sybil. "From Rachel's Aunts to Miss La Trobe: Spinsters in the Fiction of Virginia Woolf." *Old Maids to Radical Spinsters: Unmarried Women in the Twentieth-Century Novel.* Ed. Laura L. Doan. Urbana: University of Illinois Press, 1991. 85–103.

Ortner, Sherry B. "Is Female to Male as Nature Is to Culture?" *Woman, Culture, and Society*. Ed. Michelle Zimbalist Rosaldo and Louise Lamphere. Stanford: Stanford University Press, 1974. 67–87.

Ossoli, Margaret Fuller. *Woman in the Nineteenth Century, and Kindred Papers Relating to the Sphere, Condition and Duties, of Woman*. Ed. Arthur B. Fuller. Boston: Jewett, 1855.

Paden, W. D. *Tennyson in Egypt: A Study of the Imagery in His Earlier Work*. Humanistic Studies, no. 27. Lawrence: University of Kansas Press, 1942.

Paris, Bernard J. *Experiments in Life: George Eliot's Quest for Values*. Detroit: Wayne State University Press, 1965.

Paul, Janis M. *The Victorian Heritage of Virginia Woolf: The External World in Her Novels*. Norman, Okla.: Pilgrim, 1987.

Paxton, Nancy L. "George Eliot and the City: The Imprisonment of Culture." *Women Writers and the City: Essays in Feminist Literary Criticism*. Ed. Susan Merrill Squier. Knoxville: University of Tennessee Press, 1984. 71–96.

Pearson, Carol, and Katherine Pope. *The Female Hero in American and British Literature*. New York: Bowker, 1981.

Pell, Nancy. "The Fathers' Daughters in *Daniel Deronda*." *Nineteenth-Century Fiction* 36 (1982): 424–51.

Perkin, J. Russell. *A Reception-History of George Eliot's Fiction*. Ann Arbor, Mich.: University Microfilms Inc. Research Press, 1990.

Peterson, Virgil A. "*Romola:* A Victorian Quest for Values." *West Virginia Quarterly: Philological Papers* 16 (1967): 49–62.

Philipson, Morris. "Virginia Woolf's *Orlando:* Biography as a Work of Fiction." *From Parnassus: Essays in Honor of Jacques Barzun*. Ed. Dora B. Weiner and William R. Keylor. New York: Harper & Row, 1976. 237–48.

Plomer, William. "Virginia Woolf, IV." *Horizon* 3 (1941): 323–27.

Poovey, Mary. *Uneven Developments: The Ideological Work of Gender in Mid-Victorian England*. Chicago: University of Chicago Press, 1988.

Poston, Lawrence, III. "Setting and Theme in *Romola*," *Nineteenth-Century Fiction* 20 (1966): 355–66.

Pratt, Annis. With Barbara White, Andrea Loewenstein, and Mary Wyer. *Archetypal Patterns in Women's Fiction*. Bloomington: Indiana University Press, 1981.

Praz, Mario. *The Hero in Eclipse in Victorian Fiction*. Trans. Angus Davidson. London: Oxford University Press, 1956.

Prince, Gerald. "Introduction to the Study of the Narratee." *Reader Response Criticism*. Ed. Jane P. Tompkins. Baltimore: Johns Hopkins University Press, 1980. 7–25.

Pykett, Lyn. "Typology and the End(s) of History in *Daniel Deronda*." *Literature and History* 9 (1983): 62–73.

Radin, Grace. " 'Two enormous chunks': Episodes Excluded during the Final Revisions of *The Years*." *Bulletin of the New York Public Library* 80 (1977): 221–51.

——. *Virginia Woolf's "The Years."* Knoxville: University of Tennessee Press, 1981.

Redinger, Ruby V. *George Eliot: The Emergent Self*. New York: Knopf, 1975.

Rich, Adrienne. "Compulsory Heterosexuality and Lesbian Existence." *The Signs Reader: Women, Gender, and Scholarship*. Ed. Elizabeth Abel and Emily K. Abel. Chicago: University of Chicago Press, 1983. 139–68.

———. "When We Dead Awaken: Writing as Revision." *On Lies, Secrets, and Silence: Selected Prose 1966–1978*. New York: Norton, 1979. 33–49.

Richter, Harvena. "The *Ulysses* Connection: Clarissa Dalloway's Bloomsday." *Studies in the Novel* 21 (1989): 305–19.

Riley, Denise. *"Am I That Name?": Feminism and the Category of 'Women' in History*. Minneapolis: University of Minnesota Press, 1988.

Robinson, Carole. "*Romola*: A Reading of the Novel." *Victorian Studies* 6 (1962): 29–42.

Ronald, Ann. "George Eliot's Florentine Museum." *Papers on Language and Literature* 13 (1977): 260–69.

Rose, Phyllis. *Parallel Lives*. 1983. New York: Vintage, 1984.

———. *Woman of Letters: A Life of Virginia Woolf*. New York: Oxford University Press, 1978.

Rosenbaum, S. P. "An Educated Man's Daughter: Leslie Stephen, Virginia Woolf, and the Bloomsbury Group." *Virginia Woolf: New Critical Essays*. Ed. Patricia Clements and Isobel Grundy. New York: Barnes & Noble, 1983. 32–56.

Rosenberg, Brian. "George Eliot and the Victorian Historic Imagination." *The Victorian Newsletter* 61 (1981): 1–5.

Rosenberg, Edgar. *From Shylock to Svengali: Jewish Stereotypes in English Fiction*. Stanford: Stanford University Press, 1960.

Rosenman, Ellen Bayuk. *The Invisible Presence: Virginia Woolf and the Mother-Daughter Relationship*. Baton Rouge: Louisiana State University Press, 1986.

———. "Women's Speech and the Roles of the Sexes in *Daniel Deronda*." *Texas Studies in Literature and Language* 31 (1989): 237–56.

Rowbotham, Sheila. *Hidden from History: 300 Years of Women's Oppression and the Fight against It*. London: Pluto, 1973.

Rubin, Gayle. "The Traffic in Women: Notes on the 'Political Economy' of Sex." *Toward an Anthropology of Women*. Ed. Rayna [Rapp] Reiter. New York: Monthly Review, 1975. 157–210.

Ruskin, John. "Of Queen's Gardens." 1864. *Sesame and Lilies, The Two Paths, and The King of the Golden River*. London: Dent, 1907. 48–79.

Sackville-West, Vita. *Knole and the Sackvilles*. 1922. London: Lindsay Drummond, 1947.

———. "Virginia Woolf and 'Orlando.' " *The Listener* 53 (27 Jan. 1955): 157–58.

———. "Virginia Woolf, III." *Horizon* 3 (1941): 318–23.

Sanders, Andrew, ed. Introduction. *Romola*. Harmondsworth, Eng.: Penguin, 1980. 7–32.

Sandler, Florence. "The Unity of *Felix Holt*." *George Eliot: A Centenary Tribute*. Ed. Gordon S. Haight and Rosemary T. VanArsdel. London: Macmillan, 1982. 137–52.

Schaefer, Josephine O'Brien. "The Vision Falters: *The Years*, 1937." *Virginia Woolf: A Collection of Critical Essays*. Ed. Claire Sprague. Englewood Cliffs, N.J.: Prentice-Hall, 1971. 130–44.

Schlack, Beverly Ann. *Continuing Presences: Virginia Woolf's Use of Literary Allusion*. University Park: Pennsylvania State University Press, 1979.

——. "Fathers in General: The Patriarchy in Virginia Woolf's Fiction." *Virginia Woolf: A Feminist Slant*. Ed. Jane Marcus. Lincoln: University of Nebraska Press, 1983. 52–77.

Schor, Naomi. *Reading in Detail: Aesthetics and the Feminine*. New York: Methuen, 1987.

Scott, Bonnie Kime, ed. *The Gender of Modernism: A Critical Anthology*. Bloomington: Indiana University Press, 1990.

Sears, Sallie. "Theater of War: Virginia Woolf's *Between the Acts*." *Virginia Woolf: A Feminist Slant*. Ed. Jane Marcus. Lincoln: University of Nebraska Press, 1983. 212–35.

Showalter, Elaine. "Feminist Criticism in the Wilderness." 1981. *The New Feminist Criticism*. Ed. Elaine Showalter. New York: Pantheon, 1985. 243–70.

——. "The Greening of Sister George." *Nineteenth-Century Fiction* 35 (1980): 292–311.

——. *A Literature of Their Own: British Women Novelists from Brontë to Lessing*. Princeton: Princeton University Press, 1977.

——. *Sexual Anarchy: Gender and Culture at the Fin de Siècle*. New York: Viking, 1990.

Shuttleworth, Sally. *George Eliot and Nineteenth-Century Science: The Make-Believe of a Beginning*. Cambridge: Cambridge University Press, 1984.

Siegel, Carol. *Lawrence among the Women: Wavering Boundaries in Women's Literary Traditions*. Charlottesville: University Press of Virginia, 1991.

Silver, Brenda R., ed. " 'Anon' and 'The Reader': Virginia Woolf's Last Essays." Ed., intro., and commentary by Brenda R. Silver. *Twentieth Century Literature* 25 (1979): 356–441.

——, ed. *Virginia Woolf's Reading Notebooks*. Princeton: Princeton University Press, 1983.

Simmons, James C. *The Novelist as Historian*. The Hague: Mouton, 1973.

Smith, Barbara. "Toward a Black Feminist Criticism." *The New Feminist Criticism*. Ed. Elaine Showalter. New York: Pantheon, 1985. 168–85.

Southam, B. C. Introduction. *Jane Austen: The Critical Heritage*. London: Routledge & Kegan Paul, 1968.

Spacks, Patricia Meyer. *The Female Imagination*. New York: Avon, 1976.

——. *Gossip*. Chicago: University of Chicago Press, 1986.

Spencer, Herbert. *Essays Scientific, Political, and Speculative*. Vols. 13–15. *The Works of Herbert Spencer*. Osnabrück, Ger.: Zeller, 1966.

Spender, Dale. *Mothers of the Novel: 100 Good Women Writers before Jane Austen*. London: Pandora, 1986.

Squier, Susan. "A Track of Our Own: Typescript Drafts of *The Years*." *Virginia Woolf: A Feminist Slant*. Ed. Jane Marcus. Lincoln: University of Nebraska Press, 1983. 198–211.

Squier, Susan M., and Louise A. DeSalvo, eds. "Virginia Woolf's 'The Journal of Mistress Joan Martyn.' " *Twentieth Century Literature* 25 (1979): 237–69.

Stange, G. Robert. "Art Criticism as a Prose Genre." *The Art of Victorian Prose*.

Ed. George Levine and William Madden. New York: Oxford University Press, 1968. 39–52.

——. "The Voices of the Essayist." *Nineteenth-Century Fiction* 35 (1980): 312–30.

Stanton, Domna C. "Autogynography: Is the Subject Different?" *The Female Autograph: Theory and Practice of Autobiography from the Tenth to the Twentieth Century*. Ed. Domna C. Stanton. 1984. Chicago: University of Chicago Press, 1987. 3–20.

Stein, Richard L. *The Ritual of Interpretation: The Fine Arts as Literature in Ruskin, Rossetti, and Pater*. Cambridge: Harvard University Press, 1975.

Stephen, Leslie. *George Eliot*. London: Macmillan, 1902.

——. *History of English Thought in the Eighteenth Century*. 1879. New York: Harcourt Brace & World, 1962.

——. "Sir Walter Scott." *Hours in a Library*. 4 vols. New York: Putnam's, 1907. 1: 186–229.

——. "The Study of English Literature." *Men, Books, and Mountains: Essays by Leslie Stephen*. Collected with intro. by S. O. A. Ullmann. Minneapolis: University of Minnesota Press, 1956. 17–44.

Stimpson, Catharine R. "Woolf's Room, Our Project: The Building of Feminist Criticism." *The Future of Literary Theory*. Ed. Ralph Cohen. New York: Routledge, 1989. 129–43.

Stone, Merlin. *When God Was a Woman*. New York: Harcourt Brace Jovanovich, 1976.

Strachey, Lytton. "Ought Father to Grow a Beard?" *The Shorter Strachey*. Ed. Michael Holroyd and Paul Levy. Oxford: Oxford University Press, 1980. 14–20.

Strachey, Ray. *The Cause: A Short History of the Women's Movement in Great Britain*. 1928. London: Virago, 1978.

Sudrann, Jean. "*Daniel Deronda* and the Landscape of Exile." *ELH* 37 (1970): 433–55.

Sutherland, John A. *Victorian Novelists and Publishers*. London: University of London/Athlone, 1976.

Taylor, Ina. *A Woman of Contradictions: The Life of George Eliot*. New York: Morrow, 1989.

Thomson, Fred C. "*Felix Holt* as Classic Tragedy." *Nineteenth-Century Fiction* 16 (1961): 47–58.

——. "The Genesis of *Felix Holt*." *PMLA* 74 (1959): 576–84.

——. Introduction. *Felix Holt*, by George Eliot. Oxford: Clarendon, 1980. xiii–xlii.

Todd, Janet. "Who's Afraid of Jane Austen?" *Jane Austen: New Perspectives*. Ed. Janet Todd. *Women and Literature*, n.s. 3. New York: Holmes & Meier, 1983. 107–27.

Torgovnick, Marianna. *Closure in the Novel*. Princeton: Princeton University Press, 1981.

Toulmin, Stephen, and June Goodfield. *The Discovery of Time*. New York: Harper & Row, 1965.

Trevelyan, George Macaulay. "Clio, a Muse." *Clio, a Muse and Other Essays Literary and Pedestrian*. London: Longmans, Green, 1913.

———. *History of England*. London: Longmans, Green, 1926.

Uglow, Jennifer. *George Eliot*. London: Virago, 1987.

Vance, Norman. "Law, Religion, and the Unity of *Felix Holt*." *George Eliot: Centenary Essays and an Unpublished Fragment*. Ed. Anne Smith. London: Vision, 1980. 103–23.

Vickery, John B. *The Literary Impact of "The Golden Bough."* Princeton: Princeton University Press, 1973.

Vogeler, Martha S. "George Eliot and the Positivists." *Nineteenth-Century Fiction* 35 (1980): 406–31.

Waley, Daniel. *George Eliot's Blotter: A Commonplace-Book*. London: British Library, 1980.

Walker, Alice. "In Search of Our Mother's Gardens." *In Search of Our Mothers' Gardens: Womanist Prose*. New York: Harcourt Brace Jovanovich, 1983. 231–43.

Walker, Cheryl. "Feminist Literary Criticism and the Author." *Critical Inquiry* 16 (1990): 551–71.

Warner, Eric, ed. *Virginia Woolf: A Centenary Perspective*. London: Macmillan, 1984.

Watkins, Renée. "Survival in Discontinuity—Virginia Woolf's *Between the Acts*." *Massachusetts Review* 10 (1969): 356–76.

Waugh, Patricia. *Feminine Fictions: Revisiting the Postmodern*. London: Routledge, 1989.

Welsh, Alexander. *George Eliot and Blackmail*. Cambridge: Harvard University Press, 1985.

Wenzel, Hélène Vivienne. "The Text as Body/Politics: An Appreciation of Monique Wittig's Writings in Context." *Feminist Studies* 7 (1981): 264–87.

West, Paul. "Enigmas of Imagination: 'Orlando' through the Looking Glass." 1977. *Virginia Woolf: Modern Critical Views*. Ed. Harold Bloom. New York: Chelsea, 1986. 83–100.

Wheare, Jane. *Virginia Woolf*. London: Macmillan, 1989.

White, Hayden. "Interpretation in History." *New Literary History* 4 (1973): 281–314.

———. *Metahistory: The Historical Imagination in Nineteenth-Century Europe*. Baltimore: Johns Hopkins University Press, 1973.

Wiesenfarth, Joseph. "Antique Gems from *Romola* to *Daniel Deronda*." *George Eliot: A Centenary Tribute*. Ed. Gordon S. Haight and Rosemary T. VanArsdel. London: Macmillan, 1982. 55–63.

———. *George Eliot's Mythmaking*. Heidelberg: Carl Winter Universitätsverlag, 1977.

———, ed. *A Writer's Notebook 1854–1879 and Uncollected Writings*, by George Eliot. Charlottesville: University Press of Virginia, 1981.

Williams, Raymond. *Culture and Society, 1780–1950*. New York: Columbia University Press, 1958.

Wilson, J. J. "Why Is *Orlando* Difficult?" *New Feminist Essays on Virginia Woolf*. Ed. Jane Marcus. Lincoln: University of Nebraska Press, 1981. 170–84.

Witemeyer, Hugh. *George Eliot and the Visual Arts*. New Haven: Yale University Press, 1979.

Wollstonecraft, Mary. *A Vindication of the Rights of Woman*. *A Wollstonecraft*

Anthology. Ed. Janet M. Todd. Bloomington: Indiana University Press, 1977. 84–114.

Woolf, Leonard. *Downhill All the Way: An Autobiography of the Years 1919 to 1939.* New York: Harcourt, Brace & World, 1967.

Woolf, Virginia. "Am I a Snob?" *Moments of Being: Unpublished Autobiographical Writings.* Ed. Jeanne Schulkind. New York: Harcourt Brace Jovanovich, 1976. 182–98.

——. *Granite and Rainbow: Essays.* New York: Harcourt Brace Jovanovich, 1958.

——. Introduction. *Mrs. Dalloway.* New York: Modern Library, 1928. v–ix.

——. "Introductory Letter." *Life as We Have Known It,* by Co-operative Working Women. Ed. Margaret Llewelyn Davies. 1931. New York: Norton, 1975. xv–xxxix.

——. "Modes and Manners of the Nineteenth Century." *The Essays of Virginia Woolf.* Vol. 1. Ed. Andrew McNeillie. New York: Harcourt Brace Jovanovich, 1986. 330–40.

——. *The Moment and Other Essays.* London: Hogarth, 1981.

——. *The Pargiters.* Ed. Mitchell A. Leaska. New York: New York Public Library, 1977.

——. "A Sketch of the Past." *Moments of Being: Unpublished Autobiographical Writings.* Ed. Jeanne Schulkind. New York: Harcourt Brace Jovanovich, 1976. 64–137.

——. "An Unwritten Novel." *A Haunted House and Other Short Stories.* New York: Harcourt Brace Jovanovich, 1972. 8–21.

Zimmerman, Bonnie. "*Felix Holt* and the True Power of Womanhood." *ELH* 46 (1979): 432–51.

——. "Gwendolen Harleth and 'The Girl of the Period.' " *George Eliot: Centenary Essays and an Unpublished Fragment.* Ed. Anne Smith. London: Vision, 1980. 196–215.

——. " 'The Mother's History' in George Eliot's Life, Literature, and Political Ideology." *The Lost Tradition: Mothers and Daughters in Literature.* Ed. Cathy N. Davidson and E. M. Broner. New York: Frederick Ungar, 1980. 81–94.

Zwerdling, Alex. *Virginia Woolf and the Real World.* Berkeley: University of California Press, 1986.

Index

Reading Women Writing

A SERIES EDITED BY

Shari Benstock and Celeste Schenck

Library of Congress Cataloging-in-Publication Data

Booth, Alison.
    Greatness engendered : George Eliot and Virginia Woolf / Alison Booth.
        p.   cm.—(Reading women writing)
    Includes bibliographical references and index.
    ISBN 0-8014-2628-6 (cloth).—ISBN 0-8014-9930-5 (pbk.)
    1. English fiction—Women authors—History and criticism. 2. Eliot, George, 1819–
1880—Criticism and interpretation. 3. Woolf, Virginia, 1882–1941—Criticism and interpretation. 4. Women and literature—Great Britain. I. Title. II. Series.
PR830.W6B66 1992
823'.8099287—dc20   91-28120